Theologies of Religious Education

Theologies of Religious Education

EDITED BY

RANDOLPH CRUMP MILLER

Religious Education Press
Birmingham, Alabama

Library of Congress Cataloging-in-Publication Data
Theologies of religious education / edited by Randolph Crump Miller.
    Includes bibliographical references and index.
    ISBN 0-89135-096-9
    1. Christian education—Philosophy   I. Miller, Randolph Crump,
1910-
BV1464.T463   1995
268'.01—dc20   95-11226
                                              CIP

Religious Education Press
5316 Meadow Brook Road
Birmingham, Alabama 35242
10 9 8 7 6 5 4 3 2

Religious Education Press publishes books exclusively in religious education
and in areas closely related to religious education. It is committed to enhancing and professionalizing religious education through the publication of
serious, significant, and scholarly works.

PUBLISHER TO THE PROFESSION

Contents

Publisher's Introduction

There can be little doubt that the most foundational issue in all of religious education is the relation of this field to theology on the one hand and to the social sciences on the other hand. This foundational issue is absolutely pivotal because the whole way in which religion teaching is both conceptualized and enacted depends on whether religious instruction is a branch of theology or a branch of social science.

The purpose of *Theologies of Religious Education* is to explore with adequate comprehensiveness and depth the organic relationship between theology and the teaching of religion—or somewhat more accurately, the relationship between a wide variety of contemporary theologies and the teaching of religion.

If indeed the teaching of religion is a branch of theology, then theology should satisfactorily explain, predict, and verify what pedagogically occurs in the religious instruction act.

If the teaching of religion is a branch of theology, then theology should demonstrate that it can satisfactorily *explain* why certain curricula succeed or fail, why some teaching practices succeed while others fizzle, why a specific teaching practice is successful in one situation and is unsuccessful in another situation, and so forth.

If the teaching of religion is a branch of theology, then theology should demonstrate that it can satisfactorily *predict* when one specific instructional practice will work and when it will fail, when one instructional practice will be more effective than another, when various kinds of learning outcomes require the deployment of this or that instructional practice, and so forth.

If the teaching of religion is a branch of theology, then theology should demonstrate that it can satisfactorily *verify* that a desired learning outcome has actually been achieved, the degree to which it has been achieved, and so forth.

If the teaching of religion is a branch of theology, then theology should tell the religious educator *how to teach*. Thus theology should be able to satisfactorily provide the religious educator with a complete repertoire of teaching styles, strategies, methods, techniques, and steps.

If the teaching of religion is a branch of theology, then theology should satisfactorily demonstrate that it has *directly* generated and can *directly* generate instructional practices on its own rather than borrow these instructional practices from some other scientific area such as social science.

1

Another major point when considering the relationship between theology and religious education is whether a particular kind of theology such as liberation theology or Reformed theology or Thomistic theology can directly generate a *whole repertoire* of instructional practices or whether a particular theology can only generate one or a few instructional practices. Conversely, does a particular theology intrinsically rule out the possibility of using otherwise legitimate and generally accepted pedagogical practices which might be at variance with that theology?

Questions and issues raised in the preceding paragraphs are of both foundational and immediate concern to every serious religious educator. Consequently, I thought it would be especially helpful to the field of religious education to commission an edited book which would deal with the relationship of major contemporary theologies to the dynamics of teaching religion.

In order that this book offer the strongest possible case for the proposition that religious education is a branch of theology, it was necessary for me to find a person who is eminent in the field of religious education, who is knowledgeable about theology in general and major theologies in particular, and who is passionately committed to the proposition that religious education is a branch of theology. My choice was obvious: Randolph Crump Miller. More than any religious educationist in the twentieth century, Miller has consistently and forcefully advocated the theological approach to religious education. Theology, Miller has continually asserted, is *the* clue to understanding and doing religious education. And unlike almost all contemporary advocates of the theological approach to religious education, Miller is knowledgeable in theology, cites theological sources primarily, and writes from a theological perspective.

The affable Miller, by now an octogenarian, was delighted to accept my proposal. He set to work with his customary vigor and élan.

In concert, Miller and I identified the major schools of theology which would appear in the book. Our goal was to include most if not all of the primary theological schools in vogue near the turn of the millennium. Such inclusion is perforce necessary in order for the volume to possess the requisite theological comprehensiveness.

In order for the case of theological supremacy over religious education be presented in the strongest possible light, it was important to secure religious educators or others who are highly knowledgeable in the theology about which they are writing. Miller and I reviewed over and over again our list of potential candidates and finally decided on the persons who would be recruited as contributors. Miller was very successful in recruiting every person whom we had initially identified, a testimony to the recognition by the religious education community of the singular importance of the book's topic and, of course, a tribute to Miller's high standing in the field.

In order that the central issue of theological suzerainty over religious education be explored in as systematic and comparative manner possible, I asked Miller to request his contributors to make sure that their chapters deal at appropriate length with three major areas. Miller readity agreed to my request.

First, each chapter should comprise a first-class summary of the particular form of theology about which the contributor is writing.

Second, each chapter should contain a careful delineation of how that particular form of theology directly generates or at least is highly amenable to a specific instructional procedure or set of procedures.

Third, each chapter should include a top-quality summary of the specific instructional procedure or set of procedures *directly* generated by that particular form of theology, all the while interfacing these pedagogical procedures with the particular theology at selected points to show conclusively that the procedure or set of procedures are indeed a direct outgrowth of the particular theology.

When Miller had all the chapters in his hands, I asked him to assure me that each of the chapter authors had included all three axes to Miller's satisfaction and to the author's. Miller assured me that both he and the authors of every chapter were satisfied that the chapters offered as fine a presentation of the three axes as was possible for them to do.

When I received the entire manuscript from Randolph Crump Miller, I expressed to him some reservations about the quality of the writing style and substantive content in some of the chapters. However, I did not change or alter in the slightest as much as a single word or phrase of any contributor so that the views of each author would remain totally intact and pristinely pure, wholly unaffected by any outside influence.

It is my hope, as publisher of Religious Education Press, that *Theologies of Religious Education* will illumine whether or not theology is decisive in religious education theory and whether or not theology controls religious instruction practice. I further hope that this book, together with its companion volume *Religious Education and Theology* (edited by Norma H. Thompson) will form a corpus of scholarship from which can flow thoughtful and non-ideological examinations of the most foundational issue in all of religious education, namely the relation of this field to theology.

Birmingham, Alabama   James Michael Lee
July 25, 1994
In festo sancti Jacobi

Editor's Introduction

RANDOLPH CRUMP MILLER

As far back as 1943, when I began to write about religious education, I was concerned about theology and its relation to the field of religious education. I wrote that "a theology for Christian education is needed. The objectives, theory, and methods of Christian education need to be undergirded and perhaps altered by a more self-conscious theological reconstruction." Also, there was "the problem of relating content to method in an organic whole."[1]

In 1950, in *The Clue to Christian Education,* I expanded the initial insight to claim that theology should be in the background and grace and faith in the foreground. "The purpose of Christian education is to place God at the center and to bring the individual into the right relation with God and one's fellows within the perspective of the fundamental Christian truths about all of life."[2] Theology, then, must be the presupposition of any curriculum.

Since 1950 there have been new directions in both educational theory and in theology. The emphases on socialization, social sciences, and praxis are some current phases. In theology, changes in black theology, feminist theology, process theology, and other forms of thinking, have complicated the scene. Sara Little writes that "theology has become one influence among many."[3] However, theological and educational pluralism does not free educators from being theologically responsible. What is evident, as it was in 1943 and 1950, according to Little, "is that concern for theology is imperative for the educator, influencing how one selects content and chooses an appropriate and consistent process for education."[4]

We are more aware today of the need to understand cosmic history and nature theologically. "The picture of reality coming to us from contemporary science is so attractive to theology that we would be fools not to use it as a

---

1. Randolph Crump Miller and Henry H. Shires, eds., *Christianity and the Contemporary Scene* (New York: Morehouse-Barlow, 1943), 198.

2. Randolph Crump Miller, *The Clue to Christian Education* (New York: Scribner's, 1950), 8.

3. Sara Little, "Theology and Education," in *Encyclopedia of Religious Education*, ed. Iris and Kendig Cully (San Francisco: Harper & Row, 1990), 652.

4. Ibid., 652-653.

resource for reimaging and reinterpreting Christian doctrine," wrote Sallie McFague.[5] This broadens and deepens the concept of God, who is seen as the persuasive power of love with whom we are in relation , and also as the source of the entire, mind-boggling cosmos, at least from the time of the "big bang."

As editor, I appreciate the cooperation of the writers, some of whom wrote against tremendous odds of health problems and time pressures. Chiefly, I admire what they have accomplished in making significant contributions to the disciplines of both theology and religious education.

The book has three parts: church theologies, philosophical theologies, and special theologies.

PART ONE: CHURCH THEOLOGIES

The opening chapter, by SARA LITTLE, is an interpretation of Reformed theology as it affects religious education. She notes the brief dominance and the continuing minor influence of neo-orthodoxy. The Presbyterian tradition has always valued education and its instrument for faithfulness, its service of truth, and its concern for the public good. Reformed theology is always being reformed. Its emphasis on divine election combined with freedom and responsibility in an ecumenical church leads to insistence on the sovereignty of God, the need for piety, and seeing human life in relation to the power of God. She concludes with a quotation from Choan-Seng Song that theology and education should "join forces and construct education that is theologically informed and theology that is educationally viable in this world of many cultures and religions."

Thomas Aquinas provides theology and educational philosophy that have endured, although frequently modified. MARK HEATH gives a brief review of Thomas's life and then presents those theological themes that are relevant to religious education. Thomas brings together Christ and Aristotle, combines philosophy and theology, relates biblical and common law, draws virtues from both Greek and Christian traditions, and sees grace at work in nature. The primary purpose of teaching is to make God known; it is a theocentric approach to all of life. Religious education ought to be doctrinal, but it is more than conveying information about God; it is more a matter of consecrating the world.

The educational advances of conservatives have been more obvious and substantial than in the liberal churches. One reason has been the responsible scholarship and leadership of people such as KENNETH GANGEL and CHRISTY SULLIVAN. Their approach is strictly biblical without being caught in the battles about inerrancy. God is revealed in the Bible, but after

---

5. Sallie McFague, *The Body of God* (Minneapolis: Fortress, 1993), 74.

God created a good world, there came disobedience and death. Salvation through faith in Jesus Christ is the mystery that unites us with God. There is a wide diversity among conservative scholars and educators, but all stress the value of the Bible. There is no difference between secular and religious truth, for God is the God of all creation. Students move toward a Christian life and worldview within the community of the Holy Spirit.

Liturgy and ritual are at the heart of any religious community and often they are the only activities that keep a community alive in times of persecutions. CONSTANCE J. TARASAR shows how the liturgical practices of the Russian Orthodox Church have determined its nature and provided for its survival through the centuries. Both theology and religious education are *of the church,* grounded in an understanding of God and personhood, and must be communicated in their fullness. Through education, theology is acted out in ecclesial life.

PART TWO: PHILOSOPHICAL THEOLOGIES

We then turn to more philosophical theologies. HELEN GOGGIN looks at process theology, which, as Larry Rasmussen writes, "has vaulted from the minor leagues to the majors." All reality is becoming and perishing. Reality is event and not substance; all events are interrelated. We experience embodiedness, which consists of actual entities in relation. Thus all reality is social, and change, novelty, and creativity open up the possibility of freedom. The future is open, not only to human beings but to God, God is involved in but not identified with the cosmos. Goggin sees three principles for religious education: (1) reality and God are interrelated and interconnected; (2) creation is an ongoing activity of both God and world, with advance into novelty at the heart of it; (3) learning takes place within the interrelatedness of human experience.

My chapter on empirical theology deals with empirical method and its approach through experience and values. The variety in the concepts of God indicates the differences among leading empiricists. Empiricism is interpreted widely enough to include relationships, a sense of the whole, the appreciative consciousness, with a vague affective tone as the basis of experience. God is interpreted as the divine *MORE* (James), as a divine value-producing factor (Macintosh), as creative interchange (Wieman), or as creative passage (Meland). Jesus is conceived as a historical figure and the Christ event as a revelatory event in history. The church is presented in terms of community, with worship at the center. The purpose of religious education is to place God at the center and to bring the learner into the right relationship with God and one's fellows.

In a variety of revolts against more conventional theologies, existentialism presents some difficulties. DAVID WHITE and FRANK ROGERS JR. list the major tenets of existentialist philosophy and then develop its theological implications. "In Bultmann's thinking, Jesus was raised into life in the kerygma—the core of Christian truth. We as humans existentially encounter the word of God in the person of Jesus Christ—in the kerygma." The existentialists have brought passion back into the act of knowing, which is centered on a personal God. The emphasis is no longer on subject matter but on responsibility at the subjective or interior level, becoming an agent and participating in co-creating what will happen.

PART THREE: SPECIAL THEOLOGIES

In part three we turn to more particularized theologies. ELIZABETH DODSON GRAY insists that feminist theology requires a total recasting of most theology and its history. Women are missing from most of the stories. Gray is not calling for a feminine model of God or a goddess but rather for a recognition of the equality of women and men and a theology that is inclusive. She indicates how radical, even for today, was Jesus' affirmation of women. The crucifixion turns on the Father's choice to sacrifice his son, and we lose the thrust of the life-affirming message at the heart of the gospel. Our education must free us from a dominating patriarchy and the evils that come from it.

A specialized type of theology arose in Catholic circles centering on the *kerygma*. It can be compared with the biblical theology of the same period and was influential among such Protestant educators as Iris Cully. Josef A. Jungmann insisted on the centrality of Christ and the process of salvation history. But this view had weaknesses. It oversimplified the plural themes of the Bible, it disparaged the Jewish tradition and failed to do justice to the "Old" or "First" Testament. MARY BOYS provides a summary of this position and its considerable influence but regrets its attitude toward Judaism. She points to new data not available to the kerygmatic theologians that see Judaism and Christianity on parallel tracks. They came from the same womb.

JERRY H. STONE writes that "the best way to relate the ambiguous edges of human experience to God's mysterious presence is through the use of story." Stories, whether historically true or not, can lead people to incorporate them into their own life stories. There are canonical and community stories which shape our life stories. When we understand the plot and character interaction of a story, we will interpret Jesus' stories from our own perspective. When we turn to Jesus' parables, we discover that they are open-ended. They are secular in nature, but they also point to a mysterious "other," which is why the stories are profoundly religious.

DANIEL S. SCHIPANI writes that liberation theology is more oriented to religious education than any others. It is situated in a specific place within the global process of transformation: its theology is educational and its educational theory is theological. It is both theory and praxis. It sees Jesus Christ at the center of history. It is concerned for the poor and the oppressed, leading to a political and social analysis based on discerning the way of Jesus Christ in the real world. The church becomes the base community of those who share these experiences—and the old-line churches need to listen. Religious education begins with refocusing one's concerns, reorienting the approach, and developing Christian disciples as responsible citizens.

GRANT S. SHOCKLEY explores the background and current situation in black theology. It began in 1966 influenced by the Black Power movement, recognizing the gross imbalance of power and influence between black and white Americans. The powerlessness of blacks has led to a distortion of values and justice among both blacks and whites. Even in the Constitution blacks were considered only three-fifths human. It was 1954 before the Supreme Court moved, and civil rights for all entered the cultural scene in 1964-1965. Black theology developed against this background. It became more sensitive to its African roots. It has challenged blacks to work for the liberation of oppressed people, to develop religious education in a new perspective, and to achieve a black agenda, leading to a new black church paradigm.

The final chapter on ecological theology and religious education opens new vistas. Theology until recently has not concerned itself with nature. Nature was for the convenience of human beings. Theology followed the monarchical model, did not face the problem of evil adequately, did not concern itself with the environment, and misplaced the problem of human freedom. These ideas are challenged by our new awareness of ecology. William James's pluralism and a God who has an environment leading to a "strung-along type" opens up a universe in which there will be real losses and losers. Educationally, we begin with the interrelatedness of all life, organic and inorganic. The objectives include an understanding of nature, seeing it as both benign and violent, threatened by human technologies as well as greed, and yet needing technology for the healing of creation.

Thirteen theologies, all derived from the Christian tradition, provide a wide variety of starting points and conclusions, and each theology leads to its own distinctive theory and practice of religious education. There is overlapping because religious education is itself a discipline which all the writers incorporate, but the emphasis is different in each case. Each chapter is self-contained, and the reader can start wherever one's central interest is present. The total picture, however, comes only after reading all of the book.

PART ONE

CHURCH THEOLOGIES

"The major idea is that theology has deep implications for religious education and that a good theology leads to a good educational philosophy."

CHAPTER ONE

Reformed Theology and Religious Education

SARA LITTLE

Part One

Conclusions resulting from the study necessary for the writing of this chapter are threefold, offered here cautiously for testing in the interpretation of recent developments. First, there is more activity and vitality than I had thought in the writings of Reformed theologians who seem to be reclaiming and reinterpreting appropriate themes in their traditions, even including a chastened remembrance and incorporation of the neo-orthodox contribution. (My assumption, along with that of numerous commentators, had been that neo-orthodoxy is "dead.") Second, the dominant, even controlling, influence in Christian education of neo-orthodox theology for a decade in the middle of this century *is* gone. In fact, the role of theology in writings of most theorists and in educational ministry programming is much less clear now than in the fifties, and certainly could not be said to be the major influence. Finally, the question as to what the relationship of Reformed theology and Christian education should be in this last decade of the twentieth century is raised with new urgency.

The study focuses on the contemporary scene. But the conclusions stated above are not intelligible aside from at least a look at the context and background for the present situation. Who are members of the Reformed family? What is the "received tradition" of theological themes or ethos which, in a general sense, can be understood to characterize the Reformed community of faith? Given that beginning point, we can more readily approach the three conclusions through consideration of three questions: What themes or emphases

11

are being offered by Reformed theologians? What is the linkage of that content to theory and practice in Reformed church educational ministry? What critique is to be proposed of the relationship between theology and Christian education?

THE REFORMED HERITAGE

When one speaks of the Reformed tradition in general terms, one is technically including some twelve denominations in the United States,[1] a part of 354 denominations worldwide,[2] all going back to the sixteenth-century Reformation, most specifically, to John Calvin. English-speaking groups from continental Europe became known by the term *Presbyterian*, emphasizing their polity. Presbyterians are the largest denominational group in the Reformed family. For our purposes here, however, reference will be primarily to the Reformed and Presbyterian denominations in the United States.

What do we in the Reformed tradition stand for? An address given to the Eighteenth General Council of the World Alliance of Reformed Churches, meeting at São Paulo, Brazil, in 1959, is of help here. It was entitled "An Address to Our Fellow Christians after Four Hundred Years," given to commemorate the 450th anniversary of John Calvin's birth and the 400th anniversary of the definitive edition of his *Institutes of the Christian Religion*. It begins with an expression of gratitude for the whole Reformation. The two paragraphs here are from the section entitled "Gratitude for the Reformed Heritage."

When we proclaim and seem to some to overemphasize the sovereignty of God, we testify that God's indefatigable love and majestic trustworthiness are the only sure foundation for a Christian's confidence, the solid base, steady as eternity, from which Christians thrust themselves into every part of the human enterprise, there to work the will of him who sustains his whole creation. Thus Christians who emphasize his sovereignty in their confession, make serious ethical endeavor a large part of their grateful devotion, searching the Word for his will and working to make that Word the way of the world.

On this anniversary occasion, we are the thankful heirs of this tradition. We praise God for our Fathers, for their fights for all the freedoms, for

---

1. *The World Almanac and Book of Facts 1993* (New York: Scripps Howard, 1993), 718. Ten Reformed denominations participated in the major study of ministry in the United States, with four by far the largest in size. See *Ministry in America*, eds. David S. Schuller, Merton P. Strommen, and Milo L. Brekke (San Francisco: Harper & Row, 1980), 458. Ch. 15, "Presbyterian Reformed Family," 457-466, gives a helpful overview of the groups being studied here.

2. "Reformed," in *World Christian Encyclopedia*, ed. David B. Barrett (New York: Oxford University Press, 1982), 841.

their willingness to try revolutionary new forms for political and economic life, for their extension of learning and concern for education, and for their engagement in all compassionate and remedial action.[3]

Lists of distinctive Reformed doctrine are available in too many sources to be named here. Most of the important emphases are included in this address: the sovereignty of God; the life of faith and faithfulness, or the life of obedience as response to the grace of God; the authority of scripture; the importance of education.

There are other characteristics that should be noted. The address goes on to mention "Reformed repentance," reflecting the traditional concern with the doctrine of human nature. The reference to education does not do justice to the emphasis on the life of the mind as the service of God. Jack Stotts, Presbyterian theologian, puts the point strongly:

> One—if not *the*—genius of the Presbyterian tradition has been its valuing of and commitment to education as an instrument for faithfulness. . . .
> This education has been in service of the truth, which is itself in the service of goodness. "Truth is in order to goodness," we have said. Thus a mark of the Presbyterian heritage of education is its concern for the public good.[4]

An official Council Message, issued from the São Paulo gathering, refers to the "Reformed stress on divine election or calling," which holds together "the freedom and responsibility" of people who live with an awareness of God's providence and purpose.[5] Reference was made in this Message to the Reformed "ecumenical conviction," pointing out that a part of the tradition is a concern for the ecumenical church. Certainly that concern was part of Calvin's doctrine and his actions even in seeking to reconcile Calvinism and Lutheranism. Ecumenist John Mackay quotes an earlier statement of the Alliance that "it is the true nature of Presbyterianism never to be merely an end in itself, but to serve the Church Universal of Jesus Christ, the Church which is His Body."[6]

A final comment about Presbyterianism is that, historically and doctrinally, the ethos of this tradition is not that it is to be spoken of as finished, as though it had been "reformed" and could proceed from that basis. Rather, the

---

3. Marcel Pradervand, ed., *São Paulo Story* (Geneva: Alliance Offices, 1960), 177.

4. Jack Stotts, "Education for the Public Good," in *Always Being Reformed: The Future of Church Education*, ed. John C. Purdy, (Philadelphia: Geneva Press, 1985), 26-27.

5. Ibid., 21.

6. Marcel Pradervand, ed., *Proceedings of the Seventeenth General Council of the Alliance of the Reformed Churches Holding the Presbyterian Order, Held at Princeton, N.J., U.S.A., 1954* (Geneva: Office of the Alliances, 1954), 115.

term should be "always being reformed," as Ed Dowey of Princeton says in commenting on the Latin slogan *Ecclesia reformata, semper reformanda.* That translates as "the church reformed and always to be reformed."[7] A part of the church's calling and of the reforming process is for the church to confess its faith through turning again and again to the Bible in new situations. Jack Stotts comments that the Articles of Agreement when the two major Presbyterian denominations united in 1983 called for a new statement of faith.[8] Adopted in 1991 as the eleventh document in the *Book of Confessions*, this Brief Statement of Faith stands as a unifying doctrinal base for the new denomination, but also—as Reformed confessions do—addresses the contemporary situation. That double function, according to Dowey, is crucial to Presbyterians; it roots Bible in the tradition, but reinterprets the tradition in ever-new situations.

This commentary on the Reformed tradition, formulated beginning with Calvin and other reformers in the sixteenth century, points to the heritage. Variations and modifications have occurred, often in response to the points mentioned here. But before we relate these key themes to the present scene, we need to look briefly at that major theological movement from the 1930s (1920s in Europe) to the 1950s, called neo-orthodoxy.

NEO-ORTHODOXY

Neo-orthodoxy is selected for brief special attention, not because it is a continuing strand of theology parallel to the Reformed, but rather because it is a momentary manifestation of that major tradition, one that illustrates admirably the point made by Dowey about "reformed" in relation to "always being reformed." Or again, there was a monumental effort to relate the Reformed tradition to the contemporary situation. Terms also used for neo-orthodoxy, "theology of crisis," and "dialectical theology," suggest descriptively the form it took. The tale is too well known to require much review here. Disillusionment from World War I and the Depression, distrust of human effort combined with a kind of "failure of nerve," and reaction to the religious experience that liberalism placed as the foundation of Christian knowledge combined to form openness to the rediscovery of the Bible, the development of a new concept of revelation, and a major revision of educational ministry.

Emphases differed among the theologians, Karl Barth, Emil Brunner, Paul Tillich, Reinhold and H. Richard Niebuhr, and others, but all found that "the Bible is not a reference book or code of conduct. It is a book which is generically different from other books." Why is this so? Because it witnesses "to the fact and meaning of God's actions in history," thus making possible

---

7. Ed Dowey, "Always to Be Reformed," in *Always Being Reformed*, 9.

8. "A Brief Statement of Faith," in *Encyclopedia of the Reformed Faith*, ed. Donald K. McKim (Louisville: Westminster/John Knox Press, 1992), 39-40.

for human beings "the factual and experiential knowledge that God reaches out . . . in a judgment and a healing that is salvation." This reaching out is revelation, an offering of God's self in relationship.[9]

The description of several key elements in neo-orthodoxy suggests how closely related it was to the movement known as Biblical Theology, arising later than neo-orthodoxy, beginning about the time of World War II, in an effort to overcome some of the arid flavor of technical historical-critical biblical scholarship, and to see the Bible with "eyes of faith," with expectation of hearing "God speak." Many biblical scholars became involved in the movement. Probably Bernhard Anderson's *Rediscovering the Bible* summed up the prevailing views as well as any other single publication. Brevard Childs of Yale, speaking at a pastoral conference in 1982 on "The Rise and Fall of Biblical Theology," said scholars were seeking "a new way of doing theology and of doing Bible study" that would bring back a sense of "vitality and enthusiasm" as people would begin to see that the Bible could indeed "speak to a secular world."[10] The Biblical Theology movement turned out to be particularly American in focus, and, although widespread in influence, was nowhere more widely embraced than in the Reformed churches. Childs himself is still seeking to preserve some of the contributions of the movement in his "canonical" approach, as suggested in his *Biblical Theology of the Old and New Testaments: Theological Reflection on the Christian Bible.*

Theology becomes both source and norm for educational ministry in the biblical theology neo-orthodox perspective. There are probably few, if any, clearer examples of theology's being "applied" than in the Christian Faith and Life curriculum of the United Presbyterian Church in the United States of America, beginning in 1948, with Canadian James Smart, himself a biblical theologian, as editor. In his *Teaching Ministry of the Church*, Smart begins with the doctrine of the Trinity, a marked contrast to beginning with human need and experience, and relates salvation to justification by faith alone. The book turns out to be the theoretical interpretation of what was developed in the curriculum. Emphasis is on *content*, the content of the revelation through which the Christian is called to be—and trained to be—the church in the world. The purpose, then, becomes equipping for discipleship. The comprehensive Program for Church and Home of this curriculum plan called forth one of the most productive periods in educational ministry of this century. It was quite clear what discipline was in control: theology. According to Smart, religious education must ally itself with theology lest it witness to false faith. Theology is the church's way of mounting "the watchtower" and scanning "its faith and life in all directions, in order to detect the presence of blindness, unbelief, unfaithfulness, and sin, and give warning before it is

9. See my summary statement in my *The Role of the Bible in Contemporary Christian Education* (Richmond, Va.: John Knox Press, 1961), 153-54.

10. Tape of the conference, "The Rise and Fall of Biblical Theology," from Paul Vieth Christian Education Service, New Haven, Yale Divinity School, 1982.

too late."[11] But theology is more than a "watchtower"; it is the clear interpretation of the biblical message that becomes the instrument for confronting
the human person with the call to repentance and the offer of salvation. In that
confrontation, the content becomes the channel for changing the inner being
of the person who hears. The moralistic approach to the Bible is replaced with
an emphasis on beliefs, which "instruct" the conscience, and which overcome
the "deplorable incoherence" among Christians. Methods are not determined
by theology. They are chosen from among the best means of communication
developed in education—a strange failure to pursue the relation of theology
to religious education in a more stringent fashion. Nonetheless, in whatever direction one turns, one is made aware of the Reformed heritage, now
reformulated in neo-orthodox and biblical categories.

Other emphases from neo-orthodoxy, combined with other denomina-
tional interests, resulted in different educational programs. Tillich, through
Lewis Sherrill, religious education theorist in the Southern Presbyterian
Church (Presbyterian Church U.S.), influenced the development of the
Covenant Life Curriculum, beginning in the fifties, with his method of correlation. Other neo-orthodox theologians were also influential in this
Presbyterian denomination, but "predicament and theme," as Sherrill called
it in his *The Gift of Power*, became the means of relating the revelatory biblical message to the individual and the world. During this same period, in the
fifties and early sixties, neo-orthodoxy and other theologies as well had
influence in denominations other than the Reformed, but that interesting
account is outside the scope of this study. The Presbyterian Faith and Life program is the most dramatic example of the dominance of the neo-orthodox perspective in Christian education. (Note that religious education has now
become Christian education.)

CONTEMPORARY REFORMED THEOLOGY

The period since the dominance of neo-orthodoxy in the middle decades
of this century was followed by several decades of chaotic uncertainty. Just
as neo-orthodoxy was a reaction against liberalism, so the ferment, fragmentation, and loss of focus was a reaction against the overconfidence of the
fifties. Barth would probably say that the great new programs and even trust
in theology (rather than God) were only substitutions of human effort for
fearing and loving God above all things. The shift was more complex than a
theological shift. From historical and sociological perspectives, the conclusions would be that what Sidney Ahlstrom calls the "turbulent sixties"
brought new "cosmic signs" and a "fundamental shift in American moral
and religious attitudes." The years of the assassinations of John Kennedy

---

11. James Smart, *The Teaching Ministry of the Church* (Philadelphia: Westminster,
1954), 33.

and Martin Luther King, of the "death of God," and the hope from Vatican II, were times that brought "excitement and liberation to some, bewilderment and pain to others."[12] Mass media and the technological revolution, the emphasis on multiculturalism and pluralism, on globalization in theological education, and on diversity in almost any setting one can mention, combine to make *change* the key word of the last quarter of the twentieth century. Obviously, with consciousness redirected toward change, the burden on Reformed theology of speaking ever anew to the contemporary situation is a great one.

The situation is complicated when one recognizes that it is increasingly difficult to know who a Reformed theologian is. Theologians are sometimes said to be more influenced by the academy than by their heritage, to write for one another rather than for the church. Neo-orthodox theologians were identifiable, even to the point of belonging to Brunner rather than to Barth, to Tillich rather than to one of the Niebuhrs. That is no longer the case. We seem to be moving out of the time of being "between theologies," but there are other categories that seem more logical than those of denominational heritage or schools of thought—emphasis on feminism, ecology, pluralism, the oppressed, and other advocacy or special interest groups. It is a difficult task to address the question of Reformed theology in the contemporary scene. One should speak only with tentativeness.

One way to ascertain whether a person speaks from the Reformed perspective is to note the denominational tradition to which he/she belongs. Daniel Migliore of Princeton, himself an author of a new systematic theology, *Faith Seeking Understanding: An Introduction to Christian Theology*, 1991, sees in the many current publications the possibility of "new life for systematic theology." Although most of the recent theologies written by "mainline" North American theologians "display an ecumenical spirit," still, "some traits of the author's ecclesial tradition are usually evident."[13] Authors with these Reformed "traits" have been writing in areas other than systematic theology, picking up particular social concerns, or dealing with themes in which they seek to reclaim the theological vocation. What is attempted here is to pick up some of these themes or emphases by Reformed scholars in order to determine the concepts or values that may inform current educational theory and practice. The schema used here is one developed by Lee Barrett, theologian of Presbyterian School of Christian Education in Richmond.[14]

---

12. Sidney Ahlstrom, *A Religious History of the American People* (New Haven: Yale University Press, 1972), 1080,1082.

13. Daniel Migliore, "New Life for Systematic Theology," *The Presbyterian Outlook* 175:26 (July 5-12, 1993), 11.

14. The proposals here are from notes taken during a most helpful conversation with Lee Barrett in November 1993. Used by permission. He joined the faculty of Lancaster Theological Seminary in 1994.

Barrett sees five groupings in the current writings of Reformed theologians. The first consists of several authors who do indeed carry on the neo-orthodox position, in the light of current issues and interpretations tempered by use of more traditional Reformed categories. Some are influenced more by one neo-orthodox author than another, although Barth is probably still the most dominant influence. There is a substantial, steady tendency in these writers to reflect what John Leith calls gratitude for the Reformed heritage balanced by critical judgment.[15] In addition to Leith, Shirley Guthrie, Ed Dowey, Donald Dawe, and Daniel Migliore are representatives. Lee Barrett would place himself in this group. He is a United Church theologian who embodies the Reformed strand in that denomination, merger of several groups including the Reformed.

A second group is designated the "descendants of H. Richard Niebuhr." This group claims the whole tradition from Calvin down through Jonathan Edwards, Schleiermacher, and others with a theocentric emphasis, serving as mediating theologians. James Gustafson and Douglas Ottati are among the representatives.

Representing a neo-evangelical scholastic reformed Calvinism are several writers who attempt to recover some of the doctrinal dynamics of the seventeenth century, including the power of experiential conversation. Some of the spokesmen for this position are Donald Bloesch, Jack Rogers, and Donald McKim.

A fourth group of varying concerns may be grouped as Reformed liberation theologies. That is, the writers maintain the Reformed perspective, but relate various doctrines to special groups. Al Winn, Robert McAfee Brown, Letty Russell (although, if we had a feminist group, she would belong there), and C. S. Song are representatives.

Finally, there is what Barrett calls a post-liberal Reformed group of persons who are concerned about method in theology along with conceptual categories. To be placed here are David Kelsey and William Placher.

Illustrative emphases and contributions from selected writers in these five groups will inform our understanding of the theological context within which religious educators have been working since the late eighties. It is not a comprehensive overview—one would have to survey the whole ecumenical scene and even interfaith developments to sketch the spectrum of theological and religious influences—but it does suggest some of the major sources and guides currently functioning in Presbyterian and Reformed denominations as they undertake educational ministry.

Daniel Migliore is an excellent representative of this first category, the continuing neo-orthodox group. His *Faith Seeking Understanding* grew out of lectures, especially his course for Master of Divinity students at Princeton

---

15. John Leith, *Introduction to the Reformed Tradition* (Atlanta: John Knox Press, 1977), 7.

Theological Seminary. For him, the task of theology is "a continuing search for the fullness of the truth of God made known in Jesus Christ."[16] Thus it is not surprising to find that Migliore deals with major themes of Barth and other neo-orthodox theologians—the doctrine of revelation, the authority of scripture, the doctrine of the Trinity, Christology, providence, and other Reformed themes. There is a kind of conversation with recent theological emphases. For example, there had been "inflated talk about revelation in modern theology," Migliore says, but it is important to see how it is that God's self-disclosure occurs. It is far more than communication of information about God. He talks about the role of reason and imagination in revelation, picking up contemporary concerns, even as he draws on the long tradition from Calvin to center on scripture and Jesus Christ as the Word incarnate. This tendency to interweave tradition and issues that are currently being raised can be seen in several instances—the question of ecology, for example, in a chapter on "The Good Creation"; liberation theology in the chapter on Christology and elsewhere; and spirituality in "The Holy Spirit and the Christian Life." Note how he relates past and present in his statement about "the interconnectedness of life."

> Missing in the individualized, privatized, bureaucratic, and cosmetic forms of Christianity today is any real understanding of the interconnectedness of life that is expressed in all the basic doctrines and symbols of classical Christian faith.[17]

In his chapter on "The New Community," he goes on to say this:

> The Christian understanding of God as trinitarian communion and of salvation as the free participation of creatures in God's society of love highlights the importance of the church for Christian faith and theology.[18]

What Migliore does is to present a reasoned and understandable interpretation of theological doctrine in the context of contemporary issues, a move toward disproving the view "that theology is in utter disarray." He says this:

> My purpose in writing this book is to offer an introduction to Christian theology that is both critically respectful of the classical theological tradition and critically open to the new voices and emphases of recent theology. I hope that the influence of the liberation theologies of our time—especially feminist, black, and Latin American—will be evident throughout the book.[19]

---

16. Daniel Migliore, *Faith Seeking Understanding* (Grand Rapids, Mich.: Eerdmans, 1991), 1.

17. Ibid., 188.

18. Ibid.

19. Ibid., x-xi.

Leith, Guthrie, and others of this group bear out the purpose stated in Migliore, although of course with varying styles and emphases. It is the study of this group that prompted my first conclusion that neo-orthodoxy is indeed alive and well. Other writers in other categories of Barrett's schema do show the long-term impact of the movement. But for them all, there is much modification, with a much less strident voice than Barth's, for example. The urgency of Barth has been replaced by urgency in the voices of liberation theologians, but those who speak from within the Reformed tradition are not foreigners to neo-orthodoxy. However, the Biblical Theology movement does seem to have moved away from its earlier efforts to turn the "one story of the Bible" into a theology text. Influential books and curriculum texts for the church are still available, but the approach of Christian educators is informed by recent biblical scholarship and educational theory more than by the earlier movement.

Persons who are devoted to some of the values embodied in H. Richard Niebuhr's theology do not see themselves as his disciples. They draw on and develop Reformation themes that were so important to his pervasive, deep commitment to the sovereign God, to his realism as he analyzed and worked through problems of Christ and culture, to his transformationist perspective and his belief in *metanoia* as a way of life for the Christian. James Gustafson, drawing on "a broad range of scholarly and pedagogical interests" in his *Ethics from a Theocentric Perspective*, contends that

> religion is increasingly advanced as instrumental to subjective temporal human ends: desire for happiness, for success, for freedom from guilt and anxiety. . . . Both individual pieties and social pieties become instrumental not to gratitude to God, the honor of God, or service of God, but to sustaining purposes to which the Deity is incidental, if not something of an encumbrance.[20]

His view that the therapeutic has triumphed, that "cheap grace" is what is sought, plus other persuasive analyses of "our circumstances" make one ready for his theocentric theological ethics, in what he says is a clear "preference for the Reformed tradition."[21]

Given our space limitations here, perhaps the best thing to do is to quote the three elements Gustafson wishes to stress within that Reformed tradition.

> These are (1) a sense of a powerful Other, written about in the post-Calvin developments as the sovereignty of God. (2) The centrality of piety or the religious affections in religious and moral life . . . an attitude of reverence, awe, and respect which implies a sense of devotion and of duties and

---

20. James Gustafson, *Ethics from a Theocentric Perspective* (Chicago: University of Chicago Press, 1981), 18.
21. Ibid., 157ff.

responsibilities as well. (3) An understanding of human life in relation to the powerful Other, which requires that all of human activity be ordered properly in relation to what can be discerned about the purposes of God.[22]

Even the suggestion of these convictions, which cannot be explicated here, says something about their potential power.

Douglas Ottati considers some of the same themes as Gustafson, but approaches them differently. In his preference for the term "Reforming" Protestantism, he calls for a continuous process of self-critical reform and a transformational engagement with the world. He says this: "Reforming Protestantism fosters a theocentric piety that seeks to transform the world and to participate faithfully in God's all-inclusive commonwealth."[23]

Attempts at renewal and revitalization suffer from "severe internal conflicts." The cultural divide between conservatives and progressives is reflected in the church. "Reforming conservatives tend to support activities aimed at forming a distinct Christian identity," including emphasis on "Bible study, denominational heritage, prayer and evangelism." At the same time, amid "divergent impulses and the potential for conflicts," the progressives "tend to support activities aimed at engaging a cosmopolitan culture." In the midst of this "polarized ecclesiastical ethos" and the "erosion of communal contexts for education and theological discourse," the values of both conservatives and liberals are of significance. "Reforming Protestants . . . have good reasons to worry about the survival of Christian identity," but also to care about engagement, interpretation, re-evaluation of attitudes and institutions in "the intricate, encompassing, and influential web" in which we live. In the midst of this complex situation, Ottati calls for an effort to revitalize "the reforming spirit of faithful participation." One of the encouraging prospects of Ottati's position is the fact that he sees educational possibilities and implications to accompany the basic perspective set forth in his proposed direction for the future. It is to be hoped that he will develop such ideas even more fully in his forthcoming book, *A Theology for Reforming Protestantism*.

The third group of theologians, picking up that strand of conviction that Ottati calls the "conservative impulses for distinct identity formation,"[24] is represented here by Donald McKim. His *Encyclopedia of the Reformed Faith* is a major contribution to exactly that purpose. As editor, he does not draw on only one perspective or school of thought, but uses the services of persons who give commentaries on a wide spectrum of topics that contribute to understanding and valuing the heritage. His *Major Themes in the Reformed*

---

22. Ibid., 163-64.
23. Douglas Ottati, "Conservatives, Progressives and the Spirit of Reforming Protestantism," *The Christian Century,* 740. Other quotations from Ottati in this paragraph come from the same article, 740-743.
24. Ibid., 740.

Tradition serves the same purpose in an equally impressive way. Essays are from theologians representing the whole spectrum of positions referred to in this essay, beginning with John Leith's "The Ethos of the Reformed Tradition" and ending with Cynthia Campbell's "Feminist Theologies and the Reformed Tradition," along with Alan Sell's concluding reflections on "The Reformed Family Today." McKim himself deals with "A Reformed Perspective on the Mission of the Church in Society," as well as other topics. The plan is to "trace the development of major themes historically through the writings of various Reformed theologians," and to "deal with a theological topic from a Reformed perspective."[25]

In his book *What Christians Believe About the Bible*, McKim undertakes a demanding task in exploring and comparing the view of the Bible in various traditions. As he looks at the Reformed position in the perspective of its confessions, he finds that sixteenth-century Reformed confessions are more explicit in their statements about scripture than, for example, are the Lutherans. They occupy a midway position between the Roman Catholics, "who sought a blend of scripture and tradition" as authoritative, and the Anabaptist groups "who stressed the illumination of the Spirit as the only source of religious authority." In fact, for the Reformers, scripture is "self-authenticating as the Word of God." The Holy Spirit inspires, illumines, and interprets scripture.[26] In the "Theological Declaration of Barmen" and "The Confession of 1967," McKim finds continuity with the tradition, giving witness to Jesus Christ as the Word of God to which scriptures attest. But the scriptures are nevertheless "human words" and call for "literary and historical understanding."[27] Jack Rogers, in his commentary on the Presbyterian *Book of Confessions,* demonstrates the importance of interpretation of the Reformed heritage and identity in the shaping of the future, as do various other writers.

The fourth group of theologians center more on the emphasis that Ottati calls the "progressive demands for relevant engagement." Albert Winn, who wrote "The Reformed Tradition and Liberation Theology" in McKim's *Major Themes in the Reformed Tradition*, calls attention to some liberation "emphasis," representing the Reformed concern for social justice and public responsibility rather than any technical advocacy of "liberation theology." He chooses Latin America liberation theology, specifying several themes, with "trepidation," and the "humorous awareness that all lists of themes result in caricatures."[28] They number five: (1) God is on the side of the oppressed. (2) In Latin America, oppression is systemic. (3) To participate in libera-

---

25. Donald McKim, ed., *Major Themes in the Reformed Tradition* (Grand Rapids, Mich.: Eerdmans, 1992), xi.

26. Donald McKim, *What Christians Believe About the Bible* (Nashville: Nelson, 1985), 32.

27. Ibid., 33.

28. Albert Winn, "The Reformed Tradition and Liberation Theology," in *Major Themes in the Reformed Tradition*, 78. All the lists in this section are from the same essay, 77-91.

tion is salvific work. (4) The church must become the church of the poor. (5) Theology is critical reflection on praxis.

Whether or not he is a liberation theologian, many of the stands Winn has taken are suggestive of these emphases. In any case, he sees how Reformed theology could be deepened by serious dialogue with liberation technology. (1) We can be reminded of our own long history of political involvement. (2) We can be reminded that Reformed theology was origi-nally a theology of the oppressed. (3) We can be helped to take seriously neglected portions of the Bible. (4) We can be driven to reconsider the con-nection between Calvinism and capitalism. (5) We can be reminded that praxis, doing the truth, is an old Calvinist custom. But there are other Reformed emphases the liberationists need to hear, Winn says—among them, we all need to be reminded of "the reality and pervasiveness of sin" and of "the proper place of the Word of God." There is a sense of which Presbyterians *are* liberation theologians if they claim that strong emphasis in the history that calls for responsibility for and action in the public sphere for the common good.

One theologian mentioned by Winn is Robert McAfee Brown, who has taken seriously the study of "neglected portions of the Bible," and in so doing has become a prophetic voice in the Reformed tradition. Building on his own broad-based biblical scholarship, Brown has contributed signifi-cantly to the current conversations in theology, as in his *Unexpected News: Reading the Bible with Third World Eyes*. Several other persons—Letty Russell, in her work on "partnership," for example—deal with facets of the concerns of liberationists. The person who is probably the best Reformed spokesperson for liberation theology itself, rather than one who is influ-enced by it, is Choan-Seng Song, of the Reformed Church in America, as well as the Presbyterian Church in Taiwan. Professor Song, of the Pacific School of Religion in Berkeley, California, has written of narrative theology, is now working on multi-volume Christology, and speaks eloquently in *Third-Eye Theology* and elsewhere. He has some advice for educators; we will come back to him later.

Although most theologians do their work according to some assumed or explicit methodology, several theologians in various traditions are expe-cially concerned about clarification of their approaches, as in the fifth group-ing. David Tracy, Roman Catholic, in his *Blessed Rage for Order*, says to ben-efit by our "even-increasing pluralism" and to avoid the lazy tolerance of "a commonsense eclecticism that can mask intellectual chaos," he seeks to work to "articulate and defend an explicit method of inquiry, and used that method to interpret the symbols and texts of our common life and of Christianity."[29] Tracy develops a revisionist model with a description of an

---

29. David Tracy, *Blessed Rage for Order: The New Pluralism in Theology* (New York: Seabury, 1975), 3.

appropriate methodology. Some of the Reformed theologians we have considered have been serious about that task also—Douglas Ottati, for one—but
no one, so far as I know, has taken the task as seriously as David Tracy.

Of particular interest to people reading this chapter will be the current
discussions of theological education. What is its purpose? What should it look
like in the future? Reformed theologian David Kelsey has been in the midst
of these conversations for the last decade, and in his two recent books, *To
Understand God Truly: What's Theological about Theological Education*
and *Between Athens and Berlin: The Theological Education Debate,* he has
presented the most comprehensive analysis and proposals of which I know.
His care to document the historical and philosophical "mapping of the field"
of his investigations demonstrates methodological clarity. The analysis of
Athens and Berlin as two alternative models, with probing of rationale, purpose, and curriculum, leads to the conclusion that what theological education
should be about is—God. And "to understand God truly" is the purpose of
theological education. How does one go about planning an education that is
informed by that purpose? "A theological school is a community of persons
trying to understand God more truly by focusing its study of various subject
matters within the horizon of question about Christian congregations."[30]
Given that framework, one can plan for specifics. Although those specifics
are worthy of discussion, they cannot be considered here. But the value of
specified methodology is made clear.

William Placher would be a Reformed theologian whom it would be interesting to investigate as to methodology in his historical and philosophical
approach to issues. In his Stone Lectures at Princeton, 1992-93, he asks that
his audience put aside all cultural and historical images of God, looking
only at Jesus, the carpenter's son from Nazareth, to ask, "What sort of God
would that imply?"[31] He takes on the task, beginning with the Gospel of
Mark, which, in method, is "a use of the narrative shapes of Scripture in the
doing of theology."[32] In spite of difficulties, one is led to suppose that "God,
more than anything else, freely loves, and in that love is willing to be vulnerable and to risk suffering."[33] Placher says, quoting Hans Frei, that, for
Christology, "it is not that the doctrine is the meaning of the story, but rather
the story is the meaning of the doctrine."[34] This interrelation of narrative
and theology is productive in its potential for enriching understanding. A
comprehensive analysis of all Placher's work would doubtless be instructive.

There are other contemporary interpreters of Reformed theology with

---

30. David Kelsey, *To Understand God Truly* (Louisville: Westminster/John Knox
Press, 1992), 131.

31. William Placher, "Narratives of a Vulnerable God," *The Princeton Seminary
Bulletin* 14:2 (New Series 1993), 134.

32. Ibid.

33. Ibid., 142.

34. Ibid., 148.

affinities for the five groups named by Lee Barrett, or standing outside their boundaries. One of the most distinguished is historical theologian Brian Gerrish, who is particularly apt at dealing with continuity and change. A quotation from Calvin with which he begins one of this essays might be his own goal: " Our constant endeavor, day and night, is not just to transmit the tradition faithfully, but also to put it in the form we think will prove best."[35] In his emphases, Gerrish would be much like the scholars interpreting Calvin[36] and his "descendants" through to H. Richard Niebuhr, but without drawing on Niebuhr as directly as others do. The work of Canadian theologian Douglas Hall, of Lewis Mudge, Ben Kline, and numerous others would be instructive to include, but the ones selected as a sample do give at least a sense of that activity that is renewed vitality. Such a sampling is presented with the kind of trepidation Albert Winn felt in giving his "lists" of liberation themes in Reformation theology. Nonetheless, the sampling, limited though it is, gives us a basis for looking at the background of potential influence for Christian educators who work in the Reformed tradition.

Part Two

THEORY AND PRACTICE IN REFORMED EDUCATIONAL MINISTRY

Reformed themes presented in terms of historical beginnings and contemporary developments come to us as continuing emphases: the theocentric focus, the life of piety and of calling to participate in the purposes of God, the authority of scripture, and the importance of education. Variations and special concerns—liberationist themes and the relation of the church and culture, for example—can be interpreted in light of these major emphases. So we must ask: If one could get to the essential core of the ideas considered up to this point, what would that mean for Christian education? What are the applications, or better, implications for educational ministry today? What is its purpose? Its subject matter? Its agencies and strategies? Recognizing that the risk of trying to condense and simplify too much is still with us, let us consider what conceptual categories might emerge for us in education—pri-

---

35. The quotation is from Calvin's "Defense Against Pighius," quoted by Brian Gerrish in *Tradition and the Modern World: Reformed Theology in the Nineteenth Century* (Chicago: University of Chicago Press, 1978), 13.

36. In fact, Gerrish is particularly adept at relating the thought of Calvin to that of other theologians. In the essay just quoted, "Continuity and Change: Friedrich Schleiermacher on the Task of Theology," Gerrish sees much kinship between Calvin and Schleiermacher.

marily as *content* and as *perspective*. Eight major concepts of bases for work in education are suggested here.

1. *The purpose of the church, its ministry, and its education might be summarized in the first question and answer of the Westminster Shorter Catechism:*
Question: What is the chief end of man?

Answer: Man's chief end is to glorify God, and to enjoy him forever. The sexist language is left unchanged; it needs reformulation, as does the whole catechism, and even H. Richard Niebuhr's statement that the simple language of Jesus Christ is the "most intelligible key to his own purpose and to that of the community gathered around him," namely, that the goal is "the increase among men of love of God and neighbor."[37] The love of neighbor is surely implicit in the love of God. Purpose, therefore, is not a matter of speculation, but of the disposition, the will, the heart, or, as Jonathan Edwards would say, of that "true virtue" that is "love to Being in general."[38]

The theocentric perspective suggested by almost every writer we have cited is summarized here and suggested as the focal point for the Reformed tradition. Calvin says, "We are not our own. . . . On the other hand, we are God's; let us, therefore, live and die to him." The first step, then, is "to abandon ourselves, and devote the whole energy of our minds to the service of God."[39] This service motif so characteristic of Calvin and the Reformers is only a part of that "belonging to God" that brings gratitude, awe, reverence, love, joy, all a part of theocentric focus.

In fact, the theologians we have considered call the church to this biblical and historical center. If one looks at educational programs, at the content of much material, the perspective is either confused, or, as Gustafson would say, anthropocentric. The need to remember and recapture is clear.

2. *"Faith seeking understanding" is an appropriate frame of reference for Reformed educational ministry. Perhaps one should add, "faith seeking faithfulness."* The first phrase appears often in various contexts, and although it goes back at least as far as Anselm, it is heard especially frequently in Reformed circles. In fact, understanding is a key term for the words theologians would speak to educators. The act of questioning, doubting, asking why is part of what it means to be human. This understanding does not prove God's existence, nor ensure growth in faith. It does help with connecting to the Christian community and building a common loyalty and set of values for the community. It does help with working out in sometimes painful, demanding processes the understanding of what is right and good to do in particular circmstances, the determination of moral action. In other words, being faithful requires understanding of what God is calling us to be and to do.

---

37. H. Richard Niebuhr, *The Purpose of the Church and Its Ministry* (New York: Harper and Brothers, 1956), 31.

38. Quoted in *Christian Ethics: Sources of the Living Tradition*, ed. Waldo Beach and H. Richard Niebuhr (New York: Ronald Press, 1955), 391.

39. Ibid., 284.

In the major national study of church education, *Effective Christian Education*, [40] completed in 1990, Presbyterians came out valuing a "thinking" climate over a "warm and friendly atmosphere" to a greater degree than most other participating denominations. However, in the study as a whole, more people actively experienced that warm atmosphere than were stimulated by "intelligent thought and discussion." Friendliness does influence congregational loyalty, but thinking contributes more to faith maturity (as specified qualities set up for the study). People do not find much help in knowing how to deal with politics and social action, but want that help. Presbyterian youth report more than do youth in other mainline denominations that they "learn a lot." The whole study, the largest ever undertaken in the United States, is impressive in the prominence it gives to religious education by persons who report on their faith and growth in faith. It also points to the difficulty of capturing the meaning of terms like faith and faithfulness, where faith "seeks" and faithfulness is "response" to the grace of God, more than it is marked by achievable characteristics. What theologians have to say to us as we utilize findings of the psychological and sociological sciences is important—and what educators have to say about the contributions of these disciplines is also necessary.

One other reflection on faith in its relationship to education—too much attention to faith and its development seems destructive of the very hope that motivated the analysis. Or better, according to theologians, the theocentric focus becomes distorted in favor of a human-centered focus. Educators will recognize that "telling my story" activity, which, repeated too often, trivializes faith. The thing to remember, we are told by Calvin, is that knowledge of God and knowledge of self are interdependent. But note that this is knowledge *of* God, not just knowledge *about* God. It is an experienced relationship of trust, belief, and confidence within which a person comes to know who he/she is.

3. *The life of the Christian may appropriately be described as the life of piety.* Piety is a term that appears so often in the thought of recent Reformed theologians that they must have had questions raised for them in the current situation that makes them explore the heritage. Piety, for Calvin, according to Howard Rice, is "the way we exercise our Christian freedom as people whose lives have been touched by grace and who are thus keenly aware of being responsible to God." Or, he says, "Our piety is the way we live our lives responding to God's presence by attending carefully to that presence."[41] Thus, the challenge of piety is not how to be "pious," but how

---

40. *Effective Christian Education: A National Study of Protestant Congregations, A Report for the Presbyterian Church (U.S.A.).* (Minneapolis: Search Institute, 1990), 2-14, 40-42.

41. Howard Rice, *Reformed Spirituality: An Introduction for Believers* (Louisville: Westminster/John Knox Press, 1991), 46.

to "discover the joy of obedient discipleship."[42] Such an understanding of piety points to several areas in which educational decisions must be made.

One such area is that of the current emphasis on spirituality, almost a fad in educational circles. That term, according to T. Hartley Hall, is "something of an oxymoron, in that the word 'spirituality' is notably absent from the works of all the classical Reformed writers." It is a post-Vatican II concept that is now broadly related to a "popular understanding of spirituality as 'an individual's interior search for meaning and wholeness,' as both concept and practice." For Hall, the preferred term is "piety."[43] This is the kind of piety Rice was talking about as an appropriate meaning for spririituality. The development of the idea for both these writers is in terms of awareness of God's presence, of corporate social responsibility as a part of the entire Christian community, of obedient discipleship as a joyful and reverent response to God. It is instructive for those trying to meet the longing they sense in Christians for religious experience out of a "sense that modern life has become flat and without passion or a sense of purpose."[44] The emphasis on spiritual formation, too, seems to be a call for help in becoming the kind of person who does experience joy and purpose. Are we talking about Brother Lawrence's "the practice of the presence of God"? Educationally, what difference does it make as to what terms we use? Does it matter how we interpret them? Or understand them? What practices point to and substain a life of piety? Again, educators and theologians need to be in dialogue.

A second area is the relation of doctrine to the life of piety. Calvin is clear.

> Doctrine is not an affair of the tongue, but of the life . . . and is received only when it possesses the whole soul and finds its seat and habitation in the immost recesses of the heart. . . . To doctrine in which our religion is contained we have given first place, since by it our salvation commences; but it must be transfused into the breast, and pass into the conduct, and so transform us into itself, as not to prove unfruitful.[45]

Doctrine has to do with *truth*. We quoted Jack Stotts as saying "truth is in order to goodness." Religious education, which may seem to be about doctrine, is also about goodness and the "practice of the presence of God" and concern for the common good. Such an expression of doctrine, of course, is limited by our motivation, our self-interest, our sinfulness—but the life of piety is possible to one who in humility and gratitude accepts the offer of salvation. How can the educator convey that intricate understanding of doctrine?

---

42. Ibid., 47.

43. T. Hartley Hall, "The Shape of Reformed Piety," in *Spiritual Traditions for the Contemporary Church*, ed. Robin Maas and Gabriel O'Donnell (Nashville: Abingdon, 1990), 202.

44. Rice, *Reformed Spirituality*, 7.

45. John Calvin, *Institutes of the Christian Religion*, trans. Henry Beveridge, 2 vols. (London: James Clarke, 1949), Bk III, chap. vi, par. 4.

4. *Life is to be oriented toward the purposes of God.* A close corollary to a life of piety is a life oriented toward the purposes of God. For Reformed Christians, the call is to join with all those in the ecumenical circle to try to discern what God's purposes are and to join in bringing them to pass. This transformationist view had much to do with the historical involvement of Reformed leaders in political affairs, and public issues of many kinds. God created the universe and disciples are called to care for that creation, not just to maintain the church.

5. *The individual and the community are to be invited into the task of theological reflection.* At least two points are implied in this statement, reflecting an assumption amoung several theologians we have considered. One is that *all* the participants in the community of faith are to seek to relate God's purposes to life. *All* are to "do theology." This is a part of the Reformed perspective; it is related to the idea of the "priesthood of believers." There is sometimes more of a tension between clergy and laity in Reformed churches than in others,[46] although the polity would seem to suggest otherwise. Given different situations, testing points, backgrounds of knowledge and experience, the wisdom of the community is needed for the theological enterprise. A second point is that the very process of interpreting the tradition and relating it to the present is also the process by which that tradition is appropriated and reinterpreted. The contribution to the community's self-understanding is also the process by which one is educated.

What is being described is one aspect of the current emphasis on practical theology, viewed here as hermeneutical. Richard Osmer, Presbyterian educator-practical theologian, talks about the importance in congregational education for persons to have an opportunity to interpret the particular situations in their lives in such a way that they "make sense." He says this:

> It is here, in the struggle of Christians to interpret their lives in light of what can be discerned of God's purposes for the world, that we locate practical theological reflection. It is not the special province of academic specialists. It is the reflective dimension of piety. It is the theological and moral reasoning persons undertake as they seek to live out their vocations in the world.[47]

Systematic theologians serve a different purpose in the life of the church. Here, we are speaking of individual Christians and congregations. The process of practical theological reflection is carefully delineated by Osmer, beginning

---

46. See Schuller et al., *Ministry in America*, 458. This summary statement by Arthur Adams, Dean Hoge, and Lefferts Loetscher also suggests that there is "greater-than-average emphasis on a beginning minister's having . . . a learned understanding and presentation of Christianity," as well as other characteristics that bear out what has been said about distinctive characteristics of the Reformed tradition.

47. Richard Osmer, *A Teachable Spirit: Recovering the Teaching Office in the Church* (Louisville: Westminster/John Knox Press, 1990), 164-65.

with "the identification of what is going on" through stages of evaluation and analysis to "enactment of a concrete response and continued reflection on the effects that it has."[48]

7. *The teaching ministry is crucial for the church's carrying out its mission.* That commitment is clear in the life and work of Calvin is an assumption in the writings of many Reformed theologians and is even recognized as a distinctive characteristic for Presbyterians ("its genius") by Jack Stotts. What is called for here is a recovery of that tradition and a clarifying of the role of the pastor, especially in light of the invitation to all Christians to engage in theological reflection.

A move is underway to formulate what is meant by "the teaching office" in the Reformed tradition. In his *A Teachable Spirit: Recovering the Teaching Offce in the Church*, Richard Osmer offers the most comprehensive and scholarly treatment of the subject in recent years. He reconceptualizes the concept by posing three centers for the teaching office: professional theologians and seminaries, for scholarly inquiry and clergy education; representative leaders and bodies, for teaching and education on behalf of the denomination as a whole; and congregations, for practical theological reflection and lay education.[49] The ordained minister's role, then, is to "facilitate dialogue among the various centers of teaching authority in the church." Because of their "education and special relationship to the denomination," they are "uniquely qualified" for this task,[50] and for developing what Calvin called "a teachable spirit." The proposal is complex, and worthy of exploration.

8. *The faith community is called to rethink the educational ecology of the modern day—to judge old patterns and to plan for new institutions and agencies, related to one another through complementary functions in carrying out the traditioning and transformative mission of the church.* Interlocking agencies in the past helped in the education of mainline Protestants, public school and Sunday school, home and church, church colleges and journals, congregations and seminaries, as Robert Lynn so clearly pointed out in his 1989 Sprunt Lectures at Union Theological Seminary in Virginia, "Visions of Church and Commonwealth." He also said that no new educational institutions have appeared in the last century to compensate for the breakdown of the old system.

Douglas Ottati approaches this problem with the proposal that we give "vigorous, sustained and creative attention to the institutional ecology of reforming Protestantism." In fact, he offers some specific possibilities.

Expanded educational programs cooperatively supported by congregations and local judicatories, lay academies, theological institutes or "think-tanks," church-related schools, college student associations, church-related jour-

---

48. Ibid., 167. The series of stages of reflection is clearly described in the section beginning with 167.

49. Ibid., 179.

50. Ibid., 207.

nals—these are some of the institutions that might be developed. Personally, I also favor theological education for lay adults that is keyed to a congregation's order of worship.[51]

Many of these educational foundations obviously cannot be claimed to be uniquely Reformed. They are themes or emphases that emerged out of the Reformed theological stream. Many of them, with variations, are also to be found in the writings of other mainline denominational scholars. Here, they simply have the special traits that characterize the Reformed denominations, and even there we find variations within denominations.

There is no directive here as to precisely what we are to teach in educational ministry, but the implication is clear: If we want to "pass on" the tradition, there are some key beliefs and goals that are to be ignored at our peril. Of equal importance is an implicit principle in each of the eight statements: Our attitudes and perspectives probably are as important as a specific subject matter. That is an educational way of stating the principle. Those who educate with the attitude of humility and commitment to a life of piety, of joy and service, embody a transformationist approach that is more than teaching *about* the life of grateful response to God's gifts.

Given reminders of content and perspective, especially important to the developing of our theories of religious education, there is still the question: What are we to do? What practices are to be recommended? Theologians rarely risk specifying such concrete actions—although some do. Take Douglas Ottati's ideas about new institutions as a case in point. But hints are to be found, and there are some specific suggestions for practice that have already appeared as we reflected educationally on theological proposals.

Consider educational emphases on spirituality and spiritual formation, resistance to catechetical instruction or a propositional approach to doctrine, and disaffection with bureaucratic and institutional systems on which educational ministry depends. Theologians repeatedly deal with the life or piety as a key emphasis in the Reformed heritage. They question telescoping "piety" into "spirituality." But what are implications of the wide responsiveness to devotional groups, support groups, study of spiritual disciplines, uses of a spiritual director, and other practices? We need to hear the longing expressed in this personal need for religious experience, at the same time we are called to put our activities into a more theocentric context. Even the use of the language of piety may need to be questioned as we look at current perceptions. Certainly the content and procedures of our spiritual growth groups should be studied. Thus a question is raised by theology.

The emphasis on the importance of doctrine by theologians is often too lightly dismissed by educators fearful of indoctrination. But the view of doctrine as a transformative process, the call for theological reflection by

---

51. Ottati, "Conservatives, Progressives, and the Spirit of Reforming Protestantism," 743.

all believers, not just teachers or pastors, all suggest a refocusing of our look at methods and purposes. Surely understanding "what we believe" is basic to educational purpose, and surely the direct offering of interpretation by teachers is one way or one step in achieving our purpose. There is enough sophistication among educational theorists with respect to choosing models and methods of teaching to fit diverse goals for us to call that knowledge into conversation with theologians concerned about doctrine. A major problem, however, is in choice of subject matter. Looking back at the days of neo-orthodox dominance and the clarity with which doctrine was specified, we realize by way of contrast how many voices and directives come to those planning educational programs. Clarity does seem to be emerging, but we need to work together to be aware of reformed emphases within the various perspectives and to benefit from the vitality in theological thought. Perhaps this is a place where Richard Osmer's view of authority in a reconceptualized teaching office takes on a quite practical note.

Historically and sociologically, as well as theologically, we are called to disciplined and imaginative thinking about new and changed institutions. Suggestions already mentioned illustrate the point, and perhaps nothing more needs to be said here, except that the great Protestant and Reformed principles embedded in the institutional ecology of education in the past must be kept alive in our thinking. We are concerned for order, polity, form, but we must also be concerned about the relationship of the church to the public and the common good.

These three issues about educational ministry arise out of study of theological emphases. Such a moving from theory to educational practice is one way of proceeding to relate theology and education. Another way is to raise questions from the education scene and see what directions or helps are to be found in theological formulations. One such question has to do with the role of the Bible. Although both theologians and educators continue to repeat the traditional affirmation of the authority of the Bible, there is not much clarity in the Christian education enterprise as to practical implications of that statement. Work like that of Donald McKim in *What Christians Believe about the Bible* helps. We do not need a resurrection of the old biblical theology, but we need to engage in conversation with biblical scholars and theologians, so we can articulate our methodology and interpret it to people who seek for themselves clarity about the Bible.

Probably one of the most important questions to be raised is that of the influence of mass media and technology and what help is to be found from theology. Do we use computers to "teach" doctrine, so that we are at least clear about terms, names, dates, and are then free to explore meaning in a variety of ways? Do we set up groups to study TV programs and to become aware of values that are being taught, of a culture that is rapidly replacing the old Protestant civic virtue ethos? Do we go into the production venture? Do we form groups of parents who agree on what their children will not watch? Possibilities are endless. Direct answers seem hard to find in any one of the basic principles thus far enunciated, but the need for clarity about perspectives and values is obvious. And this is one place where the Reformed views of the importance of the ecumenical church is of major importance, Communities, ecumenical parish groupings, task forces need to work together to achieve some clarity, not for censorship, but for a more relevant educational ministry.

The recognition of the importance of relevance was accompanied by the other pole of the necessity for identity formation. With the context of multiculturalism and pluralism, education needs help from theology about how this identify formation is to take place. Theologian C. S. Song proposes that the division of labor between theology and education in this area particularly has proven to be "bad theology and bad education."[52] One possibility for him is to recapture the universal love for story-telling, because "doctrines alienate, while stories unite." If persons of different faith and cultures listen to each other, to myths, story-traditions, parables, we learn "how to penetrate stories to allow them to disclose their 'ultimate concerns.' " What happens is that Christians come better to understand themselves and who they are, but horizons are expanded, and we will "learn from one another to discover the richness of God's creation." For Song, rather than dwelling on metaphysical arguments, we should teach as Jesus taught. What other approaches and understandings are available? We need to work together on the answer to that question. Congregational leaders, frustrated by bombardment of information about pluralism and admonitions about doing multicultural education, underneath feel guilty about not knowing what to do about the situation, and intuitively raise theological questions. Both relevance and identity formation are important to leaders as they seek to be faithful to the Reformed emphases.

One final issue is that of whether to concentrate on developing a curriculum focused on the Reformed family or on a denomination, or to change directions and rely on independent publishers who specify goals and theological context. Ecumenical resource centers would facilitate familiarity with options and help in decision making. Historically, the curriculum plan into which twelve major denominations moved after the demise of the great denominational curricula of mid-century was a program called *Christian Education: Shared Approaches*. There were four approaches: Knowing the Word, Interpreting the Word, Living the Word, and Doing the Word. Differences were not theological, but methodological. The plan was a part of Joint Educational Development, a collaborative enterprise that quietly dissolved itself in November 1993. The need for denominational identity that came about with neo-orthodoxy in the fifties had been replaced by a new cooperative spirit, but then again the need for identity and control was raised.

---

52. C. S. Song, "Christian Education in a World of Religious Pluralism," 170. Other quotaions in the paragraph come from 170ff.

For Presbyterians, the reunion of 1983 brought with it the development of a
new plan, Presbyterian and Reformed Educational Ministry (PREM) beginning in 1988, with a major revision to begin in 1994. There are two options,
Bible Discovery and Celebrate. Principles call for Reformed education to be
biblically grounded, historically informed, ecumenically involved, socially
engaged, and communally nurtured. The principles remind us of our theological bases. But we are still faced with the dilemma of living in a pluralistic
world where we need to know our own tradition, but more. The idea of
choice among publishing agencies, with denominations limited to specifically
defined resources, as for church officer training, confirmation, new member
preparation, and the like, may emerge as a realistic approach in the present
situation. Careful attention is needed for whatever direction is chosen.

Literally dozens of other issues from the arena of practice could be
addressed to theological presuppositions. Whether the move is from theology to education or from education to theology, the conversation is needed.

EDUCATIONAL MINISTRY IN THEOLOGICAL PERSPECTIVE

The current decade finds most Christian educators willing to verbalize
the need to relate to theology and to affirm the importance of the Bible, but
with much less seriousness than was evident in the momentary theological
dominance of the mid-century. It finds theologians willing to talk about the
life of the mind in the service of God but slow to venture into reflection
about appropriate practices for implementing those values. References to
preaching are included in systematics, but mention is rarely made of teaching; there are of course dramatic exceptions, some of them noted here. Such
a critique of the relationship between theologians and educators in the
Reformed family led directly to the conclusion of Choan-Seng Song that
theology and education should "join forces and construct education that is theologically informed and theology that is educationally viable in the world of
many cultures and religious."[53] Both theology and education are open to
reform in this perspective.

This kind of observation leads to conclusion of even broader significance,
that we in the Reformed tradition must so reconceptualize the understanding
we bring to educational ministry that we will take an interdisciplinary
approach to our task.[54] That topic must be addressed in the future. We can
anticipate that doctrinal formulations will benefit from educational reflections
carried out in an interdisciplinary process, even as the process is informed by
the traditon. Thus the Reforming stance continues.

---

53. Ibid., 171.

54. James Loder has an excellent article exploring this point, explaining alternative ways
of doing interdisciplinary studies, and making his own recommendations in
"Interdisciplinary Studies," *Encyclopedia of Religious Education*, ed. Iris V. Cully and
Kendig Brubaker Cully (San Francisco: Harper & Row, 1990), 327-28.

CHAPTER TWO

Thomistic Theology and Religious Education

MARK HEATH

Part One

INTRODUCTION

The place of the theology of St. Thomas Aquinas in religious education, such as that education was in the thirteenth century, was probably small. The deeper question of what a theology of the thirteenth century might have to say about the rich variety of experiences we call religious education today is, however, of critical value. There are reasons that this is so.

The first is that for over seven centuries St. Thomas Aquinas has been cited by Roman Catholic church authorities and venerated in Roman Catholic intellectual literature, philosophical and theological, as a theologian enjoying unique worth and eminence.[1]

This singularity also has received the same special affirmation in the most recent era, beginning in the late nineteenth and continuing now almost through the entire twentieth century.

Then, too, five of his works, identified for centuries as short theological works or as sermons, have in the most recent years been reclassified and

---

1. A brief summary of the history of papal praise and commendation of the theological and philosophical work of Aquinas may be found under *Thomas Aquinas, Saint, The New Catholic Encyclopedia*, by W.A. Wallace and J.A. Weisheipl (1966), 14.

have found their place in literature as catechetical instructions. In the past few years they have become available in English translations.[2]

The Life and Work of St. Thomas Aquinas

Thomas Aquinas was a medieval friar, a Dominican, whose short life began in 1225 in Roccasecca, a town near Monte Cassino, halfway between Rome and Naples. Placed as a boy among the Benedictine monks of Monte Cassino, he began his studies and religious formation there until, at age fourteen he was sent to the University of Naples to continue studies in the liberal arts and philosophy. There, for the first time he read the texts of Aristotle and of his Arab commentator, Averroes.

In April 1244, he entered the community of the newly formed Order of Preachers, the Dominicans, just a few years after the death of their founder, the Spaniard, Dominic of Guzman. After overcoming some difficulties with his family over this decision, he was sent to Paris in 1245 and later to Cologne to study with the greatest Aristotlean scholar and teacher of the time, the Dominican, St. Albert the Great. At Cologne, in 1250, he was ordained a priest.

He returned to Paris in 1252 to prepare for the doctorate. There, he immediately began the academic regime which would be typical of his life: lecturing on the *Sentences* of Peter Lombard and on the Sacred Scriptures, taking part in public disputations and writing commentary on works of Aristotle. Such lecturing and writing were done with distinction during the next twenty years in papal curiae and theological schools in Viterbo and Orvieto, Rome and Naples, and Paris and Cologne.

In 1272 he was in Naples for the founding of a new Dominican theological school and for the organizing of the preaching of the friars in that area. For the Lent of 1273 he assigned himself to give a group of conferences on the Creed, the Our Father, the Ten Commandments, and the Hail Mary.

---

2. An English translation of the five, made from noncritical texts, may be found in Joseph B. Collins, *Catechetical Instructions of St. Thomas Aquinas* (New York: Wagner, 1939, 1953). Collins' translation are made in part from Laurence Shapcote, Westminster, Md: *The Three Greatest Prayers* (London: Burns Oates and Washbourne, 1937 and Westminster, Md: Newman, 1956, and Sophia Institute Press, Manchester, NH: (1990) and Laurence Shapcote, *The Commandments of God* (London: Burns Oates and Washbourne, 1937).

A translation of one made from the Leonine critical text with an historical and textual introduction is in Nicholas Ayo, C.S.C., *The Sermon Conferences of St. Thomas Aquinas on the Apostles Creed* (Notre Dame, Ind.: University of Notre Dame Press, 1988).

The original texts are: *Collationes super Credo in Deum; Collationes super Pater Noster; Collationes super Ave Maria; Collationes de decem praeceptis; and De articulis fidei et Ecclesiae sacramentis ad archiepiscopum Panormitanum* (Collins translates 2nd part only). Notes on authenticity and editions may be found in James A Weisheipl, O.P., *Friar Thomas d'Aquino* (Garden City, NY.: Doubleday, 1974), 392,401-402.

These took place in the afternoon of each day in Lent, in St. Dominic's Church, to congregations largely made up of university people. The sermons were taken down by his secretary, Reginald of Piperno, translated into Latin and published a short time after his death. This group of sermons, given in Lent 1273, have together in this century been published as *Catechetical Instructions.*[3]

After Lent he returned to his teaching and writing. Then, on December 6, 1273, he suddenly and abruptly ceased teaching, writing, and dictating. During the following spring on the way to Lyons for the coming 1275 General Council he died in the Cistercian Abbey of St. Mary at Fossanova on March 7, 1274. He was just under fifty years of age. So widely known was his work and the holiness of his life that he was canonized fifty years later, on July 18, 1323.

One may gain some idea of the measure of his work by glancing over the record of his writing and scholarship or by visiting a library in which his *Opera Omnia* are found.[4]

Over the centuries there have been ten more or less complete publications of the *Opera Omnia* of Aquinas. The definitive text of these works, called the Leonine Edition, of 50 Tomes (amounting to 50-60 folio volumes) is being prepared and published by the Leonine Commission, established by Pope Leo XIII in 1880. The two most accessible editions prior to the Leonine are the Parma *Opera Omnia* (Parma: Fiacacadori 1852-73) in 25 folio volumes and the Vives *Opera Omnia* (Paris: Vives 1871-72) in 34 quarto volumes.[5]

---

3. Collins, *The Catechetical Instructions of St. Thomas Aquinas*. Reginald's Latin texts were quickly turned into scholastic commentaries on the text of the Creed, Our Father, etc. Weisheipl, *Friar Thomas d'Aquino*, 401-403.

4. The most complete catalogue is that of I.T. Eschmann, O.P. *A Catalogue of St. Thomas' Works: Bibliographical Notes,* in Etienne Gilson, *The Christian Philosophy of St.Thomas Aquinas* (New York: Random House, 1956). This catalogue with notes is found also in Weisheipl, *Friar Thomas d'Aquino.* 335-405 and Wallace and Weisheipl, *Thomas Aquino Saint*, (1967), 111-115.

5. By kind of publication the works are:

1) Three long theological syntheses: *Writings on the books of the Sentences of Peter Lombard, Summa contra gentiles*, and the *Summa Theologiae.*

2) Seven major and twelve other public academic disputations which yielded publications of various length. (One, for example, *On Truth*, requires three volumes in an English translation.)

3) Commentaries on eleven books of Aristotle, especially *On The Posterior Analytics, Physics, On the Soul, Metaphysics, Ethics, and Politics.*

4) Commentaries on the text of the Sacred Scriptures: on five books in the Old Testament, principally those of the prophets; and, in the New, on the Gospels of Matthew, John, and the Letters of Paul.

5) Various polemical writings; Expert opinions, requested often by popes; Letters, liturgical pieces and sermons.

THEOLOGICAL THEMES OF RELEVANCE
TO RELIGIOUS EDUCATION

Which parts of this enormous deposit of theological wisdom is valuable to religious educators?

Apart from one question in the Disputed Question *Truth* and one article in the *Summa Theologiae*, which will be referred to later, Thomas the theologian wrote almost nothing directly about the teaching of religion.[6] His theology, however, has a role to play in this area.

Statements of his theology, while not always a canonized way of stating the faith, became an approved way of teaching the faith. In this use, his theology shaped the content and texts of catechisms and other religious education materials.[7]

One can then ask what are some of the theological tenets of St. Thomas Aquinas (as distinguished from statements of the Christian faith) which play a role in religious education.[8]

Clearly the corpus of his work is so vast and even the text of his most mature work, the *Summa Theologiae,* so comprehensive, that one can select only those few themes or theological teaching and structures which seem of importance to religious education.

Thomistic religious education is systematic.

Even the most casual acquaintance with the writings of Thomas Aquinas, and especially the works best known as associated with his name, his two *Summas*, leaves the impression that their most obvious characteristic is that of synthesis. Parts, questions, tracts, and articles march down the pages in the military formation of a dress parade, in which each unit, with its own leader and name, follows the other. Or parts, questions, and articles stand eternally in place like the elements of a Gothic cathedral: the pillars, vaults, nave,

---

6. *Truth* 3 vol. (*Questiones Disputatea De Veritate*) translated by James V. McGlynn, S.J. (Chicago: Regnery, 1953) 2 Q. 11 "The Teacher"; *Summa Theologiae* I, q. 117, a.l. Also: *II Sentences* 9, 2, and 4; 28, 5. and *Contra Gentiles* II, 75.

7. A sign of the place of the theology of Thomas Aquinas in religious education is that in both the great and authoritative catechisms of the Roman Catholic Church his work is referred to in various ways. The theological teaching of the *Roman Catechism* (or *Catechism of the Council of Trent For Parish Priests*) (1566), came to be normative for catechetical presentations of the faith for over 350 years; and the new *Catechism of the Catholic Church* (1992) will be a valuable and authorized instrument and standard for the teaching of the church's faith and Catholic doctrine in years to come. Both of these books are marked by Thomas' theological presence and the second by specific references.

8. Although no individual example perfectly fits the place assigned it in a typology, the religious education of St. Thomas Aquinas matches most closely the *Traditional Theological Approach,* identified by Harold William Burgess in *An Invitation to Religious Education* (Birmingham, Ala.: Religious Education Press, 1975).

choir, windows soaring together to form a marvelous and organic whole.

Even those who are unfamiliar with the text of Thomas Aquinas have effectively been made aware during the recent half century of the judgment that synthesis is the quality most characteristic of Thomas's theological work. In his seminal work *Christ and Culture*,[9] H. Richard Niebuhr identifies Aquinas as "the greatest synthesist in history." To illustrate the scope of Aquinas's achievement here, Niebuhr cites the following areas:[10]

1) *Christ and Aristotle*: Thomas uses the philosophy of Aristotle to provide a matrix for understanding the unity and integrity of Christian faith in all areas: dogmatic, moral, and spiritual.

2) *Philosophy and Theology*: Articles in the *Summa Theologiae* in the same subject area flow back and forth between philosophy and theology, offering the evidence that gospel and human wisdom are joined in an organic body of knowledge, each reinforcing and illuminating the other.

3) *State and Church*: Dramatically, in the *Summa*, in the treatise on law, the text moves through the biblical Hebrew and Christian gospel law to human law, preserving the distinction of each yet without tension or opposition.

4) *Christian and Civic Virtues*: The distinctions and analyses of the *Ethics* of Aristotle are used as the interpretative structures of the gospel and of the Christian virtues of faith, hope, and love. The Aristotelean virtues of prudence, justice, temperance, and fortitude are also the virtues of the Christian spiritual life.

5) *Christ and Culture*: The foundations of these two areas with their distinctions are grace and nature. In a thousand places Thomas maintains that grace does not destroy nature but builds on it; that the divine life of grace is basically in harmony with created human life; but that grace is far above culture.

Synthesis is, then, a value which the theology of Thomas Aquinas would seek in religious teaching. It ought to be characteristic of any kind of religious education, even for beginners.

Such would be Thomas Aquinas's mind. The sign that he espoused this

---

9. H (elmut) Richard Niebuhr, *Christ and Culture* (New York: Harper, 1951), x and 259; (English edition: London: Faber & Faber, 1952, 256); (New York: Harper Torchbooks, 1956). This book, itself a work of theological synthesis, was the forerunner of other books of typologies or models of theology, including official Roman Catholic studies of types or models of Christology and interpreting scripture in the church. The book has been continually available in bookstores and used in theology courses since its publication.

10. The headings are Niebuhr's. The developments of each are Niebuhr's and mine.

appears clearly in the introduction or Prologue to his most mature work, the
Summa Theologiae: It could be a manifesto of a teacher of religion at any level:

> Since the teacher of Catholic truth has not only to build up those who are
> advanced but also to shape those who are beginning, according to St. Paul:
> Even as unto babes in Christ I have fed you with milk and not meat, the pur-
> pose we have set before us in this work is to convey the things which
> belong to the Christian religion in a style serviceable for the training of
> beginners.
> We have considered how newcomers to this teaching are greatly hin-
> dered by various writings on the subject, partly because of the swarm of
> pointless questions, articles, and arguments, partly because essential infor-
> mation is given according to the requirements of textual commentary or the
> occasions of academic debate, not to a sound educational method, partly
> because repetitiousness had bred boredom and muddle in their thinking.
> Eager, therefore, to avoid these and other like drawbacks, and trusting in
> God's help, we shall try to pursue the things held by Christian theology, and
> to be concise and clear, so far as the matter allows.[11]

System in the presentation of truth about God and creation reflects their cor-
porate organic unity, which expresses the inner unity of God himself. For
Christian teachers this unity participates in the unity of Father, Son, and
Holy Spirit.

In the *Summa Theologiae*, his most synthetic work, Thomas Aquinas
worked out an expression of unified knowledge which combined in one
vision 1) the universal and necessary properties of God and creation and 2)
the contingent and free works of grace, i.e., of God's freedom and of human
free will as these are found in salvation history.

The basic structure of this synthesis is seen in the outline given by Thomas:

> So because, as we have shown, the fundamental aim of holy teaching is to
> make God known, not only as he is in himself but as the beginning and
> the end of all things, and of reasoning creatures especially, we now intend
> to set forth this divine teaching by treating first of God, secondly of the
> journey to God of reasoning creatures; thirdly, of Christ who, as man, is our
> road to God.[12]

Although he never explicitly identifies it, the source of this scheme is the
Neoplatonic doctrine of emanation-return/*exitus-reditus*, by which things
come from God and return to God.

This is unfolded in detail in the outline of the *Summa*:

---

11. *Summa Theologiae*, I, Prologue. Translations of texts of the *Summa* will be taken
from the edition published by McGraw-Hill, New York, 1964.

12. *Summa Theologiae*, I, q. 2, Prologue.

Part I: On God, and the emanation of creatures from God. This part includes the theology of God and the divine attributes and persons of the Trinity; creation and the angels, the work of the six days, man and the divine government.

Part II: The return of the rational creature to God. Human happiness; the elements of the human free act; passions, habits, and the virtues, law, grace; the theological virtues: faith, hope, and charity; and the cardinal virtues: prudence, justice, temperance, and fortitude; faith related classes of men and women.

Part III: Christ, the way of return to God. The Incarnation, Christ's attributes; the events of the infancy, childhood, and adulthood of Christ; his passion and death, the Resurrection and Ascension; the Sacraments; the Last Things.

The glory of the synthesis of the *Summa* is the fusion of all the parts of Christian teaching into a unity which observes the following:

1) It is a logical plan; yet all its divisions are so framed that there is an inner flow of movement which gives life to the logical structure;

2) The synthesis is more than a classification imposed from outside; it is an organic whole formed of the natures of things and of the events of the biblical narrative with their own intelligibility.[13]

That is, the *Summa* enjoys that logical necessity which an organized science requires, and yet it respects and incorporates the grace-contingency of the events of the history of salvation.

Upon this circuit Thomas locates the facts and deeds recorded in sacred history with all that their contingency and their dependence on the free will of God and man implies.

Thomistic religious education is theocentric.

If, for Thomas, a first quality of any teaching of religion is that it be systematic, a second is that it be theocentric. To gather this one need only ask what is the organizing principle of his system, i.e., the formal reason or reality or value that gives the system its skeleton or basic structure. For Aquinas it is clearly God and the possession of the divine being in vision.

In the *Summa*, at the beginning of his section on the human, he wrote:

Man is made to God's image and since this implies, as Damascene tells us, that he is intelligent and free to judge and master of himself, so then, now that we have agreed that God is the exemplar cause of things and that they issue from his power through his will, we go on to look at this image, that is to say at man as the source of actions which are his own and fall under his responsibility and control.[14]

---

13. M (arie) D (ominique) Chenu, O.P., *Toward Understanding St. Thomas (Introduction a L'Etude de St. Thomas d'Aquin)* (Chicago: Regnery, 1964), 301-310 passim.

14. *Summa Theologiae*, I-II, Prologue.

All religious education treats of God as the ultimate purpose of human activity, the ground of being, the meaning of the fullness of humanity, of Christ-like living, of brotherly, sisterly, and neighborly love, of the service of the poor or of the protection of the environment, etc. Each of these will be the formal reason of the synthesis which will gather into a unity all the elements of the teaching taken up in any instruction.

For Thomas, however, the relation to God is the direct and immediate reason that influences the choice of each topic of instruction and which defines the place which each tract, question, and article taken in the synthesis.

Thomas had this conviction because the nature of theology gave it to him: Theology is the study of God in himself and of all other things in their relationship to God as source and as end.

This conviction gave him reason to write long sections on the nature of God, One and Triune, of creatures coming from God and returning to God, and of the human person as the image of God.

The whole moral life, as the way of the human striving, finds its place in God as the ultimate good; and the rightness of each human action derives both from its seeking the happiness proper to its own nature and its orientation to God as the end. In the same way the moral life establishes a place for God in that the transcendence of God is the source of the goodness of the virtues and the gifts.

Finally, the nature and work of Jesus: the incarnation and redemption and the sacraments of the church are given their theocentric place as the way by which humans return to God.

Nothing is clearer in his work than this theocentric character. It was inherent in the teaching of religion for centuries before him and for seven centuries after. It was verified in the three-part model of catechetical instruction which he used in his sermons in 1273:

1. **Creed**: which contained two parts: a) God and creation and b) the nature and role of the man-God-Jesus Christ, the Savior;
2. **Code**: the commandments: the way of those redeemed by Jesus;
3. **Cult**: prayer: the way of living in union with God as taught by Jesus.

That religion teaching should be theocentric was not an innovation of Aquinas; it was the shape of the proclamation and the content of religious education for long centuries.

Thomistic religious education is doctrinal.

Overwhelmingly, Thomas Aquinas teaches that religious education, or the teaching of religion, ought to be doctrinal, that is intellectual, concerned with the knowledge of the faith.

One might object that the very statement of this reveals a fault in the theory: it seems to be deficient, lacking the purpose of religious instruction, to root the faith in life. "Where," one asks, "is there any motive to live the faith in the bare understanding of it?"

That Aquinas would think that education must be doctrinal derives certainty from the intention of all his life: to teach sacred doctrine. But sacred doctrine is primarily speculative because it deals with God and divine things and then secondarily practical, as it concerns human actions in their relation to God.

This is borne out by his understanding of faith: its object is God as First Truth and of all things in their relation to God as their source and as their end.

Contemporary religious educators prefer to think of education in faith in a more practical and pastoral sense, as about God who reveals himself not only as First Truth but in his nature as he is given in the sacred scripture as father, friend, Lord, master, teacher, judge, etc. So, its correlative, faith, is taught primarily a dynamic sense as the human response to the self—manifestation of God which invites of the believer a total response of assent, obedience, trust, reverence, and love.

The reason for this difference is that in Aquinas's mind, faith is understood in the formal sense which distinguishes it from hope and love. Faith, then, is primarily cognitive and objective; it is distinguished from the other virtues which make up the full human response to God, the God whose goodness is known only by faith.

But almost from the first page of his treatise on faith Thomas maintains that, in the structure of the human mind, truth takes the form of judgments and the composition of subject and predicate, while yet holding that the act of faith terminates not at the proposition but at the reality it conveys.

> The object of faith may be considered in two ways: First, as regards the thing itself which is believed, and thus the object of faith is something simple, namely the thing itself about which we have faith.
>
> Second, on the part of the believer, and in this respect the object of faith is something complex by way of a proposition.[15]

This ancient conviction supports the assertion of Eric D'Arcy:

> The church understands her doctrines to be objective truths, communicable without loss of meaning in propositions of human language. (This neither assumes nor entails a propositional account of *Revelation*.) That understanding cries out to be brought into fruitful intercourse with Gottlob Frege's notion of *Gedanken*. Frege was the father of modern logic, both formal and philosophical, and an essential element in his philosophy is his objectivist account of the way that *Gedanken* are: (1) The primary bearers

---

15. *Summa Theologiae*, II-II, q., 1 a. 2.

of truth and (2) transmissible without loss of meaning in propositions of
human language. . .

Time and after time (Newman) shows doctrinal knowledge to be integral
to an authentic adult faith. "That vague thing 'our common Christianity' I
disregard for the reason that it cannot throw itself into a proposition.
Christianity is faith, faith implies a doctrine, a doctrine implies propositions."[16]

Religious education, Thomas Aquinas would teach by both his example and
word, ought to be doctrinal. At times this has seemed restrictive. Yet, in the
many initiatives in Roman Catholic religious education programs which
have appeared in the centuries since 1274, and in all the languages of the
human race, in catechisms large and small, school texts and adult manuals,
men and women writers, researchers and parents have been faithful to this
charge.

Thomistic religious education is the work of student and teacher.

Scholars or students who look for a theory of religious pedagogy in the
writing of Thomas Aquinas may find materials rare. The sources are: 1)
One question of four articles in the Disputed Question Truth called *The
Teacher (De magistro)* which was debated and then written up in 1257 in the
very early years of his teaching career and 2) one article (I, q.117, a.1) in the
Summa Theologiae written in 1266, nine years later, which summarizes the
first article of the older work.

The four articles in *The Teacher* offer solutions to multiple alternate opinions related to each of the following questions:

1. Can a man or only God teach and be called a teacher?
2. Can one be called his own teacher?
3. Can a man be taught by an angel?
4. Is teaching an activity of the contemplative or the active life?

The article in the *Summa* is titled:
Can one man teach another?[17]

Little has been written about these works, their content or the importance
of the contribution they may make to teaching theory. On the one hand a
translation in English of the *De magistro* was not generally available until
1953 when it was published as part of a three volume translation of the
whole of the Disputed Question *On Truth*.[18] The only one before 1953 was

---

16. Eric D'Arcy, "The New Catechism and Cardinal Newman," *Communio* 20:3 (Fall
1993), 485-502.

17. *Summa Theologiae*, I, q. 117, a. 1.

18. *St. Thomas, Truth (De veritate)*, 3 vol., trans Mulligan-McGlynn-Schmidt (Chicago:
Regnery, 1952-54).

done privately by John McCormick, S.J., of Marquette University for a small volume, *Philosophy of Teaching of St. Thomas Aquinas,* published in 1929.

In the first paragraph of an extended summary of the teaching of the *De magistro,* Thomas Gilby writes:

> The gaining of knowledge is like the acquisition of virtue and the ordinary drawing forth, *eductio,* of physical forms in the material world. Taking a middle course Thomas rejects the two extreme views, on one hand that the learner's mind merely yields to the impressions of ideas from some higher intelligence, on the other hand that knowledge already lies dormant there and only requires to be aroused. . . . His own theory applies an inference of his general philosophy that a potential being or a "can be" is real but becomes an actual being of an "is" given the action of an efficient cause . . . a thing that itself is actual under the respect that is being considered. So knowledge can be potential and not yet actual in a mind that has yet to discover or learn it.[19]

In her commentary on the *De magistro,* Mary Helen Mayer observes the following:

> The *De magistro* notes and defines the difference between instruction and discovery; teaches that God teaches man principally in giving him his potentialities; that man can develop these potentialities through himself in the methods of discovery or, in instruction, he may accept the aid of a teacher who ministers to his nature as a physician does to a patient "applying medicines which nature uses as instruments in healing"; . . . A teacher can lead to knowledge more quickly and easily than anyone can lead himself in that the teacher, having completed an act of knowledge, presents his concepts with a symbol, and "the words of the teacher have a closer relation to causing knowledge than have the mere perceivable things outside the mind."[20]

In a later era of the history of Thomism, Jacques Maritain would summarize the argument of the first article of the *De magistro* about the cooperative action of teacher and student required for learning.

He first summarized and rejected the position of Plato, and then went on:

> The teacher does possess knowledge which the student does not have. He actually communicates knowledge to the student whose soul has not previously contemplated the divine Ideas before being united to the body; and whose intellect, before being fecundated by sense perception and sense

19. *Summa Theologiae,* I. q.) Volume I, Christian Theology, trans., notes, glossary by Thomas Gilby, O.P. (New York: McGraw-Hill, 1964), 59.

20. Mary Helen Mayer, *The Philosophy of Teaching of St. Thomas Aquinas* (Milwaukee: Bruce, 1929), 104-119 passim.

experience, is but a tabula rasa as Aristotle put it.

Yet what is the kind of causality or dynamic action exerted by the teacher? Teaching is an art; the teacher is an artist. . . . It is rather with the art of medicine that the art of education must be compared. Medicine deals with a living being that possesses inner vitality and the internal principle of health.

The doctor exerts real causality in healing a sick man, yes, but in a very particular manner: by imitating the ways of nature herself in her operations, and by helping nature by providing appropriate remedies that nature herself uses, according to her own dynamism, toward a biological equilibrium.

In other words, medicine is an *ars cooperativa naturae,* an art of ministering, an art subservient to nature. And so is education. The implications are far-reaching indeed.

But the vital and active principle of knowledge does exist in each of us. The inner seeing power of intelligence, which naturally and from the very start perceives through sense experience the primary notions on which all knowledge depends is thereby able to proceed from what it already knows to what it does not yet know. . . .

This inner principle the teacher must respect above all; his art consists in imitating the ways of the intellectual nature in its own operations. Thus, the teacher has to offer the mind either examples from experience or particular statements which the pupil is able to judge by virtue of what he already knows and from which he will go on to discover further horizons. . . .

All this boils down to the fact that the mind's natural activity on the part of the learner and the intellectual guidance on the part of the teacher are both dynamic factors in education, but that the principal agent for education . . . is the internal vital principle in the one to be educated.

The educator or teacher is only the secondary, though genuinely effective, dynamic factor and a ministerial agent.[21]

This is a long quotation; but the heart of Thomistic pedagogy: an analysis like the fresh wind from the north: the news by German psychologists in the nineteenth century which sent the teaching of religion off on a new and revolutionary tack.

Thomistic religious education can be directed to action.

A theological teaching, its ancient source Cicero and Aristotle, which Aquinas incorporated in the moral theology section of the *Summa,* unlikely as it may seem, became and continues to be for thousands of young men and women a principle which shapes their religious education, their moral training, and of the effectiveness of their social influence.

It is Thomas Aquinas's analysis of the three actions of the virtue of pru-

---

21. Jacques Maritain, *Education at the Crossroads,* (New Haven: Yale University Press, 1943), 30-31.

dence. By itself it seems a simple and straightforward analysis. In the mind of a creative thinker and leader, however, it became the most effective teaching method developed in the Christian communities in the twentieth century. The text of Aquinas:

> Assuming the definition of prudence as right reason applied to human conduct, then it follows that the chief act of prudence will be the third act of reason as engaged with conduct.
> Here the activity of reason goes through three stages. The first is *taking counsel*, which, as we have seen, is inquiry in order to discover.
> The second is *forming a judgment* on what has been discovered. So far we have not left theory.
> Practice, however, is another matter. For the practical reason, which is meant for the doing of something, pushes on to a third act, namely of *commanding*; this consists in bringing into execution what has been thought out and decided on. And because this approaches more closely to what the practical reason is for, it is a chief act of the practical reason and so of prudence as well.[22]

While this is a simple and brief description of the ways in which all humans come to decisions to act, it could also be, if broken down and then formalized with procedures for each step, a way of training men and women, especially in small groups, to reflect on their own thought processes and come to decisions about what they might and ought to do.

That this has happened is the experience of many, particularly young industrial or agricultural workers, students in high school and university and married couples. It may be the most fruitful contribution of Thomas Aquinas has made to the ministry of religious education.

Part Two

General Applications of Thomistic Religious Educational Theory

Religious Education is systematic.

Of all pedagogical characteristics of the *Summa* the most notable is that of synthesis. The fact of this in the teaching of Aquinas and the form it takes in

---

22. *Summa theologiae* II-II, q. 47 a. 6.

the *Summa* have been noted above. Why is it important? What does it mean for education today?

That a systematic and organic presentation of the faith is of supreme importance to religious education may be noted from a study of religious education materials within the Roman Catholic church everywhere in the world during the recent quarter century.

In noting an almost universal transformation of classical catechesis which began in the late 1960s, Cardinal Joseph Ratzinger observed in 1983: "One no longer has the courage to present the faith as an organic whole in itself, but only as selected reflections of partial anthropological experiences, founded in a certain distrust of the totality. It is to be explained by a crisis of the faith, or more exactly of the common faith of the church of all times."[23]

In an Apostolic Exhortation concerning the religious education effort of the Catholic church, written after the Fourth General Assembly of the Synod of Bishops, Pope John Paul II outlined some of those characteristics of instruction which define the idea of synthesis:

It must be systematic, not improvised, but programmed to reach a precise goal;

it must deal with essentials, without any claim to tackle disputed questions or to transform itself into theological research or scientific exegesis;

it must, nevertheless, be sufficiently complete, not stopping short at the initial proclamation of the Christian mystery such as we have in the kerygma;

it must be an integral Christian initiation, open to all the other factors of Christian life.[24]

These criteria are general, and therefore they can be fulfilled in various ways; indeed there is no limit to the ways in which they might be realized. They were fulfilled by Aquinas in the *Summa*. They were satisfied in the *Roman Catechism* of the Council of Trent (1566).

They are the marks of the new *Catechism of the Catholic Church* (CCC) of 1992. As the new catechism is published and the text becomes universally available, study will undoubtedly include evaluations of the ways in which that text is faithful to them.

One has already appeared, an essay: "Major Themes and Underlying Principles of the Catechism of the Catholic Church"[25] which explains that the

---

23. Joseph Cardinal Ratzinger, quoted by Bishop Christoph Schonborn, "Major Themes and Underlying Principles of the Catechism of the Catholic Church," *Living Light* 30:1 (Fall 1993), 56.

24. Pope John Paul II, *Apostolic Exhortation Catechesi Tradendae*, Vatican Polyglot Press, Rome 1979, 30-31.

25. Schonborn, "Major Themes and Underlying Principles," 54-64.

Catechism builds up a synthesis, an organic view of the faith under three aspects: 1) the principle of the hierarchy of truth, 2) the unity of the church's tradition in space and time, and 3) realism in approaching the content of faith.

Other catechisms or religious education materials in other faith traditions or in the many theological traditions of the one faith may build their syntheses on other principles. They ought not, however, lose sight of the need for organic teaching all together.

Thomistic religious education is theocentric and doctrinal.

How Thomistic religious education should in practice be theocentric is an important question for writers, editors, and teachers. The immense flood from the human sciences of opinion and theory related to religious education offers an attractive possibility to writers to design and teachers to present human-centered religious education; a course which, when taken up, could result in criticism and disappointment. The use of such knowledge, and of biblical science as well, must be judicious.

Religious education which is called Christocentric, in essence cannot avoid its orientation to God since the life and teaching of Jesus in the Bible and the liturgy is that he is pointed to the Father. Christocentric catechesis, then, is theocentric *and* Christo-con-centric.

Thus, in religious education which is doctrinal the chief quality is that it be accurate. It is here principally that successsful catechisms survive, a fact attested to by the large number of presentations of the faith which have failed after a short time.

It is here that the "catechism genre" has its strength. Although "learning catechism" was (and will continue to be) criticized because the books were the work of theologians and not educators, its strength was that what was learned had a perennial value to it. Although the memorization of incomprehensible words and phrases" seems an outrage to a child, the memorized formulas took on meanings that gave understanding to later adult life.[26]

Thomistic religious education involves teacher and student.

In the *De magistro*, the Disputed Question *On the Teacher*, Aquinas identifies several qualities and activities which provide general guidelines for

---

26. The questions raised in this section are perennial. Roman Catholics and other religious educators will be assisted by the suggestions found in:

General Catechetical Directory (Directorium Generale Catechesticum), U.S. approved translation (Washington, D.C.: U.S. Catholic Conference, 1971) and a commentary:

Berard L. Marthaler, O.F.M. Conv. *Catechetics in Context* (Huntington, Ind.: Our Sunday Visitor, 1973) and

Sharing the Light of Faith: National Catechetical Directory for the Catholics of the United States (Washington, D.C.: U.S. Catholic Conference, 1979) and

Sharing the Light of Faith: An Official Commentary (Washington, D.C.: U.S. Catholic Conference, 1981).

the practice and transaction of teaching. Joseph Collins summarizes the basic teaching in contemporary terms:[27]

> [The *De magistro*] contains the basic principles which aim to make learning functional and activated by virtuous motives:
>   The process of education is essentially one of self-activity on the part of the student; the teacher is a trained and experienced guide.
>   Learning is self-development, a form of discovery and a bringing to perfection the inner powers of the pupil.
>   Teaching, therefore, is a cooperative activity.
>   The learner must have an objective, a goal, an outcome of learning in mind.
>   The teacher must guide, stimulate, and assist the pupil to arrive at this end.

These and other canons were discovered empirically by educational psychologists in the middle years of the nineteenth century and they became staple rules for education from that time forward.

SPECIFIC TEACHING METHODS AND THOMIST THEOLOGICAL DOCTRINES HISTORICALLY IDENTIFIED

After four general observations of the way in which the theology of Thomas Aquinas might influence and shape religious education, attention turns to *specific* methods or programs in which the general principles may be seen to be shaping the instruction. The methods will be identified in their historical context.

Thomistic religious education is systematic, theocentric and doctrinal.

On several occasions before and during the work of the Council of Trent, convened intermittently (1545-1563) to respond to Lutheran and Calvinist teachings, proposals were made to provide a uniform and comprehensive manual which would supply parishes with an offical book of Catholic teaching for the faithful.[28] First mentioned in 1546 was a catechism for children and uninstructed adults. After the first approval of the idea, however, nothing was heard again until 1562 when on February 26, a commission was appointed.

The members of this commission were fathers of the council: Cardinal Seripando O.S.A. as president, Bishop Carlini, two Dominican bishops, Marini and Forcarari, and a Dominican theologian Foreiro. A team of con-

---

27. Joseph B. Collins, S. S. *Teaching Religion: An Introduction to Catechetics* (Milwaukee: Bruce, 1953), 17.

28. E. Mangenot, *Catechisme* in *Dictionnaire de Theologie Catholique 2-2 (Paris 1905)*, Col. 1917-18.

sultants was named and assignments were made to the several sections of the projected book: Creed, Sacraments, Commandments, and Our Father/Prayer. Of the twenty consultants, four were Dominicans, two Franciscans, two Augustinians, with twelve others. They were instructed to avoid particular opinions, i.e., of individuals and schools, and to express the teaching of the universal church, keeping especially in mind the decrees of the Council of Trent. The tone was not to be polemical or argumentative.

When the approved manuscript was sent to the printer, no title was attached to it. Possibly because the four parts were: Creed, Sacraments, Ten Commandments, and The Lord's Prayer the book was named a "catechism."

It was a long text. A 1909 edition of the Latin text is 470 pages;[29] a contemporary English translation makes up a quarto book of 589 pages.

Did the theology of Thomas Aquinas influence this work of religious education? Students of the text assert that it did.

The official text of the catechism provides footnotes only of the texts of the scriptures and of an occasional Father of the Church and only when he is quoted in the text. No references are made to Aquinas or any other theologian.

Two modern editors of an English translation of the catechism,[30] however, John J. McHugh and Charles J. Callan, both Dominicans, have identified by footnotes to the catechism text 332 places in the *Summa Theologiae* of Aquinas "contemporary comments and indications of pertinent passages in St. Thomas" which relate to the text.

The fact that Dominican theologians, whose professional study was in the *Summa* of Aquinas, played such an important role in the writing of the catechism offers some strong clue that, although no singular opinions of Thomas were allowed, nevertheless the substance and ways of presenting the truths of the faith were those of Thomas.

It is important to cite the *Roman Catechism* because practically every work in Catholic religious education published between 1566 and 1900 looked to this catechism for definitions, judgments, and canonized expressions of faith. The *Roman Catechism* was, of all written sources, the reason for the unity of the Catholic community during the difficult period of the sixteenth to nineteenth centuries. The authority and influence of the catechism, therefore, was immense. For those centuries it was the classic statement of Christian theology, and it was the source of the doctrinal theocentric and systematic qualities of Roman Catholic instruction. Statements, definitions, and phrases of the *Roman Catechism* found their way over the centuries into the catechisms, into children's minds, their memories and on their lips.

Because the *Roman Catechism* was more a handbook of theology than a

---

29. *Catechismus Romanus ex decreto Concilii Tridentini* (Ratisbonae, Romae, Neo Eboraci et Cincinnati Pustet 1907).

30. John J. McHugh, O.P. and Charles J. Callan, O.P., *Catechism of the Council of Trent for Parish Priests* (New York: Joseph Wagner, 1923).

catechism and, in its genre, a church success, the development of religious education took place apart from it.

Concurrent with the later years of the Council of Trent, a Dutch Jesuit theologian, St. Peter Canisius, aware of the great success the Lutherans were experiencing with this method, drew up and published three catechisms for students in Germany. In drawing up these catechisms Peter Canisius acknowledged his indebtedness to Thomas Aquinas.

Forty years later another Jesuit theologian, an Italian, St. Robert Bellarmine published two catechisms.

These books became the models which were adopted in dioceses around the world. Bishops and other writers translated them and modified them for local use. It was the Bellarmine catechism which the Roman authorities encouraged the American bishops for many years to adopt as the universal catechism of the growing nineteenth century American church. Toward the end of the nineteenth century, in 1873, the First Vatican Council approved a proposal for drawing up a uniform catechism for the whole church. The council could do nothing more about it, however, since the army of Garibaldi invaded Rome and the Council was prorouged, never to reassemble. (The 1962-65 Second Vatican was considered a distinctly new council.)

This was providential for, even as the council was meeting, there were already teachers, catechists, and psychologists in Europe and the United States who were poised to push beyond the catechism genre of instruction and to open a new era in Roman Catholic religious education.

The reason for this new activity was the birth in mid-nineteenth-century-Germany of experimental psychology and the application of this knowledge to education. This blossomed into recognition of, and sensitivity to, the developmental stages of children's learning. The centers of study, publication, and experiment in the new Catholic religious education were Germany and the United States: Munich, Washington. The active leaders were a group of priest catechists in Munich, who eventually were identified with the Munich Method and an American priest, trained in theology and pschology, Thomas Edward Shields, at the Catholic University of America in Washington.

SPECIFIC EDUCATION METHODS ROOTED
IN THOMISTIC THEOLOGY

Thomistic religious education is systematic, theocentric, and doctrinal.

The transformation of the catechism way of teaching religion was a slow process which did not really end until after the Second World War. Until then, all Roman Catholic publications of religious educational materials were systematic because they were still based on the old triad, now a quadrilateral, of Creed, (Sacraments), Commandments, and Prayer, and theocentric and doctrinal because they found their sources in the deposit of the *Roman Catechism,* enhanced by faith in the unique holiness of the Blessed Virgin Mary (the definition of the Immaculate Conception: 1854), The discussions of faith and reason and of the authority of the pope (the definition of papal infallibility of the First Vatican Council 1871-3).

These classic strengths of catechesis retained traditional Thomistic influences. They were, however, beginning with the new century, enriched by new methods of teaching religion. These came from Munich and Washington. But the influence of Thomistic thought was present here also.

Thomistic religious education involves teacher and student and can be shaped to action in dialogue with the world.

The Munich Association and Method

The first significant development in Roman Catholic catechesis in the post-Roman Catechism era and the first in which the theology or philosophy of Thomas Aquinas might have played a role in shaping curriculum or method came in Germany and Austria toward the end of the nineteenth century. It was called the *Munich Method* from the Munich Catechetical Association whose members developed it. The method was a direct offspring of a method designed by Johann F. Herbart. It came into religious education through a follower of Herbart, Tuiskin Ziller, and his student O.Willmann, who first developed an application of the Herbartian teaching method to Roman Catholic catechesis.

In this process, while the purpose of the Herbart's method, that all education should be for building character, was adopted by the Catholic catechetical leaders, much of Herbart's philosophy was left behind. The Method was in fact easily assimilated by Catholic philosophy and found a place in that of Thomas Aquinas.

In the first Catholic adoption, the Munich Method had only three steps; in later versions there were five, a new step having added before the original first and one after the third. The five, with brief identifications, were:

1. Preparation: to focus the student's attention on the topic;
2. Presentation: a Bible story, etc., which contains the lesson in concrete form;
3. Explanation: the catechesis, lesson is seen to be in the narrative;
4. Application: strengthens and deepens the truths gathered and widens them for the purpose of life;
5. Recapitulation: summary, repetition of the process in brief, etc.

The method was seen as an alternative to the presentation and explanation of a text of the catechism and deducing the behavioral lesson from the text by the teacher, and then the memorizing of the text by the student. In this new way the lesson was concrete, the process more inductive, and the teacher and student arrived at the truth together.

A. The Munich Method of teaching religion was an affirmation, after 600 years, of the transaction of teaching which Aquinas had worked out in his philosophical analysis in the *De magistro*:

1. The Method affirmed and reinforced the principle that the student is the principal cause in learning by making his/her role active rather than passive. (Later developments of the method added further activity to the learning process.)

2. It associated the teacher with the student in a cooperative activity.

3. It was concrete in that the lesson began with a narrative fitted to the child's level of understanding and development of imagination; it was a learning that was rooted in a sensory experience which moved to a intellectual reflection; and closed with an application which occupied the will and emotions.

4. It was carried on with respect for the student's free will. (Herbart seemed to teach that if the process were carried out accurately the child would invariably accept the moral lesson.)

These values of the Munich Method were observed by an American priest graduate student in Germany, Joseph J. Bierle, later a seminary profesor in Rochester, New York, who brought the method to the United States in 1919. It was then developed in manuals by two other seminary professors: R.G. Bandas of St. Paul, Minnesota, and A.N. Fuerst of Cleveland, Ohio. The method was then translated into textbooks which were used in Catholic schools everywhere for thirty years.

B. The Munich Method was also a reaffirmation, in an effective educational form, of another theological principle of Thomas Aquinas: It recognized the three steps in the act of the virtue of prudence as a way of learning and used them systematically as the basis of an educational method.

1. The Method was, from its origin, keyed to the student's forming moral judgments and resolutions. A reflection on the three central steps of the Method shows 1) the perception of a biblical or other narrative event, 2) the judgment on the goodness or evil in this concrete real situation, and 3) application and the resolution to an action.

Thomistic religious education integrates faith with other human knowledge.

Pioneers in the psychological renewal of Roman Catholic religious education in the late nineteenth and the early twentieth centuries were O.Willmann and the priest catechists of Munich of the Munich Method and Thomas Edward Shields with Edward Aloysious Pace of the Catholic University of America in Washington D.C.

Thomas E. Shields was born in Mendota, Minnesota on May 9, 1862, the sixth child in a large family of Irish immigrant farmers.[31] Although he was, as it later appeared, an unusually gifted boy, he was also so unsuccessful and backward in elementary school that he was kept out of the local grade school three times, particularly for serious defect in his reading. Then, with encouragement of the new pastor and the new teacher and special tutoring and reading he advanced rapidly. Of this ten-year experience he was to write *The Making and the Unmaking of a Dullard* as he discovered that the reason for his failure in school was not poor native ability but the poor method of the teaching in the school.

Encouraged by the pastor and teacher, he grew enough in knowledge that he was accepted into the college seminary in Milwaukee and later in the major seminary of his own diocese of St. Paul. There he stood out among his fellow students and was recognized by faculty and bishop as unusually gifted. With his class he was ordained priest on March 14, 1891, just short of twenty-nine years of age.

After a short time in service of the Cathedral of St. Paul he was assigned for further study: first in theology at St. Mary's seminary in Baltimore and then in physiology and psychology at John's Hopkins University in Baltimore, where he received the Ph.D in 1895.

He then returned to the seminary in St. Paul as the resident professor of experimental science and physiology. When he had established the program and curriculum there, he was allowed to accept, effective in fall, 1902, an appointment to the Catholic University of America as a professor of physiology and psychology.

This was the beginning of a most fruitful, creative, and active period of nineteen years which would end in his death on February 14, 1921. He was only fifty-nine.

During his three years at Johns Hopkins, he became a close and enduring friend of another young priest who was completing a doctorate in experimental psychology, Edward Aloysius Pace. They were to become, a few years later, firm colleagues in the renewal of Roman Catholic religious education.

Edward Pace was born in 1861 in Starke, Florida, seven months before Shields and studied theology in Rome, receiving ordination in 1885. On his return to Florida he served briefly as the rector of the Cathedral until he was invited to the faculty of the soon to be opened Catholic University of America. To prepare for this he studied psychology, first at Johns Hopkins University in Baltimore, where he also met Shields. He then returned to Europe and studied in Louvain, Paris, and Leipzig, where in 1891 he received the doctorate in experimental psychology *magna cum laude* under Wilhelm Wundt.

On his return he was appointed professor of psychology at the University. While there, also, he arranged for an invitation to the faculty to be given to his friend Thomas Shields, who joined him in 1902.

---

31. Justine Ward, *Thomas Edward Shields: Biologist Psychologist Educator* (New York: Scribner's, 1947). A biography by an associate and friend.

Pace soon changed his interests from psychology to philosophy, a discipline in which he was soon to become a leader in the United States. He published and edited a great deal and had a special interest in scholasticism and the philosophy of St. Thomas Aquinas, from which discipline he was able to work closely with Thomas Shields in his innovative work in the renewal of Catholic education, especially in the teaching of religion.

It is principally Thomas Shields to whom attention as a religious educator is generally given, mainly because of the great energy and work he expended in it, and in which Pace assisted him greatly.

Shield's contribution was given in all the genera of influence and work. He was full of ideas both theoretical and practical. Full of enthusiasm and evangelism for the new pedagogy, he began by writing long articles on teaching in the Catholic University of America Bulletin. Much of what he wrote was gathered up and published in his correspondence courses on teaching and in the books he wrote, which were all published by the Catholic Education Press which he founded and supported personally until the books were able to provide income from their sales.

His books were *The Making and the Unmaking of a Dullard, The Education of Our Girls, Primary Methods*, and *Philosophy of Education*.

Then he wrote eight grade-school volumes: *Catholic Education Series of Textbooks for the Schools*. With Edward Pace he founded and edited the *Catholic Education Review*.

Enjoying a wide public from his writing, he was busy year-round giving lectures and workshops especially to the teachers in the Catholic schools who were almost exclusively religious sisters.

The crown of his life was the success he achieved in providing in the University (where enrollment was restricted to men) university training in contemporary educational methods for religious sisters; in summer programs and finally in a complete university curriculum in a Sisters College, which he founded and of which he remained dean.

For this last project, Sisters College, he personally was required to secure the approval of Pope Pius X, find and purchase land, find funding for the building and persuade religious superiors of several religious communities to build houses for their sisters on the newly identified and unfinished campus. This total project called for such sustained effort that it hastened his death on February 14, 1921, at age fifty-nine.

The *New Catholic Encyclopedia* says of him: "Thomas Edward Shields was perhaps the leading Catholic educator in the United States during the first quarter of the twentieth century."

Three theological principles of Thomas Aquinas are clearly visible in the religious education work of Thomas Shields:

1. The student is the principal agent of his/her education.
2. The teaching in religion should be theocentric.
3. The religion part of the educational program ought to be the integrating

principle of the whole curriculum.

Shields often criticized Roman Catholic religious education, stating that religion was not integrated with other studies. Religion ought to be the integrating principle of the whole of the elementary school curriculum, and this would guarantee that the total instruction would be theocentric.

A close associate with him in designing the curriculum and providing sections of music to each volume, who also shared his vision of elementary education, wrote of this question of integration:

> John Dewey had written before Doctor Shields of the need of a center of correlation to link together the various subjects presented to the pupil. . . . Correlation became to Shields one of the principal leit-motifs of all his teaching. It was essential to assimilation and to a balanced development. . . . Shields held that certain fundamental values remained unchanged, among them the ultimate reality of a personal God ruling all creatures and directing them to their final end. . . . To Shields an education which ignored God and his moral laws was an incomplete affair, an organism lacking a directive principle. Thus the function of religion in the classroom was not merely to convey information about God but to consecrate human life. Religious truth must unify and illumine all the subject matter and transform the mental life of each child, guiding his actions in all possible situations that might occur. Religion to Shields was the core of all knowledge. All subjects must radiate from that central point.[32]

Thomas Shields, with Edward Pace, who collaborated with him and worked with him on some of the books, manifested this passion for integration by naming each of the books in his series *Religion* and making up each as a reader in all the subjects of elementary education to be taught in each grade. Religion was the first and principal subject in each one.

A curriculum which is both theocentric and integrated is an ideal. It is difficult to write and teach at any level. Thomas Shields sought to achieve this by providing God-centered materials which included catechetical texts with materials in the areas of instruction in each of the grade levels.

Was this desire to achieve correlation or integration around God-centered themes learned from a study of the theology of Thomas Aquinas? In her description of its intention, Justine Ward seems to think not. For Thomas Shields it was an educational ideal proposed by the educational psychologists of the time and by educators like John Dewey.

But there are many pages in the theology of Thomas which provide a basis for designing correlation and integration into a curriculum. The idea of subordination of human knowledge to divine is found in the very first question of the *Summa* in the tract *On Sacred Doctrine*.[33] The discussion of the sev-

---

32. Ward, *Thomas Edward Shields*, 218, 220-221 passim.
33. *Summa Theologiae*, I q.1, a. 1-8

eral questions there would provide a sturdy foundation and enduring vision for building a curriculum and selecting readings in the eight books of the Shields *Series*.

It is essential, of course, in using these medieval and theological sources, to transpose the treatment of sacred doctrine as theological science, and of its relationships, from medieval theology into another key altogether: that of the school and its component subjects. Then "sacred doctrine" becomes "religion" as a subject and "other sciences" become other subjects of the grade.

Having done this, the first principle of curriculum building, and transposing these insights from Aquinas, is that religion is concerned with truths which only God knows, which he reveals to us and which we know by the gift he gives us, which we call faith; while the other subjects are known by the power of our human minds and intelligence and study. Many other basic conclusions flow from that.

The first is that, because God shares his secrets with us, our human happiness depends on our knowing the truths of religion. These truths, then, are known with a sureness which depends on God's knowing himself and on his honesty in telling the truth about himself to us. Finally, we are more sure of these truths of God than we are of the truths we learn in the other subjects.

We can, however, use what we learn in the other subjects to help us understand religion better and use what we learn in religion to understand the other subjects too.

Sometimes we do not understand the truths of religion. The reason is that we are sharing God's knowledge of himself and of us and that will always be mysterious to us. We do not doubt them because God does not lie and because what God teaches us is more important to us than what we learn in the other subjects.

Such notions as these, which offer possibilities of integration of a curriculum and other teaching, are the common teaching of Thomistic theology and, indeed, of scholastic theology generally, with which Thomas Shields and Edward Pace were certainly familiar. They would unavoidably have been the theological principles of the correlation of learning of the Shields readers. They are the fundamental reason that Ward could affirm that, for Shields, religion was more than conveying information about God; it was more a matter of consecrating the world.

CHAPTER THREE

Evangelical Theology and Religious Education

KENNETH O. GANGEL AND
CHRISTY SULLIVAN

INTRODUCTION

This chapter presents two challenges to the authors: (1) To define the theological commonalities for all evangelicals with proper inclusivity, yet with adequate conservative exclusivity; and (2) to describe the philosophy and process of religious education determining whether it actually reflects our theological foundations. In effect, we shall be answering the questions "Why do we do what we do?" and "How do we do what we do?"

Students of Old Testament narrative literature will recognize the chiasm used to structure the chapter. The beginning and ending focus on the One we worship and model, with the center portions devoted to the sources of authority and instruction.

SECTION ONE: LAYING THE THEOLOGICAL
FOUNDATIONS

Whom Do We Worship?

In any theology, one must start with some understanding of what one worships. We affirm that there does exist, whether we experience or understand that existence, a being, sovereign, powerful, and good, whose nature lies beyond the boundaries of human knowledge.

As we seek to describe the object of our worship, we necessarily recognize that much remains a mystery, that those with finite minds cannot neatly define Someone Who carries the characteristics of infinity. It shouldn't surprise us that such an infinite personal Being escapes our intellectual mastery.

We tread on holy ground here, and it behooves us to step with a respectful uncertainty.

Students of God look to several sources in the search to grasp a picture of Deity: the general revelation of the world around us; the acts of God and His personal disclosures throughout history (first in oral revelation and then Scripture) which form our access to revelation at this point in redemption history, i.e., the special revelation of the Bible; and finally, tradition, the works and thoughts of others through the centuries who have poured time and energy into searching out answers to such questions.

Natural revelation

Observations of nature reveal a God Who displays immense creativity. Evangelicals accept the presupposition of the Psalmist: "The heavens are telling the glory of God; and the firmament proclaims his handiwork" (Ps. 19:1[1]). The very nature of life causes us to gasp in admiration—that this infinite variety of molecular collections, controlled in such a complex manner by endless streams of DNA, could produce organisms that live and breathe, and form themselves into societies and intertwining relationships. On the micro level, it seems no matter how small a particle we seek to define, there exists yet something still smaller.

When we move to the macro level, we sense a totally different kind of awe. What kind of God can create, in a manner incomprehensible to us, and with means which we can only speculate but never be fully sure, a universe so enormous that it takes millions of years for the light from one star to reach our eyes? We have before us a picture displaying unimaginable vastness of power and magnificence. Such a portrait helps us understand why we should attempt no images of God, for they must inevitably fall woefully short. Donald Bloesch reminds us, "A dogmatic maxim of the church fathers was *Deus semper maior* (God is always greater), which catches the spirit of the prohibition of images. For theology, God does not belong to a genus. He infinitely transcends the principles and categories of human thought"[2]

Special Revelation

Turning to the more particular revelation of the Bible, we learn that God may also be characterized in terms of holiness, righteousness, and justice. When Moses comes into contact with YHWH, he is told "Come no closer! Remove the sandals from your feet, for the place on which you are standing is holy ground" (Ex. 3:5). In Deuteronomy 28, we see blessings for obedience

---

1. All Scripture quotations from the *New Revised Standard Version Bible*, copyright 1989, unless otherwise noted.

2. Donald G. Bloesch, *Christian Foundations: A Theology of Word & Spirit* (Downers Grove, Ill.: InterVarsity Press, 1992), 41.

and curses for disobedience spelled out for the Israelites. These blessings and curses display YMWH as One devoted to righteous relationships among human beings, and between humanity and God. We also learn that YHWH devotes Himself to justice. As Erickson puts it, "God not only is personally free from any moral wickedness or evil. He is unable to tolerate the presence of evil. He is, as it were, allergic to sin and evil."[3]

The Bible also reveals that God's heart beats with compassion toward those humans who so consistently fail to live up to standards of righteousness. Time after time, we read YHWH's willingness to intercede on behalf of the suffering, of concern for the widow and orphan, of a graciousness predisposed by His covenental love (*hesed*) for His people.

We also learn, through the progress of revelations, of a plurality within the godhead, a tri-unity of persons, the Three-in-One, most commonly known as the Trinity. The mystery grows as our minds try to comprehend what the Scripture reveals, that there are three, yet only one. Many Christians believe the ultimate special revelation can be found in the incarnation, eternal God visiting the human planet in mortal flesh.

Historical Theology

Our third source of understanding God consists of the writings and thoughts of those throughout history who have wrestled with the description, the explanation of this incomprehensible being Who yet invites intimacy. In this short space, we can only describe, not defend, our theology. Our understanding of God, though, reaches through history to the early church fathers who struggled, as do we, with the concept of the Trinity as revealed through the Scriptures. The Nicene creed, written in 325 A.D. helps us set limits when speaking of God, yet does not claim to define or explain Him. These words still stand today as a basis of our theology:

> We believe in one God, the father All Governing, creator of all things visible and invisible;
> And in one Lord Jesus Christ, the Son of God, begotten of the Father as only begotten, that is, from the essence of the Father, God from God. Light from Light, true God from true God, begotten not created, of the same essence as the Father, through whom all things came into being, both in heaven and in earth; Who for us men and for our salvation came down and was incarnate, becoming human. He suffered and the third day he rose, and ascended into the heavens. And he will come to judge both the living and the dead.
> And [we believe] in the Holy Spirit.
> But, those who say, Once he was not, or he was not before his generation, or he came to be out of nothing, or who assert that he, the Son of God, is of

---

3. Millard J. Erickson, *Christian Theology* (Grand Rapids, Mich.: Baker, 1985), 285.

a different *hypostasis* or *ousia*, or that he is a creature, or changeable, or mutable, the Catholic and Apostolic Church anathematizes them.[4]

We have, then, a God of great magnificence, one of supreme power and ability to do as He may choose, and Who has, with that freedom, chosen to become entwined with human beings in an intensely personal manner. Moltmann states it well:

> When Abraham Heschel was working out the "Theology of the Divine Pathos," in order to show God's passion for Israel and his suffering with Israel, he had to propose a two-poled conception of God: God is free and not subject to anything that may happen, but he is nevertheless, through his *pathos*, committed to Israel in the covenant. He is enthroned in heaven, but he lives with the lowly and the meek. Through his "indwellings" (*shekinah*) the Almighty shares all the sufferings of his people. "God himself divides himself in two. He gives himself away to his people. He suffers with them in their sufferings. . . . "The Jewish concept of *theopathy* presupposes this distinction within the godhead. God's omnipotence must then be seen in the context of his power to suffer.[5]

Very simply, God is love (1 Jn. 4:16) and actively expresses that love to us.

What Is the State of Humanity before God?

Who are we as human beings, male and female, the recipients of that love? The answer to that question lies in our understanding of what the Scriptures mean when they speak to our original appearance: "So God created humankind in his image, in the image of God he created them; male and female he created them" (Gn. 1:27).

As we learned from our brief discussion of the nature of God, He stretches far beyond anything we can emulate. Some, however, have divided the attributes of God by classifying them as communicable and incommunicable. The communicable attributes are those which, in a partial form, humans may share; the incommunicable ones find no human counterpart.[6] Among the latter, for example, we may classify omniscience or omnipresence, for we in no way share in His fullness of knowledge or presence. However, we do share in a measure of love, a desire to see justice done, a compassion for the weak, and wrath for those who oppress the downtrodden. Apparently

---

4. The Creed of Nicaea (325), *Creeds of the Churches*, 3rd ed., ed. John H. Leith (Louisville: John Knox Press, 1982), 30-31.

5. Jürgen Moltmann, "The Motherly Father: Is Trinitarian Patripassionism Replacing Theological Patriachalism?" *God as Father?* ed. Johannes-Baptist Metz and Edward Schillebeeckx, English Language Editor, Marcus Lefebure (New York: Seabury, 1981), 54.

6. Erickson, *Christian Theology*, 266.

we find ourselves living as the image of God when we express His moral qualities.

A World Disfigured

Sadly, an observant look at our world implies a rampant disregard for divine moral qualities. We see instead constant abuse of power, corruption in all forms of government, cruelty to other humans, relentless rape of the environment, and a constant "one-upmanship" in relationships. Sensitive hearts find it difficult to read a newspaper or watch a newscast without weeping.

Not all is wicked, of course. People do perform acts of kindness; reports of altruistic actions reaffirm our hope that goodness does exist. Nonetheless, a strong core of selfishness seems to drive much human behavior.

The story in Genesis 3 helps us understand why human beings now express a defaced, but certainly not erased, image of God to the world. While most evangelicals will see this passage in terms of historical narrative, additionally it may be read as a universal example of the human determination to live independently of God. Not merely a "once upon a time" event, it has proven to be a paradigm of temptation and sin.

The story is simple and well known. The man and the woman live in Eden, a place where the two can be naked and unashamed with one another (Gn. 2:25), where they had freedom to do as they wished, except for one prohibition—not to eat of the tree of knowledge of good and evil (Gn. 2:17).

Eventually, this man and woman are approached by a serpent. Although specifically speaking to the woman, the serpent appears to be addressing a plural audience (אכלבם, for example, in v. 5). Katherine Sakenfeld, observing that all *you* verbs are plural, notes that "the Hebrew makes it clear that the man and the woman are standing together during this episode."[7] As the conversation progresses, we learn that the fruit of the forbidden tree tastes good, looks good, and the partaking of it would seem to have a useful result (Gn. 3:6). And so they chose disobedience and suffered the consequence of fallenness.

The Results of Disfigurement

As the Scriptures make clear in Romans 5, sin entered the world at that point and death with it. Furthermore, the temptation, "you shall be like God" is the archetype of all our temptation. Eugene Peterson writes, "I take it as a given that all of us would prefer to be our own gods than to worship God. The Eden story is reenacted daily."[8] Those committed to the veracity of the biblical account find no surprise to learn that its description accurately correlates with the reality of a fallen world.

---

7. Katharine D. Sakenfeld, "The Bible and Women: Bane or Blessing?" *Theology Today* 32:3, 225.

8. Eugene H. Peterson, *Under the Unpredictable Plant: An Exploration in Vocational Holiness* (Grand Rapids, Mich.: Eerdmans, 1992), 7.

Humans find themselves both from nature and from choice in a state of rebellion against the holiness and righteous standards of God. We live in a world that fights against our work with thorns and thistles (Gn. 3:18), in which men and women struggle in their relationship with each other, rather than working as intimate partners (Gn. 3:16), and creatures no longer function as they were created (Gn. 3:14). In addition death, its decay, and the grief it brings are now all inevitable (Gn. 3:19). We live as fallen creatures in a fallen world.

Does that leave us hopeless? Is the breach unbridgeable between God and humanity? We think not, and George Peters has stated this with clarity:

> It is my conviction that the fall, though horrible in its historical and eternal consequences, was a disappointment to Satan. It had not accomplished all that the fall was intended to accomplish. Man had remained man and, as such, a salvable creature. The depth of the fall had not reached the core of the human being. It did not obliterate the image of God.[9]

What Is the Relationship Between God and Humanity?

A truly biblical theology gloriously announces that the gap between human fallenness and God's holiness has been closed, but not by our own effort. We must return for a moment to our understanding of God as Triunity—Father, Son, and Holy Spirit.

In a manner of expressing love incomprehensible to the human mind, God the Son came to earth in the form of a man. Culminating centuries of hope and prophecy, He laid down His life as a ransom for us.

A Focus on Soteriology

As we briefly work through the issue of soteriology, we must necessarily keep in mind the purpose of this chapter—a description of the common ground of evangelical theology through which we determine the basis for Christian religious education. Various understandings of soteriology have divided Christians over the centuries. Scholars explore the implications of many questions: What does Scripture mean when it speaks of election? Cannot anyone call on the name of Jesus and be saved? What if people have a misunderstanding of Who He is and how He offers salvation? When did God conceive of the plan of salvation: before or after the fall?

These dilemmas and many others spark lively debates and deserve the continuing attention of theologians. However, those of us primarily engaged in Christian education must narrow our focus, concentrating on the consensus that God as God, in grace and mercy, has taken the initiative, and, in turn, called for a faith response.

Simply stated, Jesus the Messiah presented Himself as the fulfillment of

---

9. George W. Peters, *A Biblical Theology of Missions* (Chicago: Moody, 1984), 78.

the Law given by Moses to the Israelites. The ceremonies prescribed for the Levites to perform on behalf of Israel in the Tabernacle previewed the final sacrifice, after which these rituals would no longer remain necessary.

The means of salvation does not change—belief in the One Who laid down His life for us, yet who was raised from the dead so that our faith is not in vain (1 Cor. 15:14). The first verse that almost all children memorize in their Sunday School classrooms proclaims that truth with power and simplicity: "For God so loved the world that he gave his only Son, so that everyone who believes in him may not perish but have eternal life" (Jn. 3:16).

Through faith, we find ourselves re-born, adopted into the family of God, privileged to call Him "Abba, Father" (Rom. 8:15). A mystery, indeed, but one which unites us intimately with the Creator, the first steps taken to restore the original relationship between God and humankind lost in the fall.

What Is the Goal of Our Instruction and Means of Growth?

Once entered into that relationship, new believers embark on a process commonly known as sanctification (spiritual formation), with the eventual goal of living a Christ-like life. They live out that goal within the context of their work and worship with other Christians, leading to our understanding of ecclesiology.

The Goal of Maturity

Just as parents hope that the children brought into the world will grow into mature and fully functioning adults, Christian educators also hope that new believers will grow into Christian maturity. As with physical children, the process takes time; pressure to grow up too soon may lead to unhappy results. The church as a whole carries the responsibility for the nurturing process that produces mature adults. Here those of us involved in Christian education invest most of our energies.

Necessarily we must seek to define maturity in its Christian context. What does a mature believer look like? Ephesians 4:14-16 expresses it in just a few short sentences.

> We must no longer be children, tossed to and fro and blown about by every wind of doctrine, by people's trickery, by their craftiness in deceitful scheming. But speaking the truth in love, we must grow up in every way into him who is the head, into Christ, from whom the whole body, joined and knit together by every ligament with which it is equipped, as each part is working properly, promotes the body's growth in building itself up in love.

Mature Christians, then, have a solid and well-integrated understanding of sound doctrine, so that stability in fundamental truths characterizes their lives. Mature believers also relate to each other in a loving and truthful manner, always understanding that the head of each individual is Christ. Although we may function under authority structures, our relationship to God is mediated by Christ, not other people. Paul Stevens states that important point well when he reminds us that church leaders in the New Testament are not called heads of local bodies—that title is reserved for Jesus. "Therefore people find their ministries not by being directed by the leaders but by being motivated and equipped and directed by the Head himself. . . . In other words, the church is not a hierarchy but a monarchy."[10]

The mature believer works toward the good of the entire body of Christ, seeking its growth and goodness because each joins with every other in lovingly intertwined relationships. These relationships, not buildings or clerical offices or set times for services, define the church. Stanley Grenz provides a clarifying comment here: "The choice of *ekklesia* as the designation of the Christian community carries an important implication for ecclesiology. It suggests that the New Testament Christians viewed the church as neither hierarchy nor edifice, but people—a people brought together by the Spirit to belong to God through Christ."[11]

Corporate and Individual Growth

The sanctification process is both individual (a child grows in relationship with parents) and corporate (a child learns to function within the full family structure). That child must also learn relationship with sometimes irritating brothers and sisters and the oddball relative who shows up at the worst time. A vibrant family always seems to have room for one more at the dinner table and actively reaches out to those who might become part of the family circle. And the church family seeks to be part of the lives of those living outside the fold.

Evangelical ecclesiology does not mandate a set pattern for church governance but does suggest that the better model includes a multiplicity of leaders functioning as God has gifted them. Whatever pattern the local congregation might take, the key is understanding that believers today function as living tabernacles in whom the grace and glory of God resides. That glory, once removed by the presence of sin within the community, returned in the person of Jesus Christ (Jn. 1:14) and is now part of church life, both corporately and individually (1 Cor. 6:19, 2 Cor. 3:7-18). Erickson provides a helpful definition of the process:

Sanctification is the continuing word of God in the life of the believer, making him or her actually holy. By "holy" here is meant "bearing an actu-

---

10. R. Paul Stevens, *Liberating the Laity: Equipping All the Saints for Ministry* (Downers Grove, Ill.: InterVarsity, 1985), 36.

11. Stanley J. Grenz, *Revisioning Evangelical Theology: A Fresh Agenda for the 21st Century* (Downers Grove, Ill.: InterVarsity, 1993), 171.

al likeness to God." Sanctification is a process by which one's moral condition is brought into conformity with one's legal state before God. It is a continuation of what was begun in regeneration, when a newness of life was conferred upon and instilled with the believer. In particular, sanctification is the Holy Spirit's applying to the life of the believer the work done by Jesus Christ.[12]

What Is the Source of Our Knowledge?

To this point, we have freely quoted the Bible to explain and support the basic propositions of evangelical theology. We need now to turn our attention to the text itself, for a commitment to the Scriptures as the inspired and authoritative revelation of God to humankind undergirds our entire theology.

Upon confronting such a view of the Scriptures, some will surely ask, "Is this not an unnecessarily simplistic view?" We think not. Granted, this presupposition can lead to an overly literal reading of the Bible and thus to its serious misuse through decontextualized proof-texting. But properly handled, it provides the only consistent basis for theology. We condone neither bibliolatry nor the treatment of the text as some sort of spiritual "rabbit's foot"; we do commend a solid bibliology.

The Basis of Evangelical Bibliology

Let's expand on this doctrinal position. From our perspective, evangelical bibliology assumes:

• The Bible is God's revelation of Himself to humanity.

• This Bible (in the original autographs) is fully inspired by God.

• This revelation is authoritative, when properly understood, not only in matters of faith and practice, but also in matters relating to history and science.

• Proper interpretative tools, including an understanding of the principles of textual and higher criticism remain necessary to read and understand this revelation more fully.

God's Revelation of Himself

We have already touched on the fact that much may be learned of God through a study of general or natural revelation. The Bible, however, serves as God's written special revelation which provides knowledge necessary both to bring humankind into a salvation response to Himself and to give stan-

---

12. Erickson, *Christian Theology*, 967-968.

dards for behavior. Though the Scriptures surely *contain* revelation of God, that statement alone is incomplete. Evangelicals hold that the Bible also *is* revelation of God, although this cannot imply that a thorough knowledge of Scriptures means a thorough knowledge of God. As Erickson puts it,

> The God who is revealed is, however, a transcendent being. He lies outside our sensory experience. The Bible claims that God is unlimited in his knowledge and power; he is not subject to the confines of space and time. Consequently the revelation must involve a condescension on God's part (in the good sense of that word). Man cannot reach up to investigate God and would not understand even if he could. So God has revealed himself by a revelation in *anthropic* form. This should not be thought of an anthropomorphism as such, but as simply a revelation coming in human language and human categories of thought and action.[13]

Is this revelation complete? If it contains all knowledge necessary for salvation and behavioral standards, does God no longer speak to individuals today? How do we understand deep and powerful experiences during which individuals see themselves as recipients of a direct word from God?

Let us remember that Jesus Christ stands as the culmination of God's disclosure of Himself. He revealed the Father so adequately that we no longer have need for further normative revelation, i.e., revelation applicable to all humanity.

This does not suggest that personal experiences are necessarily invalid or imagined. Instead a wise person measures such happenings against the revelation already provided by the Bible. A person with a solid knowledge of the Bible has a safeguard of more objective truth against which he or she examines and judges experiences which appear supernatural. As Bloesch states, "Evangelical theology holds that Scripture has primacy not only over the church but also over religious experience."[14]

Inspiration and Inerrancy

Evangelicals affirm the inspiration of the Bible, the reality of the God-breathed text. Yet, at least forty different authors contributed to this collection, each with different styles and diverse reasons for writing. Their writings touch many different literary genres—narrative, poetry, proverb, prophecy, satire, carefully reasoned logical arguments and exquisite imagery. These features rule out the suggestions that inspiration implies mechanical dictation.

The Scriptures themselves speak of their inspiration (2 Tm. 3:16), of being spoken by the power of God (1 Pt. 1:20-21; 1 Thes. 2:12). But how does

---

13. Ibid., 178.

14. Donald G. Bloesch, *Essentials of Evangelical Theology, Volume One: God, Authority, and Salvation* (San Francisco: Harper & Row, 1978), 61.

an inspired Bible speak to the question of truth or error contained within? A full exploration of that issue would take us far beyond the guidelines of this chapter, but we must address our confidence in the Word of God.

Conservative theologians speak of the inerrancy of the original autographs. Although our texts are remarkably well-preserved, textual variants do exist and they deserve attention. As Bahnsen states, "There is nothing absurd about holding that an infallible text has been fallibly transmitted, and the fact that a document is a copy of the Holy Writ does not entail that it is wholly right."[15]

No one disputes that there are problems, areas that do not seem to reconcile clearly. Much of this arises from a misunderstanding of both the literary genre and the culture from which the original authors wrote. For example, poetry is metaphorical in nature; it is not meant to be taken as scientific truth. The problem lies much more with interpreters who work from an inadequate knowledge base, than with the Scriptures themselves. We operate from a Western perspective in which a hyperbolic statement may be regarded as grossly inaccurate. In other cultures, however, such an expression would be more readily understood as a figure of speech without a necessary rigid correspondence with reality to express ultimate truth. The writers of Scripture did not hold the same perspective as modern journalists, and it would be inappropriate at best to hold them to that standard.

We recognize that inerrancy is an easily confused term when used to describe the Scriptures and thus creates a view threatening to some. As we develop this further, we encourage the reader to keep in mind that "inerrancy" simply affirms the full reliability, dependability, and truthfulness of Scripture. Feinberg lists eight common misunderstandings:

1. Inerrancy does not demand strict adherence to the rules of grammar.

2. Inerrancy does not exclude the use of either figures of speech or of a given literary genre.

3. Inerrancy does not demand historical or semantic precision.

4. Inerrancy does not demand the technical language of modern science.

5. Inerrancy does not require verbal exactness in the citation of the Old Testament by the New.

6. Inerrancy does not demand that the *Logia Jesu* (the sayings of Jesus) contain the *ipsissima verba* (the exact words) of Jesus, only the *ipsissima vox* (the exact voice).

---

15. Greg L. Bahnsen, "The Inerrancy of the Autographa," in *Inerrancy*, ed. Norman L. Geisler (Grand Rapids, Mich.: Zondervan, 1980), 175.

7. Inerrancy does not guarantee the exhaustive comprehensiveness of any single account or of combined accounts where those are involved.

8. Inerrancy does not demand the infallibility or inerrancy of the noninspired sources used by biblical writers.[16]

Why, with these limitations, do we hold so strongly to the authority of the Bible? Precisely because these qualifications properly define the evangelical view for better mutual understanding. They apply to all books, especially those of antiquity.[17]

The doctrine of inerrancy has been confused with an insistence upon literal truth linked with a rigid dogmatism, but the two are not the same. As Bloesch notes, let us not permit modern empirical philosophy and science to impose its definition on the Scripture's own understanding of this concept.[18] *The doctrine of inerrancy does affirm that, when properly interpreted, the Bible will prove to be wholly true, to the degree of precision intended, in all areas to which it speaks.*

We consider the doctrine vital because it encourages students to search for the whole of God's truth, yet to enter that search knowing that mysteries must be uncovered. This doctrine does not control truth, but it recognizes that there exists, in a world of relativism, a trustworthy and absolute truth source.

Textual and Higher Criticism

Finally we note that the principles of both textual and "higher" criticism help in our study and understanding of the Bible. Textual criticism traces any changes in the text after it was written. Multiple manuscripts, both for Old and New Testaments, help determine the original writings with a very high degree of accuracy and therefore offer a solid foundation on which to work.

Much of the work of "higher" critics, particularly those working with form and rhetorical criticism, serve immensely well to open the literary landscape of the Scriptures as they provide unifying principles which tie various stories and scenes together. This type of criticism helps readers stand back and see the whole picture and aids in understanding how the details work within. While standing on the inspiration of the Scriptures, we seek help from all sources for a better understanding of the revealed Word.

SECTION TWO: BUILDING ON THE THEOLOGICAL FOUNDATIONS

What Is the Source of Our Knowledge?

Obviously we begin with the Bible, our *bibliology*, an understanding that

---

16. Paul D. Feinberg, "The Meaning of Inerrancy," in *Inerrancy*, 299-302.
17. Ibid., 303.
18. Bloesch, *Essentials of Evangelical Theology*, 67.

knowledge of revelation serves as a light to our path. With that light held high, we have the freedom to delve into any research which might help with the educational process.

Educational philosophies abound. Even within the evangelical camp, we don't necessarily find agreement. For example, Robert Pazmiño compares the focus and stance of four well-known Christian educators and notes that each, although well-based on biblical truth, offers a slightly different emphasis:

Educator	Focus	Stance
Frank Gaebelein	Quality formal education Academic Excellence under the authority of Scripture	Wise scholar/ headmaster
Lois LeBar	Spirit-filled formal education Teaching sensitive to student needs	Inspired teacher
Lawrence Richards	Nurturant nonformal education Discipling and modeling in the body	Enthusiastic visionary
Gene Getz	Faithful local church Education (formal and nonformal) Evangelism and edification	Discerning pastor/guide[19]

Uniformity is not the goal; we are not dealing with a uniform mass of people who can be shoved into some mold which will produce robotic educated Christians, all thinking alike. Rather, we want to become models for people who can reach into the world of learning and integrate all knowledge with biblical truth, thus producing well-rounded and holistic Christians and educators.

Truth Integration

Although one of the authors has written on this subject extensively elsewhere, it is worth summarizing the key points of the concept of truth integration here.[20]

The phrase, "integration of truth" refers to *the teaching of all subjects as a part of the total truth of God thereby enabling the student to see the unity*

19. Robert W. Pazmiño, *Foundational Issues in Christian Education* (Grand Rapids, Mich.: Baker, 1990), 149.

20. For the full explanation, see the four articles by Kenneth O. Gangel in *Bibliotheca Sarca* 135:537-540 (1978).

of natural and special revelation. Though this may seem simplistic, it requires a lifetime of effort and the best possible education a teacher can bring to this task.

We have already elaborated on the first principle of truth integration, namely, *a commitment to the authority of the Bible.* That leads us to the second principle: The integration of faith and learning demands *a recognition of the contemporaneity of the Bible and the Holy Spirit.* Here the educator explains how an authoritative and inerrant Bible relates to all aspects of the student's life. To borrow an idea from Korzybski, the great general semanticist, the "here and now" depends greatly on the "then and there." The Bible records accurately the "then and there," in most cases continuing to the "here and now."

But the Bible hardly intends to develop a distinctively evangelical view of the teaching-learning process. Evangelical educators also recognize the role of the Holy Spirit in interpreting God's truth in accordance with the words of the Lord Jesus Who said to His disciples,

> When the Spirit of Truth comes, he will guide you into all the truth; for he will not speak on his own, but will speak whatever he hears, and he will declare to you the things that are to come. He will glorify me, because he will take what is mine and declare it to you. All that the Father has is mine. For this reason, I said that he will take what is mine and declare it to you (Jn. 16:13-15).

Understanding the role of the Holy Spirit leads to the third principle in the integrative process: *a clear understanding of the nature, source, discovery, and dissemination of truth.* We understand that all truth is God's truth, but what does that mean? Simply that wherever genuine truth is found it is ultimately traceable back to the God of the Bible. And since the God of the Bible is also the God of creation, the true relationship between natural and special revelation begins to emerge at the junction of Christian epistemology. As Gaebelein wrote:

> Now Christian education, if it is faithful to its deepest commitment, must renounce once and for all the false separation between secular and sacred truth. It must see that truth in science, and history, in mathematics, art, literature, and music belongs just as much to God as truth in religion. While it recognizes the primacy of the spiritual truth revealed in the Bible and incarnate in Christ, it acknowledges that all truth, wherever it is found, is of God. For Christian education there can be no discontinuity in truth, but every aspect of truth must find its unity in the God of all truth.[21]

---

21. Frank E. Gaebelein, "Towards a Christian Philosophy of Education," *Grace Journal* 3 (Fall, 1962), 13.

We have said that thinking Christians do not fear research and experimentation. They understand that since all truth is God's truth, the more honest effort put forth by any person, regenerate or unregenerate, must ultimately result in uncovering more of God's truth. Such is the design of common grace.

The choice and/or creation of curricula looms high on the "to do" list of Christian educators, and this need leads to the fourth principle on which the integrative process is based: *designing a curriculum totally constructed on the centrality of special revelation.*

Special revelation forms the foundation for curricular design. Many Christians tend to think of natural revelation only as the study of God's creation, but in reality all beauty is God's beauty just as all truth is God's truth. Consequently, God's revelation comes in the humanities as well as in the hard sciences though it may be more easily corrupted the further one moves away from the study of hard-core measurable fields of learning.

Built upon the centrality of special revelation and corresponding integration, Christian educators emphasize the role of truth in students' lives. Students learn about themselves, interpersonal relations, family life, job skills, citizenship, and a host of other things which produce well-rounded Christian adults—the holistic view of truth in life.

With a well-rounded education centered on biblical truth, we move into the fifth principle: *a demand for the development of the Christian world and life view.* Evangelical educators agree with Gaebelein who reminded us that there is no dichotomy between the sacred and secular for thinking Christians. The teacher who understands genuine Christian education will work courageously at developing an internalization of God's truth, not just a cognitive knowledge base. And, as Arthur Holmes writes, that understanding of spiritual vitality "should make us more perceptive, more eager, more disciplined learners than we would be otherwise."[22]

This brings us full circle. I am a Christian scholar and teacher in response to the biblical mandate. The linkage between spirituality and learning is part of the relationship between faith and learning. Faith is not just the content of biblical teaching, but my continued responsiveness to God himself. So the integration of faith and learning includes integration of spirituality into my work. Like the Medievals we should work in our laboratories and libraries, develop lectures, grade papers, as an act of disciplined love for God.[23]

Eliminate the Sacred/Secular Division

We do not wish to encourage a spirit of "worldliness" here, but rather an ability to think Christianly about all aspects of life. Too many Christians

22. Arthur Holmes, "Reintegrating Faith and Learning—The Biblical Mandate," *Perspectives* (Christian College Coalition, Fall, 1993), 4.

23. Ibid., 4.

make no connection between the Sunday morning sermon on patience and the Monday morning chaos that descends into a shouting match between parent and child. By discarding the false sacred/secular division, a young mother may see that changing a diaper serves as a holy act; a businessman may understand that an ethical decision despite financial loss is as vital to his Christian life as regular participation in the sacraments; a church leader may recognize that sound management principles have use in the service of God.

Furthermore, active application of integrative principles permits the educator to draw freely from the mountains of research on teaching/learning methodologies and motivation strategies. The matter of handling John Dewey's educational practices affords us a good example. A pragmatist and a naturalist who rejected supernaturalism or absolute truth, Dewey had confidence that the adequate use of intelligence and scientific processes would wipe away disease, poverty, and evil.[24] The evangelical educator recognizes the futility of such conclusions.

However, despite this fundamental disagreement in philosophy, there is much in Dewey's processes worth emulating. Christian educators frequently draw from his understanding of group dynamics, creative thinking, controlled environment, involvement of the student, motivation through interest, and social relevance. "The intelligent approach to Dewey then, it would seem, would have to be one that excludes his godless philosophy and adapts his practical methodology."[25]

What Is Our Goal of Instruction and Means of Growth?

To some degree one may disconnect theological categories and issues of anthropology, soteriology, and sanctification. A human being is not quite so easily detachable, for a healthy person functions as a whole, not a series of disengaged parts. However, for the sake of clarity, we will deal with the educator's relationship to the sanctification process in this section, and hold off on the anthropological and soteriological questions until the next.

Corporate Sanctification

Of necessity the question of *sanctification*, or personal growth toward holiness, must be tied to the understanding of *ecclesiology*, or the corporate life of believers. The book of Romans helps define our goal and show the connection between the two.

We learn in Romans 8:29 that we are being conformed to the image of Christ, i.e., that a Christian measures his or her steps toward Christian maturity by looking to Jesus. We have now returned to our understanding of creation—men and women made in the image of God. With redemption, the possibility exists of taking steps toward achieving that original purpose. Christian

24. Kenneth O. Gangel and Warren S. Benson, *Christian Education: Its History & Philosophy* (Chicago: Moody, 1983), 292-294.

25. Ibid., 303.

educators, then, have the job of coming alongside their students and helping them move toward Christ-likeness, a heavy responsibility. Fortunately, later chapters in Romans help define the means of this spiritual formation.

Romans 12-15 give a series of imperative verbs (thirty-two in these three chapters) which explain the "how" of living the Christian life within the context of community. Romans 12:1-2 restates the need for individual commitment:

> I appeal to you therefore, brothers and sisters, by the mercies of God, to present your bodies as a living sacrifice, holy and acceptable to God, which is your spiritual worship. Do not be conformed to this world, but be transformed by the renewing of your minds, so that you may discern what is the will of God—what is good and acceptable and perfect.

The imperatives in the next three chapters of Romans following this restatement involve the practice of living out this holy sacrifice within the community of believers. Immediately we see before us the intimate interconnectedness and the necessity of not thinking too highly of ourselves. The bulk of these chapters consists of exhortations for proper and loving relationships among Christians.

A study of exhortations helps us understand that the process of Christian growth primarily takes place within the corporate setting of the church. Most of the imperatives can be obeyed only as a part of the larger church setting, not on a purely individual level. In other words, the Bible teaches that a Christian who has chosen to isolate him- or herself from the rest of the community is probably not functioning in a healthy manner (see 1 Cor. 12-14; Eph. 4:1-16; Col. 3:12-17). Ridderbos writes, "The distinguishing feature of the idea of 'body,' therefore, is that these many in virtue of this common belonging to Christ form in him a new unity with each other. They are not each one individually, but as a corporate unity, all together in him."[26]

Holistic Instruction Necessary

Where does the responsibility of the Christian educator tie in with the process of corporate unity and sanctification? With the goal of an integrated worldview, of an understanding of how to think Christianly about all of life, the Christian educator cannot afford to instruct on a cognitive level only, hoping that the material will somehow filter into the rest of the student's life. Instead, we must consider the whole person, i.e., it is necessary to teach holistically if we expect our students to learn holistically.

We teach within the context of relationship. We hold the expectation that education plays itself out not only in knowledge gained, but also in the strengthening of the body of Christ. Instruction, programs, and curricula

---

26. Herman Ridderbos, *PAUL An Outline of His Theology*, trans. John Richard DeWitt (Grand Rapids, Mich.: Eerdmans, 1975), 371.

which encourage isolationism could be discarded in favor of a design which favors community.

Teaching Community

A community demands give and take, mutuality, vulnerability, tears and joy, hurting and healing, head knowledge translated to heart loving, a sense of belonging, being needed and wanted and most of all, forgiven. Community thrives under servant leadership. Though we may teach the authoritative word of God, we need not do so in an authoritarian manner which discourages honest interaction.

Community suggests an affirmation of all members, never disregarding some because of gender, race, appearance, finances, or background. The suggestion that we live out our Christianity by means of our relationships with one another is hardly new. For example, Basil the Great wrote, "We need each other so much both for our physical and spiritual welfare that isolation is opposed to our true interests."[27] However, it is not an idea which finds a comfortable home in a culture that exalts isolationism and the idea that a "self-made" person should be admired above all others. Eugene Peterson has some interesting comments on the destructiveness of excessive individualism:

> On the "ribbon of highway" that stretches "from California to the New York Island"—the great American Main Street—the mass of people seems completely self-absorbed. One hundred and fifty years ago Alexis de Tocqueville visited America from France and wrote: "Each citizen is habitually engaged in the contemplation of a very puny object, namely himself." In a century and a half things have not improved . . . we have a self problem and that problem is responsible for everything else that is going wrong.[28]

The notion that community is important to religious instruction certainly complicates the picture—there has been a notable tendency in the evangelical community to focus on teaching content, finding contentment in cognitive achievement alone. Moving into community, into the maze of complex interpersonal relationships, necessitates leaving tight boxes and neatly defined categories behind—people don't fit very well into them. In addition, many of those to whom we seek to minister rebel against the idea of prepackaged and impersonal curriculum design.

An understanding of the primacy of community and relationship, then, makes essential a move to a small-group emphasis. To answer the question,

---

27. Saint Basil, *Ascetical Works* in *The Fathers of the Church: A New Translation: 9,* trans. Sister M. Monica Wagner, C.S.C. (New York: Fathers of the Church, 1950), 248.

28. Eugene H. Peterson, *Earth and Altar: The Community of Prayer in a Self-Bound Society* (Downers Grove, Ill.: InterVarsity, 1985), 13.

"How do we do what we do," we look to the small-group movement flourishing in many evangelical circles. Functioning under many different names—cell group, flock group, care group, mini-church, meta-church—these gatherings provide opportunities for mutual service and growth, with the emphasis upon individual rather than mass experience.

What Is the Relationship between God and Humanity?

Reconciliation between God and the people of His creation stands as the great message of Christianity. How does this message affect the work of the Christian educator?

Because we recognize that our fallenness (the Eden story) continues its battle with redemption (the Jesus story), the Christian educator continually emphasizes the process of spiritual formation. As stated earlier, growth takes place in the spiritual realm, just as it does in the physical realm. We know, however, that while the capacities of the human body may decrease with age, the capacities for spiritual growth or formation continue to increase.

Christian educators affirm the practice of spiritual disciplines to encourage individual growth toward Christ-likeness. Dallas Willard lists some disciplines of abstinence, recognizing that this list is by no means exhaustive: solitude, silence, fasting, frugality, chastity, secrecy, and sacrifice.[29] Engaging in these and other types of activities reinforces our understanding of the redemptive acts of God.

But discipline for the sake of overt act contains no spiritual validity. We both model and teach those consistent behaviors designed to help God's children grow up. Whether private or corporate, the reality and yes, even commonality of the spiritual disciplines exhibits the transformation of doctrine to life. And, like much of Christian education, practice of the disciplines must be taught as brightness not boredom. We like Foster's evaluation:

> Neither should we think of the Spiritual Disciplines as some dull drudgery aimed at exterminating laughter from the face of the earth. Joy is the keynote of all the Disciplines. The purpose of the Disciplines is liberation from the stifling slavery of self-interest and fear. When the inner spirit is liberated from all that weighs it down, it can hardly be described as dull drudgery. Singing, dancing, even shouting characterize the Disciplines of the spiritual life.[30]

Aha! Now the very presence of God sparks love in His people. Now the exhilaration of the angels finds echo on the tongues of the redeemed. Now

---

29. Dallas Willard, *The Spirit of the Disciplines* (San Fransisco: Harper & Row, 1988), 158.

30. Richard J. Foster, *Celebration of Discipline: The Path to Spiritual Growth*, rev. ed. (San Francisco: Harper & Row, 1988), 2.

doing theology has become the very essence of *being* Christian and clichés have matured into clarity.

Whom Do We Model?

As Christian educators, we enjoy the freedom to model the Master Teacher. Our confidence in the Scriptures gives us the freedom to learn from the ways He taught, how He touched people, what He expected from those around Him. Christian education, based on the life and teaching methods of Jesus, aims at the transformation of both mind and life.[31]

Let's look at this Master Teacher. How may we characterize His theology of learning, His teaching methods, His expectations of those who followed Him? As we do so, it will help us identify the common threads, the principles and practices, the interpersonal relationships which produced learning experiences.

Jesus the Master Teacher

Where could we find a better model of teaching than in the first four books of the New Testament? As we look at Jesus' teaching encounters, no clear pattern immediately emerges, no way of saying "this is done first" and "that is done next." Instead, flexibility and an intense attention to individual persons color each approach.

When a sinful woman anoints Jesus as He eats in the home of Simon the Pharisee (Lk. 7:36-50), He recognizes her great love despite a sinful life and treats her with immense gentleness and compassion. The situation in Matthew 15 stands in contrast. Here Jesus responds to the Pharisees and teachers of the law. Again recognizing the underlying motivation behind the question, "Why do your disciples break the tradition of the elders? For they do not wash their hands before they eat," Jesus, without a trace of the previously mentioned gentleness or compassion, denounced them as hypocrites. His disciples noted that the response offended the Pharisees.

When asked a direct question, Jesus might reply indirectly, requiring the questioner to think through the issue and come up with an appropriate answer. Messengers came from John the Baptist to ask Him, "Are you the one who was to come, or should we expect someone else?" The answer was not a clear "yes," but an encouragement to look at what they had seen and heard (Lk. 7:18-23). When His disciples asked, "Who is the greatest in the kingdom of heaven?" Jesus answered by drawing an object lesson from a child standing nearby (Mt. 18:1-9).

Jesus Approaches Strangers

Clearly Jesus tailored His responses to the particular audience. Look at two situations dealing with accusations of Sabbath violations in Matthew 12.

---

31. Romans 12:1-2.

First, the hungry disciples pick and eat heads of grain. The text identifies the accusers as Pharisees. Jesus rejoins by going straight to the Scriptures, using with accuracy the very tool His questioners used against Him. They saw themselves as learned and accomplished in the Law, so Jesus based His answer on their self-perception.

The second scene takes place in a synagogue. Although the more educated group would be present, we may also assume a less sophisticated audience from the local agrarian population. Jesus now addresses Himself to them. He prepares to heal a man with a shriveled hand by reminding them of their responsibility as shepherds to a sheep which might fall into a pit on the Sabbath.

A close look at the familiar story of Jesus and the Samaritan woman in John 4 may prove helpful. While this story is often cited as a model for personal evangelism, it is useful for that model precisely because Jesus picks up on the teachable moment and uses it to provide a profound change point for the woman.

Jesus approached the woman on the basis of her experience, namely the drawing of water from the well. Shocked at His approach, she expresses the shock by reminding Him of her position on the societal ladder. He immediately reveals something of His person to her, consistent with His goal of drawing all people to Himself (Jn. 12:32). He begins to paint a metaphor of water, using familiar territory to teach new truths.

Intrigued by this partial revelation of Himself, she questions Him further, seeking to place Him in her hierarchy of important people. Continuing with the water metaphor, the Lord expands it further in a direction she would be unlikely to find on her own. Although she perceives her needs as physical, Jesus discerns the real need running far deeper. He helps her acknowledge this real need by reminding her of her unholy marital situation.

She calls Jesus a prophet and takes another step in recognition of His person. The Lord continues to bring her along by addressing her religious experiences and her insecurity in worshiping as a Samaritan rather than as a Jew. When she finally expressed her belief in a coming Messiah, Jesus more completely revealed Himself as that Promised One. At that point, she makes a giant leap from self-centeredness ("Sir, give me this water so that I may never be thirsty") to other-centeredness ("the woman went back to the town and said to the people, 'Come see a man who told me everything I have ever done. He cannot be the Messiah, can he?'"). Jesus knew her; loved her; moved her.

One common denominator in each encounter—Jesus spoke the truth to the people involved. He discerned the reality behind the questions and dealt with actual issues, not superficial ones. He knew His audience, their backgrounds, their interests, the ways in which they perceived themselves. He spoke to this self-perception, whether a sinner recognizing her need for forgiveness or a scholar, comfortable in intimate knowledge of the law. He never ignored the significance of self-concept in the people He taught.

What did Jesus expect of those who accepted the invitation to learn from Him? Here we need to turn from the more general audience to those who formed His intimate circle.

Jesus Activates His Disciples

When He named His disciples, they were chosen first of all to be with Him: "He went up the mountain and called to him those whom he wanted, and they came to him. And he appointed twelve—whom he also named apostles— to be with him and to be sent out to proclaim the message" (Mk. 3:13-14).

He expected active rather than intellectual assent. *To His future disciple:* "As Jesus was walking along, he saw a man called Matthew sitting at the tax booth; and he said to him, 'Follow me,' and he got up and followed him: (Mt. 9:9). *To the rich ruler who wanted to inherit eternal life:* "There is still one thing lacking. Sell all that you own and distribute the money to the poor, and you will have treasure in heaven; then come, follow me"(Lk. 18:22). *To those whom Jesus identified as His own:* "My sheep hear my voice. I know them, and they follow me" (Jn. 10:27). *To those who understood that He was the Christ:* "Then he called the crowd with his disciples and said to them, 'If any want to become my followers, let them deny themselves and take up their cross and follow me" (Mk. 8:34). The key word jumps out: "follow,"[32] an action-oriented word touching every area of life.

Jesus Applies Strategy in Teaching

He gave His followers the opportunity to practice what they had seen by sending them out to preach and to heal (Lk. 9:1-6). After the practice session, He made them answer for themselves the question of His identity. " 'But what about you?' he asked. 'Who do you say I am?' "(Lk. 9:20). He confirmed their conclusions at the Transfiguration (Lk. 9:28-36).

He used daily life for object lessons at teachable moments. For example, the widow's mite in Mark 12 demonstrated true charity and the illustration of physical birth helps shed light on the spiritual re-birth in John 3. He encouraged His followers to take risks and try out their faith, even when they stumbled and came up short as did Peter when he tried to walk on the water (Mt. 14:22-31).

Jesus taught with active example and with an enormous amount of flexibility, displaying sensitivity to the situation. He took advantage of teach-

---

32. *Ακολονθεω, come after, accompany, go along with,* figuratively, *follow someone as a disciple (A Greek-English Lexicon of the New Testament and Other Early Christian Literature,* ed. William F. Arndt and F. Wilbur Gingrich, 2nd ed., F. Wilbur Gingrich and Frederick W. Danker [Chicago: University of Chicago Press, 1979], 31). G. Kittel (TDNT, 1:213-214) demonstrates that this word in the New Testament is limited to those who follow after Christ and that it imiplies a self-commitment in a sense which breaks all other ties.

able moments and expected those who followed Him to experience changed lives. He knew His audience intimately and drew on their individual life experiences as He brought them to change-points. He led His followers step-by-step, taking them to the next level when they evidenced readiness, quickly giving opportunities to practice the lessons He demonstrated. Though they would not have understood the principles of developmental task education, the disciples offer a realistic model of that modern concept.

Applicable Principles Uncovered

Many similar accounts abound in Scripture, but these suffice as a sampling. What principles of Christian education can we draw from this brief survey of model learning experiences? Although none of them took place in a formal setting, that does not necessarily preclude the classroom as an appropriate place for education. It *does* mean that methods which enhance the learning process should be included in the classroom experience.

First, the teacher must know the students well in order to approach them on the basis of their self-perceptions. Armed with knowledge of backgrounds, the teacher may aim with more certainty at the hearts of individuals, thus drawing closer to the goal of changed lives. These examples suggest that learning includes intensely personal experiences between teacher and learner. Invariably our Lord's teaching intentionally pulled the learner from dependence to self-directed learning. The disciples offer the most dramatic illustration.

Second, the learner must start on the basis of his or her own experience, whether drawing water at a well, dealing with illness, or enjoying an extensive educational background. The experiences provide a foundation of conscious knowledge on which to build, and they expose the need for further learning when present capabilities prove inadequate to cope with the situation.

Third, the learning experience is far more "do" than "know" oriented. The learner puts into practice as quickly as possible the lessons which have been explained or demonstrated. Intellectual assent or comprehension alone do not qualify. Practice then surfaces further needs so the learner desires more interaction with the learning facilitator. Jesus' methodology with His disciples makes this point particularly clear.

Fourth, the learning experiences consume time. It takes time to get to know people, to understand how they see themselves, to discern their experiences and their needs, to think of illustrations or stories which capture the imagination, to design practical applications so learning moves beyond mere intellectual exercise to life change. True learning appears to demand a leisurely pace. And the immediacy of application lays a foundation for our teaching today.

How does the model of Jesus speak to the issue of Christian education? Certainly not by displaying neatly organized lists of steps, guaranteed to bring immediate results. Instead we read of people, in a different culture and a different time, who grew from their learning experiences.

While circumstances may be different, evangelical Christian educators freely draw this example as we seek creativity in teaching methodology. Admittedly, change is slow; many educators continue to bore their routinely attending classes with an uninspired lesson which has no remote connection to the lives of the listeners. However, those who work on the leading edge of evangelical Christian education strive toward active involvement between the teacher and the learner. As Howard Hendricks writes, "Some of the best motivators I know never work in a classroom. They are teachers without the label—men and women who are doing discipleship and changing the lives and the perspectives of other people. Why? Because they are willing to flow into other people's lives."[33]

CONCLUSION

Active involvement, the model of Jesus freeing us to use multiple methods, a willingness to flow into the lives of others, use of small groups and community support, recognition of a truth source outside human experience—all for the purpose of encouraging Christ-likeness and an active understanding of redemption—characterize the leading edge of evangelical Christian educators today. Certainly we do not suggest that we've "got it all together" or that the push to more creative, individually oriented instruction has resulted in problem-free learning. Nonetheless, we see an encouraging movement both among present instructors and future leaders in Christian Education that is consistent with our theology. Our anthropology reminds us that we will never achieve perfection, but our understanding of God permits us to move forward in expectation of forgiving grace as we seek to impact the lives of others.

We believe Christian Education is a theological discipline informed by the social sciences. In its journey through school it visits many classes, gleaning helpful insights along the way. But its home room, its beginning and ending, can be found only in a solid biblical and doctrinal context. There it can be nourished. There it functions best. There it belongs.

---

33. Howard G. Hendricks, *Teaching to Change Lives* (Portland, Oreg.: Multnomah, 1987), 152.

CHAPTER FOUR

Orthodox Theology and Religious Education

CONSTANCE J. TARASAR

Part One

The relationship of theology to religious education in the Orthodox Church is both assumed and in the process of being discovered: assumed, because everything within the life of the church is seen through the lens of theology (knowledge of God), and being discovered, because the task of religious education in this modern era is a relatively new activity. Further, Orthodox theology itself has been the subject of a certain rediscovery or renewal during this twentieth century as its patristic roots are being recovered and its "Western Captivity" revealed.[1] There is no field of theology or dimension of church life that has not been engaged in or touched by this renewal and its attendant reappropriation or reintegration of the patristic vision. The critical theological work that has and is being done in liturgical theology, ecclesiology, church history and canon law, dogmatic theology, biblical studies, liturgical music, etc., has produced both a corpus of theological writings in modern languages that reflects upon patristic sources from historical and contempo-

---

1. See Georges Florovsky, "Western Influences in Russian Theology," in *Aspects of Church History* (Belmont, Mass.: Nordland, 1975). Florovsky spoke of the "Western captivity" and "pseudomorphosis" of Orthodox thought and called for a return to the patristic sources. See also the works of Vladimir Lossky, Alexander Schmemann, Dimitru Staniloae, John Meyendorff, John Zizioulas, Christos Yannaras, who, among others, are representative of modern Orthodox theologians who have contributed to this rediscovery and renewal.

rary perspectives and provides, as well, processes or models to guide further investigation.

The fields of religious education and pastoral theology, generally, are only at the beginning stage of this process. In these areas of study, that in many respects are "new" or have taken on new forms today, the process is one of discovering the continuity and discontinuity within the history and tradition of the church through the ages. It involves the effort of:

(a) coming to know the biblical and theological sources of the tradition (and their specific content);
(b) reflecting upon these sources in the light of the attendant context and experience of the church in which they were produced and lived-out;
(c) drawing fourth the principles and concepts that are fundamental to the life of the church in any age (at the same time, noting that which is particular primarily to the age in which it emerged);
(d) determining what kinds of transformations or re-creations from the tradition are possible in order to develop new application, consistent with the church's theology and practice, to meet contemporary needs.

From this context, I present an Orthodox approach to the relation of theology and religious education. Three basic premises provide the foundation: (1) theology and religious education are fundamentally *of the church*, (2) theology and religious education are grounded in an understanding of God in Trinity, and our relationship to God and to each other as persons, and (3) theology and religious education must be communicated in their fullness or wholeness.

The first premise, that both theology and religious education are *of the church*, means that they cannot be separated from the *life* of the church. The basic aim both of theology and religious education is not "objective" knowledge *about* God, but knowledge *of* God: i.e., the experience of communion in and with God, and therefore, with other persons and all creation. Theology and religious education, consequently, concern *Life*, life given and lived eternally in God. We seek God and desire to grow in our knowledge of God because he is the source of life. Alexander Schmemann states that theology itself "began as an inspired reflection on the liturgy, as the revelation of its true meaning."[2] It is primarily in and through liturgical *experience* that we come to know and understand God, in a process that Schmemann describes as "liturgical catechesis":

Liturgical catechesis shows us first of all the main *purpose*, the aim of religious education as it is understood by the Church. This aim is *to bring the individual into the life of the Church*. I emphasize: it is not merely the

2. Alexander Schmemann, *Of Water and Spirit* (Crestwood, N.Y.: St. Vladimir's Seminary Press, 1974), 12.

communication of "religious knowledge," not training a human being to become a "good person," but the edification"—the "building up"—of a member of the Body of Christ, a member of that new "chosen race" and "holy nation" (1 Pt. 2:9) whose mysterious life in this world began on the day of Pentecost. "And make him (her) a reason-endowed sheep in the holy flock of Thy Christ, and honorable member of Thy Church," says the baptismal prayer. Religious education is nothing else but the disclosing of that which happened to man when he was born again through water and Spirit, and was made a *member of the Church*.[3]

The second premise focuses on the inseparable concepts of the One God in Trinity and the nature of Personhood: concepts which are centered on the principles of personal relationships, freedom, love, and communion. These concepts and principles are fundamental to Orthodox theology and life and underlie our understanding of "church" and what it means to be a member of the church.

The third premise is the manner in which the theology of the church is communicated through education in its fullness or wholeness. In the early church, says Schmemann, education

was always understood as the indivisible unity of *teaching, liturgical experience,* and *spiritual effort.* It is this *unity* that, more than anything else, we need today . . . for as long as in our teaching—be it in theological seminaries or "Sunday Schools"—Bible, doctrine, liturgy, spirituality remain virtually isolated from one another, constitute autonomous "departments" loosely united within a formal "curriculum," not only does each one of them tend to become an intellectual abstraction, but none is able to reveal the *faith*, in its living concrete and truly existential fullness.[4]

For these reasons, and others, it also becomes clear that Orthodox theology cannot be addressed neatly in separate categories. When one addresses the life of *faith*, unity and integration—not division or separation—are essential. Consequently, the theological material that follows is presented in broad themes, with some overlapping among these themes. In addition, theological concepts are expressed not only through biblical and doctrinal terminology and formulas, but also through liturgical and spiritual sources, i.e. through the lived experience of faith in the church.

THEOLOGICAL FOUNDATIONS

A Vision of Life

The basic vision of Christian life is life in union or communion (*koinonia*) with God. For Orthodox Christians this vision is communicated primar-

---

3. Alexander Schmemann, *Liturgy and Life: Christian Development through Liturgical Experience* (New York: DRE-Orthodox Church in America, 1974), 11.

4. Schmemann, *Of Water and the Spirit*, 152.

ily and most powerfully through the experience of the church in its Paschal celebration wich begins with the hymn: "Christ is risen from the dead, trampling down death by death, and upon those in the tombs bestowing life" (*Paschal Troparion*).

Upon enterning the church on Easter night, after the proclamation—Christ is Risen!—of Christ's resurrection, the people begin singing a group of hymns called the Paschal Kanon. The first ode refers to the significance of our baptism: our illumination and incorporation into the life of the church, a life which is the beginning of our own passage to heaven.

This is the day of resurrection. Let us be illumined O people.
Pascha, the Pascha of the Lord.
For from death to life and from earth to heaven has Christ our God led us,
as we sing the song of victory: Christ is risen from the dead!

Let us purify our senses and we shall see Christ
shining in the unapproachable light of His resurrection.
We shall clearly hear Him say: Rejoice!
as we sing the song of victory: Christ is risen from the dead!

Let the heavens be glad, and let the earth rejoice.
Let the whole world, visible and invisible, keep the feast.
For Christ is risen, our eternal joy!

No one who has experienced the singing of these words in the church on Pascha night can read or hear them without again reliving their first Pascha or most recent Pascha. Orthodox Christians live from Pascha to Pascha, from one Easter night to the next, always recalling and reliving that vision and that saving act and revelation of God that gives us life!

During this same celebration of Pascha, the Gospel proclaims both the creation of the world by God and its salvation:

In the beginning was the Word and the Word was with God, and the Word was God. He was in the beginning with God; all things were made through him, and without him was not anything made that was made. In him was life, and the life was the light of men. The light shines in the darkness, and the darkness has not overcome it. . . . And the Word became flesh and dwelt among us, full of grace and truth; we have beheld his glory, glory as of the only Son from the Father. . . . And from his fullness have we all received grace upon grace. For the law was given through Moses; grace and truth came through Jesus Christ. No one has ever seen God; the only Son, who is in the bosom of the Father, he has made him known. (Jn. 1:1-18)

Together, these liturgical and biblical verses sum up the essence of the Christian message of salvation and provide us with the vision and aim of

Christian life. It is a vision that focuses on our passage from death to life, made possible by Christ's death and resurrection. It is a passage or journey from earth to heaven that leads to Christ himself: to the very light and life of God, where we shall see God and behold his glory in the everlasting light of his kingdom. Finally, it is a vision that includes not only us, but through us all of creation. The entire cosmos is redeemed and transformed by the resurrection of Christ who gives life to all.

The Divine Community: The Tri-Personal God

The first truth of Orthodox theology is the understanding that God is three persons: Father, Son, and Holy Spirit, who are one in essence. God exists because he is a *union of persons*—a *Divine communion* or *community of persons* united through love. A *person*, in Orthodox thought, is the specific mode in which a being or nature is realized or exists (in Greek, one would say the manner in which someone or something is *hypostasized*). In the case of God, Thomas Hopko says that the *being* (essence, nature, *ousia*) answers the question "What is God?" while the *person* (or *hypostasis*) answers the question "which one" or "who." Thus he says, "when we ask 'What is God?' we answer that God is the divine, perfect, eternal absolute, . . . And when we ask 'Who is God?' we answer that God is the Father, the Son, and the Holy Spirit."[5]

Christos Yannaras explains that "it is the *person* who constitutes the initial possibility of existence, the beginning possibility of being . . . The Person of God the Father precedes and defines his Essence; he is not predetermined by it. God is not obliged by his Essence to be God; he is not subject to the necessity of his existence . . . "He exists, since he loves and love is only an event of freedom. Freely and from love, the Father hypostasizes his Being in a Triad of Persons, constitutes the principle and mode of his Existence as a community of personal freedom and love."[6]

God, therefore, is a relational being. We can begin to discern who God is, how he acts, and something of what it means to be in a relationship of communion, a relationship of love, by reflecting on the relationships of the three persons of the Trinity. A liturgical verse from the feast of Pentecost describes how the three Persons of the Trinity relate and act together:

Come, let us worship the Tri-Personal Godhead:
The Son in the Father with the Holy Spirit,

---

5. Thomas Hopko, *An Elementary Handbook on the Orthodox Church, Vol. 1 Doctrine.* p. 141. See also the excellent article by Deborah Belonick on "Revelation and Metaphors: the Significance of the Trinitarian Names, Father, Son, and Holy Spirit" in *Union Theological Quarterly* 40 (1984), 31-42, where she addresses the question of the appropriateness of these particular names, rather than the use of Creator, Savior, Sanctifier, or Mother, Daughter, Holy Spirit.

6. Christos Yannaras, *Elements of Faith* (Edinburgh: T & T Clark, 1991), 34-35.

The Father timelessly begets the co-reigning and co-eternal Son.
The Holy Spirit was in the Father, glorified equally with the Son,
One Power, One Substance, One Godhead!
In worshiping Him, let us all say:
Holy God: who made all things through the Son.
   with the cooperation of the Spirit.
Holy Mighty: through whom we know the Father,
   through whom the Holy Spirit came into the world.
Holy Immortal: the comforting Spirit, proceeding from the Father
   and resting in the Son.
O Holy Trinity: glory to Thee!

                         (Vespers of Pentecost)

From this verse, we see that each of the persons of the Holy Trinity: Father, Son, and Spirit exists and acts differently. However, each Person never acts alone but in eternal relation to or in cooperation with the other two Persons. As Yannaras points out, the only way this is possible is through a total self-giving of oneself to others in love and the desire to freely *want* or *will* to be and act completely as One.

Yannaras also emphasizes that love is the basis of all of life, and this is true both for the Divine Community and the Human Community.

Holy Scripture assures us that "God is love" (1 Jn. 4:16). It does not tell us that God *has* love, that love is an attribute, a property of God. . . . God is a trinity of Persons . . . a dynamic actualization of love, an unbroken union of love. Each Person exists not for himself, but he exists offering himself in a community of love with the other Persons. The life of the Persons is a "co-inherence" of life, which means: the life of one becomes the life of the other; their Existence is drawn from the actualization of life as communion, from life which is identified with self-offering, love.[7]

He adds: "Since the mode by which God *is* is love, and from this mode springs each possibility and expression of life, then life must function as love in order to be actualized . . . only the person can actualize life as love, and then only as an achievement of freedom."[8]

St. Andrei Rublev's icon of the Old Testament Trinity—based upon the icon of the Hospitality of Abraham (cf. Gen. 18)—images the theological truth of this concept of persons-in-relation. The visitation of God to Abraham and Sarah comes in the form of three "strangers," imaged by Rublev (and others before him) as three angels. They are grouped around a table with their bodies forming a perfect circle, the image of the eternal. The heads of the middle figure and that on the right are turned toward the figure on the left, the

---

7. Ibid., 36.
8. Ibid.

image of the Father from whom they receive life. The middle, and central, figure is portrayed in bold colors, the same colors and vestment in which Christ—who was revealed to us concretely in human flesh—is portrayed in other icons as Pantocrator (ruler). His hand is giving a blessing over the cup in the center of the table. The garments of the other two (the Father on the left, in a pale rose, and the Spirit on the right, in a pale green) are more translucent and less visible. The whole icon is one of complete serenity, calmness, and harmonry. It is an image of communion and unity, a perfect unity of Persons united in love.[9]

The revelation of God to us is this presence of a Divine Community, a community of Persons who though distinct from one another are united fully, perfectly, eternally, in love. This Divine Community images for us what we should be as a human community. As a community of diverse persons—women and men, from a myriad of cultures, races, and languages—we are called to be united together in love. Moreover, this love in which we are to be bound together is more than an imperfect love of a fallen humanity but is joined in the love of Christ that is shared with the Father in the Holy Spirit. This is the Communion—the *koinonia*—for which we were created.

It is for this reason that the Holy Trinity, the Divine Community of Persons, is for us human persons a prototype for life in relationship and communion with others. Human persons as a community of multiple persons also share a common nature. Yannaras describe this, saying:

> God is a Nature and Three Persons; man is a nature and "innumerable" persons. God is consubstantial and in three hypostases, man is consubstantial and in innumerable hypostases. The difference of natures, the difference of uncreated and created, can be transcended at the level of the common mode of existence, the mode of personal existence—and this truth has been revealed to us by the incarnation of God, by the Person of Jesus Christ. *For man to be an image of God means that each one can realize his existence as Christ realizes life as love, as freedom and not as natural necessity.* Each can realize his existence as a person, like the Persons of the triadic Divinity. Consequently, man can realize his existence as eternity and incorruptibility, just as the divine life of triadic co-inherence and communion is eternal and incorruptible.[10]

How can this transcendence or sharing in the life of God himself take place? Bishop Kallistos Ware explains how it is possible that God is both "unknown yet known, hidden yet revealed" to us. He draws a distinction between the

---

9. Cf. Leonid Ouspensky and Vladimir Lossky, *The Meaning of Icons* (Crestwood, N.Y.: St. Vladimir's Seminary Press).

10. Ibid., 59. My italics.

transcendence or "otherness" of God and God's immanence or presence with us. He says:

> The Orthodox tradition draws a distinction between the essence, nature, or inner being of God, on the one hand, and his energies, operations, or acts of power, on the other. . . . By the essence of God is meant his otherness, by the energies his nearness. Because God is a mystery beyond our understanding, we shall never know his essence or inner being. . . . If we knew the divine essence, it would follow that we knew God in the same way as he knows himself; and this we cannot ever do, since he is Creator and we are created. But while God's inner essence is for ever beyond our comprehension, his energies, grace, life, and power fill the whole universe and are directly accessible to us.

> When Orthodox speak of the divine energies, they do not mean by this an emanation from God, an "intermediary" between God and man, or a "thing" or "gift" that God bestows. On the contrary, the energies are God himself in his activity and self-manifestation. When a man knows he participates in the divine energies, he truly knows or participates in God himself, so far as this is possible for a created being. But God is God, and we are men; and so, while he possesses us, we cannot in the same way possess him.[11]

Consequently, as human persons participate in the energies of God, but not his essence, "there is union, but not fusion or confusion." This truth enables us to understand what is meant by the concept of *theosis*, the process of deification or growth into the divine life, to which all persons are called. It is the possibility of a direct or mystical union between humanity and God.[12]

Although the language used here may be unfamiliar to some, the basic concepts about God and Personhood are few and relatively simple: in summary, they are the following:

1. God is God in Trinity: Three Persons (three *hypostases*) and One Nature (one *ousia* or essence).
2. The Holy Trinity is a Divine Community, a union or communion of persons whose existence is founded on personal freedom and love.
3. Personhood is the possibility to exist freely, to choose to determine one's own existence. to love, to give oneself freely to another, to enter into relationships, to enter into communion or a relationship of union with another in love.
4. The Holy Trinity reveals to us the perfection of life in community and calls human persons, made in God's image, to the imitation of that life of unity and holiness, in freedom and in love.

---

11. Archimandrite Kallistos Ware, *The Orthodox Way* (Crestwood, N.Y.: St. Vladimir's Seminary Press, 1979), 27.

12. Ibid., 28.

The implications of these basic concepts, particularly that of Personhood and Communion, will be expanded as other theological points are developed.

Creation and the Human Community

The search for communion (*koinonia*)[13] with God is the search for life itself. To be in communion is to be "in *Life*": the life of God who gives life *for eternity*. To be alive is to live *in God*. This is the essence of the biblical message. Human persons are created in God's own image for communion with God, for it is God who creates and sustains them in life by the power of his Word and his Spirit. This is the second truth of the faith. Alexander Schmemann, who speaks often of the world as sacrament, says:

> In the Bible the food that man eats, the world of which he must partake in order to live, is given to him by God, and it is given as *communion with God*. . . . All that exists is God's gift to men, and it all exists to make God known to man, to make man's life communion with God. It is divine love made food, made life. . . . God *blesses* everything He creates, and, in biblical language, this means that He makes all creation the sign and means of His presence and wisdom, love and revelation: "O taste and see that the Lord is good."[14]

Alexander Schmemann continues, saying that human persons, like animals and other living things, are hungry beings and exist by eating, but they alone are unique in that their hunger or desire is ultimately a desire for God.

> The whole creation depends on food. But the unique position of man in the universe is that he alone is to *bless* God for the food and the life he receives from Him. He alone is to respond to God's blessing with his blessing. . . . And in the Bible to bless God is not a "religious" or a "cultic" act, but the very *way of life* . . . the only *natural* (and not "supernatural") reaction of man, to whom God gave this blessed and sanctified world, is to bless God in return, to thank Him, to *see* the world as God sees it and—in this act of gratitude and adoration—to know, name and possess the world.[15]

Human persons, says Schmemann, are called to be "priests of creation." They are created to continually receive God's gifts as blessings and, in turn, to offer these gifts back to God as our blessing. Thus we transform our lives

---

13. See Constance J. Tarasar, "Worship, Spirituality and Biblical Reflection: Their Significance for the Churches' Search for Koinonia," in *The Ecumenical Review* 45:2 (April 1993), Geneva: World Council of Churches, 218-225.

14. Alexander Schmemann, *For the Life of the World* (Crestwood, N.Y.: St. Vladimir's Seminary Press, 1973), 14.

15. Ibid., 15.

into life in God, into communion with him. The world, he says: "was created as the 'matter,' the material of one all-embracing eucharist, and man was created as the priest of this cosmic sacrament."[16]

But the persons God has created have not fulfilled their vocation as "priests of creation." The story of the Fall of Man (Gn. 3) presents us with a third truth: it shows us that human beings opted to see the world as a "thing in itself" rather than a means of communion with God. To desire to become "like God" (Gn. 3:5) as an act of independence from God, however, is to cut oneself off from life itself.

> When we see the world as an end in itself, everything becomes itself a value and consequently loses all value, because only in God is found the meaning (value) of everything, and the world is meaningful only when it is the "sacrament" of God's presence. Things treated merely as things in themselves destroy themselves because only in God have they any life. The world of nature, cut off from the source of life, is a dying world. For one who thinks food in itself is the source of life, eating is communion with the dying world. Food itself is dead, it is life that has died and it must be kept in refrigerators like a corpse.[17]

Sin (*amartia*, literally, "missing the mark") is what separates us from God. It is our intentional act of turning aside or away from God, a "disconnection," or cutting off of our relationship with God. The result of such a disconnection is death: this is the significance of the story of the expulsion of Adam and Eve from Paradise. Sin results in death (Rom. 6:20-23), with somewhat the same results as when the cord of a lamp is disconnected from the outlet which supplies it with energy and power. As long as we are "connected" to God, to our source of energy or power, i.e. life itself, we are in a relationship of love—in communion and in life—with God, with one another, with the whole of creation.

In the Orthodox Tradition, Great Lent is that time of the year when Christians strive to understand and repent of their separation from God, and, consequently, from one another and all creation. Alexander Schmemann calls Great Lent "*a school of repentance* to which every Christian must go every year in order to deepen his faith, to re-evaluate, and, if possible, to change his life. It is a wonderful pilgrmage to the very sources of Orthodox faith."[18] Repentance (*metanoia*) denotes a change of mind, of will, of action— an actual turning around of one's life—that reflects a complete and total change affecting one's entire being. It is a true "conversion" that directs (or redirects) life toward life in God.

---

16. Ibid.

17. Ibid., 17.

18. Alexander Schmemann, *Great Lent* (Crestwood, N.Y.: St. Vladimir's Seminary Press, 1974), 9. My italics.

The Sunday immediately preceeding Lent commemorates the explusion of Adam and Eve from Paradise. The liturgical verses recall this, saying:

Adam was expelled from paradise through food;
Sitting, therefore, in front of it he cried: "Woe to me . . . "
One commandment of God have I transgressed, depriving myself of all
    that is good;
Paradise holy! Planted for me, and now . . . closed to me
Pray to thy Creator and mine that I may be filled again by thy blossom.
Then answered the Savior to him: I wish not my creation to perish;
I desire it to be saved and to know the Truth,
For I will not turn away him who comes to Me.

(Aposticha, Cheesefare Sunday)

During the Vespers of Forgiveness Sunday that inaugurates the Lenten period, the Psalm verse laments: "Turn not thy face away from thy child for I am afflicted. Hear me speedily; draw near unto my soul and deliver it" (Ps. 69). The Rite of Forgiveness, during which each penitent personally asks forgiveness of each person gathered in the church and exchanges the kiss of peace with them, reflects the fact that to be in communion with God is not an "individual" experience, but one that is both personal and communal. When we sin, we not only separate ourselves from God but from each other.

In Orthodox thought, there is a significant distinction between the use of the words "individual" and "personal." An individual, or individuality, refers to one who is isolated, self-dependent, self-centered, wishes to "go it alone" or to do things "my way." A person is always a "person-in-relation" with others, presupposes the "other" and recognizes one's dependence on others. The "Fall" of human nature, therefore, is not only a break in communion with 'God but a break in all our relationships. The tragic consequence of this "break" is death: the loss of life, life lived eternally in and with God. It is the very *image* of God in us that has suffered damage and distortion in our life and is in need of restoration.

God with Us: The Incarnate God

The next truth of the faith is that the redemption of the human nature and human persons comes through the Incarnation of God's only-begotten Son Jesus Christ,

who, though he was in the form of God, did not count equality with God a thing to be grasped, but emptied himself, taking the form of a servant, being born in the likeness of men. And being found in human form he humbled himself and became obedient unto death, even death on a cross. Therefore God has highly exalted him and bestowed on him the name which is above every name, that at the name of Jesus every knee should bow,

in heaven and on earth and under the earth, and every tongue confess that
Jesus Christ is Lord, to the glory of God the Father.

(Phil. 2:6-11)

The Feast of the Annunciation rejoices in this announcement to the whole
human race.

> Let heaven rejoice, let the earth be glad!
> For the consubstantial and coequal Son of the Father empties himself and
>   becomes a man.
> He dwells in the virginal womb, sanctified by the Spirit.
> God enters humanity; the uncontainable One is contained in a womb.
> The timeless One enters time, and what is more glorious,
> His conception is seedless, the mystery ineffable.
> God empties Himself in incarnation, for the angel proclaimed the
>   conception to the Pure One.
> Rejoice, O full of grace, the Lord is with you!
>
> *(Aposticha, Vespers of Annunciation)*

The very act of God entering time, entering this world and taking on human
flesh is incomprehensible to us; in the light of God's power, majesty, and glory,
it can only be described as a mystery of God's dispensation for our sake. It
is because God is love, creates us in love. and desires us as His beloved that
he makes such a condescension to save us. The hymn of the first Sunday of
Lent, which also commemorates the restoration of icons in the church, speaks
of this act as one of restoring humanity to its original image:

> No one could describe the Word of the Father,
> But when He took flesh from you, O Theotokos,[19] he accepted to be
>   described
> And restored the fallen image to its former state by uniting it to divine beau-
>   ty.
> We confess and proclaim our salvation in words and images.
>
> *(Kontakion, 1st Sunday of Lent)*

Several theologial truths are proclaimed in these texts. The first is that the fullness of the Godhead participates in this mystery of the incarnation of the
Son and Word of God. Freely, and because of love, God the Father sends his
only-begotten Son into the world to save humankind. The Son willingly
accepts to be humbled and circumscribed in human flesh, and the Spirt
effects his conception in the womb of a pure virgin. The second truth is
equally important: through the humility and obedience of Mary, all human-

---

19. Greek, lit. "the one who gave birth to God"; also translated as "Mother of God,"
referring to Mary the Mother of God's Son Jesus.

ity freely accepts to receive God in the flesh. It is her "yes," her "let it be to me according to your word" (Lk. 1:38), that fulfills God's initiative. As another verse from the feast of Annunciation says: "The ultimate reconciliation comes through a common consent!"—as does our consent continue through confession of faith in Christ "in words and images."[20] The third truth affirms the participation and effect on the whole creation. The church in all her feasts understands that God's creation both suffers in the Fall and rejoices in the Redemption of the world. A wonderful verse from the feast of the Nativity of Christ reflects the participation and joy of the entire cosmos in the birth of the Lord:

What shall we offer Thee, O Christ,
who for our sakes hast appeared on earth as man?
Every creature made by Thee offers Thee thanks:
The angels offer a hymn; the heavens, a star;
the wise men, gifts; the shepherds, their wonder;
the earth, its cave; the wilderness, a manger.
And we offer Thee a virgin mother!
O Pre-eternal God, have mercy on us.
(Sticheron, Vespers of Christmas)

But the church, together with all of creation, also enters into the suffering and death of Christ:

All creation was changed by fear
When it saw Thee hanging upon the cross, O Christ.
The sun was darkened, and the foundations of the earth were shaken.
All things suffered with the Creator of all.
O Lord, who didst willingly endure this for us, Glory to Thee.
(Aposticha, Holy Friday Matins)

The death and resurrection of Christ is the ultimate humiliation of the incarnate God. His self-emptying (*kenosis*) was an act of total obedience to the Father:

Christ gave himself up to death forsaking totally every tendency and aspiration for physical self-existence of the created and transposed the event of

---

20. Other translations of this kontakion of the first week of Lent say "deed and word," e.g., *The Lenten Triodion*, translated by Mother Mary and Archimandrite Kallistos Ware (London: Faber and Faber, 1978), 306. Leonid Ouspensky notes that "This word [deed] takes on a double meaning in the kontakion: that of internal and external deeds . . . it expresses the living experience of the Church, the experience which is expressed in words or in images by the men who attained holiness . . . [or the person who is able to] translate his inner santification into images, either visible or verbal." Cf. *Theology of the Icon*, Vol. 1 (Crestwood, N.Y.: St. Vladimir's Seminary Press, 1992), 164-165.

existence and life into a relationship with the Father, into his abandonment to the will of the Father, into the surrender of his "spirit" "into the hands" of the Father.[21]

Through his death on the Cross, the incarnate God entered Hades, the place of death itself. He defeated it from within: "trampling down death by [his own] death" (Easter Troparion) in order to save man whom he loved. Perhaps the most vivid liturgical verses of the entire year are those of Holy Saturday in which the poetic imagery of Christ in Hades attempts to describe the meaning of this even of salvation. The picture develops slowly and quietly during the Matins service:

Thou has slept in the tomb, O Christ, a life-giving sleep, by which Thou hast wakened all the human race from the heavy slumber of sin. (II.4)

Wishing to save Adam, Thou didst come down to earth. Not finding him on earth, O Master, Thou didst descend to Hades seeking him. (I.25)

Adam was greatly afraid when God walked in Paradise. Now, with joy he sees God stalking Hades' depths. There he fell, but here he is raised up. (II.17)

In the earth's dark bosom the Grain of Wheat is laid. By its death, it shall bring forth abundant fruit: Adam's sons, freed from the chains of death. (I.29)

O Messiah, Jesus, my King, the Lord of all, whom art Thou seeking in the depths of hell? Hast Thou come to free the race of mortal men? (I.5)

Hell, who had filled all men with fear, trembled at the sight of Thee, and in haste he yielded up his prisoners, O Immortal Sun of Glory. (II.55)

All the earth was troubled and quaked in fear. The daystar hid his brilliant face, O Word, when Thy great light was hidden in the earth. (I.26)

How could hell bear Thy coming and not shatter at once? Death is blinded by Thy splendor, O Lord. Its gloom is scattered by Thy dazzling light. (I.10)

When devouring Hades engulfed the Rock of Life, in great pain he burst asunder, and the dead held captive from all ages were released. (I.23)[22]

---

21. Yannaras, *Elements of Faith*, 109.
22. *Matins of Holy Saturday* (Syosset, N.Y.: DRE-Orthodox Church in America, 1982).

When the incarnate God by his own death enters Hades, it is not merely a dead man who dwells there, but the very life and love of God himself. And it is this very love that the Evil One cannot bear. Creation is the fruit of God's love, and now in Hades itself, the new creation, or the re-creation of the world begins as a result of the ultimate self-emptying sacrificial love of Christ. Like the image of the egg with a life growing inside, there comes a time when that life becomes so full that the shell cannot contain it. The power of the growing life inside cracks the shell from within and new life breaks forth from its "tomb." So it is when Christ who is Life, Love, and Light enters Hades. Death can no longer hold man captive, for the God-Man has filled all things with the power of his uncontainable Love. He has "trampled down death" by his own death and brought Life and Light into the tombs. During the Holy Saturday Vesperal-Liturgy, this power and joy of the Resurrection begins to be manifest, as Hell itself cries out in defeat:

Today, hell cries out groaning: I should not have accepted the Man born of Mary.
He came and destroyed my power.
He shattered the gates of brass.
As God, He raised the souls that I had held captive.
Glory to Thy cross and resurrection, O Lord!

Today, hell cries out groaning: My dominion has been shattered.
I received a dead man as one of the dead, but against Him I could not prevail.
From eternity I had ruled the dead, but behold, He raises all.
Because of Him do I perish.
Glory to Thy cross and resurrection, O Lord!

Today, hell cries out groaning: My power has been trampled upon.
The Shepherd is crucified and Adam is raised.
I have been deprived of those whom I ruled.
Those whom I swallowed in my strength I have given up.
He who was crucified has emptied the tombs.
The power of death has been vanquished.
Glory to Thy cross and resurrection, O Lord![23]

It is not surprising that the icon of the Feast of the Resurrection in the Orthodox Church depicts the Descent into Hades, for it is in Hades, as the services proclaim, where the Resurrection begins. The icon depicts the Risen Lord in bright white garments, surrounded by rays of gold representing his Glory and standing on the broken gates of hell. With arms outstretched, he

---

23. *Great and Holy Saturday: Vespers and Divine Liturgy of St. Basil the Great* (Syosset, N.Y.: DRE-Orthodox Church in America, 1976).

reaches out to Adam and Eve to pull them up out of the dark depths of the earth. Other figures from the Old Testament stand among the rocky cliffs in the background. It is not the empty tomb or one of the post-Resurrection appearances that is featured, but the power and glory of God resurrecting the human race from the bonds of hell. This is the vision that explodes in even greater Paschal joy, in the celebration of the Resurrection Matins.

On the feast of the Ascension of Christ, the God-Man, into heaven, another truth is revealed. By Christ's ascension, human flesh is lifted up to the heavens and all people have the possibility to enter again into communion with God. The verses proclaim:

Without leaving the Father's bosom and having lived with men as a man,
Today, Thou hast ascended in glory from the Mount, mercifully raising
    our fallen nature, enthroning it with the Father on high.
The angelic hosts were amazed with awe, seeing Thy great love for man. . . .
By their prayers . . . make us, Thy chosen people, worthy of this joy!
                                            (*Vespers of Ascension*)

Christ assures his disciples that he is not abandoning them but will send a Comforter, the Holy Spirit, to be with them until he comes again:

When Thou didst fulfill the dispensation for our sake
    and unite earth to heaven,
Thou didst ascend in glory, O Christ our God,
Not being parted from those who love Thee;
But remaining with them and crying:
I am with you and no-one will be against you.
                                            (*Kontakion of Ascension*)

Thou hast ascended in glory, O Christ God,
Granting joy to Thy disciples by the promise of the Holy Spirit.
Through the blessing, they were assured that Thou art the Son of God, the
    Redeemer of the world
                                            (*Troparion of Ascension*)

In the feast of Pentecost, the church celebrates the coming of the Holy Spirit and the manifestation of the Holy Trinity:

The Holy Spirit was, is and ever shall be, without beginning, without an end,
Forever united and numbered with the Father and the Son.
He is Life and life-creating, the Light and the Giver of Light, Good in
    Himself,the Fountain of goodness, through whom the Father is known and
    the Son glorified.
All acknowledge one Power, one Order, One worship of the Holy Trinity.
                                            (*Vespers of Pentecost*)

All is now fulfilled in Christ's work of Redemption and the focus now turns back to us. God himself has entered the world in the person of his Son, Jesus Christ, who

> was God before the ages, yet He appeared on earth and lived among men, becoming incarnate of a holy Virgin; He emptied Himself, taking the form of a servant, being likened to the body of our lowliness, that He might liken us to the image of His glory. For as by man sin entered into the world, and by sin death, so it pleased Thine only-begotten Son . . . to condemn sin in His flesh, so that those who were dead in Adam might be made alive in Thy Christ Himself . . . He brought us to knowledge of Thee, the true God and Father . . . Having cleansed us in water, and sanctified us with the Holy Spirit. He gave Himself as a ransom to death . . . Descending through the Cross into hell—that He might fill all things with Himself—He loosed the pangs of death. He arose on the third day, having made for all flesh a path to the resurrection from the dead, since it was not possible for the Author of Life to be a victim of corruption. So he became the first-fruits of those who have fallen asleep, the first-born of the dead, that He might be Himself truly the first in all things. Ascending into heaven, He sat down at the right hand of Thy majesty on high, and He will come to render to every man according to his works.
>
> (*Eucharistic Prayer, Liturgy of St. Basil the Great*)[24]

"He will come to render to every man according to his works." Christ has done all that was necessary to make it possible for us to restore our communion with God. However, the responsibility for our salvation is ours. As the Vespers of Pentecost ends, the congregation kneels, for the first time since the night of Pascha, for three long prayers focusing on repentance and forgiveness, our need for the guidance of the Holy Spirit, and the remembrance of those who have departed this life and who are united with us in God's love.

As at the end of every Eucharist—every Communion, where we have seen and tasted of that new life in Christ—we are reminded that our life is still "hid with Christ in God" (Col. 3:3), and we are called to return to "this world." "The church is about to begin her pilgrimage through time and history. It is evening again, and the night approaches, during which temptations and failures await us, when, more than anything else, we need Divine help, that presence and power of the Holy Spirit, who has *already* revealed to us the joyful End, who now will help us in our effort toward fulfillment and salvation."[25]

---

24. *The Divine Liturgy*, 2nd ed. (South Canaan, Pa.: St. Tikhon's Seminary Press, 1977), 131.

25. *The Vespers of Pentecost*, "Introduction" by Alexander Schmemann (New York: DRE-Orthodox Church in America, 1974), 4.

The Church as Communion

As Christians, we enter as persons into a new communion and new life with God through baptism into Christ's Body, the church, being renewed in the spirit of our minds and putting on "the new nature, created after the likeness of God in true righteousness and holiness" (Eph. 4:23-24). As such, we enter into a new relationship with all who are baptized and become members of one another. Our membership in the Body is not limited to an earthly, temporary structure, but is one that transcends space and time. Being in communion with God through Christ and the Spirit in the church, brings us into communion with those we worship and live with today, as well as with those who have fallen asleep in the Lord: *in all time*, past and present, and in every place. Our identity as persons is actualized or realized in this communion with God as we gather together as church, as a new *being-in-relationship* of which we are members-in-Christ.[26]

The church exists, as Thomas Hopko explains,

> Essentially as the divine presence of the Kingdom of God in human forms on earth, the mystery of the fullness of divine being and life, truth and love, dwelling in the community of human persons headed by Christ and animated by His spirit, the community which is dogmatically and spiritually identical and continuous in history as the gracious incarnation in men of all the fullness of divinity, and whose essential content and form is sacramental and mystical.[27]

An important liturgical dimension of this new community is remembrance (*anamnesis*). Alexander Schmemann once coined the phrase: "To love is to remember."[28] In the Eucharist, we *remember*—keep in living memory—not only the words and works of Christ for our sake, but we keep in memory and pray together with all those who are alive in Christ everywhere and at all times. To remember is to keep "in life." God continues to remember, to be faithful, to keep us in his love and consequently, in his life—even after death, for through the cross of Christ we are given newness of life. We are called in the church to love, to remember and to keep one another in life.

In all our relations, faithlessness and indifference, the absence of love and remembrance, always result in some form of death. By our thoughts, actions and memory, we either help to keep others alive—spiritually and physically—or we contribute to their death. The sin of *indifference* is that the "other" has no place in our life, doesn't *live* in our minds and hearts and, con-

---

26. Tarasar (cf. footnote 13), *Ecumenical Review* 45:2 (1993).

27. Thomas Hopko, "Catholicity and Ecumenism," in *All the Fullness of God: Essays on Orthodoxy, Ecumenism and Modern Society* (Crestwood, N.Y.: St. Vladimir's Seminary Press, 1982), 103.

28. *Orthodox America 1794-1976*, ed. Constance Tarasar (Syosset, N.Y.: Orthodox Church in America, 1975).

sequently, for all intents and purposes is *dead* for us. We kill others when for all practical purposes they do not exist for us in our life, when we don't care whether they are physically or spiritually alive or dead, when we shut them out of our life, out of any relationship, out of our consciousness, and out of our memory. Consequently, in this context, sin (*amartia*) truly is separation, the antithesis of life in Christ and communion in his Body, the church.

Remembrance in the church always begins with Mary, the Virgin Theotokos, who stands in the center of the church as love itself. It is Mary who, on behalf of all humanity, says "yes" to God and accepts to receive his Son into the world. On the icon of the Ascension of Christ to heaven, Mary stands in the center of the disciples, with an angel in white on either side as Christ ascends in his humanity to the Father. In the church building, on the iconostasis—the wall of icons separating the nave from the sanctuary—the icon of Mary with her Child is always to the left of the central doors, opposite that of Christ enthroned on the right. In liturgical texts, she is "more honorable than the Cherubim and more glorious beyond compare than the Seraphim," and is referred to as the "living Temple of God." Every image from the Old Testament Temple is used to describe her. Vladimir Lossky says:

> It is already possible to see the connection between the Mother of God, as she keeps and collects together the prophetic sayings, and the Church, as she keeps tradition. One is the germinal form of the other reality.[29]

Lossky points out that although she voluntarily accepted death, it had no more dominion over her:

> Like her Son, she was raised from the dead and borne up to heaven—the first human hypostasis in whom was fulfilled the final end for which the world was created. Thenceforth the Church and the entire universe have their crown, their personal achievement which throws open the way of deification to the whole creation. No gift is received in the Church without the assistance of the Mother of God, who is herself the first-fruits of the glorified Church.[30]

In this new realization of humanity, the person of the Theotokos and the church, the Body of Christ, are inseparably linked. Florovsky states:

> In the Communion of Saints, which is the true Church Universal and Catholic, the mystery of the New Humanity is disclosed as a new existential situation. And in this perspective the person of the Blessed Virgin

---

29. Vladimir Lossky, "Panagia," in *The Mother of God*, ed. E.L. Mascall, (London: Dacre Press, 1959), 28.

30. Vladimir Lossky, *The Mystical Theology of the Eastern Church* (Crestwood, N.Y.: St. Vladimir's Seminary Press, 1976), 194.

Mother appears in full light and full glory. The Church now contemplates
her in the state of perfection. She is now seen as inseparably united with
her Son, who "sitteth on the right hand of God the Father Almighty.". . .
The Church Triumphant is above all the worshiping Church, her existence is a living participation in Christ's office of intercession and his
redeeming love. Incorporation into Christ, which is the essence of the
Church and of the whole Christian existence, is first of all an incorporation
into his sacrificial love for mankind. And here there is a speecial place
for her who is united with the Redeemer in the unique intimacy of motherly affection and devotion. The Mother of God is truly the common mother of all living, of the whole Christian race, born or reborn in the Spirit and
Truth.[31]

Growth into the Divine Life

The process of spiritual growth into Christ or into the divine life is known
as *theosis*—i.e., deification, sanctification, transformation, growth in holiness,
growth in the Spirit. It is an effort that enables us, "while beholding the
glory of God," to grow into the likeness of God, to be changed "from one
degree of glory to another":

Now the Lord is the Spirit, and where the Spirit of the Lord is, there is
freedom. And we all, with unveiled face, beholding the glory of the Lord,
are being changed into his likeness from one degree of glory to another; for
this comes from the Lord who is the Spirit. (2 Cor. 3:17-18)

The story of the nineteenth-century Russian saint, St. Seraphim of Sarov,
provides one example of a person who manifested the Divine Light of God
in his own life. In a famous conversation with his friend and disciple
Motovilov, Seraphim spoke about the acquisition of the Holy Spirit and the
grace of God that is manifested in the divine light, such as Moses saw on
Mount Sinai (Ex. 34:30-35). Motovilov replied: "But how can I know that I
am within this grace of the Holy Spirit?. . . How I long to understand completely!" Then Seraphim took him by the shoulders and said: "My friend, both
of us at this moment are in the Holy Spirit, you and I. Why won't you look
at me?" And Motovilov replied: "I can't look at you, Father, because the
light flashing from your eyes and face is brighter than the sun and I'm daz-
zled!" Seraphim answered: "Don't be afraid, friend of God, you yourself
are shining just like I am; you too are now in the fullness of the grace of the
Holy Spirit, otherwise you wouldn't be able to see me as you do." And, he

---

31. George Florovsky, "The Ever-Virgin Mother of God, "in *The Mother of God*, 62-
63. For a more detailed overview and synthesis of Mary the Theotokos, see Chapter II of
Woman: Handmaid of the Lord, by Constance Joan Tarasar, M. Div. Thesis, St. Vladimir's
Orthodox Theological Seminary, Crestwood, N.Y., 1965. (Available on Microfilm,
Theological Research Exchange Network [TREN] #015-0051).

added, "When the Holy Spirit descends and fills the soul with the plenitude of his presence, then we experience that joy which Christ described, the joy which the world cannot take away. However, the joy you now feel in your heart is nothing compared to that which Paul the Apostle describes: 'What no eye has seen, nor ear heard, nor the heart of man conceived, what God has prepared for those who love him'" (1 Cor. 2:9).[32]

For Christos Yannaras, growth in faith is dependent upon love, and love, he says, "is neither emotionalism nor mere good intentions, but rather the supreme struggle for that self-transcendence which is, as the Church puts it, holiness."[33] The truth of the church, he says,

> is the event of the Eucharist: the transformation of individual survival into a life which is communicated as a gift of love and self-transcendence— the loving renunciation of the ego if man is to draw existence and identity from the fact that he is loved and loves. You must "lose" in order to "save," says the Gospel. . . . The truth of the Church is the destruction of every transitory self-defence and certainty in order that life be saved; it is an achievement of life and therefore a ceaseless risking, an adventure of freedom.[34]

Yannaras adds that sharing in this truth of the church presupposes "the transformation of life into a loving communion, in accordance with the triadic original of true life."

Asceticism, repentance, forgiveness, self-control or self-discipline, self-emptying or self-giving, and, above all, prayer, are some the numerous paths involved in the struggle for deification. For some, the effort takes place "in the world" in daily life at home, in marriage and family, or in the workplace; for others, the "workplace" is the monastic community, the eremitic cell or cave. Neither is judged to be the "better way" for each must work out one's own salvation. But to those who struggle for the Kingdom, the "fruit of the Spirit is love, joy, peace, patience, kindness, goodness, faithfulness, gentleness, self-control (Gal. 5:22). Fundamental, however, is love in all relationships: with God, with others, with one's own self (in mind, soul, and body), and with all of creation.

The models for growth in the spiritual life are the saints and ascetics, women and men whose whole purpose and direction in life was "to seek God and live" (Am. 5:4,6,14). The images of saints in icons reflect the inner, transfigured nature of persons who have sought the Lord, who have "put on Christ" (Gal. 3:27), and who reflect the divine light, i.e., the glory of God, in their own lives. Some pursued this search alone in prayer and fasting (Anthony of Egypt, Mary of Egypt), others within the communal life of a monastic

---

32. Valentine Zander, *St. Seraphim of Sarov* (Crestwood, N.Y.: St. Vladimir's Seminary Press, 1975), 89-92.

33. Yannaras, *Elements of Faith*, xiv.

34. Ibid., 156.

community (Pachomius of Egypt, Theodosius of the Kievan Caves), and some in their families and in service to Christ in the world (Juliana Ossorguin, John Chrysostom, John of Kronstadt, and Herman of Alaska). The countless numbers of saints are too numerous to mention here, even as "types," but the accounts of their lives are easily accessible in all Christian traditions. They are our spiritual guides and mentors in our struggle and search for God.

Part Two

THEORETICAL AND PRACTICAL IMPLICATIONS FOR RELIGIOUS EDUCATION

I began this chapter with the assumptions that theology and religious education are: (1) *of the church*, (2) grounded in an understanding of God and Personhood, and (3) must be communicated in their fullness and wholeness. I also noted, and it should now be evident, that the liturgical life of the church carries and communicates the essential truths of the church's faith and life through her worship. This is a fundamental aspect of Orthodox religious education which affect the determination of goals, the selection of content, and the context and process through which religious education is effected.

A modern-day example of the importance of worship can be found in post-Communist Eastern Europe and particularly in the territory of the former USSR. For more than seventy years, the church in Russia had no religious schools and religious instruction in classes of any sort—even in the church building. The church was not only forbidden to hold meetings of any nature but could not engage in any form of outreach to others, whether in hospitals or by various means of social service. The only church activity permitted, under strict restrictions and only in the church building, was observance of the "rites of the cult," i.e., liturgical services. Nevertheless, through even this limited exposure, the church was able to live and, indirectly, to teach. Many parents and grandparents (often secretly) baptized and raised their children in the Christian life. Under threat of reprisals, many people still came to the church services, heard the Gospel, sang the hymns, celebrated the feasts, received the sacraments, prayed before icons and venerated the saints. In spite of the severe limitations and dangers, there were also many "wonders and signs" of Christian faith and witness, as countless numbers of persons suffered as confessors and martyrs of the faith. The faith was proclaimed primarily through the living presence and witness of the ecclesial community gathered in prayer, celebration, and witness (i.e., *martyria*), whether in church buildings or in the prisons and harsh camps of the "Gulag." Thus did Christians in Russia communicate and teach each other the essence of Christian faith.

In the Orthodox Chruch, theology is more than a body of knowledge contained in books but is a living encounter with God in the context of the totality of ecclesial life. In the Book of Acts of the Apostles we read that those who gathered in Jerusalem on Pentecost and heard Peter's words

> were baptized . . . and they devoted themselves to the apostles' teaching and fellowship, to the breaking of bread and the prayers . . . fear came upon every soul; and many wonders and signs were done through the apostles. And all who believed were together and had all things in common; and they sold their possessions and goods and distributed them to all, as any had need. And day by day, attending the temple together and breaking bread in their homes, they partook of food with glad and generous hearts, praising God and having favor with all the people.

The integration of worship, teaching, and praxis within the context of personal and community life, as illustrated in the Acts, is the key to education in the church.[35] Alexander Schmemann expressed this when he stated that education in the early church "was always understood as the indivisible unity of *teaching, liturgical experience* and *spiritual effort.*"[36]

When religious education is conducted outside the context of the worshiping and witnessing community it becomes a "thing unto itself" with effects that can cause serious erosion in ecclesial life. The extreme example of this can be seen in the period of Roman Scholasticism and German Pietism where a certain reductionism took place: worship was reduced to empty ritualism, teaching to rote memorization of catechism formulas, and Christian praxis to individualistic piety and formalistic and minimalistic codes of conduct. This breakdown of the wholeness of Christian faith and life still affects church life today, both in the West and in the East.

We can be tempted to focus all our efforts on formal education, expecting new miracles to take place as a result of classes, publications, and other in structional programs. However, we can never forget that Christian education and the fullness of life in the church are intimately related and interdependent. Schmemann goes further and sets the vision of the church and its life as the goal of all religious teaching:

> The aim of all religious teaching in the Orthodox Church is to introduce the child (or the adult) into the Church, to integrate him into her life—the life

---

35. Constance J. Tarasar, "The Orthodox Experience," in *A Faithful Church: Issues in the History of Catechesis*, ed. John H. Westerhoff III and O.C. Edwards Jr. (Wilton, Conn.: Morehouse-Barlow, 1981), 236-260.

36. Schmemann, *Of Water and the Spirit*, 152.

of grace, communion with God, love, unity and spiritual process toward eternal salvation, for such are the essential aims of the Church.[37]

Basic Theoretical and Practical Factors

How can the religious educational program be envisioned both theoretically and practically within this total ecclesial reality? On the basis of the theological framework presented, several factors emerge:

1. The fundamental theological truths of Orthodox faith and life are founded on God in Trinity and the nature of personhood, which lead to understandings of church, communion, and relationships between God, human persons, and creation.
2. The church, as an ecclesial body, is the context for educating Christians in the understanding and praxis of Christian life, through its teaching, liturgical experience, and spiritual effort.
3. The church's theology and faith, as expressed in its liturgical life, provides the basic content for articulating broad educational goals.[38]
4. Religious education cannot be limited to "knowledge" factors; vision and experience (whether articulated or not) carry important "affects" that influence spiritual growth. Integrity and wholeness of the vision/message is necessary for effective communication.
5. Growth in spiritual life involves a basic comprehension of theological truths and the attitudes and values attendant to them, e.g., repentance (*metanoia*), humility and self-emptying (*kenosis*), sin, forgiveness, etc.

Conceptualizing Religious Education as Liturgical Catechesis

At the beginning of this chapter, the words of Alexander Schmemann reminded us that theology itself "began as an inspired reflection on the liturgy, as the revelation of its true meaning."[39] Schmemann also says that

the Orthodox faith has its most adequate expression in worship and that truly Christian life is the fulfillment of the grace, vision, teaching, inspiration, and power that we receive in worship. Therefore it is in the organic con-

37. Schmemann, *Liturgy and Life*, 23.
38. Cf. Constance Joan Tarasar, *A Process Model for the Design of Curriculum for Orthodox Religious Education* Ed. D. Dissèrtation, State University of New York at Albany, 1989, UMI #90-13327. Using the liturgy of initiation, i.e., the sacraments of Baptism and Chrismation as basic content, sixty theological statements were developed from an analysis of the liturgical texts and organized into ten categories involving the interrelationships of God, persons, world, and church. From a synthesis of statements in each category, twenty-nine broad educational goals were formulated and organized into the three categories of knowledge/understandings, attitudes/values, and behaviors/skills. More specific goals were then developed for different development stages.
39. Schmemann, *Of Water and the Spirit*, 12.

nection between the liturgical life of the Church and her education effort that we find the uniquely Orthodox principle of religious education.[40]

Conceptualizing an Orthodox approach to religious education, Schmemann asks:

> What then should Christian education be, if not the introduction into the life of the Church, an unfolding of its meaning, its contents and its purpose? And how can it introduce anyone into the life, if not by *participation* in the liturgical services on the one hand and their *explanation* on the other hand? "O taste and see how good is the Lord": first taste, then see—i.e., understand. The method of liturgical catechesis is truly *the* Orthodox method of religious education because it proceeds from the Church and because the Church is its goal.[41]

> Liturgical teaching consists, therefore, in explaining how everything in worship concerns *us* as the Church of God, makes us the living body of Christ, and concerns *me*, as a living member of that body. The essential role of liturgical education is to show how through participation in the *leiturgia*, the corporate and official worship of the Church, we can become witnesses to Christ in our private and public life, responsible members of the Church, or, in short, *Christians* in the full meaning of this word. The understanding of worship must lead to the assimilation of Christian doctrines and to the practice of Christian life.[42]

In one sense, the church has already conceptualized religious education in the light of its theology, having formulated a liturgical "curriculum." Every liturgical service, festal celebration and season has been intentionally constructed to communicate and celebrate the basic truths of the faith in order to lead persons into the life of God. The role of the curriculum specialist is to articulate these truths in the light of the educational task; to establish concrete goals for pastors, teachers, parents, church musicians, youth leaders, and others who have a teaching function in the church; and to assist those who are responsible for planning instruction, as well as more informal means of nurture, to faithfully interpret these goals in all areas of church life.

Four major elements are necessary to translate this conceptualization into theoretical and practical effects:

1. An ecclesial context for education and nurture.
2. A synthetic/synoptic approach to content.
3. Relational goals for personal faith and life.
4. Developmental and spiritual awareness for fostering transformative growth.

---

40. Schmemann, *Liturgy and Life*, 5.
41. Ibid., 13.
42. Ibid., 23.

An Ecclesial Context for Education and Nurture

Religious education involves the total life of the ecclesial community in its integrity and fullness. Every aspect of church life can be an opportunity for education, whether positive or negative in its teaching. Certainly the story of Ananias and Sapphira (Acts 5:1-11) had a tremendous educational impact on the early Christian community with the important lesson it conveyed about holding "all things in common" (Acts 2:44-45). Christian education is an intentional process that takes place in all dimensions of church life, i.e., worship, formal teaching, and praxis. In order for Christian education to be effective and contribute to the wholeness and upbuilding of the sobornal[43] life of the church, these contexts or dimensions must be integrally related. Whatever form or plan, whatever kind of curriculum we design must take into consideration how education takes place through the fullness of our life in community. As a worshiping community, the signs of our growth and development as a Christian fellowship, our openness and service toward others, and our witness and awareness of problems or issues that go beyond our immediate needs, all reflect the character of the educational activity that is conducted formally and informally in the church's life.

A preliminary model (see Figure 1) provides a conceptual framework for planning and implementing Christian education in the church. The contexts of (a) worship, (b) teaching, and (c) praxis are three areas of influence that the church has traditionally understood as necessary for holistic education and/or nurture.[44] Analogous terms for these contexts might be (a) church, (b) school, and (c) home and community life—referring, respectively, to the actual locations where worship, teaching, and praxis generally occur. The three interlocking circles in the model represent the three contexts; they intersect with each other to signify a relationship between worship and formal teaching, between formal teaching and praxis, and between praxis and worship. The primary focus, content and method[45] of each context is illustrated further in Figure 2. The integration of the activity in all three contexts takes place within the life of persons. The following paragraphs will describe the elements operative in each context.

---

43. Referring to the Russian word *"sobornost"* which conveys an understanding of catholicity, wholeness, and fullness, especially in regard to the church's corporate nature.

44. In addition to Schmemann's *Liturgy and Life*, see also Sophie Koulomzin, *Our Church and Our Children* (Crestwood, N.Y.: St. Vladimir's Seminary Press, 1975); and James D. Smart, *The Teaching Ministry of the Church* (Philadelphia: Westminster, 1954), 108-130.

45. Note: Much of the content which follows in the paragraphs describing the contexts of worship, teaching, and praxis is an elaboration of material taken from the dissertation noted above (note 38), and from the article "Taste and See," by Constance J. Tarasar, in *Does the Church Really Want Religious Education?* ed. Marlene Mayr (Birmingham, Ala.: Religious Education Press, 1988), 74-76.

Figure 1

A Basic Model for Orthodox Christian Religious Education

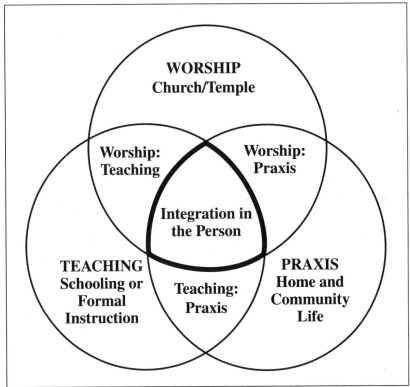

Worship

Worship (church) refers primarily to liturgical celebration in the church building, but it includes any context in which worship is the primary means of communicating the faith, e.g., a chapel or retreat setting. Worship in the church temple introduces persons to the reality of *God's kingdom and his presence among us*. In the dimension of worship, we are confronted with a *vision* and a *manifestation—a revelation* of who God is, what he has done for us, and how we are expected to respond to his love. The content of worship is the "*What*" or our Christian experience. It is here that we *encounter* God, immediately and directly, *and experience the reality* of his kingdom. In the feasts we experience, mystically and intuitively, the events and acts of salvation through which Christ has redeemed us. They are "re-presented" or *made present* to us as we enter into the words of the Scripture and the church's hymnography, e.g., "*Today* is the beginning of our salvation, the revelation of the eternal mystery! The Son of God becomes the Son of the Virgin as

Figure 2 – Contexts for the Orthodox Christian Religious Education Curriculum

The religious education program must be viewed from several perspectives or areas of influence in which religious instruction, nurture, and development occurs. To ensure a holistic and integrated approach to religious education, each of these areas needs to be considered in curriculum planning. Elements for consideration include:

	WORSHIP	TEACHING	PRAXIS
FOCUS:	The "What" Reality of the Event (World view)	The "Why" Meaning of the Event (World view)	The "How" Integration of the Event (Lifestyle)
CONTENT:	Liturgy Revelation Vision, Manifestation of God	Doctrine Explanation Exposition of the Faith	Ethics Application Realization of the Faith
CONTEXT:	Church (The Temple)	School (Formal Instruction)	Home/Community Life, Parish Fellowship

Figure 2-B Factors Guiding Implementation of the Curriculum

FORMS AND LANGUAGE:	Mystical, spiritual, intuitive, affective; Use of nondiscursive forms: symbol, imagery, poetry, and hymnography	Rational, cognitive, Conceptual, analytical	Relational, social, practical, functional
PROCESS OR METHOD:	Observation, immersion, participation, integration, reception, commemoration	Study, investigation, analysis, synthesis, reflection, discussion, etc.	Observation & application; action, rehearsal, modeling; diakonia/outreach in witness & service; spiritual life & counsel
PERSONNEL:	Worshiping community: Celebrants, acolytes, Choir, Readers, etc.	Teachers, students, peer groups, youth & adult leaders, special staff: icon painters, musicians, and others	Elder: Disciple relationships, parent:child, confessor:penitent coach: athlete; camp leaders, family, peers, community, etc.
RESOURCES:	Sources of Tradition: Scripture, patristics, liturgy, liturgical music and hymnography, iconography, saints, etc.; Community resources: ecumenical, social, etc.		

Gabriel announces[46] the coming of grace . . ." (*Troparion of Annunciation*).

The Word of God is proclaimed liturgically in many forms: in poetry, iconography, movement, color, etc. The language is nondiscursive: the imagery in iconography and hymnography, enhanced by music, rhythm and chant, darkness and light, incense, processions, and other liturgical actions, immerses persons into a new reality that is mystical and symbolic.[47] Meaning is perceived intuitively and holistically through this immersion and a new vision is grasped. Language, generally, and the sermon, in particular, is not so much rational discourse as it is a *kerygma*, a heralding or proclaiming of God's message to us. The priest takes the written word of Scripture and

---

46. Note the present tenses of the words: "Today," "becomes," "announces"; and as was quoted earlier: "*Today* Hell cries out groaning: . . ."

47. See Schmemann's comments on the Orthodox understanding of "symbol" as participation in a reality (rather than a "substitute" for something else), in *The Eucharist: Sacrament of the Kingdom* (Crestwood, N.Y.: St. Vladimir's Seminary Press, 1988), 37-40; 111; and in *For the Life of the World*, 135-151.

transforms it into a living word for us—for this moment in time and space—and exhorts us to transform ourselves by the operation of that Word and Spirit of God in our daily lives. This vision and this word provoke in us a response in faith, through our prayers and acts of thanksgiving, praise, repentance, confession, or sacrifice.

Although religious education is not the primary goal of worship, it is woven into every strand of the living fabric of the liturgical act: through sets of sung verses (*stikhira, aposticha*, the *odes* of the *kanon*), Old Testament readings (*parameya*), and the manner in which each liturgical cycle is constructed and celebrated through the integration of its reading, hymn, and actions. The "curriculum" or educational plan implied here is an intention to *communicate* as well as to *integrate* the worshiper into the life of the eucharistic community, the life in God's kingdom.

The way we educate people in worship and for worship has its own methodology. The learner acquires knowledge, behaviors, and attitudes through observing, participating, celebrating, receiving the sacaments, commemorating and remembering others. It is an active mode of learning, but it is effective only inasmuch as the worship communicates well what is intended to be sung, heard, and shared, and to the degree that the person is truly engaged in the worship. If our worship is not communicating God's revelation to us, then we need to see what must be done so that it can. Instrumental content and learning may be needed to prepare readers and singers with the proper skills and attitudes to carry out their functions in worship, to help choir directors in the choice and performance of appropriate music so that the words take precedence, to train parish council members to understand what is happening in the services and how their behavior can help or hinder, and to assist pastors in preparing worship so that it is able to communicate most effectively.

Teaching

Teaching (schooling) signifies a classroom situation in which formal instruction takes place, but refers also to less structured environments in which instruction is the primary activity, e.g., open classroom, camp class, a living room discussion with youth or adults. The *meaning* of the experience, its *rational* content, is the focus and content of formal teaching in the school.

In the teaching dimension, *explanation* is the vehicle for conveying an understanding of God's acts as expressed in scripture, liturgy, doctrine, and other sources of the content of the faith. The exposition of doctrine also provides opportunity for conscious *reflection* upon the revelation of God, and thus helps to shape our understanding of the "*Why*" of our Christian experience and make sense of our place in God's world.

In the formal teaching situation, study methods involving rational thinking, research, analysis, synthesis, and guided reflection on scripture and tradition, enable us to draw forth the concepts and principles that constitute the basis of our belief system. The classroom or discussion group is also the place where we can reflect together (in the light of what we believe) on our life as a community—both in worship and in our common action that we experience in liturgy, as well as those we experience in our families and neighborhoods. Here we can discuss the relationship between words and actions, examine alternatives for our behavior, and set goals based upon our knowledge and experience. Formal teaching is a necessary part of our church life; but it can neither be replaced by, nor should it be allowed to become a substitute for, the other dimensions of worship and praxis. Together, worship and teaching contribute to the development of a Christian *worldview*, which is assimilated or actualized through praxis in a Christian *lifestyle*.

Praxis

Praxis (home or community) refers to the family or parish fellowship but also any context in which people learn through their relationship with one another as they struggle to practice their faith. Through praxis in the home and parish fellowship, Christian experience is integrated into a person's life.

It is through the dimension of inspired and informed Christian practice that our worship and teaching are translated into action. Here we focus on *integrating* and *applying* the vision and understanding of God's revelation in our lives. If worship is the "What" and teaching the "Why" of our life as Christians, the dimension of Christian praxis is the "*How*"—the realization, assimilation, and application of the faith and belief of the community as lived-out daily through the practice of Christian ethics. Education in this dimension is personal, relational, and social. It involves the practice of skills, the acquisition of values, and the working out of attitudes that help or hinder our spiritual development as we strive for *theosis*, the process of deification that Alexander Schmemann describes simply as "the life of grace, communion with God, love, unity, and spiritual progress towards eternal salvation."

Within the fellowship of the family and faith community, we learn to transform words into deeds. We learn by imitation, rehearsal, and modeling. We learn by working side-by-side with others who are themselves trying to work out their own salvation, often becoming apprentices and disciples in the process. We learn how to serve or minister, how to care for God's creation, how to act rightly and justly, how to be patient and keep silence, how to listen, and how to speak. As we struggle to care for our own souls and to do God's will, others may learn from our effort. We may become teachers and leaders for children, relatives, friends, neighbors, and strangers. In this respect, each of us, as a member of the church, is an educator. Whether our teaching is "sound" or not depends upon the words we speak, the attitudes we assume, and the deeds we practice.

We can also learn how to transform our lives through the counsel and direction of a *staretz* (a spiritual elder) or father confessor, through reading and meditation upon the lives of saints, and through the effort of personal prayer. Monastic communities for men and women can provide both a source of inspiration as well as a model for learning and living in community.[48]

Even though praxis education is conducted more informally, it would be misleading to treat education through praxis as something that is generally unintentional or unplanned, dependent only on how persons "happen" to behave, who they are with at any given time, or what they observe at a particular moment. Education through praxis is also intentional, even if it is not planned in the same way as a classroom lesson. Parents, for example, do have aims, desires, and goals for how they want their children to grow as Christians. In nondirect but thoughtful ways parents can inculcate values and develop appreciations of people or things their children see. Responsible parents do try to guide their children intentionally to useful activities and the appreciation or moral and cultural values or direct them away from persons or things that can be harmful to them.

Certain cautions should be noted, however. We should not approach intentional planning for praxis education by scheduling "lessons" or programmatic forms of instruction. "Schooling" methods imposed in the home, camp, or informal fellowship settings generally are not very successful. However, pastors and other active Christians can help persons to become aware of their needs to assume responsibilities, to engage in their own spiritual struggles, to acquire skills necessary for witness and ministry, to foster bonds of friendship and fellowship, and to participate in acts of mercy and justice toward others. Experiences can be planned less formally (dependent more on "opportunity" scheduling than specific dates or programs) to help persons fulfill intended long-term educational goals.[49]

To restore the religious education aspect of Christian praxis, we need to teach, lead, or guide persons to an understanding and experience of family, church, community, true friendship and fellowship so that these forms of relationship or relational units can develop and assume, once again, their educational role in the church. In modern societies which exalt individualism over faithful interpersonal relationships, and where families and community units suffer continual breakdown or simply do not exist any-

---

48. See Mother Euphrasia, *"Life in All Its Fullness,"* Plenary Presentation, 6th Assembly of the World Council of Churches, Vancouver, British Columbia, July 1983.

49. Cf. Elliot W. Eisner, *The Educational Imagination*, 2nd ed. (New York: Macmillan, 1985) and John Westerhoff, "Formation, Education, Instruction," *Religious Education* 82:4 (1987), 578-591. The work of Eisner allows more flexibility to religious educators in formulating curriculum, which he defines as a "series of planned events that are intended to have educational consequences" (p.45). In the process of engaging students in activities or events, he holds that some of these benefits (outcomes) might be delineated or specified in advance in operational terms, but others—which may be general, broad, or diffuse—can only be recognized subsequent to the activity.

more, the communal life of the church can provide a healing and supportive role in the nurturing of "persons-in-relation" among the members of the church community and in the society at large.

Traditionally, the church has expressed its fundamental teachings and celebrated its common life when it has gathered together in worship. In the recent past, and in many societies today, it is often the case that the church *only* gathers for worship—and sometimes that is minimal. Fellowship and occasions for formal and informal teaching and learning have diminished as well, especially in communities where the congregation is scattered throughout a large city and its suburbs, or where there are few or no churches in the area. We need today to recover both the vision of life offered by church, and also ways of living as Christians in our own particular context. Communities of Christians must be built up and must reach out beyond themselves to build up the life of their cities, villages, and the nation as a whole. We need to educate persons within the total life of the Christian community: to learn by celebrating together, studying together and living and acting together in witness and service. All three contexts: worship, teaching, and praxis are needed for religious education in today's society. "Taste and see how good is the Lord" say the communion verse during Great Lent: i.e., *experience* and *understand*, then *act*! This is the way the Christian community shapes its life, educates each generation, and passes on its faith and traditions.

A Synthetic/Synoptic Approach to Content

Certain types or categories of theological content—e.g., biblical, historical, liturgical, doctrinal, spiritual—have traditionally formed the basis for religious education. Each contributes a particular view to the lived experience of the faith through the centuries. Together they become threads woven into one story—the story of the *church's life*, the story of *our life* as a community, the story of *my life* in God. What is important is that they not be presented in isolation from each other, for it is in the synthesis of these "subjects" that we discover the integrity of the community of faith. If presented as the "lived" experience of the church this content can be presented in its fullness and wholeness as the very essence and foundation of *life*, rather that as pieces and catalogs of information. A few examples for focus in each area can guide curriculum developers and teachers:

1. *Biblical Content.*

The content of the Old Testaments of Holy Scripture (including the so-called Apocrypha or Deutero-canonical books) is the record of a faith community—*our* faith community, the church. The story of salvation is our story, our history, our culture. I am very much a part of that history, and from the time of my baptism into Christ that story has now become *my* story. As Michael Oleksa explains, the key to the telling of sacred stories is: *"to pro-*

duce the kind of behavior that the culture considers really 'human.' "[50]

The story is remembered and celebrated in the community. It also becomes the basis for the way in which everything is said and done in the community—it becomes a frame of reference for life in common with others. From a biblical perspective, the story is used and interpreted by the community in which it emerged. Its interpretation may sometimes be altered or transformed by significant events, such as the incarnation of Christ when God himself entered history. In the context of the Christian community, it is the New Testament story that helps illumine the Old Testament story; but by looking backward, we also can see "types" of persons and happenings that help us to understand more clearly the New Testament events that brought about our salvation in Christ and the Spirit. Many people today are interested in discovering their historical and genetical "roots"; part of the task of the religious educator is to help them discover their spiritual roots through the stories of God's people.

2. *Historical and Doctrinal Content.*

Sacred stories do not end with the Holy Scriptures, but continue to grow through the stories of the church's life in history. The stories of struggles in the church, of martyrs and confessors of the faith, of heresies and councils that met to reaffirm and clarify issues of faith are also part of the history of salvation that continues up to our day and beyond. The faith that we confess today is the faith that others fought for and considered worthy of defending—even with their lives. My identity is shaped and continually strengthened by what I continue to believe and witness as a member of the church. Church history and doctrine take on meaning as they are presented and interpreted in the light of current struggles and witness in today's society.

3. *Spiritual Content.*

The lives of saints and the remembrance of our spiritual ancestors in the faith provide models and inspiration for the struggles we face in the spiritual life. Their lives and writings, their spiritual counsel help me reflect upon my own life. They help me know I am not alone in my sins and in my struggles to live in this world while striving for the kingdom. The images of these holy men and women in the icons stand together with me as I pray. They reveal the light of God in their lives and the peace and joy that comes with

---

50. See Michael Oleksa, "The Confluence of Church and Culture," in *Perspectives on Orthodox Education: Report of the International Orthodox Education Consultation for Rural/Developing Areas*, ed. Constance J. Tarasar (Syosset, N.Y.: SYNDESMOS and DRE-Orthodox Church in America, 1983), 12. Oleksa looks at the role of stories, ceremonies, the ritualist, and the *shaman* or spiritual leader in premodern societies to draw implications for religious education today.

placing one's trust in the Lord. Their personal stories manifest the many ways in which it is possible to overcome our fallen nature and the sins of this world so that I may attain the glory of the world to come.

With the help of experienced and spiritually wise people, I receive direction and guidance as I try to follow this way of repentance and forgiveness, love and truth, peace and joy. These guides—father confessors, experienced monks and nuns, and others known for their Christian life—help raise me up when I fall and cheer me when I am despondent and have lost hope. Visits to spiritual centers, retreats for youth or adults, recommended spiritual literature, and contacts with persons who are active Christian witnesses should be an essential part of any program in religious education.

Finally, our Christian life in the world must be seen as a sacramental vocation, inasmuch as the church understands all of life in God as "communion" and "blessing." The spiritual life involves service (*diakonia*) and witness (*martyria*) whenever and wherever God calls us: in our families, neighborhoods, cities, etc. Ethical and moral issues must be understood in the light of God's will for creation, for human life and personal relationship, and for the transformation and salvation of the world. Active engagement is necessary for working out understandings and attitudes that enable us to determine directions for our life and work in the world.

4. *Liturgical Content.*

To avoid repeating most of what was described and explained in the first half of this chapter, it is sufficient to say that all other content areas find their completion and expression in the integral content of worship. It is in worship that we remember and celebrate our story as God's people. As Nicholas Lossky says: "It is in the church's liturgy where all the fields of study meet, blend together, unite in one organic whole—entirely oriented toward salvation, the salvation of man, the world, the universe (cosmos). . . . If our studies do not all unite in our active participation in the liturgical life of the church, they are nothing but sterile speculation."[51] The most adequate Orthodox answer to the question "Who are the Orthodox and what do they believe?" is found in the words: "Come and see!" Only by immersing oneself in the fullness and integrity of the liturgical tradition can we truly come to know the faith. However, helping persons to become familiar, in the classroom, with the meaning of liturgical actions and texts is helpful, as is reinforcement through Christian praxis in the home. In both of these contexts, Lent and Pascha, the fasts and feasts, can be presented and understood as a series of movements of preparation and fulfillment, making life a continuous celebration of faith and communion.

---

51. Nicholas Lossky, Commencement Address, delivered at St. Vladimir's Orthodox Theological Seminary, May 1987.

Relational Goals for Personal Faith and Life

Liturgy, by its very nature, is relational. The content of liturgy—every prayer and hymn—expresses the interrelationships between God, persons, world, and church. These four concepts or categories represent, respectively, the disciplines of theology (the nature of God), anthropology (the nature of human persons), cosmology (the nature of the world), and ecclesiology (the nature of the church), as understood in a Christian perspective. When these concepts are expressed liturgically, through the prayer of the church, they are expressed in *personal* terms and relationships. For example, texts from the Service of Baptism say:

> In thy Name, O Lord of truth, and in the Name of thine Only-begotten Son and of thy Holy Spirit, I lay my hand upon thy servant (*name*), who has been found worthy to flee unto thy holy Name, and to take refuge under the shelter of thy wings. . . .

> Make her to rejoice in the works of her hands, and in all her generation; that she may render praises unto thee, may sing, worship and glorify thy great and exalted Name always, all the days of her life. . . .

> Do thou, the same Lord, delivering also this thy creation from the bondage of the enemy, receive her into thy heavenly kingdom. . . . Assign to her an Angel of light who shall deliver her from every snare of the adversary, from encounter with evil, from the demon of the noonday, and from evil thoughts. . . .

> And make her a reason-endowed sheep in the holy flock of thy Christ, and honorable member of thy Chuch, a consecrated vessel, a child of the light and an heir of thy kingdom, that having lived in accordance with thy commandments, and preserved inviolate the seal, and kept her garment undefiled, she may receive the blessedness of the Saints in thy kingdom.[52]

In every prayer, there is a relationship stated or implied: of a person with God, with oneself or other persons, with the created world (in the example above, with evil, or an angel), or with the church. Consequently, liturgical catechesis requires goals that are formulated toward personal outcomes. An example of a goal (with some suggestions for implementation in a class of teens) from the texts of the Service of Baptism might be:

Attitude Goal

To recognize and accept corporate worship as the church's response to God, the common responsibility of his people to offer thanksgiving and intercession for the whole world.

---

52. *Baptism* (Syosset, N.Y.: DRE-Orthodox Church in America, 1983), 32-33, 38-39.

Suggested contexts, methods, and modes of implementation:

Worship:
   Participate in regular services of worship: the Eucharist, Vespers, Matins.
   Participate regularly in reception of the sacrament of Holy Communion.
   Offer prayers of intercession for those you know who have special needs:
      the sick, the suffering, those who have recently departed this life.
   Offer prayers of thanksgiving and remembrance for members of your fam-
      ily and parish community.

Teaching (Schooling):
   Using a concordance, examine passages in Acts and the Epistles concern-
      ing thanksgiving, intercession, common worship, and fellowship.
   Examine the texts of the liturgy and find examples of the frequency and con-
      tent of prayers of thanksgiving, remembrance, and intercession.
   Look for examples of intercession in iconography.
   Discuss the liturgical and practical implications of the phrase: "To love is
      to remember."

Praxis:
   Create an awareness at home of the family as a little church; remember
      together at mealtime or at the end of the day those who need our prayers
      and concern.
   While watching the news on TV or reading the newspaper, make a mental
      note of the persons and events in the world that need our concern, witness,
      prayers, and service. Share your feelings and reflections about these
      with other members of your family and parish community.
   Do something concrete for another person to let them know that you
      remember them in their need or that you appreciate their work or friend-
      ship.

During such a study unit on thanksgiving and intercession, there are ample
opportunities for students to interact with each other, with the priest and
members of the parish, the choir director, and family members. They might
also engage in a project of outreach and service to others, in order to become
more aware and sensitive to those who need both our diakonia and our
prayers.

Developmental and Spiritual Awareness for Fostering Transformative Growth
   The personal character of education also requires that different approaches are needed for different developmental levels, for both children and adults.
An inclusive or synthetic understanding of the different aspects of growth—
cognitive, physical, psycho-social, etc.—is necessary as we frame and imple-

ment goals for each educational context.[53] The following example suggests how one broad educational goal can be applied more specifically to four developmental levels, and with different types of goals (knowledge, attitudes, behaviors):

Broad Goal: *To know that baptism enrolls us and makes us members of the church, Christ's Body.*

Level 1 (3-6/7 yrs.)

To know that in baptism, we belong to Christ as member of his family.

To develop an awareness of family membership and responsibilities.

To name members of our church family, their roles in this family, and the name of the church where our church family gathers.

Level 2 (7-16/17 yrs.)

To know the stories that form the basis of our faith and the history of our church.

To develop a spirit (willingness) to cooperate with others in the family, church and neighborhood.

To know the essential gifts, privileges and responsibilities of church members.

Level 3 (17-35+ yrs.)

To know the church as a *living body*—the Body of Christ—and the implications of membership in a body.

To assume responsibility for one's own personal development or growth in the faith (spriritual life, education, and skills or behaviors needed to fulfill particular functions in the church).

To relate one's membership in the church to personal choice and involvement in issues of concern to society.

Level 4 (Mid-Life and Beyond)

To know the church as a spiritual and historical reality (i.e., as a "spiritual temple; a chosen race, a royal priesthood, a holy nation, God's own people"—cf. Ephesians, I Corinthians, I Peter, and Hebrews).

To take initiative, on a regular basis, for leadership in church life and witness.

To care, in a loving, selfless manner, for members of the church as well as others in society who need help in fulfilling basic needs.

---

53. Although I used James Fowler's stages in my dissertation, I find it helpful to consult the work of a variety of developmentalists to compare particular stages. Teachers need also to rely on their own personal experience with childern of a given age, or with adults who may be influenced by a particular context (e.g., parish) in which they live.

What must not be forgotten are spiritual goals, the developmental patterns inherent in them, and how they are related to other development patterns, This is an area that is not well-developed; information and experiential examples can be found, however, in patristic and ascetical literature that may be useful for reflection on spiritual growth and spiritual stages.[54]

Communicating the Vision

In this chapter I have tried to share a vision of life that is the basis of the Orthodox vision of God, human persons, the created world, and the church. In its essence, it is a vision and experience of Communion in God. It is a relationship of love and joy in the Spirit of God with God's Son Jesus Christ. It is an anticipation and preparation of God's kingdom which, in a small way, we already "taste and see." Perhaps the primary implication for educators in the church is to understand that the transmission or communication of this vision does not take place primarily in the classroom. It is within the total life of the church family, the *synaxis* or gathering of God's people, particularly in worship, where this new life is experienced, shared, and celebrated. In my life, it is a joyous participation, and often a painful co-suffering, in a community that truly transcends space and time. Above all, it is grounded in personal relationships, in a communion that is so deep that separations from close friends thousands of mile away, and those who have already departed this life, are only temporary physical "inconveniences," for the love that binds us together in Christ keeps them as close as my thoughts and prayers. To communicate this experience, this message, this vision and joy of life in and with God, and all others in his kingdom, is the task to which we are called. What we cannot program as part of our "curriculum," we can carry in ourselves: for "we impart this in words not taught by human wisdom but taught by the Spirit, interpreting spiritual truths to those who possess the Spirit" (1 Cor. 2:13).

---

54. If *theosis* is a process of spiritual growth, then this process cannot be divorced completely from other forms of growth, especially as they concern the development of attitudes and behaviors, as well as understandings of what is desirable in terms of the aims of Christian life.

PART TWO

PHILOSOPHICAL THEOLOGY

"Above all things, we must beware of what I call 'inert ideas'—that is to say, ideas that are merely received into the mind without being utilized, or tested, or thrown into fresh combinations" (Whitehead).

CHAPTER FIVE

Process Theology and Religious Education

HELEN GOGGIN

Part One

"Limit not thy children to thine own ideas.
They are born in a different time."[1]

A Brief History of Process Thought

Is this time in history a different time, a time unlike any other? Yes it is. When the ancient power to kill has now become the power to prevent birth through a nuclear holocaust—we live in a different time. When the negative social effects of traditional coercive power/patriarchal images of God are recognized through consciousness raising activities such as the ecological and feminist movements—we live in a different time. When, through evolutionary and quantum theory, we come to understand the interconnectedness and interdependence of all of life, not as a philosophic concept, but as the essence of reality—we live in a different time. When the essence of "matter" is no longer understood as substantial, objective, static, observable or fully describable with our conceptual tools; when "time" is no longer measured in days and years but in motion and light; when "space" is no longer seen as what is between objects but as the interval through which flow the events that constitute reality; when the sub-atomic world no longer reveals mechanistic

---

1. A quote from the *Talmud* from Sophia Lyon Fahs, *Today's Children and Yesterday's Heritage* (Boston: Beacon Press, 1952), 87.

123

causality but a "conscious" freedom described in terms of "orders" with characteristics such as uncertainly, randomness, and nonlocal connections—we *are* living in a different time.

What does this mean for how God is imaged and how religious education is conducted in the church? Does this different time call for a novel response, a reconceptualization of long-held and deeply valued views of God and God's relation to the world? Scientists, philosophers, theologians, feminists, *and* many of the laity in our religious communities are saying a strong and urgent "YES" to such questions.

Over thirty years ago, Thomas Kuhn made us aware of the importance of *paradigm* changes in the advance of science in the twentieth century. Anomalies in the field of quantum theory did not fit with the accepted Newtonian view of reality, making only adjustment of present theories insufficient. The world which the particle physicists were seeing was indeed a different world. Even a scientist of Einstein's brilliance could say, "It was as if the ground had been pulled out from under one, with no firm foundation to be seen anywhere upon which one could have built."[2] According to Kuhn, such paradigm changes, far from being cumulative, are rather "a reconstruction of the field from new fundamentals," the seeing of what is there rather than what is known.[3]

Whether in science, philosophy or religion, long-held positions and beliefs which contain the truths by which people live are not easily changed. Currently the term *postmodern* is being used in theology, philosophy, science, and other disciplines to describe the new paradigms of the time in which we live. Such a term could make one think that this is a new, even "trendy" type of thinking, but it has a long history beginning in the *panentheism* of Plato's view of God as the Soul of the world and of the world as God's body. Plato taught that every creature was free and that God did not fully determine their actions. *Panentheism* understands God as involved *in* but not identified *with* the cosmos, unlike *pantheism* which identifies God with the cosmos or *theism* which sees God as totally independent of the cosmos.

For nearly 2000 years the panentheistic view of God was basically ignored or misunderstood. About 1600 a "heretical" view called Socinianism named for its founder, Socinus, proposed that God does not determine our decisions eternally and that "by making free decisions we give divine knowledge new content and thus change God."[4] But this alternative to the classical theistic doctrine was mainly ignored by historians and scholars until recently. However, in the seventeenth and eighteenth centuries, philosophers like Schelling, Krause (the first to use the term panentheism), and Fechner, who

---

2. Thomas Kuhn, *The Structure of Scientific Revolutions*, 2nd ed. (Chicago: University of Chicago Press, 1970.), 83.

3. Ibid., 85

4. Mircea Eliade, ed., *The Encyclopedia of Religion* (New York: Macmillan, 1987),168. The historical information is from this reference work.

was also a physicist, spoke about a God who does not determine what happens in history, who is *in* but not identified with reality. In the late nineteenth century and early twentieth centuries the panentheistic view of God was developed further by Bernardino Varisco, in Italy, and Charles Peirce and Alfred North Whitehead in the United States. These scholars built on this thin thread of organic thinking about God that was at odds with the accepted classical view of God's omnipotence, omniscience, and immutability.

Currently a panentheistic view of God has found an ally in a former protagonist. In the Gifford Lectures of 1989-1991, Ian Barbour surveyed the uneasy relations between religion and science and showed how the new *paradigms* referred to by Thomas Kuhn have led to a renewed interest in a fruitful relationship in this historic conflict. Barbour speaks of the new relationship of science and religion as being grounded in the process metaphysics of Alfred North Whitehead and the theology that has come out of Whitehead's thought in the writings of Charles Hartshorne, Daniel Day Williams, John Cobb Jr., David Ray Griffin, and Marjorie Suchocki, to name some of the more widely known theologians.[5] In the twentieth century, the first person to use the term *process theology* was Bernard Loomer, of the University of Chicago, writing about "the task of reconceiving the theological structure of the Christian faith."[6] In an essay written in 1964, John Cobb was the first to use the term *postmodern* for the theology based on the organic philosophy of Alfred North Whitehead.[7] Whitehead's central place in process or postmodern thought, as well as in mathematics and science, suggests that a brief introduction to his thinking should be the starting place in understanding the theology which takes its basic assumptions from his work.

Process Theology: The Philosophic Background

Whitehead's organic philosophy sees reality as *becoming* rather than being; dynamic rather than static. Reality is *event* not substance as it was understood in Newtonian physics. Even the smallest *actual entity* (the protons, neutrons, and quarks of quantum physics, or as Whitehead calls them "drops of experience" or *actual occasions*) is influenced by the past *(prehension)* and chooses *(concrescence)* in the infinitesimal present moment what it will actualize *(satisfaction)* in the future. Through this simultaneous process any actual occasion or society of occasions—the term Whitehead used for the macrocosmic level of reality—is constantly becoming and perishing. The speed at which such *"events"* take place means that, on the microcosmic level, reality has the character of fluidity rather than substance. Paradoxically on the macrocosmic level that same speed allows us to expe-

5. Ian Barbour, *Religion in an Age of Science* (San Francisco: Harper & Row,1990).

6. Norman Pittenger, "Process Theology and Christian Education," *Religious Education* 68:3 (1973), 308.

7. David Ray Griffin, William A. Beardslee, and Joe Holland, *Varieties of Postmodern Theology* (Albany: State University of New York Press, 1989), 7.

rience reality as having duration and apparent substance.[8]

How does one experience such obscure abstract statements in everyday life? Take for example the measurement of time. In any given moment of experience past, present, and future are involved. Time cannot be frozen in the present, for the present is the immediate past moving into the "not yet" of the future before we can say "it is now"! Though our lives are measured in the ordered sequence of yesterday, today, and tomorrow, experience involves flow, movement, and becoming as well as here, now, and being. Endurance, order, and the substance of self, others, and objects are experienced through perception, reason, and memory, and the aforementioned properties of the underlying quantum order. Change, novelty, and creativity flow from the freedom which is the essence of all levels of the natural order. All of these properties are a part of our experience; they are not just philosophic abstractions.

This is what Whitehead is attempting to say when he uses words like *prehension, concrescence,* and *satisfaction,* to break open traditional patterns of thinking. However, his main purpose is not to play word games but to make it clear that reality is "event" rather than composed of "basic building blocks." Freedom, novelty, and creativity are not human ideals, rather they are the essence of physical reality experienced by every aware subject—actual occasions (the subatomic world) or societies of occasions (rocks, trees, and you and I). There are no "nonexperiencing" objects. There are only experiencing subjects who *prehend* other knowing subjects as organically or internally related to them. Just as there is no actualized present and future in a process reality, so there is no "otherness"; there is only interrelatedness. However, it is important to note that "an electron in a lump of lead is not the same as an electron in a cell in a human brain."[9] The characteristics of different orders of reality are the product not only of their constituent parts but also of the relations between them. Though embodiedness gives a sense of unique individualism, persons are constituted by relatedness. All reality is social and all creation seeks unity in the complexity of experience.

Process philosophy and science have helped us to know and image a dynamic world of internally related events. Knowledge of the food chain and the growing awareness of ecological damage in our time enable us to image the strange events of the subatomic order in relation to the world which we experience. Through imagination we can feel (or *prehend*) the intimate rela-

---

8. Microcosm refers to the subatomic level of reality revealed by quantum physicists through high-powered instruments like partical accelerators. Macrocosm refers to the things and people which we experience bodily. *Contraries* such as endurance and change, novelty and stability, order and creativity apply to both levels. Whitehead saw these *contraries* as poles of a single reality rather than as contradictions. See Donald W. Oliver, "Introduction and Overview," *Process Studies* 17:4 (Winter 1988), 212.

9. Charles Birch, *A Purpose for Everything* (Mystic, Conn.: Twenty-Third Publications, 1990), 44.

tionship of all of creation which is not directly observable in daily life.

The proposition that reality is organic and fluid is, for Whitehead, more important (or interesting) than the possibility that it may be true. This vision of reality brings *satisfaction*, not as the prehension of an Absolute (an elusive goal), but as the lure toward further novelty or new ways of being. Human *satisfaction* comes at the moment of finding a more adequate representation of reality which can in turn creatively generate further understanding of self, the cosmos, *and* of God. For Whitehead, God is the source of this change, novelty, and creativity and the possibility of freedom and openness to the future.

This introduction touches upon the mere edges of Whitehead's profound vision of the many seeking the One in his great work *Process and Reality* and provides a guide to Whitehead's influence in this philosophical theology.

Basic Assumptions of Process Theology

Reality is a process of becoming and perishing, a creative movement out of which may come novelty in any given moment of time. The influence of the past continues in the present but does not restrict or control choices made by creation. Reality does not operate like a machine, as in Newtonian physics, for freedom is of its essence. Therefore neither divine decree, nor past events, determine the future within the microcosmic or the macrocosmic orders. Decisions do have consequences yet the future is always open—we are not at the mercy of determinism, fate, or chance in the form of some disembodied power.[10] Reality is social, that is, it is internally related, rather than composed of fundamental building blocks as science had earlier assumed. The central motivational factor in the cosmos is God—as persuasive love not coercive power.[11] Process theology thus adopts a *panentheistic* view of God's relation to the cosmos and proposes the concept of freedom as fundamental in understanding God's relation to the world.

God

In his book *A Purpose for Everything*, Charles Birch, the Australian biologist, raises what is the central question about God today: What do

---

10. Order is used here in the sense in which the physicist, David Bohm, would use it. He offers a theory of generative and implicate orders pervading the whole of reality interrelated in ways in which hierarchies of order no longer exist. Such orders are enfolded into one another something like a holograph. We tend to operate only on explicate orders that can be observed, rather than implicate orders that require new ways of seeing. He uses art as an example of how we are able to see new visions of reality. David Bohm and David Peat, *Science, Order and Creativity* (New York: Bantam Books, 1987), Chapter 4.

11. For a thorough discussion of the philosophic questions raised by seeing God as persuasive rather than coercive power see David Ray Griffin's *Evil Revisited* (Albany: State University of New York Press, 1991). Griffin writes with a concern that theology use "public criteria" in its arguments and not fall back on traditional circular arguments claiming revelation and no longer recognizing the human constructions that formed the tradition.

we mean when we speak of the supernatural or divinity? "The old notion of a divine being controlling the universe from outside is no longer credible. The relevant question now is, in what sense if any, is there divine activity in the universe?" The critical question is not, "Is God dead?" but rather, "Which God is dead?"[12] There are concepts of God that should die and Birch mentions several of the obvious ones—the God who can do everything, that is, who could have prevented the Holocaust and did not; the God who miraculously intervenes but rarely, if ever, does so; the God of the gaps who explains what we cannot explain; the cosmic bellhop at the end of a cosmic telephone answering all our requests; the God who requires praise and demands sacrifice; the God who is on *our* side in war and justifies the killing of one another; the God of judgment who rules by fear and punishment.

In contrast process theology, quoting Whitehead, speaks of a God who is "the poet of the world, with tender patience leading it by his vision of truth, beauty, and goodness."[13] God is described as *dipolar*, a phrase that has led to the criticism that the God of process theology is dualistic. However the two *poles* or *contraries* are a manifestation of the complementary activities of One Entity and are not in opposition to or in contradiction of one another. The mental or *primordial* pole is an image of God as the one Actual Entity who is not influenced by any other entity and who is therefore the ground of all reality, a creation that is the ongoing activity of God, not a completed action in the past. God's physical or *consequent* pole describes God as knowing not only propositionally, but as being internally affected by all that happens in the world. God laughs with us, cries with us, loves with us, feels pain when we do, enjoys satisfaction with us, and suffers the tragic results when we hurt one another and our planet.

This view of God is clarified by Sallie McFague's image of the world as God's body and God as the Soul of the world, an image, which as we saw in the historical survey that introduced this chapter, has its origins in the thought of Plato. Just as we experience our bodies, minds, and spirits as internally related, so God and creation are internally related.[14] Such an image of God is inherently incarnational, not only in Jesus of Nazareth, but also in God's continuing experience of the world. For example, just as a part of your body or mine cannot be in pain without our whole being feeling pain, so God feels creation's pain as we feel the pain in our body. All creation including God are internally related in the flow of reality. As the psalmist realized long ago there *is* nowhere that we can go where we are

12. Birch, *A Purpose for Everything*, 88.

13. Donald W. Sherburne, *A Key to Whitehead's Process and Reality* (Chicago: University of Chicago Press, 1981), 183.

14. Sallie McFague, *Models of God* (Philadelphia: Fortress, 1987), 69; see McFague, *The Body of God* (Minneapolis: Fortress, 1993).

beyond the presence of God (Psalm 139).

God contains within Godself all the possibilities which can be actualized in creation, but it is human beings and the entities of the natural order that determine which possibilities will be so actualized and which shall, at that moment, be lost. Thus, even God does not know the future which has not yet come. God knows all that is past but not what choices will be made in the present moment which in turn will affect future possibilities. This is because God relates to the world as the "loving persuasion of a tender companion"[15] not as coercive power. God is always seeking to lure us toward God's initial aims for harmony, satisfaction, and unity with Godself.

Because of the above insights, and of the critique of patriarchal religion coming from the feminist theologians, there has been a growing concern throughout the latter decades of this century about the images that describe God. Whitehead suggests that "the brief Galilean vision" of the life of Jesus of Nazareth does not

> emphasize the ruling Caesar, the ruthless moralist or the unmoved mover. It dwells upon the tender elements in the world, which slowly and in quietness operate in love. . . . Love neither rules nor is it unmoved; also it is a little oblivious to morals.[16]

If the process view is correct and God is persuasive love not coercive power then two important insights follow. First, images of God such as monarch, judge, and military conqueror need to be reconsidered. As ways of relating to one another in the world, these images encourage the valuing of power over others, including the use of violence. "Much of the tragedy in the course of human affairs can be attributed to the feeling that to control others and the course of events is to share in divinity."[17] Second, feminist thinkers have pointed out that these are masculine images and have encouraged men to see themselves as exemplifying *godly* characteristics in the exercise of power and control over women, over oppressed and marginal groups, and over the natural world. John Cobb has observed that such images of God have also meant that Jesus has not been "good news" for many people.[18]

Jesus of Nazareth

Whitehead's reference to Jesus' life as the brief Galilean vision of humil-

---

15. Randolph Crump Miller, "Theology in the Background," in *Religious Education and Theology*, ed. Norma H. Thompson (Birmingham, Ala.: Religious Education Press, 1982), 35.

16. Sherburne, *A Key to Whitehead's Process and Reality*, 178-179.

17. John B. Cobb Jr. and David Ray Griffin, *Process Theology: An Introductory Exposition* (Philadelphia: Westminster, 1976.), 53 (emphasis mine).

18. The reference here is to John B. Cobb's *Can Christ be Good News Again?* (St. Louis: Chalice Press, 1991).

ity emphasizes not power *over*, but empowerment *of* others, not coercive
force, but loving relationship, not authoritative control but the authority of
one who lived in unity with God's will. In spite of our desire to live in
such unity with God, we tend to experience God's *initial aim* for the best
possibilities in each moment as a tension between what is and what ideal-
ly could be; between the actions we have taken and those we wish we had
taken.

One of the most illuminating descriptions of Jesus' relation to God from
a process viewpoint is found in Cobb and Griffin's *Process Theology*:

> In Jesus' authentic sayings an existence expresses itself which *does not expe-
> rience this otherness* of the divine. Instead his selfhood seems to be constituted
> as much by the divine agency within him as by his own personal past. There
> is not the normal tension between the initial aims and the purposes received
> from the past, in that those past purposes were themselves conformed to divine
> aims and thereby involved in the basic disposition to be open to God's call in
> each future moment. Whereas Christ is incarnate in everyone, Jesus *is* Christ
> because the incarnation is constitutive of his very selfhood.[19]

This is not a traditional interpretation of Jesus as the Son of God, yet a better description of what it means to be a son or daughter of God could scarcely be found—that is, one who does not experience the "otherness" of God.
Such "otherness" is intrinsic to many other theological positions because
they are based on a substantive rather than a relational metaphysics. In a
metaphysics of mutuality, humanity is seen as being lured to incarnate the
Christ principle in the world through the possibilities God offers to us rather
than humanity's relation to God being seen in terms of "sin" and judgment.
We are persuaded to participate in the mutuality and openness of God's love
that was incarnated in the life of Jesus. Even though Christians live with the
Jesus story as a constitutive part of their experience, process thinkers argue
that it has been misinterpreted with respect to what Jesus taught about God.
The dualism of Greek philosophy triumphed over the humility and tenderness
of the Galilean vision.

Rosemary Radford Ruether's critique of the traditional interpretations of
Jesus illumines the above insights:

> Jesus declares that God has not just spoken in the past but is speaking now.
> . . . And Jesus does not think of himself as the "last word of God" but
> points beyond himself to 'One who will come.' Thus Jesus restores the
> sense of God's prophetic and redemptive activity taking place in the present-
> future through peoples' present experiences and the new possibilities dis-
> closed through those experiences. To encapsulate Jesus himself as God's last
> word and once for all disclosure of God, located in a remote past and insti-

---

19. Cobb and Griffin, *Process Theology*, 105.

tutionalized in a cast of Christian teachers, is to repudiate the spirit of Jesus and to recapitulate the position against which he himself protests.[20]

Process thought supports an openness of interpretation, rather than a hermeneutic based on "out-of-date" concepts.[21] God speaks through the present experience of our reality not the reality of someone else long ago. The Jesus story and Israel's story, important as they are for Christian knowing, need to be experienced firsthand not as once-for-all events in the past. This is the relational model of teaching which Jesus employed. He challenged people to come to their own knowing. Neither creation nor redemption is a once-for-all event and thus all of creation participates as co-creators and co-redeemers with God. Truth can be reconceptualized. Paradigms can change. But such openness is often thwarted by our propensity to defend beliefs and assumptions even when they are no longer true in relation to our daily experience. Here we face a dilemma. It is also true that sustained commitment is necessary to the search for creativity and truth. If creativity is of the essence, both of God and of reality, then as David Bohm has suggested, it is necessary to find a middle ground between these two extremes "to entertain a range of assumptions with trust and confidence, in which none is so sacrosanct as to lie beyond serious questioning."[22]

Spirit and the Trinity
The above quote refers to creative transformation, the movement of growth and change necessary for the enjoyment of life. Process theology finds the source of this transformation in the Logos, the Spirit of God manifested in Jesus the Christ. Using trinitarian language is not playing with numbers but speaking of the internal relatedness of the creative (primordial) and responsive (consequent) love of God. God is not three "persons" but is at any given moment a Unity of the creative, persuasive, and responsive Love at the heart of things, a Love continually incarnated in the creation, in persons, and in the life of the church as the Body of Christ. An understanding of the difference between a substance metaphysics and a process metaphysics, between externally related objects and internally related subjects enables a reconceptualization of the trinitarian formula. When we see reality as separate substantial objects rather than as subjective interrelated events then images of "Father,

---

20. Rosemary Radford Ruether, *Sexism and God-Talk*, 121-122 quoted in Carter Heyward, "An Unfinished Symphony of Liberation: The Radicalization of Christian Feminism Among White U. S. Women," *Journal of Feminist Studies* 1:1 (Spring 1985), 115.

21. This phrase comes from a conversation with Marshal McLuhan's brother Maurice, who pointed out that it does not mean old-fashioned or obsolete but rather indicates experience that is not immediate or firsthand. As soon as experience is conceptualized it is "out-of-date" because reality has moved beyond it to a new way of becoming.

22. Bohm and Peat, *Science, Order and Creativity,* 264.

Son, and Holy Spirit" tend to be seen as separate persons. However if we see reality as a process then the "events" of God's experience become unified, not as "three in One" but as a harmony of creative-redemptive Love interacting with all of creation and especially with fully conscious human responsiveness. Rationally we use analogies and definitions that divide experience into understandable segments, but intuitively we *feel* God's Spirit continually drawing us toward Unity, the purpose of the cosmic reality.

Evil, History, and Redemption

In process thought evil is what follows from choices that do not actualize God's love and redemptive activity in our interaction with one another. Human history is the making of such ethical choices. One of the most important questions for faith has always been the relation of God to evil. When tragedy strikes, people have coped by saying that whatever happens must be God's will. The events of the twentieth century have put an end to such thinking. If the violence of war, the horror of the Holocaust and Hiroshima, the oppression under which so many live or the continuing threat of nuclear annihilation be God's will, there would be no reason to believe in such a God. For if such a God could prevent evil and does not, why should such a cruel deity be worthy of our worship? But what if God is *not* "in control" of history? If that is true, then what emerges is a very different view of the problem of evil and of redemption. What if God, like us, can also be surprised at the events of history? What if, given the freedom in reality, God does not know what the future will bring? Do we then hold fast to the traditional view of God as omnipotent (is in control) and omniscient (does know what will happen but does not prevent it) because we want to think that *someone* is in control of events just as we once believed that our fathers were when we were little children? Given the continuing tragedy and threat to life in this century, together with maturity's knowledge that "fathers" (or mothers) never were "in control," should we be asking whether the God of coercive power is indeed the God who was revealed by Jesus of Nazareth whom we follow. Can we be adventuresome enough to embrace a transformation of what have been less than helpful traditional interpretations of our faith? Can we be creative and open to the continuing revelation of God? Both process and feminist theology are currently suggesting that such transformation is essential to the future of Christianity and of our planet.

Process theologians ask: Who is responsible for history, God or us? If it is indeed us—and the overwhelming evidence of experience is that such is true—then is it not time to grow up and leave the parental home of a Father God and take responsibility for one another's lives and for the world in which we live? People are starting to take this responsibility seriously today, but more often outside of the institutional church.

Whitehead recognized that evil is not so much a matter of specific actions or not observing moral codes as it is the breaking of relationships among people. The *activity* of physical sexual expression is not wrong in and of itself. "Sin" occurs when such activity breaks a marriage covenant or when pregnancy results and a child cannot be cared for responsibly or when respect for persons is denied by the use of another person for one's own pleasure, by consent or force. Whether in personal relationships or in world events, what happens in the world happens because choices are made not because it is the "will of God." In a process world every event influences every other event regardless of proximity. For example, divorce is the very personal experience of two people, but the recently published results of longitudinal research show that the adverse effects on the children involved are making a measurable difference in the welfare of society as a whole.[23]

This interpretation of evil does raise and leave unanswered many questions. There are able criticisms of this view, the more obvious being that it renders God finite and less powerful, and that God is the source of evil, given the freedom of creation. In *Evil Revisited* David Ray Griffin answers these criticisms. For example, Griffin argues that we tend to confuse *aesthetic* evil or suffering and *moral* evil or perversity. Evil which is present in the one who suffers "is evil *undergone*, not evil *intended*, it is aesthetic evil not moral evil."[24] It is this aesthetic evil which God experiences with those who suffer. A present example would be persons personally affected by AIDS. An infected person who knowingly infects another is involved in moral evil. A person who unknowingly infects another in a loving relationship participates in aesthetic evil experienced by both parties.

Where is redemption within the very real evil we all experience? Whitehead images God's redeeming activity as "a tender care that nothing be lost." He speaks of God's judgment as an activity of God's consequent nature, saving the world as it passes into God's experience. "It is the judgment of a tenderness which loses nothing that can be saved. It is also the judgment of a wisdom which uses what in the temporal world is mere wreckage."[25] Redemption is offered in the unactualized initial aims of God which are eternal possibilities. As co-creators and co-redeemers with God, men and women make the choices that actualize God's realm within history. Redemption therefore is social rather than individual. What would this mean concretely? In the early 1980s a commercial film, *Places in the Heart*, portrayed people co-creating the world in which they lived for better or worse and being co-redeemers to one another. At several places in the story, Sally Field, who plays a young widow living in the Midwest in the Depression, becomes the vehicle of redemption for other people, a black man accused of theft and a blind man who is not wanted by his family. She in turn experiences redemption through the black

23. Barbara Dafoe Whitehead, "Dan Quayle Was Right," *The Atlantic Monthly,* 271: 4 (April 1993).

24. Griffin, *Evil Revisited,* 204.

25. Sherburne, *A Key to Whitehead's Process and Reality,* 182.

man whom she had "saved" from the law, who enables her to keep her home and farm.[26] But this "redemption" is not without sacrifice, in this case the widow's participation in the back-breaking work of the cotton fields with the African Americans. Redemption comes through interrelated sacrificial effort. Redemption is social.

In solitariness lies the seeds of evil. Whitehead's oft-quoted phrase "religion is what we do with our solitariness."[27] reflects a lack of emphasis on this social dimension which is seen as much more important in our time. To be solitary is not necessarily to be religious, though individual mystical experiences are valuable in the spiritual journey. Because of God's involvement in reality, we experience God's love when we are loved and return love and as we enter into genuine mutuality with the flowing life around us. The religious quest is indeed what we *do* with our solitariness. It is our yearning to transcend separation and fragmentation.

To take the concept of redemption further into resurrection or immortality is to enter an area that is not fully developed in process theology. Whitehead saw "everlastingness" as a final unity related to the image of the kingdom of heaven and tended toward neutrality on personal immortality. Cobb and Griffin make the observation that even though process reality involves loss, there is no reason that this must be the final word because "responsive love has the power to overcome the final evil of temporal existence."[28] Daniel Day Williams speaks of resurrection as having "analogues in the human experience of forgiveness, the renewal of love, and the rebirth of hope."[29] and of the importance of seeing resurrection as victory over sin as well as death. David Ray Griffin distinguishes a postmodern view of resurrection from the view of process theology. He claims that postmodernism does not "modernize" Whitehead's ideas, as does process theology, when it speaks of the soul equated with mentality and the body equated with the physical. Postmodernism leaves room for current evidence of out-of-body experiences and the "nonlocal" connections[30] characteristic of psychic experience.

Marjorie Suchocki reminds us that the evidence of the New Testament is

26. *Places in the Heart*, directed and written by Robert Benton, produced by Arneen Donovan, distributed by Tri Star Pictures. Throughout the story different characters at different times act in redeeming ways to one another, acutalizing God's love in real life situations. The final scene in the movie is a Protestant communion service at which all the characters in the movie are present, both the living and the dead, a powerful image of our interrelatedness with the "communion of saints" who redeem one another.

27. Alfred North Whitehead, *Religion in the Making* (New York: New America Library, [1926] 1960), 16, but see 137.

28. Cobb and Griffin, *Process Theology*, 123.

29. Daniel Day Williams, *The Spirit and the Forms of Love* (Lanham, Md.: University Press of America, 1981), 169.

30. Current quantum theory speaks about particles influencing one another at great distances with no visible "cause and effect" relationship like the former "billiard ball" concept of causality.

not of the resurrection itself but of the *results* of resurrection. For Suchocki, "Resurrection depends upon the reality of God, not simply as that which God can do, but as that which God is."[31] Reflection continues on the concept of resurrection in process theology. But it should be noted that when we employ a process rather than a substantial view of universe and see reality as basically "interval" or creative Spirit then the apparent loss of substance in death may not be the end of the process itself.

Therefore when educators work from a process perspective how do the above tenets of process theology inform educational theory and practice? Griffin says that what is needed today is "a generation willing to live between Gods,"[32] that is

> a generation of religious leaders, artists, and parents who will work in terms of an idea of God that they themselves do not fully, except intellectually, feel to be God. They would teach this image through symbols, stories, doctrines, and example to the young people under their influence, with the goal that they, in adulthood, would have an understanding of God that is not only intellectually satisfying but religiously satisfying in the deepest sense of the word.[33]

Griffin's insight into the ambiguity of educating in the church today presents a major challenge for adult education in congregations and seminaries. If all religious educators and pastors attempted to teach as Griffin suggests what would religious education look like and what theory of education would guide its practice?

Part Two

PROCESS THEOLOGY AND EDUCATIONAL THEORY

Introduction

Writing about education is a concrete experience of the internal relatedness of reality. It is difficult to speak about teaching without at the same time speaking of learning, or to separate either from epistemology or the environment within which learning occurs. The multiple aspects of how we come to know anything are so intertwined that to speak of one is to speak in

---

31. Marjorie Hewitt Suchocki, *God-Christ-Church* (New York: Crossroad, 1982), 115.

32. Griffin, *Evil Revisited*, 211.

33. Ibid.

the same moment of all the others. However, if educators are to speak of education at all we must use categories and definitions and for our purposes here raise questions such as: What are the guiding principles of religious education informed by postmodern/process theology? What would the educational event look like should these principles guide its planning and execution? Why would a pedagogy based on these principles be a preferred teaching/learning situation for our time?

There are three guiding principles (other educators may choose different ones) that inform a process approach to education: *first*, reality and God are internally related and interconnected in ways not previously understood (*panentheism*). *Second*, the essence of reality is freedom and creativity. Thus creation is an ongoing activity of both God and the world, not a once-for-all event, and therefore advance into novelty is at the heart of reality (*process*). And *third*, human beings are coredeemers of the world; we are responsible for history (*God as persuasive love not coercive power*).

How do these postmodern/process principles affect a theory of religious education?

Interrelatedness of Reality
a) Epistemology

The new paradigms of quantum theory and organic philosophy have raised awareness of the interrelatedness and interconnectedness of the orders of reality. Process and postmodern approaches to theology propose the complementary view of God as internally related to reality in God's consequent nature. Each of these proposals have fundamentally altered previous ways of knowing substance, time, space and causality, and images of "divinity," making this time in history different from any other time.

Process philosophy understands knowing as a relational, constructive activity, what Bob Gowin calls "event epistemology."[34] Knowing as relational rather than propositional sees abstractions or concepts as "out-of-date." Such knowing originates in concrete "events" of which abstract concepts form the background. Concepts, propositions, categories and rational explanations are essential to the endurance of knowledge, but such need to be constantly tested in the participants' ongoing experience of life, or as Whitehead said,

> Above all things we must beware of what I will call "inert ideas"—that is to say, ideas that are merely received into the mind without being utilized, or tested, or thrown into fresh combinations.[35]

Learners need to meet ideas in many different contexts if concepts are to be owned, and thus useful. In a process worldview, knowing is informed by

34. D. Bob Gowin, *Educating* (Ithaca, N.Y.: Cornell University Press, 1981), 28.
35. Alfred North Whitehead, *The Aims of Education* (New York: Free Press, [1929] 1967), 1.

the past and lured by the possibilities offered in the present moment thereby moving into the future with openness to surprise and novelty. Coming to know is the process of exercising critical thinking, of knowing what we see rather than seeing what we know.

b) Learning

James Michael Lee reminds us that we learn about religion in the same way in which we learn about anything else using reason, perception, imagination, feelings, and intuition.[36] Learning takes place within the interrelatedness of all the aspects of human experience.

The interrelationship of Whitehead's concepts of *prehension, conscrescence,* and *satisfaction* provides the philosophical basis for his theory of learning. At the macrocosmic level of reality these are the basis for Whitehead's rhythm of education—romance, precision, and generalization—wherein learning is understood as internally motivated. It begins in activities of questioning, exploration, and wonder—the stage of romance—when what is to be known "holds within itself unexplored connections with possibilities half-disclosed by glimpses and half-concealed by the wealth of material."[37] In order to utilize such knowledge learners move into the stage of precision, consolidating their mastery over the subject with ever deepening understanding and skill. The stage of generalization is a return to romance "with the added advantage of classified ideas and relevant technique."[38] Beyond the necessary work of the stage of precision, the freedom to combine ideas in novel relationships is achieved and such creativity and appreciation bring *satisfaction.*

Whitehead does not understand "stages" as do present theorists. Learning in not improvement, it is rhythmic movement. "Growth as an improvement process presupposes a deficiency in the learner and a level of attainment to which someone else wishes [the learner] would aspire. Growth seen as a movement presupposes an urge on the part of the learner to 'advance into novelty.' "[39]

c) Environment

A learning environment designed to reflect the unity imaged by internal relation is a place where respect for persons is a key element. Learners, whether young children, adolescents, or adults are not, as Whitehead said, "portmanteaus to be packed."[40] As indicated above persons are seen as active

---

36. James Michael Lee, *The Shape of Religious Instruction* (Birmingham, Ala.: Religious Education Press, 1971).

37. Whitehead, *Aims of Education*, 17.

38. Ibid., 19.

39. Kathleen Gershman and Donald W. Oliver, "Toward a Process Pedagogy," *Process Studies* 16:3 (Fall 1987), 193.

40. Whitehead's characterization of children as "portmanteaus" predates Freire's concern about "banking education" by over fifty years. Alfred North Whitehead, "Discussion Upon Fundamental Principles of Education" (1919), intro. and ed. Robert Brumbaugh, *Process Studies* 11:1 (1984), 41-43.

agents internally predisposed to learning, having the abilities to wonder, question, and seek relationships within their world. All those in the learning event need to feel that their contributions will be valued, that it is good to be there.

d) Teaching

Teaching is often the first area dealt with in educational writing. Placing it as the summary category images teaching as completing the "loop"[41] of education which involves the teaching/learning continuum within every aspect discussed throughout the previous sections. "Teaching in the context of educating is a social event in which human beings come to share meaning."[42] Process theology sees the human person as having the freedom to actualize God's creative-responsive love in the world. Beginning with a positive outlook about the learner, the teacher offers the subject matter in love and freedom as a *proposal* to be considered and tested against experience.

Thus to teach is to relate the world of the learners to the world of the subject matter. Christian religious instruction is an incarnational activity in which scripture and tradition are brought into relationship with the lives of the learners. To paraphrase the philosopher Frederick Turner: Learners should feel the energy of the Spirit, the consciousness of nature, and the awesome responsibility of freedom; they should sense connectedness with the past in the words of the liturgy, the excitement of ongoing creation, and awe at our common heritage in the dust of the stars and God's presence in all of creation. Teachers of religion ought to be scientists and poets; scientists are increasingly teaching us about the Spirit and poets always have.[43]

Creativity and Co-creation

a) Epistemology

Process thought says that creativity and freedom are of the essence of the universe. Because this is so "no static maintenance of perfection is possible. Advance or Decadence are the only choices offered to mankind. The pure conservative is fighting against the essence of the universe."[44] Thus to know only the past—the tradition and sacred writings, the "great books" in the humanities, or the facts of science—is for Whitehead to know only "inert ideas." Faith concepts taught in childhood are often carried into adulthood because alternative views are never presented or enabling questions are never

---

41. Quantum theory speaks of the orders of reality as being like loops that double back on themselves in a never ending dance of implicate orders, creativity, and interrelatedness.

42. Gowin, *Educating*, 62.

43. Frederick Turner, *Rebirth of Value* (Albany: State University of New York Press, 1991), 124-125. Turner speaks in terms of general education. I have paraphrased his discussion in terms of religious education.

44. A. H. Johnson, "Whitehead's Philosophy of History," *The Journal of the History of Ideas* 7:2 (1946), 8.

asked. Superstition or denial become the only choices offered. However when this past knowing is thrown into creative combination with the learners' concrete experience, then learners as well as teachers are respected as knowers, and what is known can become their own. They become co-creators with God. Co-creation is the exercise of critical thinking, being surprised by what we see, rather than seeing what we already know.

b) Learning

In the first section it was noted that growth as movement understands motivation for "advance into novelty" as coming from within the learner rather than being imposed by outside forces. "Inert ideas" were seen as the failure of creativity in learning. In learning a religious tradition, doctrine and ritual can become inert ideas if they are "ideas that are merely received into the mind without being utilized, or tested, or thrown into fresh combinations." Religious education informed by a process theological approach encourages learners to be open to new paradigms of reality and to a God who is still creating and invites all of creation to participate in that exciting journey into novelty.

c) Environment

A teacher working with the concepts of process thought creates a setting in which such critical and creative thinking is encouraged. In religious education embodiment should complement doctrinal abstractions. The natural order rather than the supernatural is the arena in which God's presence is found. Each person's experience of God and life is valued. New insights are expected, welcomed, and seen as gifts from God.

d) Teaching

When creativity and freedom are seen as the essence of reality, teaching seeks to foster both attributes in the persons being taught. Teaching as a creative activity opens opportunities for learners to experiment, speculate, see visions and dream dreams. A religious educator is one who incarnates the persuasive love of God in his living. She is one who teaches about justice, caring, and the responsible use of freedom. By encouraging questioning and sharing doubts and observed ambiguities, by asking "but what if...", by accepting learners' responses as valuable, the incarnational teacher creates the accepting environment envisioned above.

Co-redemption

a) Epistemology

It matters how we know and what we know. If, in fact, we do construct the person whom we are and, to some extent, the world in which we live by our day to day decisions, then the philosophical, theological, and pragmatic concepts which we hold become very important. David Ray Griffin illustrates this point in his reference to different types of "souls" produced by different images of God. "Whereas the modern doctrines (supernaturalism and materialism) tended to produce either crusaders or power-politic realists, naturalist theism with its doctrine of divine persuasion, will tend to produce pacific souls." He uses "pacific" rather than "pacifistic" to emphasize that it is personality, not ethics, with which he is dealing. "Pacific souls are those that want to live in peace with their fellow creatures, who will therefore naturally seek forms of social order that promote peaceable relations and will naturally seek peaceful resolutions of the inevitable conflicts that remain."[45] "Pacific" souls, like the "tender Companion"[46] in process theology, will seek to be co-redeemers rather than have power over others. They will desire a quality of life that will result in satisfaction for all living things including the planet that is their home.

b) Learning

Process thought understands God as having a consequent nature, that is, God concretely experiences everything that creation experiences, thus making the past eternal in God's knowing. Each event in the world therefore increases God's knowledge. God uses actions promoting goodness, beauty, truth, and harmony to further the redemption of the world. Likewise when humans act destructively, the suffering that God feels also becomes a part of God's knowledge of the world. However, it is God who ultimately redeems whatever can be saved and, as Whitehead says, uses in redemptive ways what we see as "mere wreckage."

But if learners are to understand what redemption is they need to experience it in their own lives. The example used in the first part of this chapter referring to the film *Places in the Heart* is pertinent here. Unless we concretely experience forgiveness and caring then it is difficult to comprehend the meaning of an abstract concept like "redemption." Without such comprehension, it is also difficult to act in redemptive ways toward other people.

c) Environment

Creating a redemptive environment for teaching/learning is to do many of the things already indicated with respect to the other two basic principles. It begins with creating a learning space that is open, hospitable, affirming, caring, and forgiving.

A comparison might be made with the evaluative process of general education which is often seen as oppressive and noncreative, rather than as a redemptive experience for learners. In most religious education settings teachers do not give marks! Thus we can more easily create redemptive environments than in the regular classroom. In a faith community setting, a process approach to religious education should emphasize the state of romance. Children, youth, and adults can be introduced to a wide range of reli-

---

45. David Ray Griffin, *God and Religion in the Postmodern World* (Albany: State University of New York Press, 1989), 7-8.

46. Whitehead images God as "the Great Companion" (*Process and Reality*); Sallie McFague uses the metaphor of "Friend" (*Models of God*); and the phrase above comes from Randolph Crump Miller's chapter previously referred to (note 15).

gious knowledge without the *precision* required of scholarly activities. Whitehead saw that "whatever be the right way to formulate religious truths, it is death to religion to insist on a *premature* stage of precision."[47] A redemptive environment that encourages the participants to be co-redeemers of one another is one which initially honors the openness of the stage of romance. But each stage is essential, and it is their interrelatedness that advances learning through the rhythm of education.

d) Teaching

A teacher who works with the process concept of co-redemption envisions himself or herself as participating in such redemption on behalf of those who have come to learn, recognizing that he or she is as much in need of redemption as are those who have come to learn. The mutuality of the teaching/learning experience is modeled in a number of ways. The teacher shares his or her love of the subject in ways that enhance the learners' enjoyment of discovery. Redemptive teaching recognizes that education deals with an inevitable dilemma. How do we produce the mastery of the stage of precision without losing the joy of the stage of romance? Although any concert pianist could attest to the importance of mastery for freedom to creatively interpret the music being played, getting there has been a stumbling block for many a child practicing scales!

Enabling learners to move through the tedium of acquiring the skills for mastery of any subject requires that the novelty of the stage of romance and the satisfaction of the stage of generalization always be a part of the redemptive rhythm of education.

What would the educational event look like should these principles guide our planning and execution?

Epistemology

The primary activity in religious education is to share The Story and to hear the participant's stories[48] thereby coming to know "out-of-date"concepts in immediate relationship with the learners' reality. Myths of the human journey form worldviews while parables transform them by stimulating empathy and imagination and offering alternative ways of looking at reality. Together with scripture, the church's story and the stories of the participants' faith journeys, current scientific knowledge of reality and other religious worldviews need to be introduced. Such interrelated knowing will enable participants to test concepts of God through critical thinking. Using sociological and anthropological critique, learners can look at traditional belief systems in ways that help them to write a

---

47. Whitehead, *Aims of Education*, 39 (emphasis mine).

48. These terms are being used in the same way that Thomas Groome introduced them in *Christian Religious Education* and uses them currently in the updated shared praxis approach in *Sharing the Faith*.

"new story," a common cosmic story that speaks to humanity today.[49]

A process approach to scripture emphasizes the importance of seeing the interrelated evolving character of the faith journey of the people of Israel throughout their history. Unfortunately the teaching of the Bible in many curricula resembles a craving for fast food snacks rather than a nourishing meal. Learners need a sense of the unity of God's creative-responsive love throughout the Hebrew Bible and the Christian scriptures evolving from tribal faith, through prophetic insights, to the incarnation of the Logos in Jesus of Nazareth and continuing into the present day.

It is important that the practice of education be ethical—and a primary factor in ethical education is the offering of what is to be known. For too long "lies, secrets, and silences"[50] have been a part of the church's educational practice. There has been silence about current biblical scholarship that deals realistically with the scriptures as documents of an ancient culture. Doctrines have been turned into incomprehensible mystery through use of circular arguments based on religious clichés rather than on concepts that can be judged in the public arena. As Sophia Lyon Fahs wrote nearly a half a century ago with reference to the teaching of children:

> To build the beginnings of faith in God on a conception of the universe that our generation no longer regards as true is to prepare the way for a loss of respect for Bible; and what is worse, to court a cynical atheism when the child is old enough to learn for himself.[51]

There has not been an intention to lie (I trust!) but one may well ask whether teaching that God is in control of history and that prayers are literally answered can be born out in everyday experience. A story from Fahs' *Today's Children and Yesterday's Heritage* provides a good example of how our teaching can be misinterpreted because of lack of clarity or fear of dealing with the tradition honestly. She tells about a young boy who, although he could not swim, jumped off a dock into the water believing that if he just prayed Jesus would help him to stay afloat as he had helped Peter in the Bible. After being rescued the child's angry response was, "They lied to me in Sunday School. They said that if I prayed Jesus would always help me, and he didn't!" Though teachers or parents had not deliberately lied to this child, neither had they probably intended to teach what the child had learned.[52]

---

49. The reference here is to Thomas Berry's call for a new creation story, "The New Story," *Teilhard Studies*, (New York: The American Teilhard Association for the Future of Man, 1 Winter 1978).

50. Taken from the title of a book by Adrienne Rich, *On Lies, Secrets and Silences, Selected Prose 1966-1978* (New York: Norton, 1986).

51. Fahs, *Today's Children and Yesterday's Heritage*, 11f.

52. Ibid., 11-12. There are many other such examples in this book of "process-oriented" teaching.

We need to deal honestly with metaphors and analogies in teaching religious truth.

In a process approach a rich environment for learning includes a curriculum which is seen as "records of prior events which human beings can use to make new events happen."[53] Such a curriculum offers insights from science and welcomes firsthand experience that tests the words of scripture in the public arena. Such teachings advance the rhythm of learning in openness and mutuality respecting the inner capabilities and direction of learners to know for themselves.

Learning

Church education in a process-oriented approach engages body, mind, and spirit. Ideas that challenge the whole person are offered in dialogue and embodied through story. By using activities such as music, dancing, painting, sculpting, drama, and poetry, an aesthetic appreciation of truth is encouraged.[54] Through worship, prayer, and meditation, intuitive "faithing" is encouraged.

A concept of God is a word from the past; it is "out-of-date." It is someone else's word until it is made immediate in learners' lives; until a piece of clay images God anew or worship is reborn in a lived moment of joy and wonder. Through being aware of the internal relationship of all of reality we participate in God's ongoing creativity seeking to act in redemptive ways as we live with one another.

Environment

The space that the learners occupy should be a hospitable and open place which invites the adventure of learning. Something that is not often said is that it is as important for the teacher as it is for the learners that the environment be experienced as creative, caring, and affirming. It is a space for the hearing and telling of stories through which the "communion of saints" meets. For children, youth, and adults it is a space for action/reflection on God, the natural world and life experiences. As indicated above, for participants to feel welcome, challenged, and excited about what is being learned, the environment should be an ethical one where "lies, secrets, and silences" have no place.

Methodology used should accommodate different learning styles helping all participants to feel that this is a place where they have something to offer. When a child or adolescent or adult comes into a learning space he or

---

53. Gowin, *Educating*, 55.

54. In chapter 3 of Whitehead's *The Aims of Education*, a plea is made for the incorporation on the arts in education. Today religious educators such as Maria Harris, Gloria Durka, and Joanmarie Smith are also helping us to see the importance of the stimulation of the imagination through aesthetic activity.

she should be able to say: I know that I am welcome here. This is a place where I will be challenged to see something new. I do not feel threatened, and I know that what I have to offer will be valued. To create such a climate for learning is a natural outcome when one designs educational events from a process standpoint that enables teachers and learners alike to "sit loose" to the tradition and to play with images of God that are creative , novel, and real for today's learners.

Teaching

Those who teach out of the approach of process thinking are "mid-wife" teachers, who "assist the students in giving birth to their own ideas, in making their own tacit knowledge explicit and elaborating on it."[55] These are teachers who are co-learners with their partners in the educational enterprise. They are not afraid to speak about their doubts and questions and admit their incomplete understanding, even while sharing the faith they do hold with passion and commitment. They are teachers who are sensitive to the fragility of the faithing process and the need we all have to be secure and in control. Such teachers admit that some of their teaching will be stillborn and that "death" may occur. But as Belenky and her associates point out, midwife teachers are those who can establish a climate of connection by welcoming a diversity of opinion and by caring about their partners in the teaching/learning activity. They exercise a disciplined subjectivity ensuring that no one's contribution is overlooked or disparaged as not valuable.

The activity of teaching informed by process theology is therefore dialogical in character, giving freedom to the learners to come to their own consciousness of God's activity in their lives and the world around them. Through the telling of stories, both from scripture and from the lore of human wisdom and daily life, questions are raised that put the stories into relation with the learners' own lives. Such questioning can lead to creative reconceptualizing of long-held truths and help to preserve a healthy skepticism about fundamental convictions. A process-oriented teacher acts redemptively through incarnating within his or her teaching the freedom of God's persuasive love thereby enabling the scriptures to be heard in new ways rather than insisting on the authority of "man-made" doctrinal statements. For until the middle decades of this century most theology was written from a mas-

---

55. Mary Field Belenky, Blythe McVicker Clinchy, Nancy Rule Goldberger, and Jill Mattuck Tarule, *Women's Ways of Knowing* (New York: Basic Books, 1986), 217f. Although the following do not use this metaphor one can find this kind of teaching in the article by Eleanor Duckworth, "The Having of Wonderful Ideas," in Milton Schwebel and Jane Raph, *Piaget in the Classroom* (New York: Basic Books, 1973), in the final chapter of the third edition of David Elkind, *Children and Adolescents* (New York: Oxford University Press, 1981), in Maria Harris, *Teaching and Religious Imagination* (San Francisco: Harper & Row, 1987), and Jerome Berryman, *Godly Play* (San Francisco: Harper & Row, 1990).

culine point of view. Now important insights coming from feminist theologians and biblical scholars are making contributions to hearing the gospel in new ways that need to be shared more widely.

Why would a pedagogy based on process principles be a preferred teaching/learning situation for our time?

The reasons that a process informed educational philosophy for today's world is important are offered in the following observations. There will no doubt be other approaches for a different time in the future. The dialogue continues.

1. If our planet and its peoples are to survive, a scientifically grounded, relationally based philosophy and theology are needed which will support ecological awareness and encourage the creation of "pacific" souls. Aggression, exploitation, and oppression are no longer viable options for relationships on this planet, if they ever were! Process or postmodernism is a major current theology that fulfills this requirement.

2. It is necessary for persons to develop a sense of responsibility to construct the future. We can no longer let events occur with resignation or assign history to "God's will." Process, postmodern, and feminist theology all challenge us to take such responsibility seriously, to be coredeemers of God's world.

3. New images of God are needed. The traditional images of coercive power and patriarchal domination (so prominent in liturgy and hymnody) have resulted in fractured relationships and have become mental blocks to new ideas of truth. It is essential to redefine "divinity" and the "otherness" of God. Through process theology believers can approach religious teachings as living traditions not as an unchanging inheritance from the dead.[56]

4. For the world's peoples to have peace it is necessary to respect one another's faith communities; to acknowledge that no one has "The Truth." It is necessary to admit that, in spite of our desire for certainty, we are conscious of the beyond which always eludes our greatest intellectual systems. The rise of fundamentalism in the three major monotheistic religions, Christianity, Islam, and Judaism, make such consciousness raising particularly urgent. Process thought encourages dialogue with the peoples of the world to whom we are internally related in the evolutionary process of life.

5. Men and women need to know that although the past is eternal in God, we do not have to repeat it. God continually offers possibilities for the actualization of goodness, beauty, harmony, and peace within the world. God's initial aim is that life be enjoyable and satisfying for all of creation. But the actualization of that aim in the world is in human hands. Process theology

---

56. Edward Robinson, "Enfleshing the Word," *Religious Education* 81:3 (1986), 356-371.

challenges us to be co-creators of our world.

6. It is time to move on from the dualistic thinking of the New-
tonian/Cartesian/patriarchal worldview with its related hierarchies of
mind/body; spirit/matter; male/female; friends/enemies. In an internally
related reality there is only "us." Hierarchies are seen as an immanent general principle actively pervading and indwelling reality, rather than representing the domination of the lower by the higher.[57] Process thought could thus
contribute to the crisis in leadership in today's world. Leadership by proposal, shared leadership, and team projects are becoming better understood
in management seminars and need to be encouraged in both the church and
the boardroom.[58]

7. There is an ethical obligation that all religious teaching be grounded on
a correct notion of reality. The interrelationship of science, philosophy, and
theology in constructive postmodernism[59] helps us to fulfill that obligation.

8. There is an ethical obligation that religious teaching emphasize the
need for caring interconnection with one another, thereby helping to overcome
historic conflicts and the increasing "disconnectedness" now being experienced by children exposed firsthand or through television to a violent, hostile, and uncaring world.[60] Postmodernism encourages the development of
"pacific" souls, people who will work for a peaceful social order and resolution to conflict.

Conclusion

No human system of thought is able to heal all of the world's ills, but, to
paraphrase Whitehead, where more adequate ideas about reality which could
make a difference are available, not to share such insights is to live in a less
than ethical or loving way. Since the Second World War the Holocaust shines
a ghostly beam through the thin veneer of civilization; a prism of horror
that has fractured complacency forever. Do process thought and constructive
postmodernism provide new ways of seeing the human condition that can bet-

---

57. Bohm and Peat, *Science, Order and Creativity*, 164. Here again science comple-
ments process thought as Bohm and Peat offer a new vision of the relatedness of the
orders of reality.

58. Resources such as Harrison Owen, *Leadership Is*; Parker Palmer, *Leadership
From Within*; and John Cobb's essay "The Holy Spirit and Leadership by Proposal" in *Can
Christ Become Good News Again*? are examples of the influence of process-oriented
thinking in this area.

59. Griffin, Beardslee, and Holland, *Varieties of Postmodern Theology*. Postmodernism
has several different forms theologically and philosophically. Constructive postmodernism seeks to affirm what is of value in the modern era while seeking to correct worldviews that have led us into destructive relationships. This book provides of good overview
of the various approaches.

60. Tom Keogh, "Raging Angels," *Globe and Mail*, Toronto, 6 March 1993, D5 which
referred to Ken Magid and Carole A. McKelvey, *High Risk Children Without a
Conscience*.

ter help us to understand what it means to be co-creators with God? Can the Galilean vision of a persuasive, tender Companion who saves what can be saved and who calls us to be co-redeemers, encourage a responsible and caring way of life? Process theology offers such a vision for understanding reality and God and provides an approach to religious education that is relational, creative, and redemptive, moving with the church into the future and a new millennium.

CHAPTER SIX

Empirical Theology and Religious Education

RANDOLPH CRUMP MILLER

Part One

Empirical theology is an American phenomenon. Its leaders have been William James, Douglas Clyde Macintosh, Henry Nelson Wieman, Bernard Eugene Meland, and Alfred North Whitehead. In this first section, I will outline briefly the empirical method, the evidence that is offered, the approach through values, and the understanding of God. This will be followed by the concept of God among these leaders, as distinguished from the claims of some process theologians, and their understanding of Jesus Christ and the church. This will serve as background for the approach to religious education.

EMPIRICAL METHODS

Empirical theology uses the methods of observation, experimental testing, and reason. This is followed by imaginative construction of concepts, which are checked in terms of how they work. Experience is broader than sense experience, for it includes relationships, a sense of the whole, and what Meland called the appreciative consciousness. There is also a "vague affective tone" (Whitehead) at the basis of experience. The effects of culture and current thought patterns influence the interpretation of experience. Out of this matrix come theological concepts formulated within a historical and metaphysical perspective, enriched by models and images that are consistent with modern assumptions, leading to a naturalistic theism.[1]

Experience may be expanded in various ways. Macintosh spoke of "perception in a complex."[2] Wieman wrote that

> perception, including sense experience, can carry with it appreciation most profound, intuition most penetrating, imaginative insights to the heights, personal relations most ecstatic, awareness of deity most transforming, corporate Christian experience most powerful.[3]

James reinterpreted experience by claiming that relations are as basic to experience as the end products. Thus radical experience overcame the problems of Locke and Hume by showing the reality of connections between experienced objects. Added to this was his theory of the "fringe" of consciousness in which

> a blurred thing is just as particular as a sharp thing, and the generic character of either sharp image or blurred image depends on its being felt *with its representative function*. This function is the mysterious *plus*, the understood meaning. . . . Once admit that the passing and evanescent are as real parts of the stream as the distinct and comparatively abiding . . . and the matter presents no further difficulty.[4]

Whitehead provided another factor that enriched empirical method. His theory of nonsensuous perception, or causal efficacy, brought past mental and bodily states into the picture as they pointed to a wider world. This turned traditional empiricism on its head. First is the "vague totality" and the details are secondary. This can be tested by walking into a room full of people, or a first look at the Grand Canyon.[5]

EVIDENCE

James sought for evidence in his *The Varieties of Religious Experience*. He gathered reports of individual experiences that often seemed morbid, in which

---

1. See Randolph Crump Miller, ed., *Empirical Theology: A Handbook* (Birmingham, Ala.: Religious Education Press, 1992), 1. For an overview of the history and themes of empirical theology, see Tyron Inbody, "History of Empirical Theology," 11-35, and Nancy Frankenberry, "Major Themes of Empirical Theology," 36-56, ibid.

2. Douglas Clyde Macintosh, *The Reasonableness of Christianity* (New York: Scribner's, 1925), 200. See his *The Problem of Religious Knowledge* (New York: Harper, 1940), 163-213; see Preston Warren, *Out of the Wilderness* (New York: Peter Lang, 1989) for a current evaluation of Macintosh.

3. Robert W. Bretall, ed., *The Empirical Theology of Henry Nelson Wieman* (New York: Macmillan, 1963), 42. Wieman's reply to Miller.

4. William James, *The Principles of Psychology*, vol. I (Boston: Henry Holt; New York: Dover, 1950), 478-479, note.

5. See Schubert Ogden, in *The Future of Empirical Theology*, ed. Bernard Eugene Meland (Chicago: University of Chicago Press, 1969), 81-82; see Meland's "The Empirical Tradition in Theology at Chicago," ibid., 1-62, for a masterful summary.

surrender and sacrifice are purposely sought, so that happiness and blessedness may increase. By using extravagant experiences that may be toned down, James provided empirical evidence for his concept of God as the MORE.[6]

In 1919, Macintosh wrote *Theology as an Empirical Science*. He believed that religions and science could be brought into the same area. The evidence was to be found in "the right religious adjustment," which could establish laws of theology and the existence of God as "a divine value-producing factor." But unless this adjustment is accompanied by intensity and persistence, there may be no noticeable change.[7]

Wieman started with an inquiry: What is "that Something upon which human life is dependent for its security, welfare, and increasing abundance?"[8] As the creative good, God is the source of emerging good. Ultimately, for Wieman, the evidence points to "creative interchange" working through and with humanity. "God is the source of *human* good,"[9] rather than the creative good of the cosmos.

Meland's interpretation of the "appreciative consciousness" is perhaps the most inclusive and sensitive of the empirical theologians. Combining the insights of Henri Bergson, James, and Whitehead, Meland asserted that the appreciative consciousness combined the past and present in qualitative attainment and mystery. He made use of James's "fringe" of consciousness and "the mind as a stream of thought" as "an active theological process."[10] This approach was particularly suitable where "relations and creative possibilities form the essential stuff of meaning."[11] Influences from the past or something that cannot be treated with precision, unexpected creative novelties or

---

6. William James, *The Varieties of Religious Experience* (New York: Longmans, Green, 1902), 50, 508. Theologians "all agree that the 'more' really exists; though some of them hold it to exist in the shape of a personal god or gods, while others are satisfied to conceive it as a stream of ideal tendency embedded in the eternal structure of the world. They all agree, however, that it acts as well as exists, and that something really is effected for the better when you throw your life into its hands" (510).

7. Douglas Clyde Macintosh, ed., *Religious Realism* (New York: Macmillan, 1931), 9. Macintosh, *The Problem of Religious Knowledge*, 172-173; Warren, *Out of the Wilderness*, 103-105; See William Dean, in *Empirical Theology: A Handbook*, 116-120.

8. Henry Nelson Wieman, *Religious Experience and Scientific Method* (New York: Macmillan, 1926), 9. See Dean in *Empirical Theology: A Handbook*, 120-123.

9. Frederick Ferré, in *Empirical Theology: A Handbook*, 232. See Wieman, *Seeking a Faith for a New Age*, ed. Cedric Hepler (Metuchen, N.J.: Scarecrow Press, 1975), 266: "This excludes the subhuman cosmos except as it supports human existence; and the same applies to the ground of all being."

10. Bernard Eugene Meland, *Higher Education and the Human Spirit* (Chicago: University of Chicago Press, 1953), 51.

11. Ibid., p. 71. See Henry Nelson Wieman and Bernard Eugene Meland, *American Philosophies of Religion* (Chicago: Willett, Clark, 1936), 291-306; Randolph Crump Miller, *The American Spirit in Theology* (Philadelphia: Pilgram Press, 1974), 60-64, 75-99; see William Dean in *Empirical Theology: A Handbook*, 123-125.

high hopes operating with a certain hiddenness are not easily perceived by closed minds. It is this appreciative perception that takes one into the realms of religion and art. This kind of sensitive awareness is continuous with sense perception but enlarges its scope. It is still empirical, but with a difference.

Revelation remains a part of empirical theology, but it is not conceived as coming from a supernatural realm. It remains a source of empirical data when interpreted in William Temple's words as "the coincidence of a particularly revealing event and a particularly appreciative mind."[12] Thus, there are no revealed truths, but there are truths of revelation, which are empirically based. Revelation, then, provides data for empirical interpretation. Often there is special evidence that can be interpreted by those with sensitive minds. These moments of discernment or disclosure, which are unpredicted and unexpected, are open to further testing by others. From this perspective, there are truths of revelation, depending on the interpretation of the evidence.

VALUES

For empirical theory, there is no separation of facts and values. They are always experienced together. Values are appreciative experiences which one feels and cognizes. There are feelings which indicate levels of appreciation that carry with them a sense of obligation. We feel deeply about some realities and much less so about others, so that we place some values above others. Moreover, values come into existence through the creativity found in events. Thus, God is a creative entity which produces values and makes possible the creative transformation of whatever or whomever comes into contact with the divine. When Wieman wrote of "the growth of meaning and value" he provided a beginning concept of God.[13]

Whitehead wrote that "there is nothing in the real world which is merely inert fact. Every reality is there for feeling; it promotes feeling and is felt."[14] At the upper end of perception of values is the human person and the practice of ethics. "Personality is the extreme example of the sustained realization of a type of value,"[15] and our relation to God is to deity as "the measure of aesthetic consistency of the world."[16]

The sensitivity of the empirical theologians is perhaps summed up in

---

12. William Temple, *Nature, Man and God* (New York: Macmillan, 1934), 315, 499-500.

13. See Randolph Crump Miller, *The Theory of Christian Education Practice* (Birmingham, Ala.: Religious Education Press, 1980), 115-117.

14. Alfred North Whitehead, *Process and Reality*, cor. ed., eds. David Roy Griffin and Donald W. Sherburne (New York: Free Press, 1978), 310.

15. Alfred North Whitehead in *The Philosophy of Alfred North Whitehead*, ed. Paul Schilpp (Evanston, Ill.: Northwestern University Press, 1941), 690.

16. Alfred North Whitehead, *Religion in the Making* (New York: Macmillan, 1926), 99.

James's biting letter to James Leuba, who reduced all religious concepts to the subjective. James referred to a

> mystical germ. It is a very common germ. It creates the rank and file of believers. . . . Once allow the mystical germ to influence our beliefs and I believe that we are in my position.[17]

Whether or not it is as universal as James claimed, it is surely an element in the sensitivities of many believers.

When we begin to understand how the words empiricism and experience are used, we can espouse an empirical theology. It may be an appeal based on sense experience and always includes this, but it may be expanded to some kinds of intuition as well as bodily awareness. It is always more than observation, for it includes the participant in the process. The testing of the data may be by controlled experiments,[18] or it may be in terms of what Ian Ramsey called "empirical fit." The experiences appealed to may be mystical, more broadly empirical, or experience in all its wide variety. It may be a response to James's mystical germ. The basic assumption underlying empiricism is a realistic theology in a naturalistic framework. Once the data are established and evaluated, there is room for further speculation and the development of overbeliefs consistent with the evidence, leading some toward a process theology.[19]

GOD IN EMPIRICAL THEOLOGY

In the letter to the Romans, Paul asserted that

> what can be known about God is plain to [people] because God has shown it to them. Ever since the creation of the world his eternal and divine nature, invisible though they are, have been understood and seen through the things [God] made. So we are without excuse; for though they knew God, they did not honor him as God or give thanks to him, but they became futile in their thinking and their senseless minds were darkened (Rom. 1:19-21, NRSV).

Paul was not an empirical theologian, but in this passage he provided a base

---

17. Ralph Barton Perry, *The Thought and Character of William James* (Boston: Little, Brown, 1935), Vol. II, 351.

18. See Karl Peters, in *Empirical Theology: A Handbook*, 79-82: Nancy Frankenberry, in ibid., 43-48; Ian T. Ramsey, *Models and Mystery* (London: Oxford University Press, 1964), 17-21, 38-40. In writing of empirical "fit," Ramsey stressed the feelings of worship, wonder, and awe. "Without such an empirical anchorage, all our theological thinking is in vain, and where there is controversy and argument we are to look for their resolution where they are fulfilled, in worship." Ian T. Ramsey, *Religious Language* (London: SCM Press, 1957), 89.

19. See Miller, *The Theory of Christian Education Practice*, 72.

for such a process, as well as a warning to those who do not honor God.

Our knowledge of God comes from a wide variety of experiences. James emphasized that for the purposes of his studies of religious experience

religion . . . shall mean for us the feelings, acts, and experiences of individual[s] in their solitude, so far as they apprehend themselves to stand in relation to whatever they may consider divine."[20]

Whitehead's description was similar: "Religion is what the individual does with his solitariness."[21] But he qualified this as James might have done.

Religion is primarily individual . . . Expression, and in particular expression of dogma, is the return from solitariness to society. There is no such thing as absolute solitariness. Each entity requires its environment. Thus man cannot seclude himself from society.[22]

This protects the individual from self-delusion and offers the community the opportunity to judge the evidence, thus broadening the empirical base.

James, after examining the evidence, concluded that continuous with our experience is the divine MORE, which serves as a process of salvation operating in the universe. This is the basis for any theological reconstruction. The MORE is not defined. It is similar to the experience of Moses to whom YHWH responded by saying "I AM WHO I AM" (Ex. 3:14). All Moses could know of God was that God was present in action against the Egyptians.

Macintosh also started with the individual. He examined the evidence for the "divine value-producing factor." If one makes the right religious adjustment, by turning from sin and following the right way, God will lead one to a better life.[23] But this is not enough, and Macintosh added some beliefs on the basis of reasonable faith, supplemented finally by permissible surmises that led directly to orthodox Christianity.

Wieman began by using the word "God" to mean the creative transformation which occurs in individuals. "The 'grace of God' would then be creative transformation become dominant in the life" of human beings.[24] Central

---

20. James, *The Varieties of Religious Experience*, 31.

21. Whitehead, *Religion in the Making*, 16.

22. Ibid., 137. It is surprising that many readers overlook this passage, which provides the social impact of one's solitariness. W. H. Auden wrote that Whitehead had said "a very silly thing: 'Religion is what a man does with his solitude.'" But Auden had not read on to the statement that "there is no such thing as absolute solitariness. . . . What is known in secret must be enjoyed in common, and verified in common," 137-138. See Dag Hammarskjöld, *Markings* (New York: Knopf, 1964), xxi.

23. Macintosh, *The Reasonableness of Christianity*, 239-240; also Macintosh, *The Problem of Religious Knowledge*, 202-210, 357-382.

24. Henry Nelson Wieman, *The Source of Human Good* (Chicago: University of Chicago Press, 1946), 49; see John B. Cobb Jr., in *Empirical Theology: A Handbook*, 254-257.

to this understanding is the "creative event," which consists of four subevents. One becomes alert to qualitative meaning and integrates it with other meanings and expands its meaning so that there is a deepening of community among those who participate in this process.[25] It is both individual and corporate.

In 1971, Michael Jackson, a student at Yale Divinity School, taped two days of conversation with Wieman. Wieman insisted that human beings were the only species that have a valuing consciousness in depth and in community that could respond to creativity.

> I can't be committed to the kind of process that works with ants and bees and bugs, or dogs and horses. I must be committed to creativity as it operates in human existence, because only there does it expand indefinitely the valuing consciousness. . . . It is this indefinite expansion that deserves our commitment.[26]

Meland is often closely associated with Wieman, but there were significant differences. Meland put it this way:

> Wieman speaks of truth as a specifiable structure. I would regard specifiable structure as relevant to truth; but I would insist that truth has a more creative or dynamic structure than this formula suggests. . . . Truth as actuality in the creative event is an internal drama in every instance interweaving these persistent values that have been lived by the opportunity that is visited upon us.[27]

In a brilliant chapter on "The Appreciative Consciousness," Meland built on the thinking of James, using such concepts as "time that is lived," "the stream of consciousness," "mind as a stream of thought," "the fringe of consciousness," and "pure experience."[28] These insights led to a preference for perceptiveness over against precision in thought. The "vague" is of more significance than "exactness." Mind and body work together but the body is "a threshold to the deeper stratum of organic being . . . (and) the whole of the self is awakened with a wide awareness which renders the organism perceptive to a high degree."[29]

This leads to "a reorientation to the remote cosmic mystery as a depth of

---

25. See Wieman, *The Source of Human Good*, 58.

26. Michael Jackson, "A Conversation with Henry Nelson Wieman, April 18-19, 1971," a paper in my private files.

27. Meland, in *The Empirical Theology of Henry Nelson Wieman*, 68; see Jackson, "Conversation," 85-92.

28. See Meland, *Higher Education and the Human Spirit*, 50-57.

29. Ibid., 6. Whitehead, "The Exactness Is a Fake," in *The Philosophy of Alfred North Whitehead*, 700.

ultimacy with the immediacies of experience."[30] God is at work pluralistically in a pluralistic universe in which human beings have responsibility for
the universe as well as for each other. Meland spoke of God as "the creative
passage." He agreed with James that we live in a "multiverse" which is
"neither a universe pure and simple and not a multiverse pure and simple,"
but "the strung-along type" that recognizes the experiences of relationships as central.[31] "Not *another* world, but a *wider* world is the focus of
religious interest."[32]

The views of God that emerge from empirical methods in theology are varied, but all of them point to the increase of value, an accessible deity who is supportive of human aspirations, and a transforming entity working for a new
life in relation to God. Such a deity is finite and has an environment, and it
makes sense of the strange complexities of human life, of both the cohesion and
dissonance in the world, and even of Bernard Loomer's insistence of the ambiguity of God and life. The relations are organic and lead to creative transformation of those who relate to the MORE, whatever name we give it.[33]

PROCESS THEOLOGY

Many empiricists lean toward Whitehead's process theology, but Nancy
Frankenberry suggests three points of disagreement; first is their use of highly anthropomorphic imagery and language in speaking of God; second is
their optimistic hope for the conservation of what is good. In contrast, empiricists such as James wrote that there will be real losses, real losers and win-
ners, and something drastic and bitter at the end; third, empirical theologians are skeptical of a monistic, all-inclusive totality, and they prefer the
loose-jointed pluralism of James. Frankenberry continues,

> The idea that *immediacy and ultimacy travel together*, best thematized in the
> work of Bernard Meland, calls attention to the primal flux of experience as
> itself holy ground, generating in its vital immediacy all the sacred that we
> are apt to find in the secular.[34]

Some theologians, such as Macintosh, project their overbeliefs to include
anthropomorphic models that Frankenberry would reject. It is difficult to
get away from the language of things and substance, of nouns as representative

---

30. Meland, *The American Journal of Theology and Philosophy* (May-September
1984), 113.

31. James, *Pragmatism* (New York: Longmans, Green, 1907),148; *A Pluralistic
Universe* (New York: Longmans, Green, 1909), 325. See chapter on Ecology, 336-358.

32. Nancy Frankenberry, *Religion and Radical Empiricism* (Albany, N.Y.: SUNY,
1987), 103-104.

33. See Nancy Frankenberry, in *Empirical Theology: A Handbook*, 50-52.

34. Ibid., 52-53.

of reality. Yet we know that all reality is a process of becoming and perishing, and that verbs tell our stories. Then we can talk about creating, incarnating, forgiving, redeeming, and loving in the ongoing process in which we are living and committing to the persuading and loving of God, for God is what God does.[35]

JESUS CHRIST IN EMPIRICAL THEOLOGY

On the whole, empirical theologians have not dealt systematically with the concept of Jesus Christ, although what has been written may be significant. The starting point is Jesus as recorded in history, a meager source of information. From the beginning there was an oral tradition, but nothing was written until later. The four gospels were written by believers, which is not necessarily bad, but they were not biographies. Their purpose was to make believers of the readers. In Paul's letters, how Jesus died and rose again was more significant than his prior life.[36]

It is difficult to reconstruct a life of Jesus in the contemporary sense, although many have attempted it. It is generally agreed that we know nothing about Jesus until his baptism. He probably was born in Nazareth about 4-6 B.C.E., the first born of at least four brothers and two or more sisters (Mk. 3:21-35; 6:1-6: Mt. 13;53-58; Lk. 4:16-30). He came upon the scene by gathering some followers and preaching repentance. He wandered around Galilee teaching and doing some healing. He had great skill in telling parables, some original and some from tradition, which became a primary source for religious education. He never had a large following, and he aroused the enmity of some officials and ultimately was crucified. There was a revival of interest with news of his resurrection, however it is interpreted, and this provided the basis for faith in Jesus as Lord and Christ.[37]

Wieman interpreted the impact of Jesus in terms of the creative event.

The creative transformative power was not in the man Jesus, although it could not have occurred apart from him. Rather he was in it. It required many other things besides his own solitary will. It required the Hebrew heritage, the disciples with their peculiar capacity for this kind of responsiveness, and

35. Miller, *The Theory of Christian Education Practice*, 7-21: "God Is What God Does," *The Christian Century* (March 24, 1976), 284-287. See Jeffery Rowthorn's hymn, "Creating God, your fingers trace the bold designs of farthest space, *"The Hymnal '1982'* (New York: Church Pension Fund, 1985), 394.

36. Gerard Sloyan, in *Empirical Theology: A Handbook*, 142-154.

37. See Randolph C. Miller, *This We Can Believe* (New York: Hawthorn, Seabury, 1976), 70-74; Gerard Sloyan, *Jesus in Focus* (Mystic, Conn.: Twenty-Third Publications, 1983); Leander E. Keck, *A Future for the Historical Jesus* (Philadelphia: Fortress, 1981); Marcus J. Borg, *Jesus: A New Vision* (San Francisco: HarperSan Francisco, 1987).

doubtless much else of which we have little knowledge. The creative power lay in the interaction taking place between these individuals.[38]

After Jesus' death, this creative power was freed to dominate others through the symbols, rituals, and documents of the early church.[39]

Meland wrote of the Christ-event as a revelatory occasion in history arising from its Jewish background and resulting in a new level of consciousness, with love becoming "regulative as the appreciative consciousness."[40] From the standpoint of history we have clear evidence of "the transformation of human lives, individually and corporately, in response to this new life in Christ."[41] Love that suffers, provides justice, offers grace and forgiveness "triumphed as a saving and healing force amidst the brokenness of men and women."[42]

For Meland, a Christology that has strength and character will provide a focus for Christian themes. If it is inclusive, it will draw people into a disclosure that the revelation in Christ is a unifying and transforming event. If it is exclusive, it will ultimately be shown as a disavowal of what was given. If a Christology is lacking, some other normative measure will be relied on. It is important, therefore, to base a Christian theology on a firm Christology and the witness of scripture, for the Christ-event is a continuing revelation. The lines of communication between witness in contemporary life and in scripture must be kept open, or else "the deep lying mythos which unifies the Judaic-Christian witness will be lost."[43]

Daniel Day Williams built his Christology on the basis of God's suffering. God works in us for reconciliation. We see it in the effect of the cross and resurrection, for out of these events came the creation of a transformed humanity and a new community. The separation from God, as exposed in the death of Jesus, has been overcome. So we can accept the advice in 1 Peter:

> Cast all your anxieties on [God], because [God] cares for you. Discipline yourselves. Keep alert. Like a roaring lion your adversary the devil prowls around, looking for someone to devour. Resist him, steadfast in your faith, for you know that your brothers and sisters in all the world are

---

38. Wieman, *The Source of Human Good*, 41.

39. See ibid., 44; Sloyan in *Empirical Theology: A Handbook*, 152-154; Harold Rosen, *Religious Education and Our Ultimate Commitment* (Lanham, MD: University Press of America, 1985), 59-66; John B. Cobb Jr., *Can Christ Become Good News Again?* (St. Louis: Chalice Press, 1991); Miller, *This We Can Believe* (New York: Hawthorn, Seabury, 1976), 70-99.

40. Bernard Eugene Meland, *The Realities of Faith* (Oxford: Oxford University Press, 1962), 258.

41. Ibid., 260; see Bernard Eugene Meland, *Fallible Forms and Symbols* (Philadelphia: Fortress, 1976), 145-148.

42. Ibid., 262; See Cobb, *Can Christ Become Good News Again?* Marjorie Suchocki, *God-Christ-Church* (New York: Crossroad, 1982), 93-121.

43. Meland, *Fallible Forms and Symbols,* 146.

undergoing the same kind of suffering. And after you have suffered for a little while, the God of all grace who has called you to his eternal glory in Christ, will himself restore, support, strengthen, and establish you (1 Pt. 5:7-10, NRSV).

This is not exclusively Christian experience, for Williams believed that God is a witness in all the world and not just in one strand of history or geography. Wherever the human spirit is moved by love in preparation, knowledge, or fulfillment, there the Holy Spirit is finding a response." But then he added that "those who in faith participate in the community established by the atoning action of Jesus experience the Spirit creating a new body for its expression in the world."[44]

Gerard Sloyan concludes that what we have is an ecclesial tradition about Jesus. "The Jesus of the Gospels is the Christ of early Christian tradition." This faith in Christ we share as believers and as members of the church, based on practical experience through the ages. The empirical awareness of Jesus Christ in this sense is at the center of Christian living, and it leads to the creative transformation of human lives.[45]

THE CHURCH

The New Testament presents many models and images of the church. The imagery is so rich that any precise view is unavailable, but there is an underlying assumption that there is life together in a congregation. Certain images stand out, such as a covenant between God and the people, the fellowship of those who are called out (*ekklesia*), the body of Christ, the people of God, those who participate in the fellowship of believers (*koinonia*), and followers of "the Way."[46]

This is the community that emerged following the experience of the women and later the disciples of the resurrection. In a rather untidy way, the early church formulated its structures and views of ministry. From the beginning there were two sacraments, baptism and the Lord's Supper. Baptism was conceived organically as being grafted onto the vine that is the church, of sharing in Christ's death and resurrection, of becoming a new creation or transformed person, and of receiving the gifts of the spirit, so that we can

---

44. Daniel Day Williams, *The Spirit and Forms of Love* (New York: Harpers, 1968), 190; see 186-191.

45. Sloyan, in *Empirical Theology: A Handbook*, 154; see Miller, *This We Can Believe*, 84-99.

46. See Miller, *Christian Nurture and the Church* (New York: Scribner's, 1961), 4-15; Paul Minear, *Images of the Church in the New Testament* (Philadelphia: Westminster, 1960), 268-269 for 96 images; Loren B. Mead, *The Once and Future Church* (Washington, D.C.: Alban Institute, 1991); Sallie McFague, *The Body of God* (Minneapolis: Fortress, 1993), 205-207; Meland, *Realities of Faith*, 316-320.

say that the church is the body of which Christ is the head and all baptized people are members.[47]

Central to the early church was the Lord's Supper, also called the breaking of bread. It arose as a memorial, but soon it was more than that, for it was believed that the risen Christ was also present, It was the proclamation of a new covenant, an act of fellowship, and a way of giving thanks. The response was a renewal of commitment.[48]

Even at the beginning, sacrament and preaching were inseparable. Preaching consisted mostly of stories about Jesus and telling new ones as the corpus grew. But also there was the call to repentance, the promise of forgiveness, and the challenge to accept the gift of creative transformation offered by God through Christ.

At first, there was little to distinguish the clergy from the laity, for both groups were concerned with evangelism. The good news was spread over new lands and soon most converts were Greek speaking Gentiles. Until the canonical gospels were regularized, the stories about Jesus and the disciples continued to develop, but with the forming of levels of ministry and the Constantinian captivity of the church, a kind of rigidity set in.

Worship was at the center of life in the early church and continues to be central in the church today. It is an immediate response to the religious vision. As Whitehead wrote, "the power of God is the worship [God] inspires." But worship is more than a response to a vision; it is being in the presence of an actual entity, known or believed in, who is the source of creative transformation and is therefore worthy of worship. In worship we are seeking God and at least unconsciously becoming aware of the others who are worshiping with us. The common focus of the congregation strengthens the devotion to values and the comforting and acting of individuals in the congregation leading to moral, social, and political action.[49]

The empirical church today is the inheritor of the historical developments as the organic nature of the church continues to emerge. Tradition is interpreted from an empirical perspective. The church is wherever people gather in the name of Jesus Christ, in small or large congregations or wherever two or three are gathered in Christ's name, and then stretching out to base communities, denominations, councils of churches, and the World Council of Churches.

---

47. Miller, *Christian Nurture and the Church*, 24; Bernard Lee, *The Becoming of the Church* (New York: Paulist, 1974); Bernard Lee, in *Empirical Theology: A Handbook*, 175-202; Williams, *The Spirit and Forms of Love*, 187-191; Miller, *The Theory of Christian Education Practice*, 144-147; Henry Nelson Wieman, *Man's Ultimate Commitment* (Carbondale, Ill.: Southern Illinois Press, 1958), 163-185; Randolph Crump Miller, *The Clue to Christian Education* (New York: Scribner's, 1950), 71-89.

48. Miller, *Christian Nurture and the Church*, 23-26.

49. Miller, in *Empirical Theology: A Handbook*, 264-267; Alfred North Whitehead, *Science and the Modern World* (New York: Macmillan, 1925), 275-276. Miller, *Clue to Christian Education*, 154-169.

Local congregations have their own communities of language, based on traditions, narratives, rituals, liturgies, and symbols, which, according to Wieman, enrich their personalities and direct them to that reality which sustains, saves, and transforms them. It is a complicated process leading to self-examinations that confront their failures, sins, and self-deceptions, and may lead to forgiveness, renewal of commitment, and even to the transformation of their personalities. These congregations are always a mixture of saints and sinners, who need further understanding that may come from Bible study, preaching, prayer, and education—even from theology.

Part Two

In Part Two, I show the intertwining of empirical theology and educational theory and practice. We will look first at the learner, then at the place of relationships in the learning process, followed by consideration of several educational theories that are consistent with empirical theology, and finally at practice.

In order to equip God's people for living in God's world, we need an empirical approach to the nature of the learners. Human beings are natural creatures who have emerged from the evolutionary process and are made up of genetic and cultural inheritances. They are the creators of emerging cultures. Philip Hefner has written that

> planet earth has reached the point where the success of human beings in actualizing who we are—*self-aware creators of culture*—is critical for the entire planetary ecosystem, including the planet's nonhuman inhabitants. Our present era presents such radical challenges to us that our ability to assess our world and to construct frames of meaning that will engender wholesome behavior is seriously destabilized and confused. This is a challenge to our ability to fashion a viable system of cultural [and religious] information.[51]

Myth and ritual arose for similar reasons many generations ago to save human beings from destruction. Myth is a traditional way of telling a story of the beginning of things that provides grounds for ritual actions suitable for

---

50. Wieman, *Man's Ultimate Commitment,* 166; Miller, in *Empirical Theology: A Handbook,* 226-267.

51. Philip Hefner, *The Human Factor* (Minneapolis: Fortress, 1993), 19-21. See McFague, *The Body of God,* 110.

today, thus helping people to understand themselves and the world. We need to bring together the results of scientific discovery and our mythic and ritual inheritance. Science may provide the facts of life, but we need myth and ritual to provide direction, meaning, and purpose.[52]

Empirically, a human being is a merging of two streams: genetic inheritance and cultural information. This relationship is not clearly understood and often serious tension exists between them. Freedom has emerged out of the basic deterministic evolutionary process, probably from the plasticity that is part of the system, leading to exploring the environment, choosing between alternative decisions and behaviors, and experiencing a supportive social matrix that allows for both exploring social relationships and working for the welfare of others. Within this framework we find concern for values and the development of morality and religion.[53]

The human animal is closely related to other high-grade mammals, but the difference is clear. Human beings are talking animals who developed tools and religion about 25,000 years ago. Survival depended on physical powers, and human beings were overmatched at this level, but the development of brain power, language, and imagination made survival and dominance possible. The genetic structure is present at birth, but all else needs to be learned, including what constitutes the human mind, language, attitudes, antipathies, love, sadness, and religious faith.[54]

Whitehead stressed the sense of worth as basic to religious faith. He also interpreted human beings as co-creators, which gives them their dignity and grandeur.[55] This seems too optimistic a view of humanity. We need to recall that human beings also have a sense of failure or sin, of alienation and worthlessness, that must be faced. Most religions keep some balance between sin and redemption. This in turn brings up the human need to understand God's persuasive grace and love, which is the center of empirical and other theologies, leading to creative transformation as a continuing process. Thus we find theology in the background and grace and faith in the foreground in educational theory. Faith interpreted in terms of basic trust is essential to this approach.

Such basic truth led Meland to interpret appreciative awareness as central.

The assumption which guides appreciative awareness is that an event is never properly known apart from its context, for the relations are as real a part of its meaning as its internalized core. Thus analysis within the perspective of the appreciative consciousness must take the form of examin-

---

52. Hefner, *The Human Factor,* 21.

53. Ibid., 30.

54. See William C. Tremmel, in *Empirical Theology: A Handbook,* 155-161.

55. *Dialogues of Alfred North Whitehead,* as recorded by Lucian Price (Boston: Little, Brown, 1954), 370-371; Miller, in *Empirical Theology: A Handbook,* 270-271; Whitehead, *Science and the Modern World,* 275.

ing the parts with a full sense of their function and of their relational aspects.[56]

This is a wholistic kind of knowing that needs to be recognized as part of the educational process. It is a serious form of reflection which can be nurtured just as other disciplines can be taught.[57] The aesthetic element in religious thought is therefore recognized as essential to an empirical approach to theology and to religious education.

The learner is capable of growth. Through an increase of meaning in one's life, growth occurs, especially as the qualities of sensitivity and responsiveness increase. As meanings accumulate, experience is enriched, appreciative awareness expands, and as creative interaction between individuals and their natural environment occurs, there is growth in religious faith.[58] Wieman wrote that such increase is in scope, in enlargement of situations, in discrimination, in a refining of analytical development, and in organization, leading to both negative and positive adaptation of values in the development of interests. Conscience does not develop until a person has grown along these lines.[59]

RELATIONSHIPS

At the heart of James's radical empiricism is the recognition of the reality of relationships. It is through relationships that we grow, converse, know others, have faith in God. Such relationships are at the center of religious education. Horace Bushnell was aware of this in his discussion of the relations between parents and children and the development of morality and religion in the family. He wrote of parents:

No mock piety, no sanctimony of phrase, no longitude of face on Sundays will suffice. You must live in the light of God, and hold such a spirit in exercise as you wish to see translated into your children. You must take them into your feeling, as a loving and joyous element, and beget, if by the grace of God you may, the spirit of your own heart in theirs.[60]

Bushnell held an organic view of the family and church, with relationships as basic. At this level he was an empiricist and a process thinker, but he was pulled by what seemed to be the supernatural as well. Later, Reuel Howe, draw-

---

56. See Meland, *Higher Education and the Human Spirit,* 69.

57. Ibid., 75.

58. Rosen, *Religious Education and Our Ultimate Commitment,* 71.

59. See Henry Nelson Wieman and Regina Westcott Wieman, *Normative Psychology of Religion* (New York: Crowell, 1935), 253-255.

60. Horace Bushnell, *Christian Nurture* (New Haven: Yale University Press, 1916), 45; see Miller, "Horace Bushnell: Prophet to America's Children," *Perkins Journal* (Spring 1979), 1-8.

ing on Martin Buber's I-Thou relationship, settled on dialogue as the key element in religious education. What is called the language of relationships is a primary means of communication, and in community we discover the personal meanings of the words we hear and use. We seek "words to tell our loving." There is a grace-faith relationship between God and humanity that is at the center, interpreted and backed by an empirical theology that determines its meaning.[61]

Reuel Howe, who served on the editorial board of the *Seabury Series*, saw the connection between a relationship theology and the role of the teacher. The teacher, he wrote, (1) "is one who incarnates the Holy Spirit rather than one who teaches a certain kind of subject matter," (2) "is alert to the meanings that [the] pupil brings to the moment of learning," (3) is willing to wait, because the teacher "trusts both the working of the Spirit and the inner working of [the] pupil," (4) "is not anxious about which method of education" will be used, and (5) "speaks as a person to a person and expects a response."[62]

This approach reflects empirical theology's emphasis on an atmosphere in which the nonsensuous interpretation of Whitehead is at work, providing an environment of a "vague affective tone" in which God's persuasive love is at least available to those who are alert. Thus the learner may be brought into a right relationship with God and become subject to creative transformation. In more traditional language, the purpose of Christian education is to place God at the center and to bring the learner into a right relationship with God and one's fellows within the perspective of the fundamental Christian truths about all of life.

EDUCATIONAL THEORIES

Many emphases in educational theory are or may be made consistent with empirical theology. Education, wrote Marc Belth,

> deals with the relationship between concepts and powers nurtured in learners, and with the methods creating concepts as the inventions of intelligence, in whatever fields these methods come to be employed.[63]

---

61. See Bushnell, *Christian Nurture*, 75-101; Reuel Howe, *Man's Need and God's Action* (Greenwich, Conn.: Seabury, 1953); Howe, *The Miracle of Dialogue* (Greenwich, Conn.: Seabury, 1963); Martin Buber, *I and Thou* (New York: Scribner's, 1970); Kendig Cully, ed., *Westminster Dictionary of Christian Education* (Philadelphia: Westminster, 1963), 563-565; Miller, *The Clue to Christian Education*, 8-9; Frankenberry, in *Empirical Theology: A Handbook*, 44.

62. *Religious Education* (November-December 1959), 494-496; Randolph Crump Miller, *Education for Christian Living*, 2nd. ed., (Englewood Cliffs, N.J.: Prentice-Hall, 1963), 358.

63. Marc Belth, *Education as a Discipline* (Boston: Allyn & Bacon, 1965), 7; Miller, *Theory of Christian Education Practice*, 166-168; Miller, *The American Spirit in Theology*, 228-232.

Whatever is available to experience may be considered. Thus the data available to empirical theology can be introduced and the major task is to compare, test, and evaluate. Education, then, "becomes a way of raising and answering a question not otherwise asked, a question centering on the problem of improving the ability to think."[64] Even some children as young as seven may be helped to distinguish between literal and metaphorical language in religious thinking. This is an important step forward for all learners as they begin to understand and use models, images, and metaphors.

Religious education is also the initiation into a community which has a set of values. This is evident in the development of young children in a family. R. S. Peters made initiation the center of his theory.

> Education involves essentially processes which intentionally transmit what is valuable in an intentional and voluntary manner and which create in the learner a desire to achieve it, this being seen as having its place along with other things in life.[65]

When this is modified to include the insights of feminist and liberation theologians, through the use of more inclusive models, this can lead to a broader view of what Meland called the appreciative consciousness. which becomes

> a maximum degree of receptivity to the datum under consideration on the principle that what may be given is more than what is immediately perceived, or more than one can think.[66]

This opens up the whole area of the sense of the holy and the response of awe, and possibly an appeal to James's mystic germ. In a community that takes such experiences seriously, the sense of worth of the student is upheld, for in the values of the community one finds recognition of the worth of each individual.

In religious education, we attempt "to equip God's people for work in [God's] service" (Eph. 4:12, NEB). This leads to the requirement for proper training in the skills of creative and cooperative learning and action. First, one needs to be oriented to other people, to become aware of others' needs and concerns, and to reflect on ways in which God is at work through people. Participation training, or the techniques of group process, or cooperation in some kind of task or project may achieve this goal. It is a socializing process and the power of the community may be shared by the learner. The important element is the sense of worth as a person through the experience

---

64. Belth, *Education as a Discipline,* 13.

65. R.S. Peters, in *Philosophical Analysis and Education,* ed. Reginald D. Archambault (London: Routledge & Kegan Paul, 1965), 102; see Miller, *Theory of Christian Education Practice,* 168-170.

66. Meland, *Higher Education and the Human Spirit,* 57.

of belonging. Second is procedural training, which includes the tools for acquiring factual data, observation skills, and the utilizing of data that can be empirically verified. It includes retention of information (memory work), seeking additional information, and relating various systems to each other, especially those of the empirical sciences and theological claims.

Teachers need all of the above, plus supervision and consultation, which are practically nonexistent in many parishes. Untrained teachers are a hazard to any educational program. The problem of recruiting is little understood and asking for volunteers is risky. The best programs recruit their teachers through selective invitations. Teachers are drafted because they have potential. The words of the letter of James are sound: "Not many of you should become teachers, my brothers and sisters, for you know that we teachers will be judged with greater strictness" (Jas. 3:1, NRSV).[67]

Another view is education for insight, disclosure, and commitment. We have experiences when everything "comes alive" as "the light dawns" or "the penny drops." When one has gone through all the routes of straight thinking, or entered into a deeper appreciation of values, or been trained to be aware of the concerns of others, or learned to use certain skills, there may be moments of enlightenment which are life-transforming. Ian Ramsey suggested that the word "God" is often used in a pedestrian fashion and thus loses its power to inform, provide meaning, or inspire action. If we use logically odd qualifiers when speaking of God, perhaps there will be a breakthrough. When the right stories are told in an environment which is suitable for the stories, there may be disclosures and commitments that lead to life-transforming change. This cannot be guaranteed, but it may result in something new. The empirical "fit" for such concepts is found in worship. The moment of insight may come from other uses of language as well, frequently from providing new words to replace the well-worn customary ones.[68]

Finally, there is education as nurture. Education is what happens to a person in community, whether it is family, school, gang, neighborhood, church, or nation. Nurture is the most inclusive interpretation of education, for its purpose is "to describe the involvement of the pupil in the atmosphere and relations of a community, including knowledge about it as a means toward loyalty to it." Horace Bushnell, in his classic *Christian Nurture*, saw clearly the difference made by attitudes and emotional climate surrounding children even before words had any meaning. By the time a child is three, the parents have done half of all they can do to settle the child's moral education.

Both James and Whitehead believed that religion begins with what happens

---

67. See David R. Hunter, *Christian Education as Engagement* (New York: Seabury, 1963); see Daniel Day Williams, *God's Grace and Man's Hope* (New York: Harper, 1949), 194-195.

68. In *Religious Education* (January-February, 1962), 95; see Randolph Crump Miller, *The Language Gap and God* (Philadelphia: Pilgrim Press, 1970), 77-93.

to an individual in solitariness. James emphasized the "mystic germ" and Whitehead the rightness of things and one's duty. Both saw the necessity to return to society and the verification by others of the experience. Since religion is primarily the result of solitary experience, it is clear that for both James and Whitehead religious education starts with the individual. If there is a mystical germ in most of us, as James believed, the pupil needs to be helped to recognize it. It may be so vague and unconscious that it is difficult to identify, especially when traditional language clutters it with confusion. But the pupil can be helped to discern ways in which religious language points to the MORE. Such language may be found in the practices of religious groups where "the relation may be either moral, physical, or ritual."[70] We can work backward from the experiments with language to the mystical germ at the center of one's consciousness.

James's advice to teachers was clear.

> Don't preach too much to your pupils or abound in the abstract. Lie in wait rather for the practical opportunities, be prompt to seize them as they pass, and thus at one operation get your pupil both to think, to feel, and to do. The strokes of *behavior* are what give the new set to the character, and work the good habits into the organic tissue.[71]

Empirical theology can become the background for all of these theories, for they operate within human experience and offer a naturalistic approach to education. By making use of experience, observation, and reason, the contents of Christian belief can be examined and discussed. We learn what others think and believe, we are exposed to traditional beliefs and narratives, we learn the history of thought and events, memorize significant items from human history and the Bible, and proceed to choose according to our ability and with adequate criteria. Information and interpretation derived from expert scholarship may be accepted, but this is provisional and not indoctrination.

Furthermore, in examining the beliefs of pupils, we need to understand the evidence available to them. We accept the reasonableness of the believer on the basis of the believer's belief and the evidence available. The teacher, in such a situation, can accept the student's beliefs as they stand, but has the responsibility of providing access to further data. At this point, the teacher can introduce what humankind has found to be reasonable, thus increasing the reasonable beliefs of the students. As one is led into the further reaches

---

69. Miller, *Christian Nurture and the Church,* vii; Miller, *The Theory of Christian Education Practice,* 183.

70. James, *The Varieties of Religious Experience,* 31.

71. William James, *Talks to Teachers on Psychology: and to Students on Some of Life's Ideals* (New York: Henry Holt, 1899), 71; see "The Educational Philosophy of William James," in *Religious Education* (Fall 1991), 619-634.

of experience, new sources will become available, especially in the area of poetry, the arts, and religion. Each student will begin to think independently of the teacher and may reach new levels of insight, wisdom, and conviction. But like any good empiricist, the student will know that conceptual knowledge is always open to revision, although one's centering loyalty to God may endure.[72]

PRACTICE

Harold Rosen has applied Wieman's philosophy of creative interchange to the practice of religious education. In a carefully researched manner, he has brought out the implications of empirical theology for religious education. At points he differs from Wieman, and in his practical applications he makes good use of the writings of Sophia Fahs. In Wieman's thought, three basic categories stand out: process, which is exposure to creative interchange; content, which is a consideration of moral, cultural, and religious values; and outcome, leading to co-creativity with God.[73]

Little children are empiricists who want to touch, smell, and taste almost anything. Methods that are concrete are central. Kindergarten walks in gardens, parks, and touch museums or exhibitions are central to the teaching task. Classrooms are geared to touch and tell. Stories are about specific people, real or imaginary, whose experiences parallel theirs. They learn to communicate with other children and establish relationships that are positive. At this simple level, they are beginning to have experiences that can lead in time to an empirical theology. As they get older, these experiences become more complex and they become amenable to the use of words pointing to the same realities and processes. They begin to worship at various levels, they are exposed to the traditions of the church, they hear stories about Jesus and other portions of the Bible, they learn about empirical evidence for what we can believe, they learn about metaphors and models and that literal language may be misleading, they are given the opportunity to make commitments and to act on them in their daily lives. From then on as adults they are exposed to the same process repeatedly as they renew their commitments. But even when exposed to good educational procedures, many will reject these opportunities and withdraw. Or they will not understand religious language in this way and rebel against the whole traditional system.

Basic to all of this are relationships and dialogue. Following William James's radical empiricism that declares that relationships are as much a

---

72. Thomas F. Green, *The Activities of Teaching* (New York: McGraw-Hill, 1971), 102-106.

73. Rosen, *Religious Education and Our Ultimate Commitment,* xv. See Sophia Fahs, *Today's Children and Yesterday's Heritage* (Boston: Beacon Press, 1952); *Jesus: The Carpenter's Son* (Boston: Beacon Press, 1945).

part of experience as actual entities, a relationship theology starts with a definition of theology as "the truth about God in relation to persons."[74] It derives this in part from Horace Bushnell's treatment of the organic relations of human beings and God in his *Christian Nurture* and from Martin Buber's interpretation of *I and Thou*. Nurture takes place in community and the quality of life in such a community is crucial. This is where the church as a community of the Holy Spirit can be an effective supplement to what happens in other communities, including the family.

Thus we can speak of theology in the background and grace and faith in the foreground in religious education. Grace is unmerited and is part of the human and cosmic environment. Wieman's definition is: "The 'grace of God' would then be creative transformation become dominant in the life of" human beings.[75] The other side of grace is that God is affected by what human beings do. Grace then is the divine acceptance of what occurs among human beings, often issuing in forgiveness.[76]

Faith is a personal relationship, an attitude of trust and commitment to the reality or process that we call God. The atmosphere of family, school, church, and community is an essential element affecting what can occur in a learning situation. This affects positively or negatively what is learned.

Emerging or creative novelty becomes part of one's environment. Unexpected events occur due to chance. These occurrences become opportunities for seeking new values and achieving unexpected goals. They lead to new insights and the kind of education described by Ian Ramsey. Such education cannot really be planned, but the teacher can anticipate that some such opportunity will emerge and be ready for it.

The goals of such an educational process are in terms of discernment and commitment. If the learners are enabled to discern the processes of creative transformation and the community supports them as they face decisions in their own lives, the process may continue in spite of the opposition of other factors in the community and in the surrounding culture. And when learners experience alienation from the process or from other people, the healing power of God is available. "In Christ God was reconciling the world to himself" (2 Cor. 5:19, NRSV). Religious education contains elements of evangelism, for one purpose of the church is to lead those outside to faith in God as conceived by Christians. As long as such goals are sought by way of genuine dialogue, this is a natural way for human beings to behave.

Central to Christian thinking and education is the Bible. Although some stories appear to be simple enough, upon further thought the Bible presents immense difficulties. Its whole picture of the world stands in sharp contrast

---

74. Miller, *The Clue to Christian Education,* 7; Miller, *The Theory of Christian Education Practice,* 157.

75. Wieman, *The Source of Human Good,* 49.

76. John B. Cobb Jr., in *Empirical Theology: A Handbook,* 254-257.

to the world of today. It seems to be an irrelevant antique. It might have some esoteric value for professional theologians, but for the average person it is an ancient artifact.

But behind these difficulties, the Bible, when it is treated as literature that is alive, becomes a book of choice. It offers a challenge to the believer to choose between life and death, between the claims of Christ and the satisfaction of the self. The themes of everyday life appear through the pages of the Bible, often in strange and foreign concepts reflecting a prescientific view of the world. But the constant is the unfolding of human relations and God.[77] Theodore Wedel wrote that "a child can understand the love story of redemption of the Bible . . . if interpreted by the language of relationships."[78]

Early studies in the psychology of religious development lead to the concept of a child's "growing edge." Knowing the level of a child's overall growth helped the teacher to tailor the relationships, methods, and concepts within reach of that age-level. Later this approach was refined by the studies of Jean Piaget, Ronald Goldman, Lawrence Kohlberg, and James Fowler, so that we can speak of stages of growth as well as age-group capabilities. Although empirically based, these findings are general guidelines and do not necessarily fit every pupil.[79] There is a time for the content of the Bible to be studied, but it comes at a later time than common practice indicates. The Bible can be studied with empirical and historical methods and then be made applicable to today's world for both children and adults alike.[80]

The problem of method for religious education based on empirical theology is that any method can be used if it furthers good relationships that extend to nature, animals, other human beings, and ultimately to the cosmos. If education is to be God-centered, empirical theology will point to God as working through creative transformation resulting from creative interchange. Given this mandate, it is difficult to outlaw any method that brings people and nature together

Method needs to be guided by the rhythm of learning. Whitehead made this clear in the first pages of *Aims of Education*, where he opposed the teaching of inert ideas. He claimed that we should teach few subjects and do it thor-

---

77. Miller, *The Theory of Christian Education Practice*, 198-202.

78. Theodore Wedel, "Leadership Education," *World Christian Education* (Spring 1952), 31.

79. For earlier treatments of "the growing edge" see Randolph Crump Miller, *A Guide for Church School Teachers* (Louisville: Cloister Press, 1943, 1947), 8, 20, 27, 41, 76, 102; see Craig Dykstra and Sharon Parks, eds., *Faith Development and Fowler* (Birmingham, Ala.: Religious Education Press, 1986); Brenda Munsey, ed., *Moral Development, Moral Education, and Kohlberg* (Birmingham, Ala.: Religious Education Press, 1980); Kenneth Hyde, *Religion in Childhood and Adolescence* (Birmingham, Ala.: Religious Education Press, 1990); John H. Peatling, *Religious Education in a Psychological Key* (Birmingham, Ala.: Religious Education Press, 1981).

80. See Miller, *The Theory of Christian Education Practice*, 197-211.

oughly. "By utilizing an idea, I mean relating it to that stream compounded of sense perceptions, feelings, hopes, desires, and of mental activities adjusting thought to thought, which forms our life."[81]

Whitehead was operating within the limits of empirical method as he described the three stages in the rhythm of education. With every new entry into an educational area, the learner starts with romance, moves on to precision when romance has achieved its purpose, and then moves to generalization. But even in the stage of romance there can be difficult learning goals, as when the infant learns to speak. He wrote:

> No part of education has more to gain from attention to the rhythmic law of growth than has moral and religious education. Whatever be the right way to formulate religious truths, it is death to religion to insist on a premature stage of precision. The vitality of religion is shown by the way in which the religious spirit has survived the ordeal of religious education.[82]

The sense of value is the key to the motive power in both religion and art, leading to the sense of beauty. This sense of value leads to rising to new heights as a result of great labors. There is an inner discipline, "and the fruition is the outcome of our own initiative."[83]

Empirical theology, whether it is found in Wieman or Meland or elsewhere, leads to a similar theory of educational practice. Each person becomes one's own theologian. John Cobb Jr., has written *Becoming a Thinking Christian*, in which he challenges lay people to build their own theologies based on their understanding of experience.[84] It is the only way to avoid having a second hand theology and education, for ultimately each believer must develop one's own belief system and faith.

CONCLUSION

The future of religious education, from the point of view of empirical theology, depends on our ability to speak of God in ways that those who hear will understand in terms of their own experiences. This means being aware of the particular culture and assumptions about the nature of reality that the listener brings to the dialogue, and the capacity of the teacher to move within those limits. In a pluralistic culture there will be a rich variety of assumptions, and perhaps naturalistic theism as it develops from empirical methods will be an option for only a minority. Religious education will be

---

81. Alfred North Whitehead, *The Aims of Education* (New York: Free Press, 1929), 3.
82. Ibid., 39.
83. Ibid.
84. See John B. Cobb Jr., *Becoming a Thinking Christian* (Nashville: Abingdon, 1993). Appended to each chapter is a series of three questions aimed at helping a lay person to think theologically.

effective in so far as it enlightens those who are facing life situations. They have basic needs for love and acceptance, for some degree of structure and discipline in their lives, for the opportunity and freedom to grow, and some satisfaction about the sense of mystery in their lives.[85] The people will become dull of hearing if they are fed inert ideas. Concepts come alive and commitments arise from experience, as in a worshiping congregation, in mutually sustaining dialogue, in the solitariness where one's "mystic germ" is awakened, and in relationships with others and God in an "I-Thou" relationship. All such experiences are forms of creative interchange that lead to creative transformation, which is God at work. The priority of God in the grace-faith relationship is essential in leading us to beliefs that strengthen our commitments and undergird our actions.[86]

---

85. See Miller, *The Theory of Christian Education Practice,* 232-234; Howe, *Man's Need and God's Action,* 79-141.

86. My own position is broader than the strict empiricism I have described, for I make use of most of the insights of process theology as well. See the first two chapters of my *The Theory of Christian Education Practice,* which outlines my own approach to theology as basic to religious education.

CHAPTER SEVEN

Existentialist Theology and Religious Education

DAVID F. WHITE AND FRANK ROGERS

Part One

What is truth? How do you come to know it? These are questions that have worn many philosophical costumes in the theater of history, each robed interlocutor upstaging the last with suspicion and drama. Existentialism was one such minstrel, albeit a dreadfully challenging one, joining in the drama of seeking authentic truth. With the bankruptcy of philosophy to posit an objective, external Reality that could be known through reason (e.g., Locke), or experience (e.g., Hume), or some constructive combination of the two (e.g., Kant), existentialists raised the threatening possibility that, as far as humanity can know it, there is no objective reality that defines the essence of humanity and truth. They suggested further that knowing, itself, arises from the subjectivity of the self. Knowing is not conforming to an external Reality; it is rather, a self, standing face to face with the abyss of a meaningless universe and choosing, with decisiveness and freedom, to create one's own meaning. Figures such as Martin Heidegger, Jean-Paul Sartre, Karl Jaspers, Franz Kafka, and Albert Camus were radically challenging the Absoluteness of external truth and redefining the very concept of the essence of human knowing.

Of course, irony abounds when one tries to capture the essence of a philosophical system for whom truth eludes any external construction. As Walter Kaufmann states,

172

> Existentialism is not a philosophy but a label for several widely different revolts against traditional philosophy. Most . . . "existentialists" have repudiated this label . . . Certainly, existentialism is not a school of thought nor reducible to any set of tenets.[1]

Indeed existentialism as a loose constellation of thinkers has included theologians, artists, playwrights, politicians, and revolutionaries. Existentialism is more truly a spirit in which one relates to history and truth. Recognizing the slipperiness of this spirit and diversity of individual thinkers, it may be possible to establish a loose set of common tenets which usually reference existentialism.

In this chapter, we will discuss first those tenets of philosophical existentialism and then describe theistic appropriations of this philosophical spirit.

MAJOR TENETS OF EXISTENTIALISM

Existence Precedes Essence. Common to existentialists is the recognition of the limitations of rationality in finding any ultimacy or certainty. In the idealism of Plato there existed a realm of ideals to which everything in the temporal plane corresponded. A thing's essence is defined by the ideal. Knowing the truth entails knowing its objective essence. Rationalism sought a way from the temporal realm to the ideal world of essential truth through the path of reason.

Existentialists questioned the existence of such an ideal truth and the centrality of reason in coming to know it. For them, the human subject is not only self-evidently involved in every act of knowing; this subjectivity is the realm in which truth is known. The essence of things in the world cannot be found through appeal to an outside or metaphysical realm, only through the subjective participation in the world. Without this subjective dimension, the existence of the individual is denied by lifeless conformity to some objective, and arbitrary, construction of reality. The seriousness of the problem can be illustrated in a scene from Sartre's novel, *Nausea,*

> Bluish objects pass the windows . . . blue this great yellow brick house advancing uncertainly, trembling, suddenly stopping and taking a nose dive. . . . [It] starts up again, it leaps against the windows . . . it rises, crushing. . . . It slides along the car brushing past it. . . . Suddenly it is no longer there, it has stayed behind. . . . I lean my hand on the seat but pull it back hurriedly: It exists. This thing I'm sitting on, leaning my hand on, is called a seat. They make it purposely for people to sit on, they took

---

1. Walter Kaufmann, *Existentialism From Dostoevsky to Sartre* (New York: Meridian Books, 1962), 11.

leather, springs and cloth, they went to work with the idea of making a
seat and when they finished, that was what they had made. . . . I murmur:
"It's a seat," a little like an exorcism. But the word stays on my lips: it
refuses to go and put itself on the thing. It stays what it is, with its red
plush, thousands of little red paws in the air, all still, little dead paws. This
enormous belly turned upward, bleeding, inflated . . . is not a seat. It could
just as well be a dead donkey . . . . It seems ridiculous to call them seats or
to say anything at all about them; I am in the midst of things, nameless
things. Alone, without words, defenseless, they surround me, are beneath
me, behind me, above me. They demand nothing, they don't impose themselves: they are there.[2]

In this passage, Roquetin has realized that all objective and essential "knowing" depends on assigning names and conceptualizations to objects such as
"house" and "seat." Without these projected names and concepts the objective world becomes a stream of mere appearances. For existentialists, the
symbolic process whereby humans give meaning to things is suspended and
called into question. The existentialists have called into question the ability
of reason or any other authority be it science, society, the church, or another conventional construction of how the essential world "truly" is to perceive any objective reality apart from this stream of color and sensation. In
this world everything is absurd. Any meaning that we might assign will be
purely arbitrary or according to social convention. There is no ultimate reason or authority which compels one to choose one word over another, or
one action over another. In another passage from *Nausea* Roquetin reflects
on the possibility of meaningful action,

I feel as though I could do anything. For example, stab this cheese knife
into [another diner's] eye. After that, all these people would trample me and
kick my teeth out. But that isn't what stops me: a taste of blood in the
mouth instead of this taste of cheese makes no difference to me.[3]

Nothing can be known in its essence by appeal to a heavenly or ideal realm.
Meaning is not written into the nature of things. Authentic existence of the
self only exists in the subjective participation with history. Indeed, existence
precedes the essence of things. There is no pure essence of reality. Authentic
constructions of the essence of things are already subjectively and arbitrar-
ily determined by human existence.

The Human Responsibility for Decision. And to know truly entails
coming into existence as free individuals who then posit their own meaningful
reality. Consequently, great stress is placed on human responsibility in the

---

2. Jean Paul Sartre, *Nausea*, trans. L. Alexander (New York: New Directions, 1959),
168, 169.
3. Ibid., 166.

knowing process. Humanity chooses its own constructions of reality. We are not passive clay to be imprinted. On the contrary, we select out and put together "life-worlds." Out of the total universe in any length of moment we choose and relate to some things—those most interesting, most determinative of our fate at any given moment. Out of all of this we form our world which is meaningful for us. The principle of intentionality is central. Humans who understand themselves and the world properly discover the import of decision making. There is, after all, no ultimate necessity for dependence upon any world of ideals, or artificial social convention. What is determinative is our boldness in taking responsibility for decision making. Existence precedes essence. We are in the task of becoming through our decisions.

Existential Individualism. In existentialism, the individual, undetermined by social authority, rises to a central position in subjectively engaging with the world. An individual comes into authentic existence only through taking responsibility for one's own life-project unfettered by any social authority. Consequently, each person's mode of existence is utterly unique. As Kierkegaard proclaimed, "My category is the individual."[4] It was to this individualism which Jaspers attests when he realizes that no person can die another person's death for them. There is no general mold from which all persons are cast. A person comes to know oneself only through living one's own life and continually reflecting upon it. With Kierkegaard's metaphor, humanity is cast in a sea 70,000 fathoms deep with no external support. One either sinks in the morass of unreflective social conventionality or one chooses for oneself to swim one's own route, creating a meaningful life only in the decisions and directions one chooses for oneself.

The Wondrous Quality of Being. Given the radical individualism of existentialism can there be any discussion of authentic existence over and against inauthentic existence? Existentialists approach this by arguing that authentic existence, truly "being" is defined by the subjective quality of being rather than conformity to an external ideal of authenticity. Consider this illustration by W.T. Jones,

> If John, who does not love Mary asks, "Why should I love Mary?" we cannot tell him. Suppose we point out that she is beautiful. He will reply, "Yes, I suppose she is, but why all the bother about beauty?" And so for anything else about Mary that we might mention in an attempt to persuade him that Mary is lovable. But if he falls in love with Mary, the situation is wholly different. Then (the same applies to) the answer to the question of Being. It is not a question that we first understand and then later seek to answer. We cannot even begin to understand without already being able to

---

4. Carl Michalson, *Christianity and the Existentialists* (New York: Scribner's, 1956), 12.

answer it. That is, we cannot understand why we should wonder at Being without already wondering at it. And when we do wonder at Being, the question does not arise; the wonderability of Being shines before us. Now for Heidegger, to be human is simply to be open to the presence of Being, and the mark of one's openness to Being is one's amazement.[5]

Heidegger's understanding of authentic participation in the world betrays an almost mystical relationship that other existentialists may temper.

However, we find something of this theme of wonder in Martin Buber's conception of the I-Thou relationship. In its counterpart, the I-It relationship, a person or situation is abstracted and dealt with as objects. In these I-It relationships, people

> relate to things by looking at them, examining them, testing them. Things are measured, taken apart, and put back together again and thus comprehended. . . . To this end the observer makes a conscious effort to put a distance between himself and the thing he seeks to know. He seeks to keep his feelings and wishes from disrupting his perception. This type of knowing, exalted to a sophisticated technique, is the basis of modern science. On a less self-conscious level, it is the way men generally relate to the things and persons with whom they live.[6]

According to Buber, the I-Thou relationship is more difficult to describe. If all of a person is in it, there is nothing left over to watch what is going on so that they can later record it. Only as each remains fully present can the relationship exist. Speaking of the I-Thou relationship, Eugene Borowitz says,

> Love is a good analogy. Love is that mysterious capacity which enables two persons in the most intimate communion to remain themselves. Indeed, in their love they truly become themselves. The sign of true love is what it makes of the lovers. In love each realizes more fully the self he has been seeking as, through his beloved, the person he always knew he was he now more truly is. Such an I-Thou experience may be intimate and exalting. What is given in the I-Thou relations is the presence of the other to oneself. That is all but it is incomparably significant.[7]

Buber, of course makes ultimate claims about the nature of "finding God in the hyphen." Heidegger and other atheistic existentialists merely speak of the passionate engagement of Being in which amazement and wonder shine through. The common theme is that the quality of subjective being itself

---

5. Jones, vol 5., 290.

6. Eugene B. Borowitz, *A Layman's Introduction to Religious Existentialism* (Philadelphia: Westminster, 1975), 167.

7. Ibid., 172.

bears its own self-authenticating meaning. Knowing is choosing to be in and sustained by this self-defining moment.

The Abiding Sense of Anxiety. According to Heidegger, the human project cannot be fully realized apart from the realization of the finitude of human existence. Death is an ever-present anticipated and acknowledged end of humanity. It is in facing death that finiteness and history become clear. A life mired in convention seeks to avoid this reality of death and meaninglessness, remaining sealed in constructions of meaning that deny death's threat. With this ever-present fear of death, humans must appropriate this death by anticipating its futurity and making it a part of the present. In so doing we gain "freedom toward death." This death impinges upon our every act and thought.

The thing that points to death as a constant reality is anxiety. Anxiety is defined as a fear with no concrete object. This anxiety is a way in which our encounter with Being as such is expressed. This anxiety cannot be subdued nor should it be. Heidegger believes that our openness to anxiety enables us to transcend it. It is this anxiety which calls us to engagement with Being and decision making.[8]

Existentialism is based upon the supposition that to exist is to face the conditions of our lives which generate these anxieties about our being. According to Michalson,

> Moods have been traditionally traced back to weaknesses in man which life in the body forces upon him. A rational man, it is thought, would rise above his moods. But the existential man immerses himself in his moods to find within them a trustworthy index to reality. These moods are not the accidental product of his nervous system but a revelatory reading in his existence. . . . To exist is to take seriously these messages from deep within oneself.[9]

Authenticity confronts this sense of dread and creates meaning without suppressing either the anxiety or the reality of nothingness.

The Role of Passion in Knowing. Kierkegaard defines truth as "an objective uncertainty held fast in an appropriation process of the most passionate inwardness."[10] Kierkegaard explains that the process of rational thinking seeks to find objective truth. However, when thinking is that of an existing human being, objective truth is brought into a paradoxical relationship. Every objectivity is also an uncertainty from the standpoint of the subject. In full consciousness of its uncertainty humans are called to act. In the midst of this tension, passion emerges. This passion is an inherent part of authentic

---

8. Erich Dinkler, "Martin Heidegger," in *Christianity and the Existentialists* (New York: Scribner's, 1956), 107.

9. Michalson, *Christianity and the Existentialists*, 11.

10. Louis Mackey, "Kierkegaard and the Problem of Existential Philosophy," in *Essays on Kierkegaard*, ed. Jerry H. Gill (Minneapolis: Burgess, 1969), 45.

existence. Without it, thinking degenerates into abstraction and action becomes unreflective and arbitrary. Passion or, for Søren Kierkegaard, "passionate inwardness" emerges from and sustains paradoxical dynamics of the tension between thought and action. As Louis Mackey observes,

> Only an examined life is worth living, but without passion, the examined life easily ceases to be life at all and slips into an indefinite parenthesis of reflection. Thought and action must be held together in existence by passion.[11]

Philosophical existentialism has wielded enormous influence in the twentieth century industrial-technical milieu where people are treated as things and humanity melds together in a great apathetic mass. Existentialism calls humanity to step from behind the myths wrapped in silver which stick like confections to one's teeth. Existentialism calls us to take responsibility for our decisions. It entices us with the taunt that we can be whatever we make of ourselves. Our dreams lie before us. However, the dark side of freedom is the dread, anxiety, and fear of ultimate absurdity. According to Carl Michalson,

> Existentialism nurses an aching void, keeps the wound of man open until an authentically healing agency can be applied. Existentialism sponsors what the poet Holderlin called "a holy emptiness" which turns its atheism into a wistful stretching out for reality, a noumenal hunger, a movement of the spirit which keeps a sensitive openness upward toward God who must reveal Himself if He is to be known. What some reject as straw in existentialism may yet turn out to be a sound philosophical yearning, a yearning for a redemption to which no philosophy is either virginal or divine enough to give birth. Can the language of philosophy ever mount higher—ought it ever, need it ever mount higher than the existential passion in the porous verse of the young Nietzsche,
> "I want to know you, Unknown One,
> You who are reaching deep into my soul
> And ravaging my life, a savage gale.
> You inconceivable yet related one!
> I want to know you—even serve."[12]

THEISTIC EXISTENTIALISM

If atheistic existentialism has ignited bonfires with the ways in which humanity has ambitiously constructed meaning and guilded it with false certainty, then theistic existentialism has, alternatively, passed to us tablets of passionate religious insight. The deconstructive insight of existentialism has made the path straight from Søren Kierkegaard to the likes of Martin

---

11. Ibid., 46.
12. Michalson, *Christianity and the Existentialists*, 21, 22.

Buber, Paul Tillich, Abraham Heschel, Rudolf Bultmann, and others. It would be helpful to explore how the impact of existentialism has become woven with theology. The question implicitly asked and answered will be: How does religion proceed without certainty about an objective reality? From whence does religious truth come? Or to return to Kierkegaard's analogy: Where does one find solid rock in an ocean 70,000 fathoms deep?

Religious existentialists have affirmed that no grand system of dead orthodoxy or political ideology can stand oppressively over us as human subjects. We are indeed cast baselessly adrift in a meaningless sea of existence. Religious existentialists affirm that, indeed, we are in process of becoming—of incarnating into our essence. And in this process we must have courage to decide and choose our own authentic existence. Religious existentialism agrees that we choose our meanings from the web of existence before which we stand. However, religious existentialists enlarge our awareness of the reality before which we stand. We find ourself making meaning in relationship with nature, other people, the symbols of culture, the religious symbols of faith, the sacred texts, and the Ground of Being. The encounter with this great web of being is always an immediate experience of, and not primarily in relation to, abstracted doctrines. Our discussion will now extend to the question of how religious existentialists have conceived their relation to the main tenets of existentialism discussed earlier.

Existence Precedes Essence. Søren Kierkegaard accurately perceived the deadness of Christian Orthodoxy and vast overarching philosophical and political systems. He sought a religious faith that engaged him passionately. The faith Kierkegaard sought would be found only within one's own existence. Existence precedes essence. Other religious existentialists embraced the insight of Kierkegaard in various ways.

Rudolf Bultmann illustrates the priority of existence in his distinctive discussion of "authentic existence." In Bultmann's existential theology, humans are always in search of their essentiality. This may take the form of God, or fortune, or success, but it is always the questions humans ask about themselves. Bultmann says, "The question of God and the question of myself are identical."[13] Bultmann insisted that the existential situation of humanity is described in precisely the same fundamental manner in the New Testament and in the modern philosophy (existentialism). Both the New Testament and Heidegger spoke of the two modes of human existence. The New Testament spoke of the "unbelieving, unredeemed" existence based on what is immediately at hand, visible and tangible. The unbelieving human seeks to "attain to the future and to his essentiality by his own means and therefore having it under his own control."[14] The unbelieving person depends on what is tangi-

---

13. Heinz Zahrnt, *The Questions of God: Protestant Theology in the Twentieth Century* (New York: Harcourt, Brace and World, 1966), 228.

14. Ibid., 230.

ble and becomes enslaved to fear. Unbelieving persons attempt to achieve essentiality by their own efforts without relationship to God. On the other hand, the "believing, redeemed" person "abandons all security created by himself and bases his life on what is invisible and intangible."[15]

The believing persons understand themselves as God's creation and receive life as a gift. Such persons are set free from their own strife and security seeking. These persons are opened up to a future which is not of death, but of life. This way in which the New Testament understands the human situation is in Bultmann's view identical to Heidegger's categorization of inauthentic and authentic existence. In Heidegger's existentialism, "inauthenticity" is characterized by a human life-project, unreflectively assuming its direction from other people and their individual projects. Authenticity is characterized by a life-project which is self-consciously grounded only in its own volition. Bultmann's reading of the New Testament suggests that only a person freed by God's love can truly be in touch with authentic humanity. This is not, however, a human achievement but an encounter with Jesus Christ. Bultmann says,

> Only those who are loved are capable of loving. Only those who have received the gift of trust can show trust in others. Only those who have encountered self-commitment become capable of self-commitment. . . . It means that at the very point where man can do nothing, God steps in and acts—indeed he has acted already—on man's behalf.[16]

What is the source of this existential encounter with Jesus Christ? Bultmann, like other existentialists, eschews a body of doctrine which objectify us and reign sovereign over us. In Bultmann's thinking, Jesus was raised into life into the kerygma—the core of Christian truth. We as humans existentially encounter the word of God in the person of Jesus Christ—in the kerygma.

Human Responsibility for Decision. How do the existentialist theologians find a place to stand in the depths of absurdity? For Kierkegaard this place of certainty was absolutely not in reason. For him the quest for meaning comes down to a matter of faith. One had to simply decide by an act of volition to jump across the chasm.

Abraham Heschel speaks about one way of knowing God through "doing—a leap of action." In the risk of doing, humans know themselves to be responding to God's desires. "The final stage of human religiosity is learning to make God's need man's own, to want to the point of continual doing what God wants."[17] Hence for Heschel, Judaism as a particular way of life is authorized by its continued response to the revelation in relationship with God.

---

15. Ibid., 230.
16. Ibid., 233.
17. Borowitz, *Layman's Introduction to Religious Existentialism*, 156.

For Paul Tillich, the gulf of meaning has been bridged by God. There is both a subjective side of revelation, without which there is no revelation, and an objective side consisting of God's revealing of God's self. These two "correlate" in the concrete symbols of Christian religion. Without religion there is no revelation. In Tillich's existential theology, the New Being— Jesus Christ calls us ever in an act of will to have "courage to be." This is similar to Kierkegaard's "appropriation," and Bultmann's "authenticity" in that they call for decision toward selfhood and being. To decide is central to an existential theology.

Existential Individualism. Religious existentialism departs from Sartre's image of the lonely existentialist before the abyss. While we ultimately are left to ourselves in our life-project making, the very means to coming into selfhood is in relationship. Even my body is defined in distinction to and relation with the air surrounding it. Martin Buber suggests that the "many" are essential for the "one" to come into being. A person in a void has no possibility of becoming. In contrast to the lonely existentialism of Sartre, Buber knows that it is only in relationship that we really can know what our human project is about. For Buber, this takes form in the Covenant Jewish community. As suggested by Borowitz, Buber, in fine existentialist style, does not appeal to religious codes or a body of objective theology, instead he appeals to the personal I-Thou relationship between human and God, human and human, and humanity and all of reality.

Science has determined to transform the "I-Thou into the I-It, dogmatizing that anything which cannot be explained in terms of I-It is not really known or worthy of reliance."[18] Buber is adamant in defense of the person, the individual, the subject in an age of pressures toward objectification. The I-Thou speaks of the full legitimacy of the reality inherent in the universe.

Furthermore, God is known and accompanies all of our genuine knowing of other people. In our authentic confrontations we meet as three, for God is present. One does not prove God except by meeting with God. One does not prove other persons except by meeting and living with them. "That is why those who place certainty above all else cannot love and therefore cannot really live."[19] Religious language therefore is evocative rather than descriptive, a word world that the author can only hint at.

At any rate, the religious existentialists have always proclaimed the importance of recognizing ourselves in relation as also seen in Tillich's dipolar conception of selfhood. One pole is in the web of relationships; the other is our individual selfhood. As we are in relation we are more able to authentically define ourselves. This insight is typical of religious existentialism.

The Wondrous Quality of Being. While for Heidegger Being held a wondrous quality, for religious existentialists this became identified with

---

18. Ibid., 129.
19. Ibid., 133.

God. Similar to Buber in regard to his extraordinary sensitivity to the wonder that inheres in all things, Abraham Heschel finds three ways to full religious truth. Religious truth can be found through nature, revelation, and the holy deed. Heschel, like Buber, suggested a relationship with existence generally, but for Heschel this takes on a wondrous and shimmering quality. Borowitz interprets Heschel,

> Modern man has made himself unnatural by training himself not to be amazed, by working hard at not responding to the world in awe. That is the root affliction of an age anxious to the point of personal paralysis and moral incapacity.[20]

Heschel believes that we need to recapture that radical amazement which is most basic to faith. He is not concerned with

> "the possession of learning, erudition, but the very act of study, of being overwhelmed by the marvel and mystery of God's creation."[21] According to Heschel, "Mankind will not perish for lack of information; it may collapse for want of appreciation."[22]

We see in his words that Heschel wants humanity to be sensitive and appreciative of the magnificence and mystery of the world. This is education for reverence of Being.

Paul Tillich, in a slightly different manner, affirms the wondrous quality of being. This can be seen in his epistemological attitude. Tillich suggests that "belief-ful realism" implies the proper attitude toward reality: it is able to penetrate its surface and see the divine ground and meaning of reality. According to Zahrnt,

> A particular epistemological attitude to reality is implied in belief-ful realism. In it, the subject-object dichotomy between man and reality is overcome. To know reality does not mean domination, but union; it is something which takes place not in the attitude of standing back from reality, but in participation in it; it requires not that one should analyze something into separate parts, but that one should allow oneself to be apprehended by the whole. Knowledge cannot be separated from experience. Only by intuition can one attain to that depth of reality, or rather, can one be apprehended by that depth of reality, in which its divine ground and meaning become visible.[23]

---

20. Ibid., 151.

21. Abraham J. Heschel, "Religion in a Free Society," *The Insecurity of Freedom* (New York: Farrar, Straus and Giroux, 1966), 20.

22. Ibid., 21.

23. Zahrnt, *Question of God*, 327.

Religious existentialism has consistently expressed the value in all of created and creating existence.

The Abiding Sense of Anxiety. For atheistic existentialism there is an abiding sense of anxiety or dread which impinges upon all living and becoming. The source of this dread and anxiety is the ultimate fate of death and non-being. For religious existentialists, meaningless is as well a dreadful state. Paul Tillich articulates the human situation in regard to anxiety. For Tillich, existentialism accurately depicts the nature of human tension or anxiety. Tillich suggests that existential anxiety has three types, "anxiety of fate and death," "anxiety of emptiness and meaninglessness," and the "anxiety of guilt and condemnation." In Tillich's system, God ("being-itself," "the ground and meaning of being," "depth," the "absolute," or the "unconditional") correlates with humanity's existential alienation from being. Religion is where these two realms meet and are joined by symbols which both express and participate in being. The most important symbol is Jesus Christ who is the New Being. In Jesus we see one who most perfectly has cojoined himself with the ground of being. He is true essential being. Salvation is therefore the act wherein the cleavage between humanity's essential being and its existential situation is overcome. Tillich interprets this salvation as a healing of the self in bringing essence and existence together. Creative existentialism gives humanity the strength to shoulder anxiety and meaninglessness and the courage to express creatively the situation of modern people.

The Role of Passion in Knowing. In much of philosophy passion has been segregated and ghettoized in the process of knowing. In modern Western thought, as descended from Enlightenment influence, the premium is put upon objective knowing much removed from passion. Passion is suspect. As mentioned earlier, Kierkegaard spoke of passion as the thing that holds together existence and essence. Much of this can be seen in the "love" metaphors used frequently in existentialism. Such conceptions of knowing suggest that partners who investigate their lovers, collecting facts and statistics, really do not know their lovers. Yet once one falls in love there is no need for the facts and statistics. Indeed, one who insists on pursuing certainty through objective knowing only deadens and dulls it for subjectivity.

In religious existentialism this takes a particularly interesting form. The passion of knowing is focused on a personal God. Bultmann articulates this in a way reminiscent of many other religious existentialists. He says that the authentic person is one who is freed for authentic existence only when freed by God's love. He states, "Only those who are loved are capable of loving. Only those who have received the gift of trust can show trust in others."[24] In loving encounter with the Divine we are freed to be in true loving relationship with all of existence. For Tillich and Bultmann, it is the person of Jesus

---

24. Ibid., 233.

the Christ who invites us into loving encounter.

For Buber and Heschel, the words "wonder," "amazement," and "reverence" capture some of the meaning behind the passionate embrace of religious knowing.

These are just a few of the ways in which some theologians have worked out their theology in an existentialist framework. It should be noted that there are similarities and profound differences among them.

Part Two

Existentialism and Education

For many Christian existentialists such as Tillich, Kierkegaard, the early Barth, etc., theology did not automatically insinuate a distinct approach to religious education. But for Jewish education the matter is different. Morton Fierman says of Abraham Heschel,

> Thoughts and language (of Abraham Heschel) can only be rooted in something beyond a philosophy of education. Indeed they are. They are part of the larger tradition of Heschel's faith, which is Judaism, and a segment too of his very personal *Weltanschauung*. Certainly to some extent it can be traced to the statement in Pirke-Avoth (*The Sayings of the Fathers*): "The world rests upon three pillars, upon learning, upon worship, and upon charity." As Heschel himself writes it, "learning meant having a share in divine wisdom."[25]

For Heschel, learning, worship, and charity are not means to an end but instead are ends in themselves. Heschel, in his paper, "Essay on Youth," given before the White House Conference on Children and Youth in 1960, summarized his contention with modern conceptions of learning,

> The Greeks learned in order to revere. The modern man learns in order to use, accepting the modern maxim which declares: "Knowledge is power." This is how people are urged to study: Knowledge means success. We no longer know how to justify any value except in terms of expediency. Man is willing to define himself as a "seeker after the maximum degree of energy." He equates value with that which avails. He feels, acts, and thinks as if the sole purpose of the universe were to satisfy his needs.[26]

---

25. Morton C. Fierman, "The Educational Philosophy of Abraham J. Heschel," *Religious Education* 64 (July-August 1969), 274.

26. Abraham J. Heschel, "Essay on Youth" (New York: Synagogue Council of America, 1960), 5.

Similarly, for Martin Buber his view of education is connected with his theology of creation. In Buber's view, humanity meets the Creator, the Eternal Thou in the temporal Thou, the Ancient of Days in the unique unrepeatable situation of the present. And according to Buber, "Human life touches on absoluteness in virtue of its dialogical character." So for Buber education is in itself a religious act. Educational theory was a natural development of these traditions.

In Christian religious education circles there are those who have consciously developed religious education theory from theological clues such as Lewis Sherrill who in his book *The Gift of Power* developed the educational implications of Paul Tillich's theology and Reuel Howe who developed the thoughts of Martin Buber in a Protestant Christian context in his book *The Miracle of Dialogue*.[27] Ross and Martha Snyder have implemented a consistent existentialist religious education theory in their meaning-making workshops and in the book *On Becoming Human*.[28] However, existentialism has generally appeared in religious educational theory in the forms of themes and particular influences (see for example Thomas Groome, Paulo Freire, and Mary Elizabeth Moore).

Existentialism calls for a distinct approach to religious education. Below are themes which suggest themselves for an existentialist approach.

The Purpose of Religious Education
Responsibility. In speaking of public education generally Van Cleve Morris suggests that one goal of an existentialist education would be *an authentic society where individuals take personal responsibility* for their own values and conventions. While it is admitted that Dewey and the Experimentalists advocated a theory of experience which moved considerably away from imposing an objective body of truth upon youth, ultimately in experimentalism learning values depend upon public rather than personal criteria. An existentialist education would remind people that they are "constantly, freely, baselessly, creatively choosing."[29] According to Morris,

> A youngster who becomes fully aware of himself as the shaper of his own life, aware of the fact that he must take charge of that life and make it his own statement of what a human being ought to be—this is the individual who has been brought beyond mere intellectual discipline, beyond mere subject matter, beyond mere enculturation, . . . to the exotic but supremely human zone . . . the zone of value creation where selves create their own selves beyond the reach of teacher and textbook.[30]

27. Lewis J. Sherrill, *The Gift of Power* (New York: Macmillan, 1955) and Reuel L. Howe, *The Miracle of Dialogue* (New York: Seabury, 1963).

28. Ross Snyder, *On Becoming Human* (New York: Abingdon, 1967).

29. Van Cleve Morris, *Existentialism in Education: What It Means* (New York: Harper & Row, 1966), 111.

30. Ibid., 111.

Appropriation. Another general feature of an education that would be existentialist in character is "the epistemology of appropriation."[31] Morris points out that the etymology of the word "appropriate" is traced to the meaning "*to make one's own*." In a typical educational context knowing means adopting ideas, attitudes, or points of view. For existentialism, learning takes on a different attitude. Rather than a mere cognitive understanding of a truth, learning entails a subjectively taking hold of and putting in one's own life. For example, a student must create a become responsible for the meaning of the French Revolution for her own life. In this way history, science, literature, etc., can become personally meaningful. A religious education could affirm these aims as well as public education.

Toward Selfhood. Another statement of purpose can be found in Lewis Sherrill's book, *The Gift of Power* in which he extracts clues from the theology of Paul Tillich. According to Tillich, humanity is alienated from self and each other and God. These are the underlying sources of the existential anxiety. In articulating a religious education from Tillich's theological clues, Sherrill suggests that *the nature of Christian education would be for the purpose of attaining selfhood*. He also states that, "As man encounters God, the nature of the responses which the self makes to the divine Self indicates the nature of the changes taking place in the depth of the human self."[32] A religious education would facilitate this encounter and encourage positive responses to God. This would enable healing of the self and Communion.

Future Orientation. In a discussion on educational alternatives, Buber suggests that Plato, Dewey, and himself offer different views of the future. Education from Plato's framework proceeds from a view of timeless truth, fixed and changeless. He indeed offers a goal of perfection to strive after in the future, but it is not in any way connected to the present existential situation. Dewey, on the other hand, emphasizes a view of life as changing, guided by intellectual action. He offers little connection to the future. Buber, offers an existential connection to the present and to the future. This concern frames his overall educational task. Quoting Lionel Etscovitz,

> Educationally speaking, a program is prophetic if it places before the student the opportunity to explore the future in terms of where he himself stands and what he himself can decide. Such a program may even include within it certain conditioning forces such as the goal-values of Plato. But the thrust of the program, if it is genuinely prophetic, must be to provide for human choice and change, human decision and transformation, both personal and communal.[33]

---

31. Ibid., 120.
32. Sherrill, *Gift of Power*, 157.
33. Lionel Etscovitz, "Religious Education as Sacred and Profane: An Interpretation of Martin Buber," *Religious Education*, 64 (July-August, 1969), 284.

Thus, a religious education so conceived would include a vision of possibility but must never lose sight of actuality. Such an approach would encourage a *dialogical inquiry into the future*—meeting rather than receiving the future.

Subject Matter. As generally conceived, the existentialist educational task would not be the discovery of subject matter but instead the discovery of responsibility! Learning in an existentialist mode would be the vivid awakening of the learner to the sense of being personally accountable for one's life.

Subjectivity or Interiority. Existentialist philosophers and theologians alike have discussed the situation of objectification of humanity. Existentialism suggests that in such a world we come to see ourselves also as things. An existentialist religious education awakens us to our subjectivity and thus value. Sartre starkly and dramatically emphasized human loneliness as "I." As subject, we are distinct from all existence—our essence unknown and uncertain.

Religious educators have emphasized instead our connectedness to all being. They have stressed that we only know who we are in relationship to God, to others, to the air around us and the ground beneath our feet. Religious educators have stressed exploring this relationality. However, there still remains the existential subjectivity which places responsibility and freedom firmly in our laps. A religious education conceived in this mode would not give information, or stuff the student with facts, but rather would evoke and awaken the student. Religious education in this mode would affirm, as Ross Snyder says, "incarnating in his life story. The Eternal birth which occurred at one point in history, must occur in him if he is to really exist."[34] "I" is the central reality of life. Psychological sciences, linguistic philosophy, and even Whiteheadian theology have taken the "I" out of their system and substituted various impersonal occasions or mechanisms.

As Snyder affirms, "To be an agent is to take an attitude toward what is happening, and participate in co-creating what will happen."[35] A religious education conceived in this mode would be concerned with awakening this consciousness.

Arousing Subjectivity. If a chief aim of existentialist religious education is an emerging selfhood, the question of how to arouse this sense of self arises. In correlation to the existentialist philosophy, any program of instruction would *cultivate an affective sensitivity*. In this scientific age where reason is cool and detached, passionate involvement is viewed negatively. But to the existentialist, involvement means the experience of "getting personally implicated in the situations of life."[36] According to the existentialists, our emotions have been neutralized by external criteria for value. Learning

34. Ross Snyder, "Toward Foundations of a Discipline of Religious Education," *Religious Education* 62 (September-October 1967), 400.

35. Ibid., 401.

36. Morris, *Existentialism in Education*, 116.

in the existentialist mode means being aroused by questions of value, good and bad. It means "awakening to the normative quality of experience—in a book, in a teacher's remark, in a classroom situation."[37] There are various ways in which existentialists envision this arousal of awareness.

Importance of Immediacy of Experience. Religious educators theorizing from an existentialist philosophical perspective agree with each other by and large in eschewing large, preformed, philosophical or theological ideologies. Therefore it is always important for meaning to be formed in the context of immediate experience with nature, self, God, and others. In these encounters, as one participates with another one grows in selfhood and understanding. Ross Snyder says,

> A new church begins with a vivid program of enlarging the area of experiencing, with more perceptions in situation (the only place you can get them), with more sensing. Away with word games played on Sunday morning. Away from all free-floating abstractions. For the first act is perception. And to "see" a world means to organize a felt-seen life world.[38]

For Snyder, experience is not limited to seeing or thinking but is a total body experience, he adds,

> Perception is by a total body—a bodied consciousness, a selfed body. Not by a disembodied spirit. But "body" is not merely physical; it is the all that we are, including the active residues of our expectancies, memories, ideas, feelings. Such body is mostly preconscious (and should remember that we are educating mainly a preconsciousness). But [is] also conscious. Man is not a dualism of unconscious and conscious—even though conflict may seal off certain clusters. Nor is he a dualism of body and self—though not all bodies are selfed (merely organic life, for instance). . . . There is an inner personal region which is an intending, a choosing, a taking attitudes toward what is happening.[39]

Abraham Heschel also conceives of the importance of immediate experience in religious education. He says,

> The secret of effective teaching lies in making a pupil a contemporary of the living moment of teaching. The outcome is not only the retention of the content of teaching but also of the moment of teaching.[40]

Heschel sees this immediacy in terms of the relationship not only of pupil and subject but pupil and teacher as well. He says, "It is not enough for the pupil to appropriate the subject matter, the pupil and the teacher must go through

---

37. Ibid., 119.
38. Snyder, "Foundations," 397.
39. Ibid.
40. Heschel, "Religion in a Free Society," 6.

significant moments, sharing insight and appreciation."[41] Heschel further explains that

> the teacher is not an automatic fountain from which intellectual beverages may be obtained. He is either a witness or a stranger. To guide a pupil into the promised land, he must have been there himself. . . . What we need more than anything else is not textbooks but text-people. It is the personality of the teacher which is the text that the pupils read; the text they will never forget.[42]

Such themes are also pervasive in Martin Buber, Reuel Howe, and other existentialist religious educators.

Religious Education as Dialogue. As noted many times in the course of this discussion, existentialism decries numbing external systems of thought as oppressive to the human situation. However, relationality has always been affirmed by existentialists as pregnant with potential meaning. Martin Buber's thinking has been the chief articulation of the value of dialogue in relationship with God, humans, and nature.

For Buber, God is not to be equated with a specific meaning. God is the presence of potential meaning and direction in life. Therefore, humanity meets God through relations with nature and especially with other humans. The failure to relate to humanity and nature thus becomes basic to humanity's failure to relate meaningfully to God. Buber says, "You cannot really love God if you do not love men, and you cannot really love men if you do not love God."[43] Buber's conception of the I-Thou dialogue between humans and all of existence is a theme central to an existentialist conception of religious education. According to George Kneller,

> A dialogue is a conversation between persons in which each person remains a subject for the other, a conversation, in Buber's terms, between an "I" and a "Thou." The opposite of a dialogue is an act of verbal manipulation or dictation in which one person imposes himself on another, turning the latter into an object of his will expressed in speech.[44]

Such a theoretical element suggests itself as a method as well as a general principle.

---

41. Ibid., 55.

42. Abraham J. Heschel, "The Spirit of Jewish Education," *Jewish Education* 24: 2 (Fall 1953), 9.

43. Martin Buber, *Hasidism and Modern Man* (New York: Harper Torchbooks, 1966), 233.

44. George F. Kneller, *Introduction to the Philosophy of Education*, 2nd ed. (New York: Wiley, 1964), 80.

Role of Community. Lewis Sherrill has defined religious education conceived in theological assumptions of Paul Tillich as

> the attempt, ordinarily by members of the Christian community, to participate in and to guide the changes which take place in persons in the relationships with God, with the Church, with other persons, with the physical world, and with oneself. The ends of such a religious education are . . . that persons might attain to increasing self-understanding and self-knowledge and an increasing realization of their own potentialities; and that they might sustain the relationships and responsibilities of life as children of God.[45]

Sherrill agrees with the other theorists of existentialist religious education that within the faith community there is profound encounter where God as Spirit is present as participant. Religious education as means to the end of community is involved, according to Sherrill, with introducing other persons to Christian community, to the Bible and Christian heritage, and should prepare the way for personal response to revelation of God, as well as participating in purposeful action and counseling with participants during periods of crisis.[46] In existentialist religious education the faith community is the hothouse for meaning making. In this context of care and encounter one finds symbols, myths, ideas, and stories which help one make meaning in one's own life.

Practices of Religious Education Generated by Existentialism

Responding to an existentialist religious education theory, whose fundamental insight is the inherent responsibility of the subject to appropriate meaning, certain practices suggest themselves for consideration in an existentialist approach to religious education.

Curriculum. Generally, whatever curriculum might be chosen would be specifically related to an individual's unique project. In other words, curriculum would be available for appropriation by individuals. Currently in contemporary conventional curricula, a few possibilities which suggest use for an existentialist education would be *music, dance, drama, creative writing, painting, etc.* These subjects encourage self-expression. Such artistic products should be the authentic expression of what a student sees in his own world. These subjects most naturally "awaken decision-making awarenesses in the learner."[47] In traditional educational philosophy there is a serious body of knowledge which takes priority over the learner. If this serious content is seen as somehow written into the nature of reality then it must certainly be mastered.

---

45. Sherrill, *Gift of Power*, 82-83.
46. Ibid., 85.
47. Morris, *Existentialism in Education*, 125.

By contrast, *extracurricular experiences* are undertaken in a much different attitude. According to Morris, they are technically speaking, "play." They are undertaken on the student's own terms. The student outranks the subject matter in importance. Morris suggests that "play, like Kierkegaard's irony, releases subjectivity."[48] In such activity we find students feverishly studying history, math, science because it fits in with their subjective project.

The Role of Teacher. Regarding existentialist pedagogy, two approaches suggest themselves as suitable for teaching for the goal of subjectivity in the context of freedom from objective truth. One is the *Socratic method of inquiry*. Another approach is less of a teaching style than an attitude and is found in the I-Thou *dialogue proposed by Martin Buber*. In Socrates' approach, to students he incessantly asked questions (enough to infuriate the fellow citizens so they finally sentenced him to death) of people. Although he sometimes asked questions to which he knew the answers, as in *The Meno* when by artful inquiry he got an ignorant slave boy to formulate the Pythagorean theorem, his chief method and posture was as the "seeker after truth" as he sought answers to questions to which he was as ignorant as fellow learners. Socratic inquiry does not approach the student with ready-made answers which the teacher manipulates onto the subjective plane of the learner. An existentialist doctrine requires that the subjectivity of the learner be respected and indeed cultivated. In this method the existentialist teacher is always seeking for new appropriations of truth for herself.

Although similar to the Socratic method in a desire to respect the subjectivity of the student, Buber's dialogue requires a different role for the teacher. Buber not only opposed personal tyranny in the classroom but also opposed tyranny of impersonal knowledge. If knowledge was construed as an objective body to be learned then the role of the teacher was simply as mediator passing on the subject matter to the learners. In this traditional role the teacher as well as the students are devalued.

> The teacher, Buber said, must familiarize himself fully with the subject he teaches, and take it into himself as the rich fruit of human activity. When the teacher has made the subject . . . a part of his inner experience, he can present it to the pupil as something issuing from himself. Then teacher and pupil can meet as persons because the knowledge the teacher offers is no longer something extended to him but an aspect of his own condition.[49]

This role of teacher rests on trust and honesty as well as vulnerability. The teacher must be willing to approach students as co-equal human subjects

---

48. Ibid., 131.
49. Kneller, *Philosophy of Education*, 81.

and allow them to reject or accept the offerings of the teacher.

In sum, the fundamental insight of existentialism is that in order for a "fact" of science, history, literature, etc., to have meaning the student must first have a life trajectory, or at least a launching point. Otherwise, facts are compiled as in an encyclopedia irrelevant to the life of the student. Kierkegaard used to say that you cannot learn from history until you have a life, an existence, of your own against which to judge history.[50] History is no better judge than contemporary human society. Nothing can claim a position of sovereignty except the baseless subject aware of what is going on in his own life project.

Religious Education as Meaning Making. Religious education in the existentialist mode envisions for itself the task of *"midwife," facilitating the making of meanings*. In Sherrill, this task is primarily seen in terms of encounter with the symbols and biblical stories of God's revelation. These symbols, themes, and stories become the means of communication and interpretation of reality and making meaning for one's life. For Martin Buber, the Hasidic tales become the means for this meaning-making task.

The religious educator who has perhaps remained most consistently within the realm of existential construction of being is Ross Snyder. He uses an approach which he calls, "ministry of meanings." According to Snyder,

> We are battered by the flood of programmed sensations from ceaseless masscomm, by the omnipresent sounds and movement of megalopolis, by intense awareness of worldwide history-making going on every day, man needs "organizers." Myths, images, a few ideas, which enable him to comprehend and order the multiplicity and chaos into pattern, habitat, meaningful world. . . . So the second great thrust of phenomenology is toward what we call a ministry of meanings. We cannot give another person a meaning, for the essence of meaning is felt significance.[51]

In Snyder's meaning-making workshops he led people in guided experiences of listening to and responding to, for example, stories such as of Bonhoeffer's life experience. Response to these encounters takes the form of artistic expression and ultimately the appropriation of meanings. He says,

> An . . . implication is that Christians are meant to create culture forms. And we better embark wholeheartedly on our vocation. For without meanings processed into compelling "art" forms, we are leaving contemporary man in the lurch, and prodigal to the essential task the religious leader is to perform for civilization.[52]

50. Morris, *Existentialism in Education*, 141.
51. Snyder, "Foundations," 398.
52. Ibid., 399.

Snyder's Institute for Meaning Formation is designed to foster interiority. In small groups participants write essays about their lives and share with interpretation in the groups. Mary Elizabeth Moore has summarized Snyder's steps through which participants are led:

> 1) lived moment—discussing an experience significant to the person; 2) psychohistory—a record of several lived moments during a period of time, along with the feelings that were part of these moments; 3) manifesto—a record of a time when the person risked self; and 4) saga—an account of the person's own life journey with the holy or "wild energies of God." As these essays are shared, participants are invited to reflect with their group ultimately helping each other give birth to meaning and reflecting on the decisions and strengths that sustain each person through difficult times.[53]

According to Snyder, humanity needs myth, symbol, models of existence as tools to help us criticize what is here and to envision a new future. Humanity draws symbol, myth, and ritual from culture and creates symbol, ritual, myth for culture's use. These symbols are birthed directly from experience, dialogue, and reflection.

Congenial Methods. In *Teaching from the Heart*, Mary Elizabeth Moore explores methodology appropriate for such an organic existence. The five educational methods she explores seem to be congenial to an existentialist religious education. The methods are case study method, Gestalt method, phenomenology, narrative method, and conscientization. While Moore is a process theologian, these methods could with some modification be quite compatible with existentialist methodology.

The methods exemplified in Moore's book are in dialogue with her process theology. But, as methods, they hold much potential for education in an existentialist mode. They are congenial to an existentialist education in that they are attempts to represent the complexity of existence out of which participants would choose meaning. This is in contrast to transmissive approaches in which systems of doctrine are prior to students as subjects.

Case Study: According to Moore:

> The case study approach is basically an attempt to learn from a particular, concrete slice of existence. It generally takes the form of presenting a description of a particular situation. Students are then asked to reflect on the situation presented, to interpret, and to come to some judgment or decision regarding action. . . . In short, case study method involves reaching into a particular case and drawing out truths.[54]

---

53. Mary Elizabeth Moore, *Teaching from the Heart* (Minneapolis: Fortress, 1991), 99.
54. Ibid., 28.

In relation to existential thought, such a method becomes an individual opportunity for dialogue with a slice of reality and other people. This then becomes an opportunity for students to appropriate meanings as they become evident for themselves and their fuller being. However, as mentioned earlier, becoming a self is not a cold analytical process but takes on the nature of passionate inwardness. It is not certain that one could, nor is it necessary that one should, fully explain one's passion to others. Existentialism denies the supreme role of reason in deciding our essentiality. The case study process in an existentialist education would not be a purely cognitive process but would be instead a complex encounter.

Gestalt Method: Moore says,

> Basically, the Gestalt approach presents many ideas in proximity to one another so that learners can put the ideas together in some sort of unity. The presentation does not follow a linear pattern toward a particular kind of unity, but sets forth a variety of images and concepts for the learners to draw together.[55]

One of the insights of Gestalt is that learning involves the whole person—cognitive, affective, mental, and physical. Education in an existentialist mode would affirm the holistic nature of learning. For this reason, existentialist education has been thought of as "encounter education." In an existentialist mode, the subject is actively inclined toward being in direct relation to his or her personal projects. Such a teaching method might invite participant learners to offer personal insights. In the complexity of dialogue with other learners or multiplicity of sources, one's personal learning may be reformed in some unity based on one's life project.

Phenomenological Method: We have already noted the significance for phenomenology in the origins and formation of existential philosophy and theology. Moore defines this method as

> reflecting on experience and letting conclusions emerge from those reflections . . . [this involves] bracketing, or suspending judgments, in an effort to avoid reductionism in the study of experience and to discern intentions, or meanings.[56]

It is an attempt to get behind all of the layers of imposed meanings we attach to phenomena. Such an approach has been mentioned in relation to Ross Snyder and meaning formation. In this approach the emphasis is on experiencing relation with an event, describing it, theorizing about it, and practicing or testing the theories. Snyder uses a phenomenological method in

---

55. Ibid., 61.
56. Ibid., 95.

approaching biographical materials. The student responds to such an experience as an encounter suggestive of possible meanings for her life. Moore suggests such an approach to biblical studies where students meet traditional sources of authority subject to subject.

Narrative Method: Moore says that,

> Narrative is a significant mode of human communication, a bearer and critic of culture, and a potentially profound and far-reaching educational method.[57]

It has already been mentioned that one element of religious education in an existentialist mode is the use of symbol, myth, and ritual. Although we may "exist" before we have "essence," we find in narrative our roots and our essence. Narrative is a way in which we link together meanings that we discover in existence. We do not find meaning apart from narrative, and we do not appropriate meaning without forming a narrative. Narrative communicates complexity of existence in a way that cannot be conveyed in a linear abstracted manner. Kierkegaard spoke of irony as the means by which humans transit from the aesthetic to the ethical stage and humor the way from the ethical to the religious awareness. Kierkegaard found great resource in storytelling as a way of communicating complex and multivalent truths. For existentialism, narrative is a way to communicate some of the relational complexity of life as one person tells her story to another, and we all form our individual stories. An existentialist critique of narrative would warn against the hegemonic oppression of a master narrative. Such a narrative has been in effect in Western history subjugating minorities and women and silencing their stories.

Conscientizing Method: One of the most important developments in educational method in this century is described by Paulo Freire as conscientization. It includes a movement from action to reflection toward the goal of justice. The first step in Freire's method is to name the world. This was a time to listen to the life worlds constructed by the peasants. The next step was to discern the meaning of those words, especially related to the social structures of oppression. The third step is to define the problem in the social structures. The final step is to formulate strategies for action and to act. The pedagogy is a cycle and continues from action to reflection. This approach is being espoused now by many religious educators including Thomas Groome, Maria Harris, and Daniel Schipani. Groome has noted that this pedagogical approach embodies the belief that to educate for justice is to educate justly. Harris includes much more of the affective domain in her approach including the steps of silence, political awareness, mourning, bonding, and birthing.[58]

---

57. Ibid., 132.
58. Ibid., 173.

This approach to religious education would correlate nicely with the concerns of theorists like Buber, Ross, Snyder, Heschel, Sherrill, etc. In such a manner, the conscientization approach moves from a position of existence to further definition of essence. It is in fact a method of meaning making. Theology grows out of praxis.

Conclusions: Existentialism, as a spirit of relating to life and history has been characterized as melancholic befitting its founding Dane, Søren Kierkegaard. It has not been a story of cheer and light, but the goodness of its message has been cloaked in angst, fear, dread, meaninglessness, and death. But for those with eyes to see and ears to hear its language of passion, existentialism has lifted oppressive burdens of dead orthodoxy. In the halls of established religion, existentialism has been the embarrassing orphaned child who is spoken of in whispers. For religious education, existentialism has taunted with the beckoning insights of subjectivity, responsibility, relationality, and encounter. There are few today who approach religious education purely from an avowed existentialist perspective. But existentialism continues to gain homage paid in footnotes and mystical Heideggerian references. However, the fundamental insights of existentialism remain like a wart on the forehead of religion—impossible to totally ignore. Existence does precede essence! Education for subjectivity must be a part of our consideration as religious educators.

PART THREE

SPECIAL THEOLOGIES

"The priority of God in the grace-faith relationship is essential to sound Christian education leading to both belief and action. This is as it should be, and it is the basis for hope for the Christian education of the future."

CHAPTER EIGHT

Feminist Theology and Religious Education

ELIZABETH DODSON GRAY

Part One

The Challenge of Feminism

Feminist theology is not one possible theology among a pantheon of male theologies. Feminism is such a drastic critique of the entire Christian tradition that it calls for the almost total recasting of that tradition and the reconstruing of its history.

Feminism points out the obvious but previously overlooked fact that Christianity is one of the many religious traditions in which it has been the males who have "named the sacred" from the viewing point of their own male life experience. Like Narcissus of Greek mythology, the male has looked into a pool which has made the religious tradition a reflection of himself.

This is what feminists mean when they call the received tradition "andro-centric": It embodies the perception of the entire world through "male-colored" glasses. The absurdity of this interpretation of the human situation usually eludes us, until we realize that it is like left-handed or brown-eyed people assuming that their brown eyes or left-handedness gave them the only "keys to the kingdom."

The Power to Name How Things "Are"

Adam in the Genesis story is portrayed as "naming all the animals." This is an elegant parable to convey the truth that infant humans, female and male, are born into a whole social construction of reality done from the standing point of the male body and the male life experience. Of their socially dominant gender the generic male can say, like Adam, "Everything is named, everything is thought, from my point of view." And all of us, having been born into and socialized within this "Adam's world," feel what patriarchal history for centuries said: "This is the way the world really *is*," for we have never experienced life another way.

Our language itself reflects Adam's world. So-called "generic" language has perpetuated the illusion that all of the human species is made visible in the words *man* and *mankind*. Our language is like a Rorschach test, imaging back to us reflections of even uniquely male genital experience in statements such as "the *thrust* of his thinking," " a *penetrating* statement," "a *seminal* book," even "*seminars*." Yet male consciousness, like the Washington Monument to "the father of our country," has left us blissfully unaware of the frequently phallic nature of the sculpting of its monuments as well as its words.

In the long history of thought, Adam's world has given us male-constructed philosophy, male-constructed psychology, and, yes, male-constructed theology. It has been men who have "erected" these great conceptual systems. Thus traditional Christian theology has imaged the generic human in the form of the male, and also imaged the divine in the form of the male. Michelangelo's portrayal of a bearded God reaching out the finger of creation-energy to fill Adam with life has been accepted in Western culture as an icon, a visual summary, of the theological statement that "God created man in his own image."

But when we take account of the sociology of knowledge, and notice *who* is *doing the knowing*, we realize that the "flow of creation" really happened as the *reverse* of what we earlier perceived. It is actually the human male who has created God in *his* own image. Yes, like Narcissus of old, the male sees only himself in the cosmic reflecting pool of ultimate mystery.

Unrepentant Male-Reflective Christian Theology

The feminist theologian Mary Daly says somewhere that when God is male, then the male is God. The sociologist Peter Berger writes, "Religion legitimates social institutions by bestowing upon them an ultimately valid ontological status, that is, by *locating* them within a sacred and cosmic frame of reference."[1] What Daly and Berger are saying is that when ultimate reality is imaged as being male, then male power—expressed in male political leaders, male corporate CEOs, and males as "heads" of patriarchal families—is made to seem credible and "natural."

So male-reflective Christian theology is not innocent. It is deeply implicated in the history of the creation of patriarchal structures of male power in the home, in the church, and in the structures of economic, political, and social power in the wider culture. Feminist scholars, from Mary Daly to

---

1. Peter L. Berger, *The Sacred Canopy: Elements of a Sociological Theory of Religion* (Garden City, N.Y.: Anchor, Doubleday, [1967] 1969), 33.

Rosemary Radford Ruether to Elisabeth Schüssler Fiorenza, to dozens of others, have written and published on these themes.[2]

But male Christian theology still seems curiously unrepentant for the blatant way Christianity has been constructed "in the image of him."[3] This leaves Christian women, as in the lament of the ancient Hebrews, "singing their song in a strange land," a land not their own.

THE DENIGRATION OF WOMAN

The Mark of the Divine

Christian piety and theology have always taken for granted that we humans are created in the image of God (Gen. 1:26). This has been the starting point for Christian self-understanding of our humanness, that somehow we bear the mark (or image) of the divine. Such theology in recent decades has undergone a feminist deconstruction exposing its roots in male perspectives and self-interest. Nonetheless we must recognize that this "image of God' theology has been extremely important over the centuries to the Christian church and to the Western world in constructing how various kinds of humans were "named," labeled, and thought about.

But women's problem with the Christian tradition is not just that it is all "in the image of him." It is also that from this male standing point, women were named as Other, as inferior, evil, unclean, "grotesque." So it is important that we examine more closely just how this denigration of women developed over the centuries and was articulated theologically.

Are Women Also in the Image of God?

Jane Dempsey Douglass, professor of historical theology at Princeton Theological Seminary, raises an interesting question: "Why," she asks, "did the doctrine of the image of God in all humanity not serve in the past to break down distinctions based upon gender and race?"[4]

Answering that question, she points out that from the very early years of

---

2. For a survey and summary of this history, from pre-Christian times in the classical world to the present day, see Rosemary Radford Ruether, *Gaia and God: An Ecofeminist Theology of Earth Healing* (San Francisco: Harper San Francisco, Harper Collins, 1992), especially 115-201.

3. God's statement of self-revelation to Moses, "I am who I am"—or "I will be whoever I will be" (Ex. 3:14), is interpreted by Thomas Aquinas in *Summa Theologiae* (I q. 13, a. 11; also Scg I. 22, par. 10) as "*He* who is," as if this were God revealing to Moses the maleness of God's ontological nature. See Elizabeth Johnson, *She Who Is: The Mystery of God in Feminist Theological Discourse* (New York: Crossroad, 1992), 241-243.

4. Jane Dempsey Douglass, "The Historian of Theology and the Witnesses." Nathaniel Taylor lectures, Yale Divinity School, 1990. The quotations are transcribed from tapes of lectures.

the Christian era "theologians have taught that humanity was created in the image of God. But they have seemed ill at ease explaining how *women* bear that image. Adam is seen as created in the image of God, a God who is seen as man-like, or as having no gender. But when human sexual differentiation is taken into account, the image becomes problematic."

Over the centuries there has been a continuing struggle in Christian theological circles over how to explain that women also are made in the image of God. Douglass points out that strongly contributing to this difficulty was what the apostle Paul wrote in 1 Corinthians 11:7b-9, "Man is the image and reflection of God, but woman is the reflection of man. Indeed, man was not made from woman, but woman from man. Neither was man created for the sake of woman, but woman for the sake of man" (NRSV).

"Some of the Church Fathers, like Gregory of Nyssa [b. c325] and Augustine [354-430], developed double-creation schemes. There was a purely spiritual creation of humanity [Gen. 1] before there was the creation of bodily differentiation [Gen. 2]. But then," says Douglass, "having done this, the female was then seen as reflecting the image of God *less fully* than the male because of her different and inferior bodily nature."

Douglass reports that Chrysostom (c. 345-407) and other Eastern Mediterranean theologians working out of Antioch "lean heavily on 1 Corinthians 11:7 to argue that 'ruling' and 'governance' are a critical part of the image of God. And it is men that are endowed with that capacity to imitate God's ruling. Again this view militates against the fullness of God's image in women," observes Douglass.

Pronouncing Women Inferior

It turns out that Aristotle (384-322 BC) is quite important in this discussion about women and the image of God. It was Aristotle who had said: "The female is a female by virtue of a certain lack of qualities—a natural defectiveness—a 'misbegotten male' " (*On the Generation of Animals 2, 3*).

Uta Ranke-Heinemann is professor of the history of religion at the University of Essen. In *Eunuchs for the Kingdom of Heaven: Women, Sexuality and the Catholic Church* she writes: "These belittling notions of woman as a kind of flower pot for the male's semen were worked up by Aristotle into a theory that lasted for thousands of years. Aristotle, Albertus Magnus, and Thomas Aquinas see things this way: According to the basic principle that 'Every active element creates something like itself,' only men should actually be born from copulation. The energy in semen aims of itself to produce something equally perfect, namely, another man. But owing to unfavorable circumstances women, i.e., misbegotten men, come into existence. Aristotle calls woman '*arren peperomenon*,' a mutilated or imperfect male."[5] She continues: "Thomas

---

5. Uta Ranke-Heinemann, *Eunuchs for the Kingdom of Heaven: Women, Sexuality and the Catholic Church*, trans. Peter Heinegg (New York: Doubleday, 1990), 187.

says that women do not correspond to 'nature's first intention,' which aims at perfection (men), but to 'nature's second intention, (to such things as) decay, deformity, and the weakness of age'" (*Summa Theologiae* I q. 52 a. 1 ad 2).[6]

Nine centuries after Aristotle's death, in the year 585 AD, a gathering assembled in a general council for all of France, the second Synod of Mâcon. Forty-three Christian bishops and twenty men representing other bishops debated, among other things, a most peculiar topic: "Are women human and fully 'person' (*homo*)?" When a vote was finally taken, in the infinite wisdom of the males present, women were officially declared human![7]

Margaret Miles, professor of historical theology at Harvard Divinity School, writes of this discussion still being carried on in the Middle Ages. In *Carnal Knowing: Female Nakedness and Religious Meaning in the Christian West* she says, "In the Middle Ages Aristotle's doctrine of woman as a misbegotten and deformed male crossed easily into Christian speculation about Eve and her secondary and derivative creation."[8] After all, it was said, God created Adam first, so women must be second-best.

Thus Christian theology functioned for centuries as a potent cultural force declaring women inferior beings. You might think this was surely sufficient denigrating to do to one half of the human species—the half that conceives and bears the next human generation. But no, Christian theology went further, declaring women to be evil, defiling, dangerous, even grotesque.

Proclaiming Women Evil

Using the powerful negative image of Eve, the one who "led Adam" into disobedience and so the one by whom sin came into the world, women were portrayed by generations of Christian theologians as both inheritors and perpetuators of human evil and disobedience.

Tertullian (c160-c230) said: "Do you know that each of you women is an Eve? . . . You are the gate of Hell ['the devil's gateway,' it is sometimes translated], you are the temptress of the forbidden tree, you are the first deserter of the divine law."[9] Echoes of Tertullian's words persist in Christian thought of subsequent centuries.

---

6. Ibid., 188.

7. Gregory of Tours, *History of the Franks*, trans. O.M. Dalton. (Oxford: At the Clarendon Press, 1927), 8, 20; 344-345; also Charles Joseph Hefele, *A History of the Councils of the Church from the Original Documents*, trans. William R. Clark, vol. 4 (451-680 AD) (Edinburgh: T.& T. Clark, 1895), 406-409.

8. Margaret R. Miles, *Carnal Knowing: Female Nakedness and Religious Meaning in the Christian West* (Boston: Beacon Press, 1989), 162; see also Maryanne Cline Horowitz, "The Image of God in Man—Is Woman Included?" *Harvard Theological Review* 72: 3-4 (July-October 1979), 175-206.

9. Tertullian, "On the Apparel of Women," in *The Ante-Nicene Fathers: Translations of the Fathers Down to A.D. 325*, eds. Alexander Roberts and James Donaldson (Buffalo: Christian Literature, 1885), vol. 4, 14.

Medieval "theologians, philosophers and medical authors discussed the question of whether woman is a 'monstrous creation.' "[10] Of this discussion Margaret Miles says: "Figured as Eve, the perversely bent rib, every woman was seen as essentially grotesque, though the revelation of her hidden monstrosity could be prevented by her careful adherence to socially approved appearance and behavior."[11]

"One of the most prominent features of the grotesque," writes Miles, "is sexuality and the sexual organs, and female reproductive functions, as we will see, were in the medieval period the quintessential terror that must be 'conquered by laughter.' " She cites the work of Michel Bakhtin, one of the major scholars of the grotesque. "Bakhtin identifies the three main acts in the life of the grotesque body as 'sexual intercourse, death throes, and the act of birth.' 'Birth and death are the gaping jaws of the earth and the mother's open womb.' "[12]

In the medieval world, Miles says, "Pregnancy and birth provide images of 'natural' grotesqueness. 'Woman with child is a revolting spectacle,' Jerome wrote in the fourth century, a judgment with which countless medieval authors concurred. Pregnancy, like menstruation," writes Miles, "reveals that a woman's body is not the 'closed, smooth, and impenetrable' body that serves as the symbol of individual, autonomous, and 'perfect' existence. In menstruation, sexual intercourse, and pregnancy, women's bodies lose their individual configuration and boundaries."[13]

In both Judaism and Christianity women were declared befouled and contaminated by our natural body functions of menstruation and childbirth. A woman was so contaminating of the sacred liturgical space presided over by male priests that a woman was exiled or banned during times of menstruation and birth and required to undergo a special cleansing ritual before she could be allowed back into the sacred space of worship.[14]

Deciding Sexual Intercourse with Women Is Evil

But here the Christian theologians have created a problem for the heterosexual male.[15] If women and women's bodies are so horrible and defiling, then what about men having sexual intercourse with women?

In his book *Power and Sexuality: The Emergence of Canon Law at the Synod of Elvira*, historical theologian Samuel Laeuchli examines how church

---

10. Miles, *Carnal Knowing*, 160-161.

11. Ibid., 152.

12. Ibid., 153.

13. Ibid.

14. See Leviticus 15:19-31; 12:1-8, and also the service for the "churching of women" ("Thanksgiving after Childbirth") in the Book of Common Prayer, 1928. 305-307.

15. See Ranke-Heinemann, *Eunuchs for the Kingdom of Heaven,* for booklength documentation of the lengthy tradition of Christianity of pronouncing sexual intercourse to be evil.

leaders in Spain in 309 at the Synod of Elvira for the first time create an explicitly antisexual code and called upon men to rise spiritually above their sexual bodies. "In the image of manhood which these canons presuppose, the woman as a sexual being was excluded."[16] "Sexuality," says Laeuchli, "becomes synonymous with evil. The sexual act becomes abhorrent and people either flee into deserts or write books on the perfection of virginity."[17]

But it was Augustine (354-430) in his *Confessions* who gave these antisexual views what was to be their classic formulation.[18] Augustine wrote of *concupiscence*, or what is usually translated "sexual desire" or "lust." He proposed a biological theory about the transmission of original sin from one generation to the next. Augustine was speaking to the problem of how Eve's sin could be our sin. How could her sin be transmitted to us? His answer was *concupiscence* or lust. In the act of sexual intercourse, something spoils the act (and indeed spoils the whole human race). That something was and is sexual desire.

Augustine was building a theological case for the necessity of baptism. Baptism, he said, washes away that original sin transmitted to us from our parents' sexual desire. Baptism, then, is the recommended spiritual cleanser for bleaching out the stain caused by our parents' erotic impulses at the time of our conception. So baptism is his solution to a problem which Augustine himself created. It was a sort of spiritual antibiotic, cleverly constructed to match the lethal "virus" he had theologically conjured up.

So here is a Catch-22, a religious system created by men that labels our women's bodies so carnal and sexual and evil that normal heterosexual desire for women finally contaminates both the men and their children. Note however that women may procreate without experiencing any sexual desire. Since it is males who must experience such desire in order to become erect and ejaculate, what Augustine has created theologically becomes a formidable problem for the Christian heterosexual male. Augustine has, in effect, launched a powerful theological boomerang, one that returns to wound whatever male uses it.

But there was a way to avoid this wounding, and males for centuries have used their standing point as "the namer" to avoid taking responsibility for their own sexuality. They have done this by psychological projection, disowning their own sexual desires and erotic imagination, and projecting them "out" onto women. For generations men were able to blame women as the source

---

16. Samuel Laeuchli, *Power and Sexuality: The Emergence of Canon Law at the Synod of Elvira* (Philadelphia: Temple University Press, 1972), 104; cited in Carter Heyward, *Touching Our Strength: The Erotic as Power and the Love of God* (San Francisco: Harper & Row, 1989), 44.

17. Laeuchli, cited by Heyward, *Touching Our Strength*, 167n.

18. See, for example, Margaret R. Miles, *Desire and Delight: A New Reading of Augustine's Confessions* (New York: Crossroad, 1992).

of all "carnal desire," and in this way they avoided facing up to their own lustful fantasies and whatever it was that they as males were doing with their own sexuality. Thus they neatly avoided taking any responsibility and viewed women instead as the source of this now-declared evil. "All witchcraft comes from carnal desire, *desire which in women is insatiable*," wrote the authors of *The Hammer of Witches* in 1487 just after the start of the Inquisition.[19] It is difficult for us today to read that pronouncement with a straight face. In court records in the United States today there are literally thousands of cases of rape, incest, and pedophilia by males.[20] There is a minuscule record of such offenses perpetrated by women. "Insatiable carnal lust" *in women?*— who do we think we're kidding?[21]

The Culpability of the Christian Tradition

Feminist scholars Jane Dempsey Douglass, Carter Heyward, Margaret Miles, and Uta Ranke-Heinemann, among others, have dug deep into the literary records of the Christian tradition and unearthed these terrible antisexual and antiwoman pronouncements. Their scholarship helps women today understand that the difficulties women may have with self-esteem, self-confidence, and self-assertion are more than just their own individual or personal issues. These issues are culture-wide. They are widely shared wounds, which trace their origin to messages about women promulgated continuously and with great priority and intensity throughout the long history of our Christian tradition.

Feminists have concluded that *Christianity's contempt for women and their bodies has been an essential backdrop legitimating the violence against women*. Rosemary Radford Ruether, for example, says: "Historical Christianity defined women as inferior, subordinate, and prone to the demonic. These images justified almost limitless violence against them whenever they crossed the male will at home or in society. Woman as vic-

---

19. Jakob Sprenger and Heinrich Institoris, *The Hammer of Witches* (1487), I Q. 6. The two were German Dominicans and Sprenger a professor of theology in Cologne. Pope Innocent VII appointed Sprenger and Institoris as inquisitors of heresy in his "Witches Bull" of 1484. *The Hammer of Witches* is intended to be a commentary upon the "Witches Bull." (Ranke-Heinemann, *Eunuchs for the Kingdom of Heaven*, 238, 229, 235).

20. Feminists today argue that these crimes should be tried and punished as crimes of "power" and "violence." But such crimes also involve sexual lust out of control. So in seeking to *understand* such crimes, I feel that the sexual component of both the motivation and the crime cannot be ignored.

21. An interesting glimpse into the perennial problem of male sexual lust in the second through fifth centuries of the Christian Church in North Africa (Tertullian, Cyprian, Augustine) is provided by Margaret R. Miles. See "Patriarchy as Political Theology: The Establishment of North African Christianity" in *Civil Religion and Political Theology*, ed. Leroy S. Rouner (Notre Dame, Ind.: Boston University Studies in Philosophy and Religion, Vol. 8, University of Notre Dame Press, 1986), 169-186. See also her *Desire and Delight.*

tim is the underside of patriarchal history."[22]

The full extent, intensity, and duration of this violence toward women is only now being unearthed by feminist scholars. During "the Witch-Burnings," hundreds of thousands of women were burned at the stake (or drowned) as witches. This continued for more than two centuries (1484-1692) in the Catholic and Protestant Christian West. In addition, evidence in literary and ecclesiastical records shows there have always been the violent assaults of incest, child abuse, wife-battering, religiously sanctioned child-beating, marital rape, acquaintance rape, stranger rape, war rape, and individual killings of women.[23]

All these forms of violence create and sustain a theologically and religiously sanctioned culture of ongoing oppression into which women are born, grow up, and are expected to find a place, their "woman's place." In other cultures the violence toward women has its roots in different (but still male) social and religious traditions. But in the Christian West such violence is rooted in the denigration of women which is powerfully and continuously articulated by the Christian antiwoman and antisex tradition. It is important we be clear in our own minds that in all this violence, *the perpetrators are not just individual males who are violent. It is the entire tradition which is culpable of doing structural, theological violence to women*.

Because it has been the entire tradition, it is very important now that the entire tradition genuinely and explicitly repent for this violent and damaging patriarchal past and for all the hurt it has caused women. I want this repentance to be "out loud," articulated loudly and clearly in our regular church services and in our church pronouncements. And I want change.

JESUS AND WOMEN

Jesus' Radical Affirmation of Women

The Christian tradition as it developed in the centuries after Jesus has been woman-hating. Yet if one looks to some of that tradition's earliest written materials—the four gospels about Jesus' life—no greater contrast to this woman-hating Christian tradition can be imagined than Jesus' own interac-

---

22. Rosemary Radford Ruether, "The Western Tradition and Violence Against Women," in *Christianity, Patriarchy and Abuse*, ed. Joanne Carlson Brown and Carole R. Bohn (New York: Pilgrim Press, 1989), 37.

23. For a detailed study see Lawrence Stone, *Family, Sex, and Marriage in England, 1500-1800* (New York: Harper Collins, 1983) and especially his later work based on a collection of documents Stone discovered late in his career from the Court of Arches, an ecclesiastical appeals court having jurisdiction over family cases from 1600 until 1857: *Road to Divorce: England 1530-1987* (New York: Oxford University Press, 1990) and two volumes of case studies, *Uncertain Unions: Marriage in England, 1660-1753* (New York: Oxford, 1992) and *Broken Lives: Separation and Divorce in England, 1660-1857* (New York: Oxford, 1993).

tions with women. Rachel Conrad Wahlberg[24] has focused on these interactions, and it is she who has given me fresh eyes to see that Jesus is not only *not* woman-hating, but in the gospel accounts of his words and actions he is radically woman-*affirming* in ways totally at odds with both his own time and with the subsequent Christian tradition.

When I was growing up as a Southern Baptist my reading of the gospels was supplemented in sermons by briefings on certain aspects of Jesus' social context. But other aspects of that social context were never discussed. For example, I learned that in order to understand the gospel account of Jesus' conversation with the Samaritan woman at the well (Jn. 4:7-30), I needed to be aware of the tradition of enmity between Jews and Samaritans.

What was *not* discussed was the traditional customs governing conversations between men and women in that day. Jesus and all men were prohibited by social custom from speaking to women not already known to them.[25] So I never really saw how radical a social departure Jesus' conversation at the well really was.

Truly "Disciples," Not First-Century Groupies

Women, unless accompanied by a man, were also enjoined by social custom to stay in the immediate surroundings of their own home.[26] Without awareness of these social customs, I lacked the background to understand or appreciate the life-transforming commitment being made by the women who "followed" Jesus as he traveled (Lk. 8:1-3). They were truly "disciples," not first-century Palestinian groupies or hangers-on.

I was instructed, for example, in the Sabbath rules of Judaism. I had to understand these to grasp the explosive impact of Jesus' actions as he "broke" Sabbath rules. But I never heard in childhood sermon or seminary classroom about similar rules and customs narrowing the worlds of women in New Testament times. So I was unprepared to understand the equally explosive impact Jesus had when he disregarded the conventions governing male/female relationships in his day.

For example, Jesus talks *theology* with the woman at the well. He did this at a time when men not only did not talk to women in public but women were not allowed to study the Torah. This must have meant that women were always excluded as participants in religious discourse. But when Jesus visits Mary and Martha, he encourages Mary to leave Martha in the kitchen and join the men in talking theology (Lk. 10:38-42). Later, after the death of

---

24. See Rachel Conrad Wahlberg, *Jesus According to a Woman* (New York: Paulist, 1975) and *Jesus and the Freed Woman* (New York: Paulist, 1978).

25. Ranke-Heinemann, *Eunuchs for the Kingdom of Heaven*, 120.

26. The only exception was an emergency, when a child or an animal was missing and must be found. See Pheme Perkins, *Jesus As Teacher* (Cambridge: At the University Press, 1990).

their brother Lazarus, Jesus does not rebuke Martha for upbraiding him for his being absent and thus unable to heal her brother in his mortal illness. Instead Jesus engages now Martha (who earlier had been the one who labored in the kitchen) in a serious theological discussion of death and resurrection, saying finally, "*I* am the resurrection and the life" (Jn. 11:1-26).

Women as Hearers and Doers of the Word of God

When a woman from a crowd shouts out her affirmation of his mother's womb and breasts—"Blessed is the womb that bore you, and the breasts that you sucked!" (Lk. 11:27-28)—Jesus responds with the amazing affirmation that a woman is more than her uterus, indeed more than her reproductive function.[27]

In a time when women gained social value for having children and especially male children, and were seriously devalued for being "barren,"[28] it was a radical thing for Jesus to reject the image of woman as a biological and reproductive vessel only. Jesus is affirming that a woman is also a serious "choosing" human agent who can choose to "hear the word of God and do it" (Lk. 11:38). Women are affirmed as Hearer and Doer of the Word.[29]

So after our Christian churches repent of all the woman-hating in our Christian tradition, something else I want is the preaching, the educational activities, and all of local church life to make crystal-clear to children (and to everyone) just how radically *woman-affirming* the churches' founder, Jesus, really was.

Jesus and the Apostolic Role of Women

A great deal has always been made within Christianity about being an apostle (see 1 Cor. 15:3-11) and the apostolic commission of "Go and tell." An apostle is someone who is sent, usually with the "apostolic" task of going and preaching, or proclaiming the good news of Jesus.

It seems to have escaped the serious attention of a male-obsessed tradition that women were the very first apostles, the first to be commissioned by Jesus himself to go and tell. It is to the woman at the well that Jesus first says he is the Messiah: "I who speak to you am he" (Jn. 4:26). She then, the gospel says, goes and tells other people so convincingly that they *believe* (Jn. 4:28-30)! Thus this woman at the well *is an apostle*, perhaps the first preacher of Jesus as the Messiah.

Equally surprising is how the Christian tradition from as early as we can glimpse it (1 Cor. 15:5) has downplayed the "apostolic" role of women in the

---

27. See Wahlberg, *Jesus According to a Woman*, 43-47.

28. See, for example, Luke 1:5-25; also Genesis 16:1-2, 21:1-7.

29. Wahlberg, *Jesus According to a Woman*, 43-47; also Elisabeth Schüssler Fiorenza, *In Memory of Her: A Feminist Theological Reconstruction of Christian Origins* (New York: Crossroad, 1983), 146.

resurrection narratives. But women are the first witnesses of Jesus' resurrection (Mk. 16:1-8; Mt. 28:1-10; Lk. 24:1-11). And here in these resurrection narratives those same words of apostolic commission occur. In Mark 16:7 the angel says to the women, "*Go and tell* his disciples"; in Matthew 28:8, "They ran to *tell*"; in Luke 24:9, "They told this to the eleven"; and in John 20:14-18, when Mary Magdalene sees Jesus outside the empty tomb and mistakes him for a gardener, Jesus again says, "*Go and tell* the others." Women are "sent" as apostles by Jesus!

But for the Faithfulness of These Women . . .

Had it not been for these women's faithfulness, there would not be an Easter morning account of the resurrection, since the male disciples had all run away and did not come to the tomb. And when the women told Jesus' male followers of their experience of him raised from the dead, the men would not even believe the women—"but these words seemed to them an idle tale, and they did not believe them" (Lk. 24:11). The gospel traditions let us glimpse the fact that even at this critical juncture the women were not believed, nor were they viewed as credible witnesses.

This may be why Paul, trying to be convincing to Christians at Corinth about Christ's resurrection and his own apostolic credentials, does not mention the risen Christ's Easter appearances to the women. Certainly these Easter appearances first of all to women would certainly never have been created later by pious tradition[30] because these accounts were so truly countercultural. Furthermore, like Peter's denial, they cast in a bad light the male disciples who later became leaders in the earliest Christian communities. So, precisely because they are *not* what a pious male-dominated tradition would have found congenial or useful, these accounts are undoubtedly authentic.

Jesus' Use of Female Metaphors to Speak of God

Look also at the images for God which Jesus is recorded in the gospels as using. Everyone touched by the Christian tradition has heard a lot about God (and Jesus) as "the good shepherd." The God-as-shepherd image has become an icon, and is celebrated in innumerable stained glass windows. Likewise we all know the story of "the prodigal son" and its related image of God-as-loving-Father grieving a lost son.

But both of these oft-repeated and oft-pictured images of God occur in the same chapter of Luke's gospel (Lk. 15) alongside another image of God which Jesus used, an image of God as like a woman (15:8-9). This latter

---

30. The historical facticity of specific events in Jesus' life is a persistent concern of New Testament scholars. A tendency of the early church to embroider upon events to underscore its message, as in the Christmas narratives, is already evident in the gospels. This tendency became even more evident in the additional gospels which by the early fourth century the church had decided were not authoritative or "canonical."

image is scarcely ever referred to in prayer or sermon nor is it portrayed in stained glass as an icon suitable for contemplation and comfort. This is the story of the woman with the lost coin.

The common theme in Luke 15 is lostness and foundness: a lost sheep, a lost coin, a lost son. Each time what has been lost has been found, and the words of the refrain echo each other: "Rejoice with me, for I have found my coin (my sheep, my son) which I had lost. Even so I tell you, there is joy before the angels of God [in heaven] over one sinner who repents."

The Absurdity of the "Maleness" of God

It is not simply that in Luke 15 Jesus is recorded as giving his hearers a female God-image, an image which has been largely ignored throughout Christian history. It is also that *Jesus himself was gender-inclusive in his own chosen God-images*. This renders rather absurd our contemporary debates about the maleness of God and the use of gender-inclusive language about God. It indicates instead that we have not really "seen" the biblical Jesus as he appears in the gospels. The truth is that *the male-obsessed church through the ages has restricted our symbolic universe to only male God-images in language and story*, something the gospels indicate Jesus himself never did.

There are also probably no stained glass windows commemorating Jesus' image of himself as a mother hen (Lk. 13:34; Mt. 23:37). Here Jesus suggests he is like a *female* parent, even a female *animal* parent, who is gathering her offspring under her wings. This image of Jesus also is clearly neglected by the male-dominated Christian tradition because it did not fit their idealized image of Jesus as the God-man. Can you imagine such a one as a mother-hen? Apparently Jesus could.

Reproductive Blood and Birth: Contaminating or Sacred?

Jesus lived in a religious culture which declared women "unclean" or religiously polluted and polluting when they menstruate or after they give birth. It is interesting how Jesus responds when he himself is made "unclean" (according to that culture) because he has been simply touched (and hence "polluted") by the woman with the issue of blood which has been ongoing in her for many years (Mk. 5:24-34).

Jesus did not rebuke her for touching him and making him unclean. Nor did he pull away from her or send her away. Instead she was healed, and Jesus told her to go in peace. So Jesus also breaks decisively with the taboo of women's uncleanness.[31]

Because Jesus grew up in a religious culture which had named women's natural process of giving birth as unclean and defiling of sacred space, he must have learned those attitudes about women's bodies, menstruating, and giv-

---

31. Wahlberg, *Jesus According to a Woman*, 31-41.

ing birth. Yet when Jesus chose a metaphor for spiritual conversion and transformation, he chose *giving birth* (Jn. 3:3-8 only). How remarkable![32]

When Jesus uses the birth image as the metaphor for "coming into new life in the spirit," there is respect and reverence in his words for the birth process which women experience. How could subsequent Christian tradition hallow those words "born again" into a very influential theological formula, yet still continue in Roman Catholic and Episcopal liturgical menus to keep the women-denigrating "cleansing" services until the 1970s? Jesus' respect for the birth-process was not able to be translated into the male-obsessed tradition but was instead spiritualized so that the theological denigration of women's actual bodies could be continued.

The Jesus Who Is Respectful of Women's Bodies and Minds

What do I conclude from all this in the gospel accounts about Jesus and women? I conclude that Jesus is a good model for full adult relationships— a model which unfortunately the male-dominated church was unable to follow but instead chose to abandon.

Jesus alone among the men in the gospel record did not accept the first-century mold for women. He took women as seriously as he took men. He never patronized women or demeaned them[33] or constricted them to "their place" as defined by the social conventions of his day. He rejected stereotyping women as "birth vessels" or kitchen helpers. He used female images for God and for himself, and he chose as his metaphor for conversion women's unclean birth process: "being born anew" or again.

Jesus treated women, women's bodies, and women's life-processes *respectfully*. Can you imagine what Jesus' reaction would be today to the worldwide epidemic of violence against women in the forms of pornography, rape, incest, battering, war rape, and murder? Then, ask yourself, Have you ever heard from the pulpit such a sermon—about Jesus' reaction to present-day violence against women?

Jesus was respectful of women's minds. He talked serious theology to them about the Messiah and the resurrection. He is respectful of women's spiritual capacities, which responded to his life and message, and he repeatedly gives women the apostolic commission to "go and tell."

Tampering with the Evidence

That women were active in this role in the earliest Christian communities is testified to by Paul who in Romans 16:7 names a person, for centuries referred to by the male name *Junias*, as "prominent among the apostles"

---

32. Wahlberg, *Jesus and the Freed Woman*, 42-64.

33. Jesus' encounter with the Syrophoenician woman (Mk. 7:25-30) is a possible exception. But note that this is also a memory of the only theological argument Jesus is ever recorded as conceding—and to a woman!

and "in Christ before I was." The story of the naming of that person is a cautionary tale, because a woman-denigrating tradition was reworking the evidence in subsequent centuries.

For approximately the last millennia it has been assumed that Paul's words referred to a male apostle. But in very recent years Bernadette Brooten, while reading John Chrysostom's *Commentary on Romans* (written late in the fourth century—his dates are 345?-407), noticed that Chrysostom wrote of there being a woman apostle, *Junia*. "To be an apostle," he wrote, "is something great. . . . How great the wisdom of *this woman* must have been" (emphasis added).

Brooten realized she had made a truly exciting discovery—the presence of corroborating nonscriptural evidence from the early centuries that *they* knew then that there had been at least one woman apostle in earliest Christianity.[34] This is shocking to us only because for the last thousand years or so (she found) the church has said (and taught) that only men were apostles.

There is an ambiguity in Paul's Greek at Romans 16:7; his use of the objective case includes both male and female. Brooten came to understand that Paul and his intended readers knew—as did Chrysostom and a millennium of subsequent Christians—that Junia was a woman who was an apostle "in Christ before me." But, she found, by about 1200 the fact of Junia being a woman was no longer mentioned. Apparently the church could no longer imagine that such a prominent early apostle was female, so the male form of the name *Junia* was created, even though there is no evidence in antiquity of the male form of that name!

So Martin Luther, writing in the early 1500s in his influential commentary on *Romans*, assumed this apostle must be a man. By the nineteenth century Roman Catholic and Protestant scholars almost without exception spoke of Junias. And soon the maleness of all in the New Testament who were called apostles had become a further argument against the ordination of women to the priesthood.

"What reasons have commentators given for this change?" Brooten asks herself. "The answer is simple: a woman could not have been an apostle. Because a woman could not have been an apostle, the woman who is here called apostle could not have been a woman."[35]

Finally now, after Brooten's research and nearly 1600 years later, the *New Revised Standard Version* of the Bible has set this bit of the New Testament record straight. But the fact that a woman apostle was "erased" and converted to a male (and a correction was needed for the NRSV) is a tiny bit of profound evidence of the pervasive male resistance and unbelief about

---

34. Bernadette Brooten, "'Junia . . . Outstanding among the Apostles' (Rom. 16:7)," in *Women Priests: A Catholic Commentary on the Vatican Declaration*, ed. Leonard Swidler and Arlene Swidler (New York: Paulist, 1977), 141-144.

35. Ibid., 142.

the role of women within the early church.[36]

Notice also what has happened to Mary Magdalene in Christian tradition. Mary Magdalene is one of the most prominent of these early Christian women and prominent in the gospels.[37] Yet the tradition subsequently portrayed her as a former prostitute. Elisabeth Moltmann-Wendel points out that this "tradition" about Mary Magdalene has no New Testament basis and is a subsequent fabrication.[38] This time it was a woman so *important* as a confidante of Jesus, a leader and a significant contender with Peter for prominence in the earliest Christian movement[39] that she could not be erased. So she was instead demeaned and trivialized by this attack upon her reputation.

Participants in the Basileia of God, God's Dawning New Age

The relevant category for Jesus does not seem to be whether someone is "created in the image of God" (as it is for the Church Fathers). What mattered to him is whether someone is participating in the *basileia* of God, God's dawning new age. Women are recorded in the gospel stories of Jesus' life and ministry as full participants in that new age, that *basileia*.

The gospel accounts tell of women being early recipients of the good news (gospel or *euangellion*) about Jesus as Messiah and Risen Lord. Women are reported to be hearing the Word of God and doing it. Women (as well as children and men and finally the dead) are being healed by Jesus, in what his followers saw as the signs of the presence in their midst of the power of God and God's *basileia*. Women are actively going and telling, witnessing, spreading the Word, converting others, and traveling about as disciples with Jesus' band. Then after his resurrection, women are described in The Book of Acts and in Paul's letters as being important leaders in the earliest Christian communities.

"Woman, You Are Freed" (Lk. 13:12)

Rachel Conrad Wahlberg notes that when Jesus healed the woman with the terribly bent back, he does not say, "You are healed," but instead he says,

---

36. Such unbelief extended into the twentieth-century. Helmut Köster of Harvard Divinity School pointed out to me that Hans Lietzmann, the outstanding philologist of early twentieth-century New Testament studies, could not believe that the person named *Junias* could be a woman. "The name *Junias* is not in evidence anywhere else . . . the short form never occurs. But because this person so named is designated as an apostle, one has to posit that this was a man, even though the name *Junias* never occurs anyplace else in antiquity" (*An die Romer [Handbuch zum NT]*, 4th ed. [Tübingen, 1933 (1906)], 125—this passage translated by Helmut Köster).

37. Stories of Mary Magdalene were carried on by the Gnostic tradition in works dating into the second century, including *Gospel of Thomas, Dialogue of the Savior, Gospel of Philip, Gospel of Mary*, and *Pistis Sophia*.

38. Elisabeth Moltmann-Wendel, *The Women Around Jesus*, trans. John Bowden (New York: Crossroad, 1982), 64-65.

39. See Schüssler Fiorenza, *In Memory of Her*, 50-53.

"Woman, you are freed."[40] Wahlberg says that Jesus frees women from "labels, limitations, and low expectations."[41]

Therefore, if we take Jesus seriously, a new relationship between women and men emerges as a possibility. Relationships can be symmetrical and mutually empowering for both sexes because women and men are radically equal and equally active, just as the creative will of God intends us to be (Gn. 1:27). Fully freed women are not simply objects in others' lives but are fully human and active, thinking and feeling and doing their days— "subject" in their own lives. Such women can be perceived by men as a serious threat to the masculine identity and social power of males. Tertullian at the end of the second century, Cyprian in the third, and Augustine in the late fourth century—all were Christian bishops who were important in shaping our Christian tradition and who perceived and railed against women as just such a threat.[42]

But fully freed women can also be welcomed by secure males who are able to share power and can enjoy being companioned by equal and active women partners. Throughout his public career Bill Clinton has welcomed Hillary Rodham Clinton as a fully powerful co-architect of his political journey, while she has also maintained her own separately active and equal public and professional life. I once heard a man asked what was in it for men if women claim their power. His answer was startling in its simplicity: "It's a better tennis game with a better partner." Precisely!

JESUS' CRUCIFIXION

Making Jesus into a "Salvation Machine"

As a feminist I do not find the figure of Jesus in the four gospels problematic for women. What I do have difficulty with is what the church did after his death with the life, the persona, and the message of Jesus.

In his lifetime Jesus was a social and religious radical, breaking down prohibitions which worked against women, lepers (Lk. 7:22), the sick (Jn. 9:2), working on the Sabbath (Mk. 2:27-28), healing on the Sabbath (Mk. 3:1-5), and so on. His preaching centered on social justice (e.g., Lk. 4:18-27; Mt. 6-7; Mt. 26:35-40).

But in the decades immediately after Jesus' death, the apostle Paul became the foremost interpreter of Jesus and a great missionary figure in the spread of what would become what we know as Christianity. Paul and most subsequent theologians centered not primarily upon Jesus' life and message but instead upon Jesus' death *and their interpretation of that death.*

Through their theologies of the cross, they made Jesus into a "salvation

---

40. Wahlberg, *Jesus and the Freed Woman*, 15-29.
41. Ibid., 1.
42. See Miles, "Patriarchy as Political Theology."

machine." They became obsessed with Jesus' death as a way of individual salvation. There was little or no social justice component to that message.

The "Blood on the Cross" Message of Individual Salvation

All that was the beginning of the "blood on the cross" message of individual salvation which I experienced in the Southern Baptist Church of my childhood. In the racially segregated South of that time, I knew people who could tell you the day and hour when they were "born again." But these same folk were totally oblivious to the great injustices of racist attitudes. They were supportive of the "Jim Crow laws" which created the legal basis for segregation. They were blind to the violence of lynchings and rape.

These white Christians celebrated the suffering of Christ's "passion" as salvific. But they did not see any connection of that suffering with the suffering of African-Americans.

Its lack of social justice, however, is not the only problem of the cross-obsessed preaching I grew up on. Certainly another major problem is in its underlying theology, which has focused so single-mindedly upon the cross itself. The cross, either in its starkly plain Protestant form or in its Orthodox and Catholic devotional form of the crucifix, has for centuries been the central icon of Christian faith and devotion. Jesus as the Christ "dying for our sins" is seen as the critical moment in salvation history. As someone has said, such theology is necrophilic, death-affirming rather than life-affirming.

A "Double Whammy" for Women

Feminist theologians writing in *Christianity, Patriarchy and Abuse* have focused on this glorification of suffering and self-sacrifice, especially as the theology of the cross combines with the social messages given to women. Joanne Carlson Brown and Rebecca Parker sum it up: "The central image of Christ on the cross as the savior of the world communicates the message that suffering is redemptive" and therefore it is implied that "our suffering for others will save the world."[43] And "this glorification of suffering as salvific [is] held before us daily in the image of Jesus hanging from the cross."[44]

This honoring of Jesus' suffering may inspire a few men to heroic martyrdom—a few like Gandhi, Martin Luther King Jr., and the archbishop of El Salvador, Oscar Romero. But for most men that glorification of suffering is more than blotted out by the culture's messages that men should live instead to further their own self-interest, power, career, money, and sexuality.

But the culture gives to women a different message than it gives men. Women are told, "Give yourself, submit yourself, Eve was created as a helpmate for Adam, and you should really live through taking care of

---

43. Joanne Carlson Brown and Rebecca Parker, "For God So Loved the World?" in *Christianity, Patriarchy and Abuse*, 2.

44. Ibid., 8.

your husband and children." It is a culture's call to self-sacrifice, a message intended however only for women.

Then on top of that message Christianity is teaching that to live a life of self-denial and self-sacrifice is to follow the way of the cross. And to do this is to find the experience which is at the heart of our salvation.

The "double whammy" for women is overwhelming. Making suffering sacred is, for women, an invitation to practice what feminist theologian Carter Heyward calls "theological masochism."[45] Or as Sheila Redmond says, "The focus on the need for redemption creates a sense of unworthiness and, eventually, guilt."[46]

So theologically induced "bad feelings" are piled onto women's culturally induced bad feelings about their second-class status and "evil" bodies. Little wonder then that feminists have identified low self-esteem as an important psychological problem for most women in this culture!

Seeing "That Old Rugged Cross" in a New Light

As women's voices have begun to be heard and women have started "naming the suffering, so as to begin the healing," women and also some men have begun to tell excruciating stories of childhood incest, physical and sexual abuse.

It is in this context that women are now taking a new and hard look at "that old rugged cross"—and what we see now is "divine child abuse," proclaimed as necessary and salvific. What we see is *not* Abraham's hand restrained by God from a sacrificial slaying of his son but instead God said to be for his own purposes *intentionally* killing a son. As Brown and Parker say, "To argue that salvation can only come through the cross is to make God a divine sadist and a divine child abuser."[47]

And if God abuses children, why shouldn't parents do this also? Philip Greven is an intellectual historian at Rutgers University. In his writing he traces the powerful and terrible intertwining of American Protestant colonial theology and the Calvinistic heritage of harsh physical abuse of children.[48] Brown and Parker say, "When parents have an image of a God righteously demanding the total obedience of 'his' son—even obedience to death—what will prevent the parent from engaging in divinely sanctioned child abuse,"[49] especially to force "obedience" to parental will?

"The image of God the father demanding and carrying out the suffering and death of his own son," Brown and Parker say, *"has sustained a culture of*

---

45. Carter Heyward, *The Redemption of God* (Washington, D.C.: University Press of America, 1982), 58.

46. Sheila A. Redmond, "Christian 'Virtues' and Recovery from Child Sexual Abuse," in *Christianity, Patriarchy and Abuse*, 77.

47. Brown and Parker, "For God So Loved the World?" 23.

48. Philip Greven, *The Protestant Temperament: Patterns of Child-Rearing, Religious Experience, and the Self in Early America* (New York: Knopf, 1977); and *Spare the Child: The Religious Roots of Punishment and the Psychological Impact of Physical Abuse* (New York: Knopf, 1990)

49. Brown and Parker, "For God So Loved the World?" 9.

abuse and led to the abandonment of victims of abuse and oppression. Until this image is shattered, it will be almost impossible to create a just society."[50]

This suggests a direction toward a just society which was never glimpsed by Walter Rauschenbush and the Social Gospel movement, *or* by Martin Luther King Jr. and the Civil Rights movement, *or* by Reinhold Niebuhr and Christian ethical realism, *or* by World Council of Churches manifestos, *or* by the popes in their encyclicals. *All these founder in their attempts to come to grips with injustice because they do not comprehend their own faith-commitment to the glorification of violence in the cross.*

Creating a Fascination with Violence and Pain

The Swiss psychiatrist Alice Miller, in her book *For Your Own Good: Hidden Cruelty in Child-Rearing and the Roots of Violence*, explores the psychological processes by which the violence by one generation of parents, particularly fathers, toward their children begets in their sons of the next generation similar violence in turn toward their own children.[51] In three extended case studies she explores how childhood experiences of brutalization created monstrously violent and brutal adults.

In one of these cases, Miller examines all that is known of Adolf Hitler's early life. In his brutal treatment by his father she finds the psychological origins of his violence against Jews.

Then, Miller asks, how could one such "wounded" man, Adolf Hitler, reach by his speeches so quickly and so deeply into the emotions and psyche of an entire people and win such total commitment to the Nazi cause?

Such a vast and rapid transformation was possible, Miller says, only because Hitler himself was a part of and also speaking to a nationwide population of adult survivors of childhood violence. Most of his German hearers had experienced childhood physical abuse similar to his own.[52]

The fact that the "Our-sin-is-laid-on-Him" atonement theology has for so many generations and centuries moved so many Christian hearts[53] raises

---

50. Ibid.

51. Alice Miller, *For Your Own Good: Hidden Cruelty in Child-Rearing and the Roots of Violence* (New York: Farrar, Straus, Giroux, 1983), 3-106.

52. Ibid., 142-197.

53. The *Messiah*, by George Frederick Handel gives us a window into this. See part 2— "Surely, He hath borne our griefs," "And with His stripes we are healed"—"All we like sheep have gone astray; we have turned every one to his own way. And the Lord hath laid on Him the iniquity of us all."—and just preceding the paean of praise in the Hallelujah chorus to "the Lord God Omnipotent" who "shall reign forever and ever," there is a celebration of God's righteous wrath and abusive power: "Thou shalt break them with a rod of iron; Thou shalt dash them in pieces like a potter's vessel"—and immediately the hallelujah celebration of God's power over all.

With new eyes we can see here the demand for total obedience by an authoritarian parent, the violence of an abusive father, and the induced guilt/shame of the abused child which becomes the "sin" laid upon Jesus.

an important questions: Is this too a consequence of harsh and abusive physical discipline for children in Christian homes? Greven has gathered the historical records documenting a centuries-old tradition of such violence toward children among many Christian groups.[54] Had our own childhood been less violent, wouldn't we find the father-son violence inherent in Christian atonement theology either bizarre or repulsive?

When I was coming into teenage in my Southern Baptist religious context I could never understand why the "blood on the cross" theology (as I came to call it) *never* resonated in my spiritual being as did the truth of God's love manifested in the creation of the world. I knew the presence of that loving God in my own experience, "calling" me, upholding me, "visiting" me in translucent moments of God-encounter. Today I wonder if my lack of such resonance for "blood on the cross" came from my personal experience of a nonviolent child-rearing, for which I am very grateful to my parents.

But those who do experience violent child-rearing add on other additional consequences. Childhood abuse catapults both genders into more extreme gender-stereotypic behavior. Girls become more docile and submissive women, easy candidates for further victimization. Boys become more aggressive and brutally violent men.[55]

A large proportion of men in prison for violent crimes (including rapists, murderers, serial killers) were themselves physically and/or sexually abused as children. Being abused or neglected as a child significantly increases the risk of being arrested for a violent crime.[56] It may come as news to advocates of "law and order" that probably the most effective thing we could do about stopping violent crime would be to stop fathers and grandfathers, uncles and older brothers, the man next door and the older boy next door, from physically and sexually abusing male children!

How are we to stop the abuse of children while at the same time our most sacred icon for religious contemplation is Jesus hanging on the cross, ordered there by his heavenly Father: Do you know the story of the young boy with behavior problems at school? He was sent from one school to another, finally becoming "good" in a parochial school. His grateful but curious parents (who were not Roman Catholic) asked him what was different about his new school, and he said, "Did you see that guy nailed to the wall? I figured that if God would do that to his own son, guess what He could do to me!"

---

54. Greven, *The Protestant Temperament.*

55. Elaine Hilberman Carmen, Patricia Perri Rieker, and Trudy Mills, "Victims of Violence and Psychiatric Illness" *American Journal of Psychiatry* 141 (1984), 378-383.

56. Cathy Spatz Widom, "The Cycle of Violence," *Science* 244 (1989), 160-166.

Part Two

CHANGING AN ENTIRE TRADITION

Making Women Visible

How do you take on a tradition that reflects the male image like a Narcissus pool, and remake it over into a tradition that is also *in her image*?

The answer reminds me of the riddle about "How do two porcupines make love?" The answer is, "With difficulty!"—because the problem of the male-centeredness of the Christian tradition goes well beyond male generic language, biased history, and celibate theology. "You have to git man off your eyeball," as Shug suggests in *The Color Purple*, "before you can see anything a'tall."[57]

Some women feel that the only way to break the hold of that male image on our unconscious is to incorporate the female image of God into our theology and especially into our worship. They reason that imaging the great I AM in its female face (Goddess, Gaia, The Great Mother, Sophia, Wisdom, and so on) is the ultimate antidote to the denigration of women as inferior and evil. To see the female in the God-space cracks open the unconscious male imaging of God which is our deep legacy from thousands of years of patriarchy. As we learn to reverence the female in the divine, they argue, we are opened up to reverence the divine in the human female.

This is not a pathway that appeals to me. I feel it only compounds patriarchy's error in socially constructing God in its own gender image.[58] I cannot see that the Mystery of creative energy which has brought into being 193 billion galaxies has male form, and unfortunately for my participation in "the pathway of the Goddess," which seems so very meaningful to many women, I do not think it helpful philosophically or theologically to clothe that Creating Mystery now in female form, even in image or metaphor.

Cleansing the Temple

We may or may not add female images to the divine. But it is imperative, if we care about the psychic health of the young people we are rearing in our churches, that we *totally strip the male language/image/metaphor from our references to deity* in worship and in church life.

We must also *deconstruct the male-identified biblical text*, making clear the male voices of its authors and the male viewing points from which they

---

57. Alice Walker, *The Color Purple* (New York: Washington Square Press, Simon & Schuster, 1982), 179.

58. See Elizabeth Dodson Gray, *Patriarchy as a Conceptual Trap* (Wellesley, Mass.: Roundtable Press, 1982).

speak. And we must *stop coating scripture with sacred varnish* in the pious words, "This is the Word of God." Instead, we must introduce patriarchal texts (or follow them) with prayers of repentance for the sin of the idolatry of the male which such texts embody.

We must do this to empower our girl children with affirmation. But we must do this also for our boy children, if we want them to be able to relate to the women in their lives (mothers, sisters, wives, colleagues, children) without the distorting filters of misogyny, which have for millennia beclouded and crippled male life-attitudes.

A Church Where Women Are Visible and Honored

In the 1970s our family attended Sunday services at the chapel of Wellesley College, the local women's college, under the pastorate of Paul Santmire. I gradually became aware how totally he had reworked the quite traditional service.

When a hymn had no objectionable male language or metaphor, we sang it from the hymnal. When we sang a hymn printed in the leaflet, it was because Paul had quietly reworked the words.

Then I began to realize that any illustration or anecdotes he used in sermons were all about women, never men. Paul was sensitive to the needs, expressed and unexpressed, of Wellesley College's students to have inclusive language and also to be visible themselves as a gender in his sermons. Finally, I realized that the stained glass windows in the Wellesley College chapel were all about women.

For too long we have expected women not to mind being invisible in our tradition. In our culture we have expected women to do the additional psychological work to "find themselves" in the male figures who are the main characters in the faith, the church, the culture, the stained-glass windows, and in the male-generic language and literature of our religious and national traditions.

Where Women Are Major Figures, Not Mere Bystanders

I remember a story told by Joseph Campbell, the great scholar of myths. He was teaching at Sarah Lawrence College and after a lecture about the mythic literature surrounding King Arthur, a woman student asked him about who in all the Arthurian saga she as a woman could identify with. Surprised, Campbell said that of course she could identify with the hero's mother, the hero's wife, the hero's sister, the hero's daughter. "No," the woman student said, "you don't understand!—*I want to be the hero.*"

There you have it. It is no longer sufficient for women to identify with the bystanders and the supporters in the hero's life. Women want to be the hero themselves. It is men's turn now to have to do the psychological work involved in "finding themselves" in a heroic figure of the other gender, the heroic female.

What we want now are adulatory sermons and services about Mary Magdalene. Like Peter she was a prominent early Christian leader—and one of Jesus' closest friends. So she is a figure we all, both men and women, should try to emulate.

Let us celebrate the first apostle, the woman at the well. Can we, either male or female, be as effective an evangelizer as she was?

I want an Easter morning that says flat out that the men had all deserted, and only women witnessed and attested to the resurrection that Easter morn! I want stained glass windows that show the risen Christ surrounded by only those women!

And while we are at it, let us show the women who were present at the Last Supper, cooking in the kitchen. Someone has quipped, "If there was a meal, you better believe there were not just men present!"

I am also tired of looking at Christian art with Jesus in the center and a grouping of disciples "boundaried" by the male gender. This is not true to the gospel records or The Acts of the Apostles.

Church Life as a Massive "Latent Curriculum"

We have a huge job to open up not only the language but also the stained glass window, the preaching, the storytelling, the celebrating. We need this opening up because *everything* in the life of the church is a learning experience for us as adults as well as for children. Church life itself is a *massive latent curriculum* in which everything that happens is teaching someone something.

So we need to *never* refer to Abraham without also naming Sarah and Hagar, never refer to Isaac without Rebecca, and so on. When we talk about Francis of Assisi, we need also to talk about Hildegard of Bingen—who left a considerably larger literature about her own form of creation spirituality, a literature neglected by Christians for centuries!

What I want is that at least half of every worship service and every curriculum makes women as visible as men—the women of the Bible and the New Testament, the women in church history, and the women and women's issues in contemporary life. Women are half the human species. "Women hold up half the sky," as a Chinese saying puts it, and we will no longer be invisible and marginalized in church worship or preaching or in church lore—or in curricula.

A Celebration of Women

When I was growing up in my Southern Baptist Church, every fall and spring our church had an in-gathering to benefit overseas missions. As a young child I would go with my mother early in the morning to the huge kitchen in the church's basement. While the women of the church cooked, the janitor set up long tables and we children rolled out the long paper tablecloths and set the tables with the silver and glasses, salt, pepper, sugar, and paper napkins.

It was a big operation involving many people, and at dinner time 300 to 400 men and women and children gathered in our church to eat a festival meal and to celebrate the memory of two great missionary figures, Lottie Moon in the fall and Ann Judson in the spring. We were celebrating *women* as heroic religious figures! After dessert had been served I heard both men and women (including our much revered pastor) praise and eulogize a woman, either Lottie Moon or Ann Judson, who had heard and followed the call of God to Christian service.

I look back now on this and I realize how important those celebrations of women were in shaping my life. I concluded as a young girl that if I chose in my life to respond to the call of God, my home religious community would applaud and honor me as they had honored Lottie Moon and Ann Judson year after year.

Changing a Tradition of Celebrating Men

I still find it sad that males, when they created a religious system around themselves, chose primarily to honor what it is *men* do. How else are you to explain the fact that women's experience of giving birth has *never* been honored as sacred (even though it brings new life and the only ongoing life our species knows in time)? Instead, women's natural bodily functions of menstruation and giving birth were declared "unclean" and "defiling" to the religious sanctuary.

Jesus honored women's giving birth and spoke of the new life we are called to as "being born again."[59] But the male-dominated tradition seized upon Jesus' words and used them to create male *imitation-births*, calling the "baptism" of infants their *true* birth, the time when they are "born again, into the family of God." This, it is implied, is the being born which really counts, *not* the birth from one's own mother. But ask yourself, "In which birth did God actually give you the gift of life?"

Mary Daly, in her scathing satire of the Looking Glass,[60] made many women aware of how the sacred rituals done by males *imitate* and *co-opt* many of women's sacred life-experiences. The feeding which women do at home became the communion presided over by men at church, and so on.

Going Beyond the Ancient and Crippling Hatred of Women

I say that it is time now to go back and resacralize these women's experiences which male religion has imitated and co-opted, and to do it with new and fresh eyes. To do less is to dishonor God's creation of woman. We can be filled with the spirit of Jesus, our founder, and be no longer stuffed with the ancient and crippling hatred of women which has dominated our woman-denigrating tradition.

---

59. See Jesus' dialogue with Nicodemus, John 3:1-10; also John 1:12-13.
60. Mary Daly, *Beyond God the Father* (Boston: Beacon Press, 1973), 195-198.

I want ritual that celebrates the sacredness of women giving birth. I want to celebrate in church not just Mary birthing Jesus but all women birthing all children. I want to expand the traditional celebration of the Advent season and Christmas to celebrate the sacredness of women's bodies—not just women's wombs but women's breasts, vaginas, vulvas, clitorises—all that God has provided to us as women and without which no human generations continue to be born on this earth.

We do not have to image the godhead as female in order to celebrate the God-given natural body of the woman. I am convinced this celebration has already begun in our extensive use in our Christmas celebrations of wreaths, which (let's face it) are *not* celebrations, as I was once told, of the Alpha and Omega—but celebrations of the rounded circle of the woman's vagina, which makes birth (including Jesus' birth) possible.

I want curricula which point out the absurdity of the story of Eve born out of Adam's body (thus reversing what happens in natural birth where men *always* come out of women's bodies). I want curricula which make clear the misogyny in the Genesis 2 account which labels women's natural pain in childbirth the result of Eve's "curse" for sin.

I want curricula to point out that while a baby is half the father's genes and half the mother's genes, once that DNA template or blueprint is formed, every molecule and atom of that growing embryo is built out of the real body and real blood of that gestating mother's body. This is how actual life is gestated and born in each of us.

I want church curricula to point out that modern biology has "revealed" to us that all fetal life is initially neutral—it can become either male or female. If at a certain time a triggering process occurs, this sets in motion the development of the male genitalia for the fetus. Without that triggering process the fetus goes on to become female. Aristotle and Thomas Aquinas and the Christian tradition for centuries had it backwards and wrong, thinking men (and Adam) came first and women were "deformed males." These mistaken speculations were used again and again to exclude women from priesthood and to put down women as "imperfect" while men were being touted as perfect. Modern biology has overturned all that erroneous theological speculation, and the church would now like to be able quietly to forget its centuries of derogating women in this way. But such a long history of Christian misogyny cannot now simply be ignored; it must be corrected.

I also want curricula which honor the sacred feeding that comes from women's breasts. Breast milk is women's blood with the red blood cells removed, and it sustains life in infants and also passes on her precious antibodies. We as faithful Christians may be given pause when we realize that birthing women can say to their children in truth, not metaphor, the hallowed words of the communion service: "This is my body, given for you; this is my blood, the blood of life, given for you."

A Life-Affirming Tradition for Ourselves and Our Children

Jesus said, "I have come that you might have life, and have it more abundantly" (Jn. 10:10). To be a life-affirming tradition, we must lay aside our sacralizing of death and suffering and put the affirmation of life at the core of our tradition.

For Jesus as we know him from the gospels, abundant life was social justice, a banquet feast to which everyone was invited (Lk. 14:15-24; Mt. 22:1-14). Jesus' message and life continued a liberation tradition begun in Moses ("I have seen the affliction of my people"—Ex.3:7) and continued in the eighth-century prophets ("Let justice roll down like water"—Am. 5:24). The account in Luke's gospel of Jesus' first sermon in a synagogue tells us he read Isaiah 61:1-2, "He has sent me to proclaim release to the captives and recovering of sight to the blind, to set at liberty those who are oppressed, to proclaim the acceptable year of the Lord" (Lk. 4:18-20). Of the discipleship of caring which he expected from his followers, he said, "I was hungry . . . thirsty . . . a stranger . . . naked . . . sick . . . in prison. As you did it to one of the least of these, you did it to me" (Mt. 25:31-46 NRSV).

I want a Christian education which focuses on the historical Jesus and his startling message of liberation and diversity and inclusion, because that message and example would be relevant in a positive way to our contemporary struggles with racism, sexism, heterosexism, classism, and speciesism. Can we help Christian young people, both female and male, to imagine who Jesus—with his startlingly inclusive patterns of relating to women, the poor, the outcast, the marginalized—calls upon *us* to include in our Christian communities?

I also want a religious education that is body-affirming and sexuality-affirming. And I would also like us to honor the body of the Earth. Sallie McFague's book *The Body of God*[61] is pointing us in this direction, toward images of God which are neither anthropomorphically male nor female, but which include and affirm the diversity and wonder of this entire created life-system of which we are but one part.

Can We Leave Behind Hierarchy?

Can we invent a religious education which does not *assume*, and therefore teach, hierarchy (men over women, humans over other species, humans over nature and the planet, God over all)? Can we learn to teach, with reverence, the biospheral cycles of the Earth when we teach creation? To teach about the creation of the Earth in this way is to say that our created world came not by God's verbal fiat (Gn. 1) but by the Creator's incredible participation in billions of years of an evolutionary process. It is this process which has given rise to our present biological and ecological existence as selves in bodies within a natural context we call the living Earth-system.

---

61. Sallie McFague, *The Body of God* (Minneapolis: Augsburg Fortress, 1993).

Can we internalize God's concern for other species in this Earth-system as well as for us? (There are fragments in our heritage which suggest this: "When the rainbow is in the clouds, I will look upon it and remember the everlasting covenant between God and every *living creature of all flesh that is upon the Earth*" [Gn. 9:16].)

Can we discover the *"creation-based value"* of every species, which is established in that covenant with the entire creation, a creation of which we are only a part and not its Lord and Master? Can we climb down from the high illusion we have of ourselves as "king of the castle" and in "dominion" over all the other species?

Can we write some curricula filled with real biological data about our Earth and our life-partners on it, as well as with some genuine theological humility about our place in the divine scheme of things? We talk about humility as a Christian virtue, but it has seldom been practiced in our theology!

Can we teach Jesus in religious education in a way that would make it obvious to our children that they should be "in solidarity with the poor"? Can we take Jesus' death away from those who would climb to heaven on his drops of blood? Can we finally see Jesus' death as what happened to a social revolutionary—and call our young people to the struggle against many oppressions, instead of focusing only on the dying?

Joanne Carlson Brown and Rebecca Parker have written, "We do not need to be saved by Jesus' death from some original sin. We need to be liberated from the oppression of racism, classism, and sexism, that is, from patriarchy."[62]

Fruits of the Patriarchal Spirit

The patriarchy of male power over female submission has done great harm by imposing itself upon Christian theology. This same patriarchal pattern also permeates male/female power relationships in the family. Much of the resulting harm in families has been hidden and is only now coming to light. Again, the daunting question is: Can we change the power relationships between male and female in the Christian family?

Patterns of wife-beating have been legitimated by the patriarchal imbalance of power and validated by scripture.[63] The classic biblical text on the subject is from the apostle Paul: "Wives, be subject to your husbands, as to the Lord. For the husband is the head of the wife as Christ is the head of the church, his body, and is himself its Savior. As the church is subject to Christ, so let wives also be subject in everything to their husbands" (Eph. 5:22-4). The

---

62. Brown and Parker, "For God So Loved the World?" 27.

63. Susan Brooks Thistlethwaite, "Battered Women and the Bible: From Subjection to Liberation," *Christianity and Crisis*, 16 November 1981. Also R. Emerson Dobash and Russell Dobash, *Violence Against Wives* (New York: Free Press, 1979).

most important twentieth-century Protestant theologian Karl Barth voiced similar views: "Woman is ontologically subordinate to man."[64]

But this is woman. What happens to children within these skewed power relationships in the Christian family? Judith Lewis Herman's ground-breaking work in *Father-Daughter Incest* highlights the profile of the incestuous father as being a pillar of the church, a pillar of the community.[65] She also is clear that the common thread in the profile of the abuser is the imbalance of power between the father and the mother.[66]

The religious issues of incest survivors are explored empirically in *Christianity and Incest*, by Annie Imbens and Ineke Jonker. Nineteen Dutch women, survivors, were reared as children in Holland in very Christian homes, both Protestant and Roman Catholic. Hear their voices, the voices of girl-children now grown to adulthood, speaking about their childhood sexual abuse which took place in Christian homes:

Question: *What aspects of religion did you experience as oppressive?*
Answer: Obedience, and that as a woman, you were always inferior to a man. You had to be subservient all the time, self-sacrificing.[67]
Question: *What connection do you see with religion?*
Answer: My father had very "Christian" ideas about women: women were supposed to be submissive, obedient, and servile. I used to wonder how incest could happen in such religious families. Now I think that families who practice their religion so strictly live in a closed system, a vacuum. . . . My father was religiously dogmatic. A certain image of women was fostered by the church, which enabled men to treat their women that way.[68]
Question: *What aspects of religion did you experience as oppressive?*
Answer: My father often said the commandment: "Honor thy father and

---

64. See Karl Barth, *Church Dogmatics*, ed. G. W. Bromiley and T. F. Torrance (Edinburgh: T. & C. Clark, 1956-1962). III/4, 116-240. Of Barth's views Mary Daly writes, "Barth goes on and on about women's subordination to man, ordained by God. Although he goes through a quasi-infinite number of qualifications, using such jargon as 'mutual subordination,' he warns that we must not overlook the 'concrete subordination of woman to man' (175). He writes, 'Properly speaking, the business of woman, her task and function, is to actualize the fellowship in which man can only precede her, stimulating, leading, and inspiring. . . . To wish to replace him in this, or to do it with him, would be to wish not to be a woman.' In case the point is not clear, he adds the rhetorical question: 'What other choice has she [than to be second] seeing she can be nothing at all apart from this sequence and her place within it' (171). This is justified as being the divine order, according to Barth." (Daly, *Beyond God the Father*, 202.)

65. Judith Lewis Herman with Lisa Hirschman, *Father-Daughter Incest* (Cambridge, Mass.: Harvard, 1981), 71-72.

66. Ibid., 78-79.

67. Anni Imbens and Ineke Jonker, *Christianity and Incest* (Minneapolis; Fortress, 1992), 93.

68. Ibid., 39-40.

thy mother." . . . I was completely abandoned to his will because I obeyed those commandments.[69]

Question: *What connection do you see with religion?*

Answer: Sometimes I asked my father why he kept making me do this. Then he said, "All women are the same as that first woman, Eve. You tempt me. In your heart, this is what you want, just like Eve." I used to pray "God, let it stop!" But God didn't intervene, so I thought, either it really was God's will, or I really was as bad as they said, and this was my punishment.[70]

Question: *What do you associate with these words?: Forgiveness.*

Answer: *Forgiveness*—that was the worst. I had to forgive him "70 times 70 times." It can't be forgiven, even if he were to ask for it—but he never has—even then I couldn't talk about forgiveness. He was a grown man, wasn't he? I was just a child.[71]

Perhaps now we will understand this summary statement by Imbens and Jonker: "*Sexual abuse of children is the ultimate consequence of the gender power relations in our society that we call normal.*"[72] And it is precisely these gender power relations which, from Ephesians to Karl Barth, Christian spokesmen have declared not only normal but God-given and ontologically established.

"I Was Just A Child"

Such haunting, poignant words! But they fill our hearts with the realization that we have been teaching our children power relationships which are simply sick. These teachings poison us and wound deeply. Sometimes it is as brutal as incest. Sometimes it is as quiet as the devastated lives of women silenced and stunted, women whose potential and promise given them in their God-given DNA is never allowed to flower into anything approaching the full expression of their talents.

And then there are all the young boys, who grow into men poisoned into arrogance and male entitlement—and into abuse. What we have done is poison the well from which our children drink.

"*I was just a child.*" This is no mere child's play, this need for a feminist religious education which teaches and models equality and not hierarchy in the Christian family and the so-called "family of the church." This is deadly serious, because the harvest of the past in pain and stunted lives is very real and has been carefully hidden and silenced, with Christianity as its powerful accomplice.

You cannot have a children-friendly tradition until you have a woman-

---

69. Ibid., 40.
70. Ibid., 66.
71. Ibid., 34.
72. Ibid., 119.

respecting tradition. You cannot affirm life, without affirming women, and you cannot raise whole and life-affirming children without affirming women because children love their mothers and need to be nurtured by them. Therefore it hurts children when Christian theology, ritual, and praxis denigrate and abuse their mothers—just as it hurts children to watch battering husbands/fathers beating their mothers.

"I was just a child." Jesus said, "Let the little children come to me. Do not stop them, for it is to such that the *basileia* of God belongs" (Mk. 10:14 NRSV). And again, "If any of you put a stumbling block before one of these little ones who believe in me, I would be better for you if a great millstone were fastened around your neck and you were drowned in the depth of the sea" (Mt. 18:6 NRSV).

How about a new commandment which says, "Honor the children, not the parents"? How about an Eleventh Commandment which says, "Thou shalt not commit incest."[73] How about a commandment that says, "Spare the child and throw away the rod"?[74]

"I was just a child." Do we care enough about our children in an emerging feminist world to challenge all the powerful men and the male-identified women in our Protestant and Roman Catholic traditions to really make the changes necessary to raise our children in a healthy, life-affirming and woman-affirming tradition? I don't know.

Another Reformation
What I am calling for is another Reformation of Christendom, freeing us this time not from the power of pope and priest but from the power of patriarchal males whatever their position. To urge this is to challenge nearly all of our tradition, and it is an awesome challenge. And a part of me fears for the challenge and also for the response.

"It is essential that our religious ideas and images function to heal and empower us, rather than reinforce the dynamics of self-denial, self-hate, child abuse, and oppression," writes Rita Nakashima Brock.[75] In these words she says it all. Our Christian tradition—its ideas, ritual, theology, practice *and its religious education*—must "function to heal and empower us." That is what our Creator had in mind for us. That is what the Jesus who called the children to him certainly had in mind.

Feminism is God's call to us, in this generation, to open up to radical change so that our tradition may be true again to Jesus, and become life-affirming for all.

---

73. The Eleventh Commandment is a movement within Quaker congregations initiated by anthropologist Dana Raphael of Westport, Connecticut.

74. This commandment is inspired by the work of Philip Greven. See his *Spare the Rod.*

75. Rita Nakashima Brock, "And a Little Child Will Lead Us: Christology and Child Abuse," in *Christianity, Patriarchy and Abuse*, 54.

CHAPTER NINE

Kerygmatic Theology and Religious Education

MARY C. BOYS

In all likelihood, "kerygmatic theology" was never a household word. Yet it enjoyed a certain currency in mid-twentieth century, only to be eclipsed by other theological perspectives in the past twenty-five years. Indeed, one is hard pressed today to think of influential books and articles explicitly kerygmatic in orientation and method. Thus, this essay in part revolves around a three-fold question: What was kerygmatic theology, what happened to it, and why?

Another set of questions also frames this study: How and why did kerygmatic theology influence the education of Christians, especially during its peak years in the 1950s and 1960s? A concluding inquiry invites reflection on its present status: If today kerygmatic theology seems to languish in the appendix of theological discourse, might it not still play a significant role in religious education, albeit without the recognition it once enjoyed?

In pursuing these queries, it is necessary to proceed chronologically, examining first the development of kerygmatic theology and the principal educational movements to which it gave rise. Only then is it appropriate to assume a more critical posture by assessing its theological and educational contributions and deficiencies, particularly as they have become apparent in this last quarter century of deepened scholarship on the relationship of

230

Judaism and Christianity. This stance makes it possible, finally, to explore what seems to be kerygmatic theology's revival in *The Catechism of the Catholic Church* (promulgated December 8, 1992).

The Origins of Kerygmatic Theology

Kerygmatic theology takes its name from the Greek term *kerygma*, "preaching" or "proclamation." It refers to those theologies emphasizing the core content of the Christian proclamation of faith (see Mt. 12:41; Rm. 16:25, 1Cor. 1:21; 2:4; 15:14; 2 Tm. 4:17; Ti. 1:3).

Two major developments in the European churches—the so-called "biblical theology" movement[1] and the liturgical movement[2]—shaped kerygmatic theology. Although the former exercised greater influence in Protestant circles and the latter in Catholic circles, the two movements intersected at various points, most notably in their common stress on "salvation history" (*Heilsgeschichte*).[3]

Thus, a brief word about salvation history. Although a fully developed understanding did not develop until the nineteenth century, antecedents appear in Irenaeus and Augustine, as well as in the work of seventeenth-century theologian Johannes Cocceius.[4] At the heart of this concept is the formulation proposed by J. C. K. von Hofmann in the nineteenth century that God is progressively revealed in history.

The fundamentals of Hofmann's formulation, although given varying emphases and interpretations by subsequent theologians, remained constant among all who operated under the rubric of "salvation history":

- God is revealed in history.
- God's self-revelation is progressive, that is, it moves through successive stages.
- The progressive nature of revelation is evident in the way in which the New Testament fulfills and completes the Old Testament. Thus, the Bible records the history of salvation.
- Christ is the focal point of God's progressive self-revelation. All is fulfilled in him.

Often linked with salvation history was a typological reading of the scrip-

---

1. For a review and analysis, see Brevard S. Childs, *Biblical Theology in Crisis* (Philadelphia: Westminster, 1970).

2. See Virgil C. Funk, "The Liturgical Movement (1830-1969)," in *The New Dictionary of Sacramental Worship*, ed. Peter Fink (Collegeville, Minn.: The Liturgical Press, 1990), 695-715.

3. A movement studied in detail in my *Biblical Interpretation in Religious Education: A Study of the Kerygmatic Era* (Birmingham, Ala.: Religious Education Press, 1980).

4. See Irenaeus, *Adversus haereses* 4:14,3; Augustine, *De catechzandis rudibus*; Cocceius's *Summa doctrinae de foedere et testamento Dei* is summarized in Hans W. Frei, *The Eclipse of Biblical Narrative: A Study in Eighteenth and Nineteenth Century Hermeneutics* (New Haven: Yale University Press, 1974), 46-50, 173-176.

tures.[5] Although not restricted to Christian usage—Isaiah employs it to console the exiles from Judah by imaging a new and greater exodus (Isaiah 43:16-18)—it has often functioned as an apologetic tool grounded in the dictum of Augustine: "In the Old Testament, the New Testament lies hid; in the New Testament, the Old Testament becomes clear."[6] Consequently, the types of the Old Testament are mere shadows of the realities of the New Testament "antitypes." "The type," said Jean Daniélou, "is like a flash of lightning which lightens the gloom of the future without in any way changing the present order of things."[7] Thus, the near-sacrifice of Isaac on Mount Moriah prefigured the sacrifice of Christ on Calvary, Leah and Rachel prefigured the synagogue and church, King David, the Lord's anointed, prefigured Christ the King, and so on.

Typology had been a favorite method of the early Christian writers in their apologetics. In the "Epistle of Barnabas" and Melito of Sardis's "Homily on the Passover" typology was employed with a vengeance as a way of asserting the superiority of a Christian reading of Israel's history: Israel misread its own scriptures because it interpreted them too literally and thereby could not see "the Christ." Such literature, with its frequent use of typology, has come to be regarded as part of the extensive literature known as *Adversus Judaeos* (Against the Jews).[8]

Although typology need not be used to assert the superiority of the New Testament, it played that role for some associated with the biblical theology movement. Moreover, typology has obvious liturgical uses.

Biblical Theology, the *Kerygma* and Christian Education

The "biblical theology movement" was roughly contemporaneous with and akin to neo-orthodox theology. Associated particularly with German Old Testament scholar Gerhard von Rad and Swiss New Testament scholar Oscar Cullmann, the principal contours of this movement helped to shape kerygmatic theology.[9] In particular, four characteristics of biblical theology also

---

5. Typology is a mode of interpretation in which a present event, person, situation, or thing suggests a likeness to an event, person, situation, or thing in the past. See P. Joseph Cahill, "Hermeneutical Implication of Typology," *The Catholic Biblical Quarterly* 44 (1982), 267.

6. *Questions on the Heptateuch*, 2.73.

7. Jean Daniélou, *From Shadows to Reality: Studies in the Biblical Typology of the Fathers* (Westminster, Md.: Newman, 1961).

8. See "The Epistle of Barnabas," in *The Apostolic Fathers*, ed. Kirsopp Lake, vol. 1 (Cambridge: Harvard University Press, and London: W. Weinemann, 1952). For the text of Melito's "A Homily on the Passover," see Richard A. Norris Jr., *The Christological Controversy, Sources of Early Christian Thought* (Philadelphia: Fortress, 1980), 33-47. For an important study of the context in which these writers lived, see Robert S. MacLennan, *Early Christian Texts on Jews and Judaism*, Brown Judaic Studies 194 (Atlanta: Scholars Press, 1990).

9. See James Barr, "Biblical Theology" in *The Interpreter's Dictionary of the Bible*, Supplementary Volume (Nashville: Abingdon, 1976), 104-111.

played a significant role in kerygmatic thinking: (1) a stress on the unity of the Bible, with the Old Testament seen as preparation for the New Testament;[10] (2) a contrast between Hebrew and Greek ways of thought;[11] (3) an accentuation on word studies,[12] (4) the importance assigned to God's progressive revelation in history.[13]

Biblical theology, like its cousin neo-orthodoxy, developed in part as a response to liberal theology and to the way "liberals" had studied the Bible. Likewise, among a number of Christian educators, biblical theology served to restore a more theological basis to a field which had been under the sway of theorists such as George Albert Coe and Sophia Lyon Fahs, neither of whom assigned the Bible a central role. The role of kerygmatic theology is most evident in the work of Iris Cully.[14]

Cully makes the *kerygma* central to her existentialist approach to Christian education. She premises that the organic functioning of the church community involves the production of *didache* (teaching), and this teaching is in turn derived from and based upon the *kerygma*. *Kerygma* both forms the church and is formed by it:

> The *kerygma* yields teaching, expressed in the words of the confessions and the activity of the sacraments, intellectualized in doctrine, and made relevant to the immediate situation in terms of ethics. The kerygma further yields teaching through the fellowship—explaining the redemptive experience, nurturing children, and strengthening the community for witnessing in the world.[15]

The church fails when it emphasizes the *didache* alone. Ethical teaching can be found in other religions and philosophies. But it is the "dynamic in back

---

10. Here "salvation history" is the clear hermeneutical principle; it was, in Cullmann's terms, "the factor binding all the texts together" (*Salvation in History* [New York: Harper & Row, 1967], 297).

11. Von Rad, for instance, claimed that Hebrew thinking was thinking in historical traditions, whereas Greek thinking was more metaphysical in nature (*Old Testament Theology, I* [New York: Harper & Row, 1962], 116). See also T. Boman, *Hebrew Thought Compared with Greek* (London: SCM, 1960); O. Cullmann, *Christ and Time*, rev. ed. (Philadelphia: Westminster, 1964), 50-53.

12. Exemplified most fully by Gerhard Kittel et al., *Theological Dictionary of the New Testament,* 10 vols. (Grand Rapids, Mich.: Eerdmans, 1964). (Original volumes in 1932, *Theologisches Worterbuch zum Neuen Testament*).

13. Promulgated particularly by George Ernest Wright, *God Who Acts: Biblical Theology as Recital* (London, SCM, 1952).

14. See also Randolph Crump Miller, *Biblical Theology and Christian Education* (New York: Scribner's, 1956). Sara Little (*The Role of the Bible in Contemporary Christian Education* [Richmond: John Knox Press, 1961]) offers an excellent appraisal of, among others, Miller and of another prominent scholar, James D. Smart, who exercised leadership in the influential *Christian Faith and Life Series.*

15. Iris V. Cully, *The Dynamics of Christian Education* (Philadelphia: Westminster, 1958), 59.

of the Christian teaching"—the *kerygma*—that is Christianity's unique insight. Thus, teachers must not be unduly preoccupied with "how to" because "Christian nurture is dynamic and the gospel will not be reduced to a set of five steps. . . . The 'what' conditions the 'how.' "[16]

Methods for Christian teaching, moreover, should be life-centered rather than "experience-centered." The latter connotes present experience, whereas the former suggests participation in life events which are made present by means of remembrance. When children can see their needs and problems against those of biblical personages, they will discover a focus beyond themselves that offers perspective. So, although one may begin with the child's existential situation, it is necessary to offer the broader context of the *kerygma* in order to provide historical depth, which in turn deepens present experience. Cully concludes:

> The proclamation of the good news that God has come into human life to save his people in a new and wonderful way through Jesus Christ is as living a message today as it was when first spoken. All the teaching that arises from it shares in its vitality. But the teaching must remain rooted in the proclamation. The teaching too is good news. Only dynamic methods can fully carry it so that the work of bringing light and life to men [and women] may continue.[17]

The Liturgical Movement, Kerygmatic Theology, and Catechetics

In contrast to the biblical theology movement, which had played a mediating role in twentieth-century Protestant theology, the liturgical movement in Catholic circles emerged as a counterpoint to nineteenth-century scholasticism, and thus functioned as a progressive force.[18] The confluence of liturgical renewal and kerygmatic theology is most obvious in the work of Austrian liturgical scholar Jesuit Josef Jungmann (1889-1975).

---

16. Ibid., 117.

17. Ibid. See also her subsequent *Imparting the Word: The Bible in Christian Education* (Philadelphia: Westminster, 1960). An interpretation of her work may be found in Kendig Brubaker Cully, *The Search for a Christian Education-Since 1940* (Philadelphia: Westminster, 1975). In this citation and others which use exclusive language, I have added the complementary noun or pronoun.

18. Mark D. Jordan, "Scholasticism," in *The New Dictionary of Theology*, ed. Joseph A. Komonchak, Mary Collins, and Dermot A. Lane [Wilmington, Del.: Michael Glazier, 1987], 936-938) argues that the term scholasticism does not denote any one thing, set of concepts or procedures. However, the definition Jordan cites from Martin Grabmann seems to match most closely what Jungmann and his colleagues were reacting to: "Scholastic method applies reason or philosophy to the truths of revelation in order to gain the greatest possible understanding of the content of faith. It strives for a 'systematic' and 'organic' representation of the whole of saving truth, while seeking to resolve any of reason's objections against it" (937).

His 1936 work *Die Frohbotschaft und unsere Glaubensverkündigung* fired the first volley, so to speak, of the kerygmatic movement. Its purpose was to restore Christ to the center of theology.[19] The need for this restoration, Jungmann believed, was in part necessitated by the state of theology. He argued that because theology—by which he meant scholasticism—had to be concerned with truth questions, and therefore with distinctions, definitions, proofs and solutions, it was primarily at the service of knowledge. Such theology, in his view, did not adequately allow for exploration of the implications for *living a* Christian life. What was needed was an approach more oriented to the task of *proclaiming* the faith:

> Basically the proclamation of the faith needs knowledge only about the way which leads to God, about its beginnings and critical turns, about its ramifications and its endings. Its proper subject is and remains the Good News—what was called the *kerygma* in primitive Christianity. Dogma must be known; the *kerygma* must be proclaimed.[20]

Theological analysis, therefore, had a subservient function when it came to the proclamation of faith. The method of proclamation differed from scholastic theology because it was not to be concerned with "reproducing the ontological order" of all things, but with the *economy of salvation*.[21] Thus, it preferred the "original, simple modes of expression of Sacred Scripture" to the sharply defined language of the School.[22]

What Jungmann proposed was the proclamation of the faith in which the economy of salvation was "above all else" the central theme. Were this to be done, a number of transformations would result. The objective Christocentrism of Catholic doctrine would become a "vitally dynamic subjective presentation." Those influences that had obfuscated the proper Christocentric outlook over the centuries would recede because emphasis on the life-giving mission of Jesus would correct the one-sided emphasis on his divinity that had arisen during periods of christological heresy. Moreover, grace would again be

---

19. All references will be to the English translation, W.A. Huesman and Johannes Hofinger, eds., *The Good News Yesterday and Today* (New York: Sadlier, 1962).

20. Ibid., 33-34.

21. The phrase "economy of salvation," so important in kerygmatic theology, has a long history of usage. Based on the Greek term *oikonomia*, it has various connotations; Jungmann and others drew particularly upon its meaning as the "plan of salvation," for which Ephesians 1:9-10 is the central text: "With all wisdom and insight God has made known to us the mystery of his will, according to his good pleasure that he set forth in Christ, as a plan (*oikonomia*) for the fullness of time, to gather up all things in Christ, things in heaven and things on earth" (NRSV). For an excellent analysis of the phrase, see Catherine Mowry LaCugna, *God for Us: The Trinity and Christian Life* (San Francisco: HarperSanFrancisco, 1991), 24-52.

22. Huesman and Hofinger, *The Good News*, 35.

viewed within the totality of Christian doctrine. In short, heightened attention to the proclamation of faith would revolutionize the lives of Catholics by restoring the position of Christ as mediator, a primacy too long obscured in the multiplicity of devotions.[23]

A later work, *Glaubensverkündigung im Lichte der Frohbotschaft*, reiterated and refined many of the arguments Jungmann had put forward in the 1930s.[24] Again, he stressed that the divine plan must be placed in the foreground and that the various commandments derived from this plan be relegated to the background. Jungmann did not think that theologians needed to begin anew but rather to fit the parts properly into the whole, that is, into the picture of a new divine order which was an "unchanging background and fixed framework for the multifarious searchings and struggles that pass across the stage of life."[25] To describe this totality, Jungmann suggested:

> It is salvation history, begun in the old covenant, reaching its climax in the fullness of time and continuing in the history of the Church until the second coming of our Lord. St. Paul calls it the mystery hidden in God before the beginning of time, but now revealed to his saints. He calls it God's decree, or plan, the purpose of which is to gather together in Christ all things that are in heaven and on earth (Eph. 1:10). Elsewhere this totality appears as God's gracious call (κλησις Eph. 1:18; 4:1, etc.) to the human race, or as the assembly (εκκλησιγ) of those who have heard and obeyed the call—the holy Church.[26]

The person of Christ always stands in the center, because he is the "source of light from which all other doctrinal points are brightly illumined."[27] In Jungmann's view, however, this had not always been the case with scholasticism. Whatever gains it had made possible, he believed scholasticism had also tended to concentrate on a "multitude of isolated pieces of knowledge" and thereby obscured the "true message concerning the facts of salvation history." In his analysis, Christianity was first and foremost a "fact," and only secondarily a doctrine. Because theological science had "overburdened the *kerygma* with things of second and third rank," Jungmann offered an impassioned plea to restore the original and unified power of the *kerygma* as it had been evi-

---

23. Apparently, it was this claim that troubled certain officials in the Vatican. The superior general of the Jesuits, Ladislaus Ledochowski, avoided the condemnation of *Die Frohbotschaft* by withdrawing the book from the market. Only in the 1960s would it recirculate. See Jeremy Hall, "The American Liturgical Movement: The Early Years," *Worship* 50 (1976), 472-489; and Johannes Hofinger, "J.A. Jungmann (1889-1975): In Memoriam," *The Living Light* 13 (1976), 354-356.

24. Joseph A. Jungmann, *Announcing the Word of God* (London: Burns and Oates, 1967). References taken from this translation.

25. Ibid., 17.

26. Ibid.

27. Ibid., 18.

dent in the preaching of the early church.[28] This meant avoiding all "excessive splitting up of the substance of faith:" and all "rank growth around the fringe." Dogmatic theology had its place, but "amidst all the complexities of distinctions, theses and hypotheses, the *leitmotiv* of salvation-history must be preserved. The kerygmatic climaxes must once more come into their own."[29]

It is evident why Jungmann's proposals, as well as those of his followers, have typically been categorized under the rubric of kerygmatic theology. His focus on the core of Christian proclamation—the kerygma—was an attempt to reorient theology by highlighting the centrality of God's salvific plan fulfilled in Jesus Christ:

> *Kerygma* is a biblical concept meaning "that which is preached." It denotes, therefore, the content of preaching, that is what Christ himself proclaimed and what his apostles proclaimed abroad as his heralds: that the kingdom of God had entered the world, thus disclosing salvation to mankind [humankind]. It denotes the original preaching, at first addressed to those who did not yet believe, but which was also intended to provide the core and basis of all subsequent guidance and instruction of believing Christians, and which ought to become all the more clearly sounded in those places where the paths of faith have become overgrown and where a fresh need has arisen for orientation and sign-posting. The *kerygma* is the announcement of facts, above all of the facts through which God himself has intervened in human history and uttered his call to [humankind].[30]

Jungmann's proposals incited a controversy about whether or not this kerygmatic theology was a separate branch of theology. Shortly after the publication of *Die Frohbotschaft*, several articles appeared in the journal he edited, arguing that kerygmatic theology would suffice for priests in pastoral ministry whereas "scientific theology" would be the preserve of academicians.[31] Jungmann's own view on this was not entirely clear until his book of 1955, *Katechetik*, in which he stated: "The efforts to bring about such a renewal do not imply a special kind of theology but a clear and effective presentation of Christ's message itself."[32]

Jungmann's clarification raises a central point for this essay: *kerygmatic theology was less a distinct theological movement than an appeal for more attentiveness to the core of faith in the doing of theology. Engendered by a pas-*

---

28. Ibid., 46.

29. Ibid., 62.

30. Ibid., 59-60.

31. See F. Lakner, "Das Zentralobjekt der Theologie," *Zeitschrift für katholische Theologie* 62 (1938), 1-36 and J.B. Lotz, "Wissenschaft und Verkündigung," *Zeitschrift für katholische Theologie* 62 (1938), 565-501.

32. Joseph A. Jungmann, *Handing on the Faith* (New York: Herder and Herder, 1959), 398.

*sion for revitalizing the lives of Christians, kerygmatic theology was less a
method than a strategy and more of a manifesto than a system. With roots in
Protestant pietism and Catholic liturgical renewal, it reflected little interest
in philosophical sophistication: Its language was that of the scriptures, and
its aim hortatory rather than didactic.*

This pastoral orientation of kerygmatic theology suggests why it would be
taken up with great enthusiasm by Catholic educators.

The Metamorphosis of Kerygmatic Theology into Catechetical Theology

Kerygmatic theology received its purest translation into Catholic education through the indefatigable efforts of Jungmann's student and brother-
Jesuit, Johannes Hofinger (1905-1986) and in the six international catechetical study weeks Hofinger helped to inspire and direct between 1959
and 1968.[33]

Hofinger took up virtually every kerygmatic theme which Jungmann had
sounded and presented it to catechists throughout the world. The motifs of salvation history echoed clearly. Consider his recommendations for teaching the
Bible:

'The Old Testament is essentially our "pedagogue in Christ" (Gal. 3:24). We
will choose from it the preparation for the "mystery of Christ." We must continually point out the imperfection of the Old Testament. It had to be so,
Christ not having come. In elementary teaching for children, it is recommended, after the example of the greatest catechists, to pass immediately
from the story of the Fall and the promise of a Savior to the fulfillment of
that promise (the Annunciation to Our Lady). If there is sufficient time,
one may, in teaching adults (missionary catechesis) deal with some other passages of the OT but always from a Christian angle (Christological).[34]

Hofinger disclosed his theoretical groundwork in greatest detail in a chapter
on "Kerygmatic Theology: Its Nature, and Its Role in Priestly Formation."[35]
He defined kerygmatic theology as that which is more definitely oriented to
the preaching and teaching of the Christian message. It explicitly emphasized
the *dynamic* aspect of the Christian message rather than the rational aspect on
which scholastic theology concentrates. Consequently, Hofinger argued, scholas-

---

33. These international study weeks began in 1959 in Nijmegen (the Netherlands).
The 1960 session at Eichstätt (Germany) represented the highpoint of kerygmatic catechetics. The other four weeks—Bangkok (1962), Katigondo ([Uganda] 1964), Manilla,
(1967), and Medellin (1968)—took up the themes from Eichstätt with varying degrees of
emphasis. For documentation and interpretation see Michael Warren, ed., *Sourcebook for
Modern Catechetics* (Winona, Minn.: Saint Mary's Press, 1983), 23-109.

34. Johannes Hofinger, "Our Message," *Lumen Vitae* 5 (1950): 265.

35. In *The Art of Teaching Christian Doctrine: The Good News and Its Proclamation*,
rev. and enlarged ed. (Notre Dame, Ind.: University of Notre Dame Press, 1962), 245-260.

tic speculation must be supplemented by a study of scripture and of the Fathers in order to bring out the meaning, nature, and character of the Christian message:

> The scholastic rational approach admittedly is of great assistance in the correct teaching of Christian doctrine, and therefore the Church wisely demands a sound use of this approach in theological training. But correctness is not the only aspect of genuinely Christian preaching. Christ's heralds must proclaim a message which is, finally, not for the mind alone, but for the whole man, for life and action.[36]

Hofinger offered four qualifications to this assertion. First, kerygmatic theology is not a new branch of theology but rather a "functional orientation" of theology. Thus he preferred to speak of "the kerygmatic approach to theology" rather than "kerygmatic theology." Second, the kerygmatic approach is not opposed to scholasticism but a complement to it.[37] Third, "kerygmatic theology" is not intended as a practical theological course for seminarians lacking academic gifts but, on the contrary, as a mode of theology that stressed for all students the religious values of Christian doctrine. Nor, fourth, should "kerygmatic" theology be regarded as a "lay theology" in contrast to the scholastic theology used in seminaries and university faculties of theology.

In a word, for Hofinger kerygmatic theology *is* catechetical theology. It merges with religious education in regard to content because it answers "*ex professo* exactly those questions which now are the focus of catechetical interest: the right selection of material, the organization of the catechetical material, the special relation to the whole in which the individual parts of the material are to be presented."[38]

Hofinger's conviction about the inextricable link of kerygmatic and catechetical theology offers the contemporary reader a critical clarification both about the "location" of kerygmatic theology and the character of the catechetical movement. At least in Catholic circles, the kerygmatic approach to

---

36. Ibid., 249.

37. "Scholastic theology aims primarily at an intellectual elaboration of Christian doctrine . . . [whereas] 'kerygmatic' theology aims at the religious appreciation and the missionary proclamation of the revealed truth. . . . Scholastic theology is, in principle, concerned with the whole of revealed truth (cf. *Summa Theologica*), although its preference is for those parts of revealed doctrine that offer the richest material for . . . a rational elaboration of the revealed truths that draws heavily on philosophy. But the kerygmatic approach limits its interest more to those aspects of revealed truth which are in a special way meant to be lived and proclaimed. . . . Scholastic theology offers us a precise formulation of Christian doctrine; it assures orthodoxy; it develops the gift of a clearer discernment between truth and error in doctrinal matters. The kerygmatic approach, on the other hand, develops especially the sense of the substance, the relations and the religious values of Christian doctrine. It gives us the ability to pray, to meditate, to appreciate, to live Christian doctrine. (Ibid., 254-255)

38 Ibid., 259.

theology exercised far more influence on the educational scene than it did on the theological plane precisely because from the outset its orientation was primarily pastoral.

Nevertheless, some major Catholic theologians have relied on salvation history as an important theological concept, most notably Karl Rahner, Joseph Ratzinger, and Hans Urs von Balthasar. In Rahner, for example, the theme of God's progressive self-revelation is evident. For him the Old Testament represented a period in salvation history which was not only fulfilled by the coming of Jesus, but effectively ended; "the OT period was closed by the new covenant in Christ Jesus."[39] As the "prehistory of the new and eternal covenant, in which the OT has been annulled yet incorporated," it can only be fully and correctly interpreted from the standpoint of the new covenant, because its true nature is only disclosed (2 Cor. 3:14) in the revelation of it τελος (end) (Rm. 10:4).[40]

Similar themes emerge in the writings of Joseph Ratzinger, a fact of enormous consequence for the contemporary Catholic world because of his influence on the *Catechism of the Catholic Church*.[41] In a brief work written with Karl Rahner, Ratzinger distinguishes various biblical theologies. One emanates from historians, another is a New Testament theology of the Old Testament ("a new interpretation in the light of the Christ-event which does not arise from the purely historical consideration of the Old Testament alone"), a third is theology of the New Testament done by historians, and the fourth is the Church's theology of the New Testament "which we call dogmatic theology." What distinguishes this dogmatic theology from biblical theology is tradition.[42]

Ratzinger develops his understanding of biblical interpretation in a recent essay in which he takes issue with the philosophical foundation of historical-critical method (which he associates particularly with Martin Dibelius and Rudolf Bultmann). Texts, he argues, need to be placed in their historical context, but only if they are then seen in "light of the total movement of history and in light of history's central event, Jesus Christ" will they yield proper understanding.[43] What is apparent in this essay, and was foreshadowed

---

39. Karl Rahner, "History of Salvation," in *Encyclopedia of Theology: The Concise Sacramentum Mundi*, ed. K. Rahner (New York: Seabury, 1975), 1506-1518. Quotation, 1512-1513.

40. Ibid., 1516.

41. Joseph Ratzinger is the head of the Congregation for the Doctrine of Faith, from which the catechism has been issued.

42. Karl Rahner and Joseph Ratzinger, *Revelation and Tradition* (New York: Herder and Herder, 1966), 44.

43. Joseph Ratzinger, "Biblical Interpretation in Crisis: On the Question of the Foundations and approaches of Exegesis Today," in *Biblical Interpretation in Crisis: The Ratzinger Conference on Bible and Church*, ed. Richard J. Neuhaus (Grand Rapids, Mich.: Eerdmans, 1989), 20-21. The subsequent essay by Raymond E. Brown ("The Contribution of Historical Biblical Criticism to Ecumenical Church Discussion," 24-49) offers an insightful complement to Ratzinger's essay.

in the one previously cited, is Ratzinger's reluctance to grant historical criticism a significant role in the church's interpretation of scripture.

Something of von Balthasar's understanding of the relation between the Testaments is evident in the second chapter of his *A Theology of History*, "The Son and Salvation History." He claims that the creative element marking the leap from Old to New Testament is the love with which Christ obeys, "a love which is so perfect that it breaks out of the old principle of servile obedience and makes the Law the servant of love."[44] In von Balthasar's view, the "Old Covenant is a sketch of future achievement, compulsion is the foundation of a future freedom, and form the vessel of a content yet to come."[45]

Without doubt, Rahner, Ratzinger, and von Balthasar are of enormous significance for twentieth-century Catholic thought and may well be the principal reason that salvation history and kerygmatic theology retain a measure of influence today. In the main, however, those who theologized from the kerygmatic/catechetical point of view did not dominate the academy. Other theological frameworks and methodologies developed that took into account the growing unease of biblical scholars with the assumptions of salvation history. Because, however, the *kerygma* was transfigured into catechetics, catechetics must be understood as first and foremost a theological perspective with little grounding in educational theory and practice.[46] Those who offered leadership, especially in its foundational period (ca. 1960-1975), tended to be theologians with pastoral rather than academic interests.

So the kerygmatic approach was essentially carried on through catechetics. In fact, the principles articulated at the Eichstätt study week in 1960, although modified in significant ways, have enjoyed a tremendous staying power in catechetics.[47] They are:[48]

---

44. Hans Urs von Balthasar, *A Theology of History* (New York: Sheed and Ward, 1963), 55. German original, 1959.

45. Ibid. In his later work (*Man in History: A Theological Study* [London: Sheed and Ward, 1968; German original, 1963]), von Balthasar suggests that postbiblical Judaism is without "any possible inner development"; he writes: "An Israel after Christ is not only a theological contradiction; it is also a historico-philosophical one. In order to continue to exist it must somehow detemporalize itself: around the "letter" of the law or the "spirit" of wisdom or enlightened Gnosticism. Its institutions, its temple cult, and its priesthood together with sacrifices are bound by time and cannot return (even in today's state of Israel): thus it can replace its former institutions only by secularized ones. In the Qumrân the end is already visible" (172).

46. See the discussion of the educational implications in James Michael Lee, *The Shape of Religious Instruction: A Social Science Approach* (Birmingham, Ala.: Religious Education Press, 1971), 31-34.

47. For an analysis of the "cousin" terms *catechesis and catechetics*, see my *Educating in Faith: Maps and Visions* (San Francisco: Harper & Row, 1989, 109-110). I detect no consistent, clear distinction between the two.

48. What follows is the text of the Eichstätt document as adapted by Michael Warren in *Sourcebook*, 34-38.

1. Catechesis carries out the command of Christ to proclaim God's message of salvation to all people.
2. Catechesis proclaims the merciful love of the Father for us and proclaims the Good News of God's Kingdom.
3. Catechesis is Christ-centered, reflecting the fulfillment in and through Christ of the Father's loving design.
4. Catechesis proclaims that Christ continues to live and work in his church through the Holy Spirit and the ministry of his shepherds.
5. Catechesis emphasizes that worship is the heart of Christian community life.
6. Catechesis teaches us to respond to God's call by an inner change of heart manifested in a life of faith and hope and of loving obedience to his commands.
7. Catechesis makes Christians aware of their responsibility for the world and the betterment of its condition.
8. Catechesis leads the Christian to share the faith with others.
9. Catechesis, following God's method, proclaims the "wonderful works of God," which show forth the truth and especially the love contained in them, moving the heart and inspiring the whole of life.
10. Catechesis embraces a fourfold presentation of the faith: through liturgy, Bible, systematic teaching, and the testimony of Christian living.[49]
11. Catechesis adapts itself to the life and thought of peoples, shows due appreciation of their laudable views and customs and integrates them harmoniously into a Christian way of life.
12. Catechesis introduces the catechumen into a living community and helps him or her to strike root in it.[50]

These principles received wide dissemination, whether in the brief, popular manual for teachers (especially volunteer teachers in Confraternity of Christian Doctrine [CCD] programs), *The ABC's of Modern Catechetics*[51] or in the four-year textbook series for Catholic secondary school students, the *Lord and King* series[52] or in numerous articles in the European journal *Lumen Vitae*. Occupying a central place, often explicitly, was the notion of the four-fold presentation of the faith (#10). For example, this notion was the organizing principle of the *Lord and King* series authored by three alumni of the

---

49. In a later section of the document, the authors write: "There is no genuine religious formation without education to *action*, and above all, formation of conscience." (See the "Appendix," in *The Art of Teaching Christian Doctrine*, 273).

50. "Moreover, because Christian life unfolds itself day by day in the Church, the catechist must avoid forming in his [and her] followers an individualistic personality. To this end, he [and she] must bring them into contact with the parish *community* and above all with its liturgical life. (Ibid., 274.)

51. Johannes Hofinger and William J. Reedy, *The ABC's of Modern Catechetics* (New York: Sadlier, 1962).

52. Vincent M. Novak authored the books for the first two years, John Nelson the third year, and Joseph Novak the fourth year. See especially V.M. Novak, *Teachers Guide, Lord of History* (New York: Holt, Rinehart and Wiston, 1966).

Lumen Vitae school. The first year text featured the biblical (*Lord of History*), the second year the liturgical (*Jesus Christ: Our Life and Worship*), and the third year the doctrinal (*The Church: People of God*), and the fourth year the sign of witness (*Christian Witness: Response to Christ*). This series was used in nearly 65 percent of Catholic secondary schools in the mid-1960s.

The four signs reappear in the national catechetical directory for U.S. Catholics *Sharing the Light of Faith*, although the fourth is referred to as "natural signs," which the faithful should test and interpret in a "wholly Christian spirit."[53] The salvation history motif, however, was less evident, although echoes can be perceived in the exhortation that "major themes of the Old Testament are also to be known as preparing for Christ" and in the notion that the Old Testament set the stage "for a broader and deeper covenant, God's fullest self-revelation in Jesus Christ."[54]

In short, kerygmatic theology disappeared, as it were, into catechetics. Or one might say that the kerygmatic approach to theology metamorphosed into the catechetical movement, at least in its early phases (ca. 1955-1970). In its emphasis on the vitality of Christianity, it offered a more dynamic understanding of faith than had either scholastic theology or the question-and-answer format of the catechism. With its teaching on the unity of the divine plan, it enabled large numbers of Catholics who were taking up the Bible for themselves for the first time to find coherence in the diverse biblical writings, and particularly to find a way to connect the Old and New Testaments.[55] In its stress on Christ as the center, it offered a sort of "hierarchy of truths," thereby emphasizing the central aspects of God's saving ways and giving less stress to more marginal beliefs and practices.[56]

---

53. *Sharing the Light of Faith: National Catechetical Directory for Catholics of the United States* (Washington, D.C.: The United States Catholic Conference, 1979), #s 42-46. Quotation #46.

54. Ibid., #s60 and 53.

55. Most Catholics mistakenly thought they were forbidden to read the Bible themselves, a misconception directly linked to a decree in 1546 from the Council of Trent. The decree in actuality forbade the *private interpretation* of scripture, a prohibition intended to counter the authority of the church's interpretation of scripture over against the claims of Luther that the "godly though unlearned" layperson might grasp the true sense of scripture. Tragically, the vast majority both within and outside the Catholic church understood Trent's decree as forbidding the *private reading* of scripture. See F.J. Crehan, "The Bible in the Roman Catholic Church from Trent to the Present Day," in *The Cambridge History of the Bible*, vol. 2: The West from the Reformation to the Present Day, ed. S.L. Greenslade, (Cambridge: Cambridge University Press, 1963), 199-237.

56. This phrase originated in the Decree on Ecumenism (*Unitatis redintegratio*) of Vatican II, promulgated in 1964, #11: "When comparing doctrines with one another, they [Catholic theologians] should remember that in Catholic doctrine there exists an order or 'hierarchy' of truths, since they vary in their relation to the foundation of the Christian faith" (cited in Austin Flannery, ed., *Vatican Council II: The Conciliar and Post-Conciliar Documents*, vol. 1; cf. William Henn, s.v., "Hierarchy of Truths," in *The New Dictionary of Theology*, 464-466).

However, as biblical studies and theology matured and as the catechetical movement moved into other phases, the kerygmatic "era" largely
passed. The theological tenets which had seemed so exciting to Jungmann,
Hofinger, and their numerous disciples appeared increasingly insufficient
to sustain a revolution in religious education.

Religious education flowered in ways less rooted in kerygmatic theology,
although the close connection between liturgy and education evident in the
many writings flowing from the restoration of the catechumenate in 1972
honor Jungmann's insights in a profound manner.[57]

Kerygmatic Theology: A Critical Assessment

In large part, kerygmatic theology's failure to take hold in the academy may
be attributed to serious flaws in one of its principal concepts, salvation history. In my 1980 book I argued at length that new theological thinking on revelation, christology, the relationship between the Testaments and ecclesiology "cast heavy shadows" on salvation history.[58] More recently, systematic
theologian Bradford Hinze has perceptively identified a related series of
problems with salvation history.[59] The first difficulty lies in the imprecision
of the term and a second with its distortion of the diversity of literary genres
within the scriptures. To link historical and prophetic motifs, as does salvation history, overlooks the sapiential, parabolic, and cultic genres. Thus, by
"superimposing one plan or order on the historiography of the Bible as a
whole," salvation history "levels the plurality of narrative patterns at work in
the scriptures."[60]

Moreover, salvation history not only force-fits pluriform texts into a uniform interpretative schema but also represses discontinuities. A prime example is the relationship between God's covenant with Israel and with the
church. Hinze writes:

> Promise and fulfillment motifs and a typological method of exegesis can
> gloss over a multitude of questions that arise when one scratches the surface
> of texts and examines the different plots and structures of argument at
> work. What is the role of the Jews in salvation history? Must the Jews be cast
> as those who reject God's plan and will in order to present Jesus as the
> inauguration of a new covenant? Is it possible to portray Jesus as the epit-
> ome of the Jewish tradition and trajectory without denying the specific

---

57. Among the most notable, James B. Dunning, *Echoing God's Word: Formation
for Catechists and Homilists in a Catechumenal Church* (Arlington, Va.: The North
American Forum on the Catechumenate, 1993). Also, Philip J. McBrien, *How To Teach
with the Lectionary* (Mystic, Conn.: Twenty-Third Publications, 1992).

58. Boys, *Biblical Interpretation in Religious Education*, 141-202.

59. Bradford E. Hinze, "The End of Salvation History," *Horizons* 18:2 (1991), 227-245.

60. Ibid., 235.

character of Christianity? These are important issues for New Testament exegesis as well as for Jewish-Christian dialogue.[61]

Other theological questions arise in regard to salvation history. Hinze poses six: (1) Is the God of salvation history portrayed in such exclusively anthropomorphic ways that it becomes difficult to acknowledge other ways of imagining God? (2) Is the concept of salvation history sufficiently future-oriented, that is, is the promise-fulfillment motif stressed to the detriment of eschatology? (3) Is its christology distorted or myopic, without adequate reference to the Spirit? (4) Does salvation history adequately account for the political and social dynamics of biblical texts? (5) As the account of salvation history has been told, has it been largely a story about men, with women playing only subordinate, supporting roles? (6) Does salvation history sufficiently account for the role of creation, nature, and cosmos in the biblical witness and in today's world?

Hinze's conclusion is worth citing at length:

> The Bible testifies to God's economy of salvation at work in nature and history. But this economy is mystery, not map, for the God of the future also bids us into unchartered territory. The pilgrimage is aided by these revered, received writings. They tell us who we are and who we are called to be. However, these saving traditions are not exhaustive: they suggest, but they neither tell all, nor detail the end.[62]

A Fundamental Problem: The Kerygmatic Approach as Supersessionist

Building on my earlier arguments and on Hinze's, let me develop in somewhat greater detail what I believe to be a fundamental problem with the kerygmatic approach to theology as it was translated into the catechetical movement: its disparagement of Judaism, premised on the assumption of God's progressive self-revelation and its use of the promise-fulfillment motif.[63] In short, the kerygmatic approach is *supersessionist*: it shares in that longstanding, but now outmoded, view of Christians that they have replaced—superseded—the Jews as God's people because of the Jews' rejection of Jesus Christ.[64]

As a consequence, those influenced by the kerygmatic approach inter-

---

61. Ibid., 236-237.

62. Ibid., 245.

63. See Jon D. Levenson's exploration of why Jews are not interested in biblical theology (*The Hebrew Bible, the Old Testament, and Historical Criticism* [Louisville: Westminster/John Knox, 1993]), 33-61.

64. See my "A More Faithful Portrait of Judaism: An Imperative for Christian Educators," in *Within Context: Essays on Jews and Judaism in the New Testament,* ed. David Efroymson, Eugene J. Fisher, and Leon Klenicki (Collegeville, Minn.: Liturgical Press, 1993), 1-20.

preted the "Old" Testament—what I prefer to call the "First" Testament—reductionistically, presented Jesus in a simplistic fashion, and distorted the emergence of Christianity from Judaism.

Even my choice of terminology—"First" Testament instead of "Old" Testament—reveals discomfort with the kerygmatic/catechetical approach. Admittedly, the term is far from poetic, but it avoids both the connotation of outmoded and superseded that so often accompanies "Old" Testament, and the linguistic imprecision of the more recent terminology of "Hebrew Bible."[65]

Those influenced by the kerygmatic approach failed to recognize that the way our Christian ancestors interpreted the First Testament is not the only possible way those scriptures might have been read—indeed, that a Christian reading of the First Testament is pervasively shaped by a distinctive christological perspective. The Christian appropriation of the First Testament is a second reading, as it were, from a confessional point of view. In particular, the experience of the resurrection reoriented the disciples of Jesus. It provided a new "lens" by which they understood God's relationship to them. Accordingly, they searched their scriptures with "christological eyes," looking for images, stories, and expectations that would help them understand and give voice to what God had done in their midst. They discerned a new layer of meaning in those texts. But this layer was not the primary layer. Rather, it flowed from the "surplus of meaning" intrinsic to a classic text. Monika Hellwig has aptly summarized this process:

> There is, in other words, a general acknowledgement by those who have studied theology that the Hebrew Scriptures have as their primary meaning that which is discerned therein by Jewish piety and tradition—a meaning that is complete without the New Testament. The meaning that Christians discern there, in the light of their experience of Jesus the Jew and his impact on their world, is a reinterpretation, not the primary and evident meaning of the Hebrew texts themselves.[66]

---

65. The first attestation of "old" testament dates from the late second century in Melito of Sardis, ca. 180 (*ta tés palaias diathékes biblía*); see Roland E. Murphy, "Old Testament/Tanakh—Canon and Inspiration," in *Hebrew Bible or Old Testament? Christianity and Judaism in Antiquity*, ed. Roger Brooks and John J. Collins, vol 5 (Notre Dame, Ind.: University of Notre Dame Press, 1990), 11-30. "Hebrew Bible" avoids the negative connotation of the past, but does not do justice to the Aramaic passages (and Greek texts, if one is taking the Orthodox and Roman Catholic canons into account). André Lacoque has suggested that "Prime" Testament is fitting (" 'Old Testament' in Protestant Tradition," in *Biblical Studies: Meeting Ground of Jews and Christians*, Stimulus Books, ed. Lawrence Boadt, Helga Croner, and Leon Klenicki (New York: Paulist, 1980), 120-146. His proposal is similar to the argument I follow, that of James A. Sanders for "First" Testament ("First Testament and Second," *Biblical Theology Bulletin* 17 [1987], 47-49).

66. Monika K. Hellwig, "Bible Interpretation: Has Anything Changed?" in *Biblical Studies: Meeting Ground of Jews and Christians*, 175.

The experience of the resurrection refocused in an illuminating manner what the disciples already knew from the tradition. The resurrection of Jesus served as a catalyst for seeing more than they had seen before. As Paul van Buren suggests, promise-fulfillment—a schema dearly beloved by kerygmatic theologians—is inadequate because it does not do justice to the "genuine novelty-within-continuity" to which the Apostolic Writings [a term van Buren prefers to New Testament] bear witness; we might more fittingly speak of *promise and confirmation* rather than promise and fulfillment:

> To confirm is to corroborate, to ratify. It means to say Yes. When the Church, in its Apostolic Writings and in its witness through the centuries, confirmed and confirms Israel's Scriptures, it says Yes to their witness. It says *Amen*, so be it. It cannot then intend to replace that witness with its own. Rather, it adds its witness to that of Israel's, with the intent of confirming Israel's witness. It does so because it believes, with the Apostle to the Gentiles, that 'all of the promises of God find their Yes in [Jesus Christ]' (2 Cor. 1:20).[67]

Christians will indeed discern in the First Testament the face of Jesus the Christ—not because references to Jesus are part of the literal level of the texts, but because at the canonical and ecclesial levels their insight "reads" a new dimension.[68]

Such a distinction permits a far more sensitive and appropriate Christian interpretation of the First Testament. Gail Ramshaw suggests a liturgical hermeneutic to counter the kerygmatic "two-step" interpretation in which (1) the First Testament contains promises which were fulfilled in Christ, and (2) Christianity is part of the fulfillment, whereas Judaism is not. Far more satisfactory, she argues, is the addition of a third step: the Spirit in the worshiping assembly. So the readings of the Easter Vigil, for instance, are (1) narratives of the Jewish people; (2) imaginative images

---

67. Paul van Buren, *A Christian Theology of the People Israel* (New York: Seabury, 1983), 27-29. Van Buren argues that the church cannot be itself without confirming God's choice of, covenant with, and promises to Israel.

68. Here I am following the distinctions proffered by Raymond E. Brown (*The Critical Meaning of the Bible* [New York: Paulist, 1981], 23-44): the *literal* level of a biblical text is not only what the final human author meant, but also the intention of the redactor; the *canonical* level of the text refers to the meaning the text has when joined to other books in the canon; the *ecclesial* level refers to the meaning of the text as it is taken up into the life, liturgy, and theology of the community shaped by its scripture. The literal level is the "conscience and control" of the other levels. Sandra M. Schneiders offers an important qualification in her argument that the literal sense is the religious meaning of the text which is actualized in numerous ways and at varying depths throughout Christian history. A clear implication of this argument is that the exegete is obligated not simply to establish what an author said but to inquire into the questions behind the text ("Faith, Hermeneutics, and the Literal Sense of Scripture," *Theological Studies* 39 [1978], 719-736.)

of Christ's resurrection, and (3) language describing this year's baptismal community.[69]

Further, Ramshaw suggests three different techniques for a Christian interpretation of First Testament texts.[70] The first technique draws upon the First Testament for *context* in order to provide *clarity*. Often, for instance, one needs to understand the First Testament language to make sense of the Second, such as knowing the postexilic context of Isaiah 40 in order to understand Mark 1:1-8 about John the Baptist. A second technique involves *metaphor* for the purposes of *enrichment* of understanding. This is most easily seen in the Easter Vigil readings, which are neither "an exercise in *Heilsgeschichte*," nor a historical background but "metaphors for the resurrection":

> That the world is created; that Noah is saved from the flood; that Isaac is saved from the knife; that the Israelites are saved from Pharaoh's army; that the dry bones are revived: these are images for Easter Day, metaphoric parallels for the gospel story of Jesus' empty tomb and for the church's baptisms.[71]

The third technique Ramshaw suggests, *parallel by contrast*—the contrast of the life of Christ's salvation with the death of the human condition—is especially susceptible to antisemitism because it casts the stories of the First Testament in a negative light. It can provide "the simple-minded exegete with texts that condemn Judaism as the evil to which Christianity offers the good."[72] Precisely because it is the most difficult to manage, it ought to be used sparingly. Nonetheless, Ramshaw sees it as effective when, as in the First Sunday in Lent (Cycle A) the fall of Adam and Eve is paired with Christ's temptation: "the tale of humankind's seeking ourselves to our own loss is contrasted with Christ's worshiping God to our gain. With these contrasting stories of choosing death or life, Christians begin Lent."[73]

Another major oversight in the kerygmatic reading of the "Old" Testament is its failure to acknowledge the rich tradition of textual interpretation in Judaism. This is hardly surprising; because as a general rule Christians are abysmally ignorant about the ways Jews have interpreted *Tanakh* over the

---

69. Gail Ramshaw, "The First Testament in Christian Lectionaries," *Worship* 64 (1989), 503. See also *SIDIC* 21:3 (1988) for a special issue on "Problems of Typology: Reading the Jewish and the Christian Scriptures."

70. Ramshaw applies these techniques to the lectionary, but I believe they have wider applicability. Note that we have come full circle from Jungmann, with a liturgist now making a proposal with considerable implications for the teaching of scripture.

71. Ibid., 507.

72. Ibid., 509.

73. Ibid., 508.

ages.[74] They have virtually no knowledge of the manifold traditions—Talmud, Midrash, medieval Bible commentaries, medieval Jewish philosophy, Kabbalistic texts, teachings of Hasidic masters and prayers, to use the categories established by Barry Holtz[75]—by which Jews interpret their scriptures. In fact, if one premised an understanding of Jewish interpretation solely on the view of the kerygmatic theologians, he or she would conclude that nothing had happened since the first century.

As a consequence of their reductionistic interpretation of the First Testament, the kerygmatic theologians (among others) vastly oversimplified their presentation of Jesus. In their well-intentioned effort to restore dynamism to the presentation of Christian life, they had made Christ the "center" by suggesting that all history led up to him, a sort of evolutionary ascent. This provided, for example, a clear portrait of Jesus as the long-awaited messiah to whom the prophets had so clearly pointed but whom the Jews had failed to recognize.

But the reality of this history is far more complex. Israel's history and literature reveal diverse meanings of "messiah," primarily because Judaism itself was so diverse.[76] First-century Jews held many different, even mutually exclusive, images and beliefs about messianism. There were, as Catholic scholar Clemens Thoma has phrased it, a "rich palette of messianic notions within Judaism at the time of Jesus. . . . The conclusion is evident that there is no fully established, universally portrayed Jewish messianic figure which should be contrasted to the human Jesus."[77]

In short, Jews had no one script, no straightforward list of prophecies about the nature and function of "the messiah." Messianic language, more-

---

74. Here I use the term that is an acronym of the Jewish canon, divided as it is into three parts: Torah (*Torah*), Prophets (*Neviim*) and Writings (*Ketuvim*). See "Bible" in Dan Cohn-Sherbok, *A Dictionary of Judaism and Christianity* (Philadelphia: Trinity Press International, 1991), 13.

75. Barry Holtz, ed., *Back to the Sources: Reading the Classic Jewish Texts* (New York: Summit Books, 1984). Also Burton L. Visotzky, *Reading the Book: Making the Bible a Timeless Text* (New York: Anchor Books, Doubleday, 1991); and Frederick E. Greenspahn, ed., *Scripture in the Jewish and Christian Traditions* (Nashville: Abingdon, 1982).

76. Hence Jacob Neusner speaks of "Judaism*s* and their messiah*s*" [my emphasis]; see J. Neusner, William S. Green, and Ernest Frerichs, eds., *Judaisms and their Messiahs at the Turn of the Christian Era* (Cambridge: Cambridge University Press, 1987). Also, James H. Charlesworth, ed., *The Messiah: Developments in Earliest Judaism and Christianity* (Minneapolis: Fortress, 1992).

77. Clemens Thoma, *A Christian Theology of Judaism*. A Stimulus Book (New York: Paulist, 1980), 134. Cf. Henning Graf Reventlow (*Problems of Biblical Theology in the Twentieth Century*: Philadelphia: Fortress, [1986], 50): "However, the traditional model of the 'messianic promises' which find their fulfillment in the New Testament in Jesus Christ has long since come to an end in serious scholarly discussion as a result of the exegetical developments described above."

over, was but one way of imaging God's salvation, and it was not the most important. When the early church called Jesus the "Christ," it added new layers of meaning to the term and made it more central than it had been in Judaism. So to call Jesus our messiah is a claim of faith, not a self-evident axiom of prophecy.

Similarly, the kerygmatic approach tended to obscure the complex dynamics by which Christianity emerged from Judaism. The emphasis on Christ as the fulfillment of the promises of the covenant implicitly suggested that once he had come the distinct identity of Christianity was established. In reality, however, it was considerably more complicated.

A host of studies testify to new understandings of Christian origins that quite definitely alter the conventional account. They may be summarized as follows:

- Early Judaism admitted of many variant streams, one of which eventuated in Christianity. Judaism as we know it today ("rabbinic Judaism") also emerged from the same source, but the emergence and separation of these two streams were extremely complex. It is as if "Jesus' movement-become-Christianity" and "the Pharisaic movement-become-rabbinic Judaism-become Judaism" are fraternal twins, carried in the same womb of early Judaism, but who grew up to look (and be) quite different.
- The emergence of Christianity from formative Judaism did not happen "in a flash" but as the result of differences over certain "flash points" (temple, circumcision, dietary laws, status of Torah, monotheism).[78]
- At least until the mid-second century (and in many places well past that), the boundaries between "Judaism" and "Christianity" were not nearly so fixed as most have imagined.[79]
- Writings such as the Gospel of Matthew, for example, which seem to position Jesus over against "the" Jewish community, are better read as intra-Jewish debate. So the polemical dimension of many New Testament writings must be seen in certain cases (e.g., Mt. 23) as reflecting a community's heated, conflicting claims about the authoritative reading of the tradition.[80]

---

78. See James D.G. Dunn, *The Partings of the Ways: Between Christianity and Judaism and Their Significance for the Character of Christianity* (London: SCM, and Philadelphia: Trinity Press International, 1991).

79. "I want to advance the proposition that for many Christians, there was no break at all with Judaism—not in 70, not in 150, indeed not even in 370, some three hundred years after virtually all previous scholars have told us the final break took place" (John Gager, "The Parting of the Ways: A View from Early Christianity: 'A Christian Perspective,'" in *Interwoven Destinies: Jews and Christians Through the Ages*, A Stimulus Book, ed. Eugene J. Fisher (New York: Paulist, 1993), 67.

80. See Anthony J. Saldarini, "Deligitimation of Leaders in Matthew 23," *The Catholic Biblical Quarterly* 54:4 (1992), 659-680.

• In any case, polemics must be understood in the literary context of the ancient world.[81] Later readers must thus relativize what appears to be extremely hostile language.

Many of these insights were not available to the kerygmatic theologians, as they are the fruit of more recent biblical and historical scholarship. They represent, however, a considerable body of knowledge that simply must be taken into consideration today if we hope to offer an understanding of Christianity grounded in a faithful portrait of Judaism.

Kerygmatic Theology Redivivus: *The Catechism of the Catholic Church*

Given the richness of this recent scholarship that has seemingly laid to rest so many of the supersessionist assumptions of the kerygmatic theologians, it is particularly disappointing to see them reappear in so important a document as *The Catechism of the Catholic Church.*[82]

The *Catechism*, a lengthy narrative, is organized in four books. The first, "The Profession of Faith," centers on the creed and the second, "The Celebration of the Holy Mystery," explains the liturgy and sacraments. Book Three, "Life in Christ," takes up the relationship of law and grace, giving special attention to the Ten Commandments. The concluding book, "Christian Prayer," discusses the centrality of prayer and offers a commentary on the Lord's Prayer.

Obviously a document of such extent and complexity cannot adequately be analyzed in the context of this essay. Yet, because its incorporation of kerygmatic theology and its salvation history motif is striking, it is important to note the connections. *By so doing, it becomes clear the kerygma lives still in religious education.*

In certain respects one can detect a sort of tension when the document speaks of the Old Testament. On the one hand, the catechism speaks of it as an "indispensable part of Sacred Scripture. Its books are divinely inspired and retain a permanent value, for the old covenant has never been revoked."[83] Yet its purpose seems to be entirely preparatory: "Indeed, 'the principal pur-

---

81. See Pheme Perkins, "Irenaeus and the Gnostics. Rhetoric and Composition in Adversus Haereses Book One." *Vigilae Christianae* 30 (1976), 193-200 and Luke Timothy Johnson, "The New Testament's Anti-Jewish Slander and the Conventions of Ancient Polemic," *Journal of Biblical Literature* 108:3 (1989).

82. See John Paul II, "Apostolic Constitution on Publication of Catechism of the Catholic Church," *Origins* 22:31 (January 14, 1993). For background, see the special issue of *The Living Light* 29:4 (Summer 1993) and the symposium articles in *The Living Light* 30:1 (Fall 1993).

83. *The Catechism of the Catholic Church* (Città del Vaticano: Libreria Editrice Vaticana, 1992) #121. The official English translation has not yet been released, although it has been published in French (original), Spanish and Italian. The citations used here are from an advance copy sent to bishops of the United States on December 4, 1992.

pose of the Old Testament economy was to prepare for the coming of Christ, the Savior of the world.' Although the books of the Old Testament 'contain incomplete and provisional things,' they nonetheless bear witness to the whole divine pedagogy of God's saving love."[84] The reference to the "divine pedagogy" is premised on God's progressive self-revelation:

> God accomplished his plan of revelation "by deeds and words intrinsically connected with each other." This plan involved a specific divine pedagogy: God's gradual self-communication prepared humanity by stages to accept the supernatural self-revelation that culminated in the person and mission of the incarnate Word, Jesus Christ.[85]

The link between divine pedagogy and progressive revelation is clear also in a later declaration that "God gave the letter of the law as a tutor to lead his people toward Christ. But the law, powerless to save a human race deprived of the divine likeness yet awakening a growing awareness of sin, kindled in the people a desire for the Spirit."[86]

Because of this progressive self-revelation, there is a unity of "the two Testaments [that] proceeds from the unity of God's plan and revelation. The Old Testament prepares for the New and the New Testament fulfills the Old. The two shed light on each other and both are the Word of God."[87] The promise-to-fulfillment schema is evident in the assertion:

> The coming of God's Son to earth was so vast an event that God wished to prepare for it over the centuries. He made all the rites and sacrifices of the "first covenant" and all its figures and symbols converge in Christ. Through the mouths of the prophets who succeeded one another in Israel,

---

Henceforth, only paragraph numbers will be cited. The phrase "the old covenant has never been revoked" evokes the statement of Pope John Paul II to the Jewish Community in Mainz, Germany [then West Germany] on November 17, 1980: "The first dimension of this dialogue, that, the meeting between the people of God of the Old Covenant, never revoked by God (cf. Rm. 11:29), and that of the New Covenant, is at the same time a dialogue within our Church, that is to say, between the first and the second part of her Bible" (in Eugene J. Fisher and Leon Klenicki, eds., *Pope John Paul II on Jews and Judaism 1979-1986* (Washington, D.C.: United States Catholic Conference, 1987), 35. Interestingly, in speaking to the Jewish Community of Australia in November 1986, the Pope uses the phrase "Hebrew and Christian Scriptures" (*John Paul II on Jews and Judaism*, 96; cf. n. 65, above).

84. #122. The quotations within are taken from the Second Vatican Council's "Dogmatic Constitution on Divine Revelation" (*Dei verbum*) #15; (see Flannery, *Vatican Council II: The Conciliar and Post Conciliar Documents*).

85. #53.

86. #708.

87. #140.

God announced the Messiah's coming, and even awakened in the hearts of pagans an obscure hope for this coming.[88]

As might be anticipated in light of such a claim, typology plays a significant role in the catechism. These three passages in sequence offer the framework:

> The Church, as early as apostolic times, and then constantly in her Tradition, has illuminated the unity of the divine plan in the two Testaments through typology, which discerns in God's works of the old covenant prefigurations of what he would accomplish in the fullness of time, in the person of his incarnate Son.
>
> Christians read the Old Testament in the light of Christ crucified and risen. Such typological reading discloses the inexhaustible content of the Old Testament, which does not allow us to forget that it retains its own value as revelation, as our Lord reaffirmed. In addition, the New Testament must be read in light of the Old. Early Christian catechesis made constant use of the Old Testament. According to St. Augustine, the New Testament lies hidden in the Old, while the New Testament in unveiled in the New.
>
> Typology indicates a dynamism toward the fulfillment of the divine plan, when "God will be all in all." Nor do the calling of the patriarchs and the exodus from Egypt, for example, lose their proper value in God's plan, from the mere fact that they were intermediate steps.[89]

What these passages attest to is the perdurance of the kerygmatic theologians' supersessionist reading of the Old Testament. One can almost hear Hofinger's admonition, cited above that "we must continually point out the imperfection of the Old Testament." At the same time, there is an effort to honor the Old Testament: it is "indispensable," its contents "inexhaustible," it "retains its own value as revelation." The New Testament must be read in its light.

Clearly, however, even though the "old covenant" has not been "revoked," it has no real reason to exist after Christ. It is as if the *Catechism of the Catholic Church* simply does not recognize the existence and vitality of Judaism today. Would a Jew recognize the description of Judaism in this catechism? I think not: it exists merely as preparation. Ironically, an earlier document (1985) had noted that "mutual knowledge must be encouraged at every level. There is evident in particular a painful ignorance of the history and traditions of Judaism, of which only negative aspects and often caricature seem to form part of the stock ideas of many Christians."[90]

---

88. #522.

89. #s128-129.

90. Commission for Religious Relations with the Jews, "Notes on the Correct Way to Present the Jews and Judaism in Preaching and Catechesis in the Roman Catholic Church,"

Whatever the value of this catechism, its grounding in the assumptions of kerygmatic theology lessens its worth. Kerygmatic theology indeed played a valuable role in focusing attention on the dynamic quality of the Christian message, but its supersessionist premises have themselves been superseded by sounder scholarship. We can be grateful for its contributions even as we acknowledge its limitations. Only by so doing will the *kerygma* resound in greater depth.

---

in Helga Croner, *More Stepping Stones to Jewish-Christian Relations: An Unabridged Collection of Christian Documents 1975-1983*, A Stimulus Book (New York: Paulist, 1985) #27. Also of note is this document's more nuanced (if still problematic) discussion of typology (#s3-9), which it notes "makes many people uneasy and is perhaps the sign of a problem unresolved."

CHAPTER TEN

Narrative Theology and Religious Education

JERRY H. STONE

A rabbi, whose grandfather had been a pupil of Baal Shem Tov, was once asked to tell a story. "A story ought to be told," he said, "so that it is itself a help," and his story was this. "My grandfather was paralyzed. Once he was asked to tell a story about his teacher and he told how the holy Baal Shem Tov used to jump and dance when he was praying. My grandfather stood up while he was telling the story and the story carried him away so much that he had to jump and dance to show how the master had done it. From that moment, he was healed. This is how stories ought to be told."

Martin Buber, as related
by Johann Baptist Metz

Part One

THE SIGNIFICANCE OF NARRATIVE THEOLOGY

The best way to relate the ambiguous edges of human experience to God's mysterious presence is through the use of story, say the narrative theologians. They agree with the rabbi in the prologue above that the story of religion "ought to be told so that it is itself a help." My essay explores what it means to "tell a story," and how the telling of a story provides an approach to religious education that helps to heal a paralysis of the mind, if not always of the body.

What Is Narrative Theology?

For many narrative theologians, the culture that nurtures us largely shapes our religious and social beliefs. We use our language, itself a cultural product, to write and tell our stories to the next generation, and in this way we pass on our beliefs and establish a tradition.

This is nothing new, for we have always transmitted our Western cultural tradition through narratives. Homer's epic poems, *The Iliad* and *The Odyssey*, gave personal definition to the Greek aristocratic warrior; Virgil's *Aeneid* set the political direction for the Roman statesman; and the biblical writings brought divine inspiration to the devout Jew and Christian. All of these texts included basic stories that plotted sets of events and characters within frameworks of time and space; they were narratives that gave definition and vitality to human cultures.[1] Most narrative theologians affirm this understanding of cultural and religious development; they find the heart of a culture's meaning in its narrative tradition. Thus narrative *Christian* theology, which is the focus of this chapter, looks to the narratives in the Bible and the broader Christian tradition for the richest expression of religion.

The Unique Contribution of Narratives to Religious Expression

Artful narratives resonate more vibrantly with our personal experience than do theological statements and moral pronouncements. Every good teacher knows how a summary, condensation, or interpretation of a narrative can diminish its vitality. Students miss the nuanced levels of meaning in *Hamlet* by resorting to a "Cliffs Notes" summary as a substitute for reading the play, just as they miss the meaning of *Moby Dick* by reading a review rather than engaging the richer levels of the novel itself. Aware of this, narrative theologians believe that we come closest to authentic religious meaning when we involve ourselves in the full narrative flow of a religion's literary tradition.

Robert Alter cites the *Genesis* story of Joseph and his brothers as an example of biblical narrative as a source of spiritual and psychological meaning.[2] The Joseph story relates how God engages the world through human characters of mixed virtue and vice, and how God's purposes will finally prevail

---

1. I follow James Hillman here: a narrative story with a *plot* tells us the "why" of the story; it explains character motivation and the interrelationships among characters and events. On the other hand, a simple story relates a series of sequential events without explaining the character motivations. James Hillman, "The Fiction of Case History: A Round," in *Religion as Story*, ed. James B. Wiggins (Lanham, Md.: University Press of America, 1975),129-132. As Hillman points out, E.M. Forster explains that an "order" of events describes what happened, whereas a "plot" tells us why events and characters interrelate as they do. Thus Forster can say, "'The king died and then the queen died,' is a story." "'The king died and then the queen died of grief,' is a plot." A story answers what happens next, a plot tells us why. E.M. Forster, *Aspects of The Novel* (1927, reprint ed., Harmondsworth: Penguin, 1962), 37-38.

2. Robert Alter, *The Art of Biblical Narrative* (New York: Basic Books, 1981), 12.

through the actions of the characters even though temporarily diverted by the brothers' betrayal of Joseph and by Tamar's deception of Judah (Gn. 37-39). Alter says "The implicit theology of the Hebrew Bible dictates a complex moral and psychological realism in biblical narrative because God's purposes are always entrammeled in history, dependent on the acts of individual men and women for their continuing realization."[3] Thus fully to grasp God's purposes we must appreciate how those purposes unfold in human characters through a sequence of events, in other words, how they unfold in narrative form. Since God's purposes are entrammeled in the flow of history and ambiguously unfold through imperfect persons, we can no more reduce biblical meaning to a set of theological ideas or moral principles than we can reduce the flow of life's meaning to such terms.

We reduce and distort biblical meaning in many ways, for example, we distort the intent of Jesus' sayings when we abstract them from the narrative context of his life. Jesus' familiar pronouncement, "Greater love hath no man than he who lays down his life for his friends" (Jn. 15:13), is sometimes quoted at military funerals to eulogize the fallen war hero and to extol the glories of war along with a love for the cultural values which war seeks to preserve. But Jesus' pronouncement has a different meaning in the larger narrative context of John's gospel. Jesus himself is the one who will lay down his life for his friends, and he has called them to withdraw from the glories of the world with its love of cultural values. In contrast to soldiers who are called to fight for the glory of their country and culture, Jesus says to his friends, "If you were of the world, the world would love its own; but because you are not of the world, I chose you out of the world, therefore the world hates you" (Jn. 15:19). Moreover, the Christian meaning of Jesus' call is only fully understandable within the context of the biblical narrative as a whole, that is, the role of Jesus as the main character in the biblical plot which unfolds God's action from world creation to the consummation of the divine kingdom. For narrative theologians, these are the reasons why we best understand the text within the full flow of its storied context.

Meaning and Truth in Narrative

A narrative need not be historically true in order to carry meaning. Herman Melville's fictional account of Ahab's pursuit of the great white whale, Moby Dick, presents us with a more frightening demonic dimension than do some narratives considered to be historically true. Further, Eric Auerbach has shown us that some passages in Homer's epic poems, while mythic, resonate with our sensibilities more vibrantly than do many of the ostensibly historical narratives in the Bible.[4] Still, many religious people make faith com-

---

3. Ibid., 12.
4. For this comparison of Homeric and biblical narratives, see Eric Auerbach, *Mimesis* (Princeton: Princeton University Press, 1953), ch. 1, "Odysseus' Scar."

mitments to stories not only because the stories hold vibrant levels of personal meaning but also because they believe them to be true in *both* a symbolic and a realistic sense. For most traditional Jews and Christians the Bible contains "true" stories in a way that Homer's epic poems do not.

While most narrative theologians agree that the biblical narratives contain historical truth, they often disagree on the nature of that truth. Exactly how some of the most significant biblical narratives depict true events (the resurrection and ascension stories of Christ for example) gives rise to broad disagreements. Does the truth of Christ's resurrection reside in the described events themselves? Or does its truth lie in the believer's *own* "resurrection" through a "born again" experience so that it does not actually matter whether Christ's resurrection occurred literally as described in the Bible? For my purposes, the basic Christian narratives, such as the story of Christ's life, death, and resurrection, are taken to represent in some significant way events that happened in the real world, events that Christians can justifiably believe as true either by faith or by reason, or by both. Just how such a belief can be justified as true is a matter of considerable complexity about which even the most sophisticated thinkers disagree, and to explore the philosophical and theological discussions of this issue would involve an extended diversion from the theme of my essay. Suffice it to say here that some responsible scholars have made reasoned arguments for the rational justification of basic Christian beliefs as true while other scholars believe that Christian faith does not require rational justification since its foundation is in a faith response.[5] (I will return to this issue of how narrative is related to truth in my discussion of "pure" and "impure" narrativists.)

The cultural linguistic approach to meaning in narrative. Many, but not all, narrative theologians follow the cultural linguistic approach which places almost exclusive emphasis upon culture and language as the shaping forces of the meaning found in religious experience.[6] For these theologians, human

---

5. For an excellent account of the problems involved in the justification of beliefs as true, see Laurence BonJour, *The Structure of Empirical Knowledge* (Cambridge: Harvard University Press, 1985). Although BonJour does not approach this matter from a Christian point of view, his insights can be helpful for scholars seeking to work through a rational justification for Christian beliefs. For a rational justification of religious beliefs from a specially Christian point of view, see William P. Alston, *Perceiving God: The Epistemology of Religious Experience* (Ithaca, N.Y. and London: Cornell University Press, 1991). Another important contribution to this issue is Alvin Plantinga's two-volume work, *Warrant and Proper Function* and *Warrant: The Current Debate* (New York: Oxford University Press, 1993).

6. The cultural linguistic theologians are broadly divided into two schools, the "Yale school" and the "Chicago school." The "Yale school" stresses culture and language as the primary shapers of both meaning and truth as found in the writings of George Lindbeck at Yale Divinity School. See his *The Nature of Doctrine: Religion and Theology in a Postliberal Age* (Philadelphia: Westminster, 1984). The "Chicago school" looks to a more universal philosophical explanation of cultural-linguistic sources of theology, such as found in the writings of David Tracy at the University of Chicago. For a discussion of

experience can grasp little if any meaning behind or beyond that which is articulated in the cultural linguistic process. A leading cultural linguist, George Lindbeck, cites Helen Keller's personal testimony to illustrate this perspective. Deaf and blind from infancy, Helen Keller testified that her raw experience lay within her as a vast field of chaotic sensations until she learned a language through which to organize and give meaning to it.[7] If Ms. Keller's experience is true for human experience in general, it suggests that we do not first have recognizable religious experiences then find language to describe them. Rather, language itself, expressed in a cultural context, is primary in shaping the religious experience and the meaning we find in it.

The narrative theologians who adopt this cultural linguistic outlook see stories as the richest linguistic form in which religious meaning is culturally transmitted. They shift the focus from the inner experiences to which stories might point to the power of stories themselves to create and shape those inner experiences, thus adopting a perspective similar to that of Helen Keller. My own childhood experience of reading "A Wise Old Dog," a story in my first-grade reader, illustrates the point. Here is a summary of it:[8]

> Bran, a farmer's dog, has a puppy who runs into the cornfield where he falls into a deep hole half-filled with water. Bran jumps in to save her puppy, takes him in her mouth and treads water to keep both their heads above the water. The sides of the hole are too steep to climb out and there is no bank to stand on. With the pup in her mouth Bran cannot bark for help, not even when the farmer misses his dogs and calls for them. At last the farmer remembers the deep hole in the cornfield and comes to the rescue, pulling out his wet and cold dogs just in the nick of time. Later that day when his children come home from school, he tells them about the misadventure. "Good old Bran," they all exclaim, bringing the story to a happy, loving ending.

I loved Bran for what she did, and the story seemed to create the sentiment it evoked in me: love as personal concern and ethical action. I believe that reading the story provided me with more than an external expression of my already existing experience and knowledge of love; I think it partially *generated* within me the awareness of love as concerned action. The story itself was a help in creating the meaning of the experience, just as the rabbi said in the prologue to this chapter. (My purpose here is to stress the *influence* of culture and language on the shaping of meaning and truth; it is not to adopt

---

these two approaches to narrative theology, see Gary Comstock, "Two Types of Narrative Theology," *Journal of The American Academy of Religion* 55:4 (Winter 1987), 687-717. For the definitive cultural linguistic position, see Lindbeck, *The Nature of Doctrine*.

7. This account of Helen Keller is taken from Lindbeck, *The Nature of Doctrine*, 34.

8. The story appears in *The Laidlaw Readers* compiled by Herman Dressel and others (Chicago and New York: Laidlaw Brothers, 1928), 35-46.

the more radical view that meaning and truth can be reduced to cultural linguistic terms.)

The dispute between "pure" and "impure" narrative theologians regarding truth in narrative. Following the cultural linguistic school, "pure" narrative theologians such as Stanley Hauerwas and Stephen Crites claim that we have no recourse to knowledge outside the biblical narrative to ascertain its truth; the particular truth of the narrative is so interwoven in the strands of the story that it can hardly, if at all, be separated from it. Whatever the meaning of a story, about the closest we can come to its truth is through our participation in the narrative to realize its "truth for us."

Contrariwise, "impure" narrativists such as Julian Hartt assert that narratives cannot authenticate themselves as true, therefore, believers make faith assertions about the truth of the objective historical events to which the stories point, events such as the physical resurrection and ascension of Christ.[9] Hartt believes that even though the biblical narratives were written and are now read as products of human culture, they nevertheless contain propositional truths about God's presence in the world that transcend cultural and linguistic boundaries. For Hartt, the ascension of Christ refers to a historical event beyond the story itself that is affirmed in theology, doctrine, and creed as a propositional truth.

Hartt's view reflects the traditional Christian understanding of canonical biblical literature in which this canon contains realistic stories that provide us with a picture of God that is not only meaningful to our inner experience but is also *true* as a proposition in the real world beyond our experience. Until recent times, this canon established the meaning of God's action in history and provided a historical standard by which Christians could assess their own cultural and historical perspective, according to Hans Frei.[10] Moreover, says Frei, the traditional Christian interpretation of the seemingly diverse biblical stories disclosed a unified and continued narrative of

---

9. For a good discussion of these issues, see *Why Narrative?: Readings in Narrative Theology*, Stanley Hauerwas and L. Gregory Jones, eds. (Grand Rapids, Mich.: Eerdmans, 1989). See especially the exchanges among Hauerwas, Hartt, and Stephen Crites, 279-319. Hauerwas says that we cannot come any closer to the truth than a careful reading and faithful response to the story; we cannot assert a transcendent truth to which the story refers. To the contrary, Hartt asserts that we can assert a transcendent truth which the story discloses to us. See also Gary Comstock's account of these issues in his "Two Types of Narrative Theology." Comstock refers to Hartt's assertion that Christians mean more by Christ's resurrection than just how they as readers feel in faithful response to the narrative. Comstock quotes Hartt: "When we are seriously and affirmatively engaged with the Christian faith we not only *believe* the Gospel is true, we *claim* it is true, and we assert its truth . . . using Acts 13 as a model we should say that the point and climax of the narrative is the assertion of the resurrection of Jesus as an actual event." 120-121.

10. Hans W. Frei, *The Decline of Biblical Narrative* (New Haven: Yale University Press, 1974), see especially ch. 1.

God's action in human history. This narrative of God's involvement with human beings was found in a figural, or typological, interpretation of the biblical narratives so that the Hebrew scriptures themselves (The Old Testament) prefigured the appearance of Christ in the New Testament. The Christ who came as the lamb of God to be sacrificed in the sinner's stead was the same Christ who appeared as a lamb from the bushes to be sacrificed by Abraham in Isaac's place. Thus a single, overarching biblical narrative connected the many separate biblical narratives that related God's continuing engagement with the world. (I will discuss later the problems which arise with such an all-encompassing interpretation of the many different biblical narratives.)

The Impact of Modern Liberalism on Narrative Theology (and Religious Education)

Hans Frei also describes how the above interpretation of biblical narratives began to decline in the eighteenth-century as scholars realized that the biblical world of miracles and supernatural events described in the Bible could no longer be accepted as part of the real world. Because of this, metaphorical and demythologized interpretations of the narratives began to replace the earlier realistic understandings of them. This movement included two theological giants of the last two centuries, Friedrich Schleiermacher and Rudolf Bultmann, who shifted the significance of Christ away from the biblically narrated world of miracles and supernatural happenings to the "inner meaning for us" of Christ's death and resurrection. This "inner meaning" resided in the believer's feeling of "absolute dependence" on God (Schleiermacher) and in the "existential" transformation of the believer's spiritual life from death to life (Bultmann).[11] For Bultmann, the biblical narrative of Christ's life, death, and resurrection was a mythic narrative that the modern believer living in the scientific age could not accept without a sacrifice of intelligence. Still, Bultmann said, this narrative carried an inner truth which the believer experienced "existentially" in her own death to a self-centered life and rebirth into a life of outgoing love. Thus the demythologized "existential" meaning of the resurrection story replaced the more realistic understanding of it. The narrative events were now regarded as cultural products of a primitive mythological worldview, events more similar to fictional descriptions in a novel than to a chronicle of historical happenings.

Modern theological liberalism was born with this change. God no longer

---

11. Friedrich Schleiermacher, *The Christian Faith*, trans. and ed. H.R. Mackintosh and J.S. Stewart (Edinburgh: T. & T. Clark, 1948). For Schleiermacher's own understanding of "the feeling of absolute dependence," see ch.1, with special attention to sec. 4, 12-18. For Bultmann's famous view of demythology and existential interpretation, see his formative essay, "New Testament and Mythology," in *Kerygma and Myth*, trans. Reginald H. Fuller, ed. Hans Werner Bartsch (New York: Macmillan, 1957), 1-44.

reigned as the transcendent "other" who mysteriously entered into the realm of human experience through external events, rather, God was reduced to the immanent "inner experience" of modern believers. Although Bultmann himself insisted that the transcendent "otherness" of God was disclosed to inner experience, the liberal movement's near equation of divine and human experience seemed to dissolve the real presence of God's "otherness" into the believer's subjective experience. Moreover, since liberalism interpreted biblical narratives as symbolic expressions of an inner religious experience, the particular narratives in their realistic forms no longer held exclusive truths. Their authority now resided in their power to resonate with the innate religious consciousness shared by all believers. Thus a narrative's content might not always describe real events, but its symbolic meaning could arouse the reader's religious consciousness.

This liberal view thrives today in modern-day religious movements such as the "New Age" religions, Unitarianism, and much of modern Christianity. These movements shift the center of God's presence from the narrated world of the scriptural text to the world of the believer's personal experience. This helps to explain why, earlier in this century, many Christian educators under the influence of the liberal vision moved from a biblical to an experientially based approach to religious education, or as Randolph Crump Miller phrased it, from a "God-centered to a learner-centered curriculum with emphasis upon the divinity of human beings to the near exclusion of theology."[12]

In sum, the liberal movement in Christian education, whatever its strengths, set its curricular focus on contemporary human experience to the near exclusion of the divine/human encounter as unfolded in biblical narratives. Exactly what this relationship between contemporary human experience (our life stories) and the biblical narrative (canonical story) *should* be is a central issue for narrative theologians. I will now articulate a view of this relationship as I will apply it to the theory and practice of religious education.

Narrative Theology as Three Kinds of Story: Canonical Story, Life Story, and Community Story

Narrative theology moves beyond the canonical, or biblical, story to include the believer's personal life story within the context of the Christian community story. Since Christian education relates past tradition to the modern Christian experience in similar ways, we need to understand these three forms of story in order to apply narrative theology to Christian education. I follow here Gabriel Fackre's grouping of narrative theology into canonical story, life story, and community story. As Fackre points out, these three

---

12. Randolph Crump Miller, "Theology in the Background," in *Religious Education and Theology*, ed. Norma H. Thompson (Birmingham, Ala.: Religious Education Press, 1982), 18-23.

kinds of story bear a striking resemblance to the three forms of authority in traditional theology: scripture, human experience, and tradition.[13]

Canonical story refers to the canon of biblical literature which a Christian community accepts as the authentic account of God's engagement with the world. This does not mean that the truth is "carved in stone" on the infallible text as the advocates of biblical inerrancy claim. God's purposes as expressed in the canonical literature do transcend the human scene, but they also unfold within the ambiguities of a human history to which the biblical writers themselves were subject. As creatures of their own history, the writers encased the narrative of God's action within their particular cultural and personal situation. Accordingly, each of the four gospel writers presented the narrative of Christ's life from his own perspective. But as Julian Hartt says, Christian biblical narrative is canonical in that, however artfully and humanly crafted many of the stories may be, they refer to and describe a presence of God in and through Jesus Christ that transcends the stories themselves. Without *some* such reference to the presence of God in Christ as a propositional truth, whether made in faith or with rational justification or with some combination of both, Christianity loses its essential reason for being.

Life story refers to the separate life story of each person, a story that influences the development of the person's character and that provides direction for moral action. Narrative theology focuses on how life stories merge with canonical and community stories to shape the moral character and action of Christians. And yet, while this interrelation of stories has been fundamental to the positive growth of the ongoing Christian tradition, it has also been the source of considerable conflict in this tradition. For example, when Martin Luther stood before the Diet of Worms to defend his writings in 1521, he pitted his own life story and his understanding of the canonical story against the community story of the established church. He declared, "Unless I am convicted by Scripture and plain reason . . . I do not accept the authority of popes and councils, for they have contradicted each other . . . my conscience is captive to the Word of God, I cannot and will not recant anything, for to go against conscience is neither right nor safe. God help me. Amen." Whether or not Luther was justified in his position, his declaration is a classic expression of canonical and life story in conflict with community story.

Community story refers to stories of communal life as they unfold in the various branches of Christendom such as Roman Catholicism, Eastern Orthodoxy, and Protestantism. Particular community stories provide the

---

13. Gabriel Fackre, "Narrative Theology: An Overview," *Interpretation: A Journal of Bible and Theology* 37:4 (October 1983), 340-352. For a more extended discussion of personal life stories and their larger relationship to the stories embodied in the Christian tradition, see George W. Stroup, *The Promise of Narrative Theology* (Atlanta: John Knox Press, 1981), especially ch. IV, "The Narrative Form of Personal Identity."

framework within which the individual members live out their own life stories. In some cases the life story is in close harmony with the community story, as in a vigorous monastic or Amish community. In other cases dramatic conflicts break out between the community and life stories as we saw above in the case of Martin Luther.

Narrative theology explores how these three stories meet in individual Christians, how they integrate themselves in one person, clash in another, and are met with indifference by still another. It is probably safe to say that many contemporary Christians have drifted away from any meaningful connection with the traditional stories, and therefore respond to them with considerable indifference. A major task for religious education is to examine how it might address the problem of integrating these three stories, a task which I shall address in Part Two of this chapter.

Concerns about Canonical Stories

Before moving to Part Two, however, I want to interject some words of caution about the inherent dangers in a zealous allegiance to canonical stories. If we accept Julian Hartt's position that the Christian canonical story refers to a propositional truth about God's presence in the world, this acceptance can encourage the fanatical believer whose dogmatic adherence to a canonical story compels him to persecute or suppress the nonconformists. Adherence to the mythology of the Nazi Third Reich is an only too recent example of the affirmation of a canonical story turned tyrannical. In a commissioned study of Hitler and his Nazi inner circle during their last few days, H.R. Trevor-Roper compares Heinrich Himmler, the S.S. Commandant, with Cardinal Robert Bellarmine, the Jesuit "Grand Inquisitor" (1542-1621). Both men, each living in his own canonical story in a different time and place, believed that no punishment was too drastic for those who obstructed the "right" canonical way. Even more, Cardinal Bellarmine believed that punishment was good for the heretics. Trevor-Roper quotes from the Bellarmine correspondence in which Bellarmine wrote that heretics should be liquidated as an act of charity for them, "since if they live longer they will only deceive others, and thereby intensify their own damnation."[14]

Another concern is that advocates of one canonical story sometimes make damaging interpretations of other canonical stories even though they refrain from actively persecuting and suppressing those who follow those other stories. For instance, we have seen how some Christian scholars give a typological interpretation of the scriptures in which the entire biblical narrative is understood as a unified expression of God's action in Christ. Michael Goldberg, a Jewish scholar, has reasonably charged that the desire to find Christ in the Old Testament scriptures has given rise to superficial, inaccu-

---

14. H.R. Trevor-Roper, *The Last Days of Hitler*, 3rd ed. (New York: Collier Books, 1973), 81-83.

rate, and hurtful interpretation of Jewish scripture.[15] Still another problem occurs within the Christian community itself with its many splits into churches, denominations, sects, and cults, each group reading the canonical story in its own dogmatic way to suit its particular purposes.

Issues such as these raise again the problem of truth in narrative which I have already discussed. Can there be a single, over-arching canonical story that is true and meaningful for all humankind? If not, are all canonical stories, both religious and secular, relative to the culture that gives birth to them? A continuing awareness of these problems of meaning and truth is important in our discussion of the significance of narrative theology for religious education. We will confront them again in our consideration of a praxis approach to Christian education.

Part Two

THE SIGNIFICANCE OF NARRATIVE THEOLOGY
FOR RELIGIOUS EDUCATION

I turn now to the significance of Christian narrative for religious education. I begin with the ancient Greek concept of praxis, which provides just the right framework for understanding how the three forms of narrative presented in Part One, canonical, community, and life, relate to religious education.

The Place of Narrative in a Praxis Understanding of Education

For Aristotle, praxis meant reflective action informed by the practical knowledge and skill learned within a tradition that enabled a person to transform a tradition's meaning into the present context. To act out of such practical knowledge was to exhibit virtue, the quality of moral excellence. The virtuous person knew how to make the correct moral response in each situation as it arose; he was a good family member in a household context, a good citizen in a political context, and a good religious person in a sacred context. The virtuous person learned the skills of moral living through the cultural tradition, and the purpose of education was to provide the means to accomplish this. In the aristocratic warrior society of Homeric Greece, a tutor (*paidogogos*: pedagogue) trained the male child in the arts of war, sports, play, and social behavior to be just the right person with the right skills to do the right thing

---

15. Michael Goldberg, "God, Action, and Narrative: *Which* Narrative? *Which* Action? *Which* God?" in *Why Narrative?* 348-365.

in every situation. The child was not just taught *about* spears, shields, and chariots; he was also taught how to use them. He was not just taught *about* proper social manners; he was also taught how to conduct himself as guest or host in the house and at the table. The ancient Greeks looked to Odysseus (Ulysses) as their ideal for this virtuous style of life. To develop character meant to nurture a child on the model of Odysseus, for Odysseus knew just how to act in every situation.[16] Thus a person learned to be virtuous through incorporating the practical knowledge of his particular cultural tradition; he learned to discern virtue more as a way of life than as an abstract good. Alasdair MacIntyre develops this thesis in his important book, *After Virtue*. He proposes that we do not become virtuous through rational and moral thought itself; rather, virtue is generated within the context of our cultural tradition. We learn how to be a good Greek warrior or a good Christian from the tradition embedded in our particular community.[17]

A major objection to this praxis perspective is its apparent relativism. It seems to provide no grounds for deciding who is the morally better person, the Greek warrior or the Christian saint. The question of meaning and truth is once again before us. If the cultural context establishes values, does this mean there are no universal values that transcend the culture? While this important but probably unresolvable debate continues on (I make summary statements about it in footnotes 5 and 17), I will focus here on how a praxis approach to religious education directs us into our own narrative tradition, more specifically, into our canonical and community stories as inspirational sources of virtue to enlarge our own life stories.

From a praxis perspective, to be virtuous in a Homeric or a Christian world would mean to incorporate the canonical stories into one's own life story within the context of the community that embodied them. Following this approach to Christian education today, a praxis approach will include a

---

16. For a formative account of Greek education, see Werner Jaeger, *Paideia: The Ideals of Greek Culture*, 2 vols., 2nd. ed. (Oxford University Press, 1974). See esp. Vol. I, 22-23 on Odysseus. For a popular and shorter, yet scholarly, account of Greek, Hellenistic, and Roman education, see Henri I. Marrou, *Education in Antiquity* (Madison: University of Wisconsin Press, 1982).

17. Alasdair MacIntyre's important book, *After Virtue* (Notre Dame, Ind.: University of Notre Dame Press, 1981), is in the center of the contemporary dispute about the source of virtue. He affirms Aristotle's understanding of virtue and rejects the eighteenth-century Enlightenment view which attempted to establish the power of human reason to justify a moral position independently of a cultural tradition. Strong rejoinders to MacIntyre have been made by scholars who are unwilling to jettison the Enlightenment position to the extent that he does. For an interesting debate between MacIntyre and Richard J. Bernstein on these issues, see *Soundings: An Interdisciplinary Journal* 67:1 (Spring 1984). Bernstein defends the Enlightenment perspective, pointing out that without final appeal to rational criticism, morality remains relative to the cultural situation and therefore vulnerable to tyrannical abuse. In this essay, I will attempt to avoid the pitfall that Bernstein warns against.

social context in which the community stories support the interplay of canonical and life stories. Narrative theology can contribute to this model of religious education by developing creative forms of interplay among the three forms of Christian story.[18]

Some might object, however, that the breakdown of the modern community story makes such an interplay of stories extremely difficult, if not impossible. Modern society, both inside and outside the Christian community, is largely nurtured by a popular culture of diversity that promotes habits, values, and lifestyles that often seem alien to vital Christian community. If this is true, can traditional educational methods successfully integrate Christian canonical stories into a popular community culture deeply antagonist to it? After all, the Homeric canonical narratives began to lose their power to influence the life stories of the Greeks as archaic Greece made the transition from an aristocratic warrior society to a more urban democratic society in the emerging "Golden Age" of the Athenian city-state. The late Roman Empire experienced a similar fate as its social structures changed, and so has our modern mass culture. MacIntyre observes, our modern mass culture has ceased to identify itself with its traditional moral community just as the late Roman Empire did. And yet, as barbarism and darkness overtook the Roman Empire in the fifth century, Benedictine monasticism emerged as a new form of community in which the moral life was sustained, says MacIntyre.[19] The Benedictine monastic order embodied a new community story which integrated the canonical and life stories of the monks. MacIntyre then asks whether some such community, taking its own new form, might arise on the modern cultural scene.

Whether contemporary Christian groups can create their own community stories is problematic. Still, my own teaching experience in adult education and undergraduate courses tells me that some students *are* concerned about the vital interconnections within their Christian tradition, community, and personal lives, and *do* seek ways to integrate them. We religious educators should meet this challenge with creative responses.

The Forms of Narrative in a Praxis Understanding of Education
I will now consider specific forms that narrative theology might take in a praxis understanding of education. My proposal for these forms of narrative as teaching aids is not meant as a set of directives for broad curricular revision, rather, it is directed toward those teachers and students who have the interest, energy, and talent to explore these particular ways in which the

---

18. For an excellent and extensive discussion of a praxis approach to religious education, see Thomas H. Groome, *Sharing Faith: A Comprehensive Approach to Religious Education and Pastoral Ministry: The Way of Shared Praxis* (San Francisco: Harper Collins, 1991). See especially Part II to end, 133-449.

19. MacIntyre, *After Virtue*, 244-245.

Christian community life of faith might be enrichened. Of course there are other important directions for Christian education to explore as well.

The use of biographical narrative in Christian education. To know how to be virtuous on the model of Odysseus would involve knowing the stories about Odysseus in Homer's writings. To know how to be virtuous on the model of Jesus would involve knowing the stories about Jesus in the New Testament. It would also involve knowing the biographies of Christian heroes through the centuries, including modern figures who personify the ideal Christian life within our own community contexts.

Teaching biography as theology is uniquely important because the lives of inspirational people, both living and dead, can speak to our character and our convictions in a unique way, says James McLendon. McLendon defines "convictions" as "those tenacious beliefs which when held give definiteness to the character of a person or community."[20] Convictions go beyond our acceptance of the religious beliefs and moral principles we might learn in a classroom situation. Convictions involve our fundamental sense of what it means to be a person, including possible dimensions of our moral intuition that have not been consciously formulated. When we take a moral stand on an issue, convictions are the "unseen weight on (our) moral scales." Convictions include not just what we say we believe but what we are convinced about. "For as men are convinced so will they live, and similarly with convinced communities," says McLendon.[21] Moreover, McLendon reminds us that in or near our present communities persons appear from time to time whose lives embody the convictions of our community, persons who share the vision of our community and invest it with new power. Such lives can serve as models for our community and for each of us. By getting to know these heroes through their biographies (their life stories), both we and our communities become involved with them; *our* souls begin to resonate with their souls; we participate with the heroic souls of a Dag Hammarskjöld, a Martin Luther King Jr., a Clarence Leonard Jordan, or a Charles Edward Ives. In this way we gain the practical knowledge that helps us to participate in our tradition; we engage in a praxis mode of education with the help of biographical narratives.

Education as reenactment rather than imitation of the lives of our heroes. To implement this biographical approach would involve us both as teachers and learners in thoughtful reenactments of our hero stories within the context of our own community and personal stories. I speak here of reenactment and not imitation. We do not imitate the lives of our heroes, repeating the particular things they did, rather, we interpret the meaning of their lives

---

20. James McLendon, *Biography as Theology: How Life Stories Can Remake Today's Theology* (Nashville: Abingdon, 1974), 34.

21. Ibid., 35.

for our lives and apply that meaning in ways relevant to our particular situations. We blend interpretation and application in "play," or *Spiel*, on the model of artistic expression, says Hans-George Gadamer.[22] Just as Laurence Olivier's interpretation of *Hamlet* brings Shakespeare's play into a fresh and unique expression, so the living Christian community brings its traditional stories into fresh and unique expressions. We might call this process "praxis as reflective action."

As I have said in another essay, "True play as mimesis does not 'mimic' the external characteristics of the original; rather, it reenacts, or re-presents, the original by evoking its essence in contemporary forms. Thus, the modern passion play 'mimics' to the extent it acts out Christ's passion week in a literal, surface presentation of the gospel narrative."[23] In contrast, to reenact the story of Jesus in our own teacher-learner situations would be to evoke the essence of his life story in our own forms just as Laurence Olivier evoked the essence of *Hamlet* in his own form. Such reenactment happens in all the great performing arts; it can also happen in great religious education. For such a reenactment of our heroes' lives to be successful, we must find *internal* connections among the biographical stories and our own life and community stories. To reenact Martin Luther King's heroism does not mean that we repeat the externals of his actions. Our own social situation probably does not call us to move to the front of city busses or organize "sit ins" to desegregate restaurants. But surely there are subtle forms of discrimination in our own social worlds that call for the reenactment of King's spirit in new forms, that ask us to let his "soul" emerge through our "souls." So we read King's biography for inspiration, realizing that knowledge of the externals of his story will do little to enhance our religious lives until the internal "soul connection" is also made.

Nearly all educators would agree that students do not really "know" rules and principles simply by memorizing them, rather, they *know* them when they can *apply* them, when they can *reenact* them in a praxis way in different contexts. Yet these same educators often teach stories about our great religious past and its heroic figures as if memorizing the stories somehow will enhance our religious lives. Such memorized knowledge of stories may provide the groundwork for this enhancement, but experience has shown us that such knowledge does not in itself enhance.

Of course narrative theology cannot provide a manual of procedures for applying our religious tradition to life and community stories in a praxis way, but it can point religious education in some helpful directions. One

---

22. Hans-George Gadamer, *Truth and Method* (New York: Seabury, 1975). See especially 91-99; see also Gadamer's subject index for the many references to play.

23. See my description of *mimesis* in "Christian Praxis as Reflective Action" in *Legal Hermeneutics: History, Theory, and Practice,* ed. Gregory Leyl (Berkeley: University of California Press, 1992), 106.

such direction is clinical psychology, a counseling practice which can guide us in making internal connections between our canonical stories and life stories.

Narrative theology, clinical psychology, and Christian education. "Clinical psychology" here means the professional practice of personal counseling, which is a form of mental therapy grounded in varied and often undoctrinaire mixtures of such movements as Freudian and Jungian psychology, B.F. Skinner's behaviorism, and Carl Rogers' client-centered psychology.

Clinical psychology and religious education share similar narrative concerns in the way they interrelate canonical, community, and life stories to bring about personality change. Counseling patients have "tales to tell," says James Hillman.[24] The therapist's role is to "cure" the patient by aligning her personal life story to a larger frame of psychological theory that functions something like a canonical story. Whatever the chosen canon of theoretical psychology, perhaps some combined Freudian and Jungian view on how to interpret life stories, it is assumed to have power to transform the patient's life once she begins to understand her own life story in light of this more authoritative canonical story. The therapy usually proceeds somewhat as follows: the counselor empathetically hears the patient's life story, then reinterprets it within the accepted canonical story. The patient presumably improves through engaging her life story with the larger traditional story, and through discovering internal connections between her own experience and the counselor's interpretation of that experience. In therapy influenced by the Freudian school, for instance, the counselor may seek to disclose to the patient that her inability to establish meaningful and lasting personal relationships is somehow related to her unfulfilled childhood relationships with her parents and/or other significant adults. In this way the patient's cure involves a reenactment of her past relationships in her present relationships.

Applied to the religious education process, this would mean a reenactment of the traditional Christian stories in the present community and personal life stories as I have already discussed. It just will not do for teachers to present the Christian tradition to students as an external body of material to be learned as an end in itself. The power of a tradition to transform our lives does not reside in its surface meaning as presented in the classroom anymore than the power of a bowl of cereal to nourish us resides in its surface presence on the breakfast table. The issue for education focuses on our capacity to ingest the traditional stories as nourishment for our own life stories, not just our ability to recall them as surface events spread before us on a tableful of memories. To ingest a story means to *interpret* that story within the context of our own lives, to transmute it into forms that energize our own self-expression.

---

24. Hillman, "The Fiction of Case History: A Round," Sec. 4, "Stories in Therapy," 136-141.

Even our most intimate personal stories are more than a string of past events that we remember. My own life story is a recollection of happenings that I *interpret* within a story-frame of meaning, and through that interpretation these happenings carry a mythic power to change my life. My interpretation of my life story can debilitate and destroy me, or it can refresh and occasionally renew me. Unconscious levels of meaning can emerge in my inner pilgrimage through my past, perhaps a suddenly remembered mother's action or father's expression which I now interpret and transform into imaged meanings that influence my present sense of self in a way that transcends the original events themselves.

Our interpretations of our life stories shape our sense of selfhood, and through the innate human drive to reach beyond ourselves we raise the question of the larger stories to which our life stories belong, the canonical and community stories which shape again our already-shaped life stories. It is in this context that religious education, just as mental therapy, is called upon to interpret the many-layered and interrelated meanings of stories. To interpret a story requires an understanding of the structure of a story, a knowledge of how a story is put together in the form of plot and character interaction within a sequence of time. It is essential to understand the form of the plot, for the plot provides the framework within which the characters unfold and are given shape. Since the purpose of religious education is to shape character, and since we are all characters in the larger Christian plot, it behooves us to understand exactly how plots work, which is the subject to which I now turn.

The role of the plot in the interpretation of our life stories. The plots we find in literature and in our lives *do* shape our vision, for some plots make us happy and others make us sad; some plots encourage us and others discourage us; some plots heal us and others make us ill. And from the religious perspective, some plots save us and others damn us. But our readings of stories, be they from literature or life, do not always find the plots that actually exist in the stories; we sometimes create, or at least alter, the plots. For example, liberal theology interprets the plot of Jesus' life story differently than does evangelical theology.

What sorts of plots do we religious educators give to (or find in?) our stories? We might agree that the plots we find in stories are mixtures of the stories themselves and our own projections into them. Most of us partially distort our personal history as we tailor it to fit our own self illusions. Even the revered Augustine arranged his life experiences to express the plot he wanted to develop in his autobiography, *Confessions*. Moreover, after we interpret our own life and community stories within some plot context, we then try to project that plot understanding onto our interpretation of the traditional Christian canon. We have already seen how the liberal tradition did this (just as every other tradition did and still does in its own way). Thus we not only interpret our past history according to a chosen plot line, we also seek to *live out* our present lives according to that chosen plot.

To amplify this point, I will describe some of the plots different people find in their life stories, looking especially at life stories expressed in the following plot modes: comic, tragic, tragi-comic, and picaresque.[25] People who interpret their lives in the comic mode often organize and manage themselves and their environment to bring about personal improvement and material success. They arrange their lives to reach the desired end, which is exactly what a plot is: the order and arrangement of events toward a desired end. Shakespeare's comedy, *The Taming of the Shrew*, is a classic example. Petruchio establishes a conditioned environment in which Kate is changed from a shrew to a loving and obedient woman, and the two of them presumably live happily ever after as man and wife. (And I do mean *man* and wife; whether Kate's change is "for the better or for worse" is problematic given the current feminist consciousness.)

We find a similar comic pattern among some practitioners of Behaviorist psychology. The behaviorist canonical story interprets human existence as comical in that the patient is healed through positive reinforcement, which is to say that the environmental context is rearranged to evoke fresh responses from the patient which lead to the desired personality changes. In this way, failed life stories are presumably changed into successful life stories.

Many people do frame their personal life stories in the comic mode. They organize and manage their lives and environment so as to bring them material profit, professional success, a happy domestic life, and even spiritual peace of mind. Christian churches are filled with people who interpret their lives in the comic mode. What is more, they often project this vision onto their understanding of the gospel accounts of the life of Jesus. Like Shakespeare's Petruchio, Jesus establishes an environment in which his followers become loving and obedient persons, and they all live happily ever after. As a teacher of religion, I have found that many students not only interpret their own life meanings from a comic perspective, they also understand the life of Jesus from that same perspective. (I shall return to this topic later.)

On the other hand, some people adopt a more tragic mode of living. Such a person connects past episodes of personal defeat with his present situation, living out his life as a succession of setbacks and moral struggles involving calamities such as alcoholism, broken relationships, professional failures, and mental illness. He conjures up endings of disappointment, depression, and sometimes ruin (as self-fulfilling prophecies?). Like a modern Oedipus, some "oracle" presumably plagues him so that even the good things that happen seem to hold more threats than promises. In the deep irony of his tragic life, every success seems burdened with its own load of failure.

25.This discussion of plot borrows extensively from James Hillman's excellent essay cited above.

Still another person lives her life in a picaresque mode, never reflecting on whether she can change for better or for worse. She opportunistically manipulates the world about her to seize the most for herself in every situation. She never personally engages in loving relationships or commits her life to significant causes. She never changes. She lives and dies as the superficial and detached, even roguish, character that she is.

The role of religious education in relating stories. As already said, most of us cast our own life stories into some plot form, then seek to relate these stories to larger community and canonical stories. Given this, *a major task of religious education is to guide the process of relating stories.* Such guidance involves both an understanding of the plot contexts of life stories as described above, and of canonical and community stories. With such an understanding, effective education can unfold the inner plot connections among stories. As we saw earlier, the external application of canonical and community stories to life stories is by itself insufficient. For a teacher to recite the biblical account of Jesus' life and teachings as an external model for students usually does little good. The teaching process should move toward a *self-realization* of Jesus' vision which involves a knowledge of the internal plot connections between Jesus' story and our stories.

Relating stories in the comic mode. When religious educators interpreted the biblical story in the comic mode, as many did under the influence of liberal theology earlier in this century, they tended to view the teachings of Jesus as moral principles to be learned within a progressive community environment. Thus the so-called liberal "gospel of success" entered religious education. The more tragic themes of the life of Jesus, which included his struggle with the satanic forces, his own dark, apocalyptic predictions about the fate of the world, and his disappointments and defeats, were demythologized and glossed over in order to retain the steady and assuring focus on the positive elements in the Jesus story. Accordingly, the task of religious education was to further the kingdom of God by nurturing a "kingdom of maturing personalities," as Carroll Wise phrased it years ago.[26]

Moreover, many nationally popular religious personalities and authors spoke and wrote in this liberal comic mode, telling us that our life stories could be harmonized with this larger "happy" canonical story which seemed to carry authority in both religious and secular forms. Norman Vincent Peale's *The Power of Positive Thinking*, Bruce Barton's *The Man Nobody Knows*, and Joshua R. Liebman's *Peace of Mind* exemplified this liberal mood. On a parallel track, much of the curricular material for primary and elementary religious education was closer in spirit to the fulfilled and satisfied world of the "Dick and Jane" books than it was to the world of biblical stories. The

---

26. Carroll Wise, *Pastoral Counseling: Its Theory and Practice* (New York: Harper and Brothers, 1951). For an interpretation of the significance of Wise's work, see my essay, "Christian Praxis as Reflective Action," in *Legal Hermeneutics*.

"Dick and Jane" story also related comfortably to the secular community stories of the time. In the social-political realm from the "New Deal" to the "New Frontier," politicians and social engineers proclaimed that modern technology and proper management of personal and natural resources would build a better tomorrow.

The limitations of the comic mode of interpretation. While this liberal interpretation was not entirely wrong, it also was not completely right. But whatever the merits of the liberal comic mode of interpretation, most contemporary religious educators seem to agree that it carried more meaning for yesterday's religious education curriculum than it does for today's. Among the reasons for this change might be the waning of the dominant "Waspish" middle-class mentality and the rise of our modern pluralistic culture, the frustrating and inconclusive Vietnamese war, the failure of large government social programs to improve society so strikingly symbolized by the planned destruction of the failed St. Louis high-rise housing project, Pruitt-Igoe, and even more recently by the failure of the Army Corps of Engineers with all its trained personnel, state of the art technology, and dams and levees to control the "great Mississippi flood" of 1993!

Whether we know all of the particular reasons for this move away from the progressive mood of liberalism, we can conclude that modern historical events have introduced negative, even tragic, elements into our public life which have tempered the progressive spirit. Almost every promise of improvement seems to hold its corresponding threat. Will nuclear energy save the world or destroy it? Will the refinements in medical technology also create conditions for financially wasteful and socially unjust distributions of medical services that will elude the controls devised by both private enterprise and government? The questions go on, themselves raising our awareness of the tragic elements in our public community story without further elaboration here.

As we move through the 1990s into the next century, a time laden with ambiguities and uncertainties, we religious educators should look again at the relationships between our secular and religious stories. Perhaps the most escapist approach to this relationship would be to teach canonical stories in a comic mode to students living in cultural narratives that seem to unfold along other plot lines, one of which is the tragic plot. Just how, then, might an awareness of tragic elements in our Christian canonical story be relevant to teaching religion in the modern cultural situation?

Tragic elements in Mark's Gospel plot. Narrative theology with its focus on story detail and plot helps us to see that the biblical story need not, indeed ought not, be monochromatically read in a comic way. Tragic elements are there, too, especially in The *Gospel of Mark*.[27] Mark's tragic theme

---

27. I summarize here my more detailed account of the tragic elements in Mark's gospel in my article, "The Gospel of Mark and *Oedipus The King*: Two Tragic Visions," in *Soundings: An Interdisciplinary Journal* 67:1 (Spring 1984).

unfolds as the gospel writer builds in misunderstanding, denial, desertion, betrayal, and doubt. Jesus' disciples repeatedly misunderstand him, and in the end they desert him while Peter betrays him. Tragic irony appears even more starkly when Jesus confidently predicts the outcome of his own crucifixion, then expresses doubt about it in his cry from the cross "My God, my God, why hast thou forsaken me?" (Mk. 16:34). Christ is the tragic hero who experiences setback, who himself does not (cannot?) arrange the environment and condition the people around him so as to bring about successful worldly endings. This tragic dimension of Jesus' life speaks compellingly to people of today who experience similar endings in their own human enterprises.

Of course Mark's gospel is not unremittingly tragic, for it assures the reader that Christ will rise again and that God's kingdom will be realized through the tragic events of the Passion week; the tragic hero who suffers is also the comic hero who recovers (a literary mixture that has given rise to the genre of tragicomedy). Still, as Paul Tillich cautioned us in his sermon "Born in The Grave," when we read in the Apostles' Creed that Christ " 'suffered . . .was crucified, died, and was buried . . . rose again from the dead,' we already know when we hear the first words, what the ending will be: 'rose again'; and for many people it is no more than the inevitable 'happy ending'."[28] Tillich opposed this superficial interpretation that many people seem to make, for he believed that the Christian message embodied an unrelieved tension between comedy and tragedy which is easily lost when the preoccupation with Christ's resurrection obscures his crucifixion and death. For Tillich, Jesus experienced the full impact of death in his cry of forsakenness from the cross just as does the tragic hero.

Thus a narrative theology sensitive to plot forms can lead us into tension-filled and richly textured understandings of our stories and challenge us as educators to find the internal connections among these stories in their canonical, community, and personal forms. So long as our canonical stories remain stories from the past that we accept on authority and tradition alone they will continue to die a slow death, for the modern erosion of traditional authority as an alien law from outside or above our conscience is not likely to subside in the minds of most thinking, sensitive people. This is nothing new. Here again, Tillich told us decades ago that human creativity can never flourish so long as persons attempt to live entirely by their own law (a false autonomy) or entirely by an alien law from outside their own rational and moral experience (heteronomy, a law enforced by an arbitrary religious system). Rather, Tillich said, creative expression emerges when human laws resonate with the divine law and thus unite with their own spiritual depth (theonomy).[29]

---

28. Paul Tillich, "Born in The Grave," in *The Shaking of The Foundations* (New York: Scribner's, 1955), 164-168.

29. Paul Tillich, *Systematic Theology*, Vol. I (Chicago: University of Chicago Press, 1951), 83-86.

Translated into the terms of narrative theology, this means that creative expression emerges when life and community stories resonate with canonical stories and thus unite with their own spiritual depth. What could be more relevant for Christian education than the emergence of such creative expression?

Understanding and Communicating the Canonical Story in a Contemporary Educational Context

We have seen that we must understand how the narrative structure, especially the plot form, unfolds in comic and tragic modes in order to develop internal connections between the canonical stories and our present lives as teachers and students living in modern religious and secular communities. This requires us to comprehend the narrative structure, including the plot form, in which the fundamental theme of the canonical gospels is expressed, namely, the theme of salvation (soteriology is the theological term). I will now explore how a narrative approach can enhance our comprehension of salvation in an educational context.

According to Michael Root, salvation "presumes two states of human existence, a state of deprivation (sin, corruption) and a state of release from that deprivation (salvation, liberation), and an event that produces change from the first state to the second. It presumes then the sufficient conditions of a narrative: two states of existence and an event that transforms the first into the second."[30] Salvation is a process over a period of time in which a person moves from one state of existence to another. The biblical narrative unfolds in a problem/solution, tension/resolution scheme; the tensions of human sin and corruption are resolved in a series of sequential events involving the heroic character, Jesus Christ. Since salvation involves this sequential process, "Narrative is not merely ornamental in soteriology (salvation), but constitutive," says Root.[31]

The meaning of salvation can be described in summary statements, of course, but since it happens over a period of time rather than as a static event, we cannot reduce its essence to a doctrine any more than we can capture the flight of a bird in a still photograph. (This may explain in part why an official doctrine of the atonement has never developed in the Christian tradition.) Thus the heart of the canonical story is not a doctrine to be learned or a principle to be handed down through instruction. Rather, it is a story to be incorporated into the believer's own life story which also unfolds over a period of time.

Narrative theology's question for religious education now becomes: "How can education incorporate the canonical story of salvation into life stories?"

---

30. Michael Root, "The Narrative Structure of Soteriology," in *Why Narrative?* 263. My discussion of soteriology draws heavily from Root's essay.

31. Ibid., 263.

For Michael Root, the answer involves a *retelling and a reliving of the canonical story in augmented forms*. In the early church before canonization when the gospels were being formed, the gospel stories were passed down through retelling the stories in augmented forms that brought out particular interpretations. This augmentation preserved the integrity of the original stories while it expanded them to fit within the life story of the new narrator or writer. In fact, the verb "augment" means "to make greater; to expand." Thus each of the gospel writers both preserved and expanded the original story of Jesus from the perspective of his own experience of Christian life in his particular community of believers. Root explains the process in this way:

> The problem that an "atonement theory" seeks to solve is how the story of Jesus is the story of redemption, at least for those who bear a certain relation to it. If this special relation is understood as a kind of inclusion, then the task is to elucidate the relation between the one sequence in the story, the life, death, and resurrection of Jesus, and another sequence now included in the story, the life and redemption of the Christian. Again, we have a task of narrative interpretation, of the explication of the relation between two sequences within an allegedly unitary story.[32]

Root is saying here that a dynamic atonement theory which speaks to *our* salvation joins the sequence of events in the Jesus story with the sequence of events in each of our life stories. In other words, the process of salvation involves *internal connections* among the different stories. For religious education to accept the challenge of finding internal connections between the gospel story of salvation and our modern life stories is one thing, to accomplish such a task is another. Many conservatives view the biblical narrative as the crystallized Word of God for unmodified application to our lives; for them, the "true colors" of the message should not be blended in any way with the "colors" of our own life stories. At the other extreme, many liberals distort the original story beyond recognition in their transformation of it to meet the needs of their own modern lifestyles; the "true colors" fade beyond recognition.[33]

---

32. Ibid., 267. Root goes on to say that some scholars, such as Frank Kermode, agree that the gospel writers augmented the stories of Jesus, but that after their gospels were canonized, the texts became "frozen" into the canonical form, and as such were no longer open to augmentation, but only to interpretation through exegesis. Root's references to Kermode are from Frank Kermode, *The Genesis of Secrecy: On the Interpretation of Narrative* (Cambridge: Harvard University Press, 1979), 81, 98. Kermode says the following about the gospel writers' augmentation of the original story of Jesus: "It is quite widely agreed that the evangelists used methods continuous with those by which, before the establishment of the canon, ancient texts were revised and adapted to eliminate or make acceptable what had come to be unintelligible or to give offense," 81.

33. In his discussion of augmentation, Root refers to Hans Frei's description of the theology of Karl Barth as a retelling and reliving of the gospel story which preserves the

Still, this is the challenge that narrative theology presents for religious education, and although it is a difficult task, it is surely not an impossible one. It is probably true that many Christians are more concerned about relating to their family worlds and professional careers than to canonical religious stories. Yet in my own experience as a teacher of undergraduate and adult education classes I have known many teachers and students of all ages who are concerned about the meaningful augmentation of the Christian story into their own stories. These people can relate *internally* with Augustine, joining him in his prayer, "Our hearts are restless until they find rest in Thee."

The plain fact is that there *are* teachers and students who work together in an educational context to move toward this richer religious end. For instance, in my religion classes I have often juxtaposed biblical narratives and modern novels as a meaningful way to approach the religious dimension. The purpose is never just to compare and contrast the texts, rather, it is to explore the inner currents of our own life stories in relation to the worlds depicted in the biblical stories and the novels. Although the gospel story moves in one stream while the chosen novel moves in another, we are readers try to swim for a while in each. Feeling along below the surface waters of both gospel story and novel, we sometimes touch upon similar currents in the deeps and shallows of the two of them.

I take as an example Margaret Atwood's novel, *Surfacing*,[34] where much of the meaning unfolds in water symbolism. The protagonist (whose name is not given to us) embarks on a journey of self discovery by returning to the Canadian lake on which she spent part of her childhood. As her search for selfhood develops, she dives into the lake's depths in search of pictographs on a submerged cliff wall that might connect her with her past and her father; she sees instead her dead father's image and a fetus image, the child she has presumably aborted. She confronts herself through these encounters, and her self-transformation begins. She divests herself of her old self in order to re-clothe her new self and thus undergoes a ritual cleansing to uncover a primitive state of existence within her that lies beneath the cloak of her cultural past. She returns to her parents' cabin and destroys her visible attachments to the past: clothes, photograph albums, the whole lot. But her ordeal is only a temporary withdrawal to cleanse herself. She now surfaces to reen-

---

integrity of the original text. I agree with Frei. But Barth has come under intense criticism from both the radical liberals and the biblical literalists. The liberals charge that the biblical world so drenches his mind that he is insensitive to the real challenges of the modern world. On the other hand, the biblical literalists charge him with playing fast and loose with the textual meanings. (At some point in his colorful theological career, I suspect that Barth had something very funny to say about this.) For Frei's assessment, see Hans W. Frei, "An Afterword: Eberhard Busch's Biography of Karl Barth," in *Karl Barth in Review: Posthumous Works Reviewed and Assessed,* ed. H. Martin Rumscheidt, *Pittsburgh Theological Monograph Series* 30 (Pittsburgh: Pickwick Press, 1981), 110.

34. Margaret Atwood, *Surfacing* (New York: Fawcett Crest Ballantine Books, 1972).

ter her old world in a new way (although hesitatingly and tentatively).

If we are of a mind to, we can find elements of our own life stories in her story and surface with her, understanding the rebirth of life as a narrative process. When this happens, Atwood's narrative prepares us for an expanded awareness of many of the canonical Christian themes: the fall, Augustine's distorted will and corruption of culture, the cleansing and renewing waters of baptism, the return to the primal innocence of Eden in the tradition of St. Francis, and finally the hesitant reentry into the fallen everyday world of ambiguity and doubt.

But ironically enough, my point is almost lost in the making of it, for the really important connections among stories are never made through an external account of the similarities as I have just done. Rather, the significant interrelationships among stories are the internal connections that come through retelling and reliving the stories in one's own context, through the augmentation of an original story into one's own story. This is the point of the rabbi's story in our prologue. His paralyzed grandfather has to jump and dance to tell the story about his teacher who jumped and danced. Grandfather internalizes and augments the story.

But to point this out is also to raise the great unanswered (unanswerable?) question that arises for *all* education, whose Christian formulation is this: "Why is it that one student can draw together a gospel, a novel, and his own life story into the same orbit while another cannot or will not?" Educators seem unable to provide a formula answer for this question, nor can they even guarantee specific results through their partial answers. Jesus himself reflected on being "born again" by commenting that "the wind blows where it wills, and you hear the sound of it, but you do not know whence it comes or whither it goes; so it is with everyone who is born of the spirit." Read in the light of Jesus' own life, this passage seems to tell us that the process of religious education and personal growth is itself an ongoing story that cannot be reduced to a formula which brings guaranteed results. Rather, it is a story that evolves in a tragicomic form filled with frustrations, disappointments, and set-backs that nevertheless in the long haul holds together to help make the world a better place for us all.

Narrative Theology, Religious Education, and the Mystery of God's "Otherness"

While religious education must relate the Christian vision to our life in the everyday world, it will teach little other than sociology or psychology if it ignores the transcendent "otherness" of God. Indeed, to be a vital Christian *in* the world requires some awareness of the mysterious God who, while creating and sustaining the world, also transcends the world. This dimension of God's mystery is especially relevant for us educators, because religious education's subject matter is none other than this God who is shrouded in mystery. If we gloss over this mystery in our teaching, then we do nothing in the classroom that cannot better be done by the experts in the secular class-rooms.

The unfollowable presence of God along the liminal edges of human experience sensitizes us to the pervasive presence of mystery and prevents us from reducing God to our own pictures of (him/her/it?). Many people know the title of J.B. Phillips' book, *Your God Is Too Small*, but fewer have thought through its full meaning. For the literalist, the straightforward account of God's action in the written word often divests the divine presence of real mystery. For the extreme liberal, God at times becomes little more than the mirror image of that liberal's own modern life story, which seems to confirm Ludwig Feuerbach's well-known claim that the concept of God refers to no more than a projection of human thought.

Narrative theology can help to convey the sense of God's transcendent "otherness," the sense of God's mysterious "being" whose fullness eludes our human conceptions of it.[35] We religious educators can use good novels to evoke this sense of God's "otherness." Novels often remind us of the "numinous" dimension of God, a presence along the parameters of human experience that can never be entirely contained within human experience itself. Herman Melville's *Moby Dick* is a classic example. We know that the awesome surfacing and then disappearance of the great white whale, Moby Dick, is not literally meant to be a supernatural presence. Yet as the plot unfolds, it presents us with a sense of "otherness," with a "world of inscrutable things, unknown depths, and unanswerable questions that communicate to us through equivocal signs and portents."[36] Melville builds into his narrative an almost unendurable tension between the presence and absence of the whale, and interlaces this tension with the presence and absence of God to Moses. God says to Moses:

> Behold, there is a place by me where you shall stand upon the rock; and while my glory passes by I will put you in a cleft of the rock, and I will cover you with my hand until I have passed by; then I will take away my hand, and you shall see my back; but my face shall not be seen. Exodus 33:21-23

In an obvious literary play on this Exodus passage, Melville reflects on the dissection of a whale:

> Dissect him how I may, then, I but go skin deep; I know him not, and never will. But if I know not even the tail of this whale, how understand his head? Much more, how comprehend his face, when face he has none. Thou shalt

---

35. For excellent discussions of the sense of "otherness" in narrative, see Giles B. Gunn, "American Literature and the Imagination of Otherness," in *Religion as Story*, 65-92 and Stephen Crites, in "Angels We Have Heard," *Religion as Story*, 23-63.

36. I think this is a quotation from some commentary or essay on Melville's novel, but I cannot locate its source.

see my back parts, my tail, he seems to say, but my face shall not be seen. But I cannot completely make out his back parts; and hint what he will about his face, I say again he has no face.[37]

In both *Exodus* and *Moby Dick* the sense of transcendence described in the above passages is generated by the unfolding narratives themselves. The narratives point to a mysterious God who cannot be reduced to a simple law giver and enforcer of morality. The *Exodus* narrative does contain moral pronouncements, such as the Ten Commandments, and it exhorts the reader to follow them. Yet moral pronouncements and exhortations to follow the laws, taken as ends in themselves, usually thrive best in the flat, gray worlds of places like Dorothy's Kansas in *The Wizard of OZ*.[38] Of course religious education must stress moral development, but such teaching loses its vitality when it legalistically stresses moral principles and religious teachings pulled like brass buttons from their richly mysterious spiritual fabric. This is a major point in Jesus' parables of *The Laborers in the Vineyard* and *The Prodigal Son*. Morality is not rejected in these two parables, rather, it is transformed by a spiritual presence capable of regenerating life.

Religious education does itself a disservice when it fails to grasp how biblical narratives always place human morality and love within the numinous context of God's mysterious "otherness." The God who gives Moses the Ten Commandments is hidden in the clouds on Mt. Sinai; this God tells Moses to warn the people not to come too close, for God's "otherness" might break out against them (Ex. 19:23-35). Time and again through the biblical account of God's centuries-long engagement in human history, God's mysterious "otherness" brings into question the rational and moral formulations of human beings.

To discourse on the role of mystery in religious education as I have done here is one thing, to experience mystery through the full-bodied unfolding of it is another. A sensitive use of narratives can help us to discover this transcendent dimension, not as an object we can reduce to a formula or fence in like a flower garden, but rather as an illusive presence on the edges of our experience that, although largely unnamed and uncontrolled, can move us beyond ourselves in order to take a fresh look into ourselves.

On Teaching the Parables of Jesus: A Postmodern Approach to the Educational Process

Finally, I want to show how a careful reading of a unique form of biblical narrative, the parables of Jesus, can enhance the educational process. James

---

37. Herman Melville, *Moby Dick* (New York: Signet Classic, 1961), 363.

38. I borrow this image of Dorothy's Kansas from Linda Hansen's "Experiencing the World as Home: Reflections on Dorothy's Quest in *The Wizard of OZ*," *Soundings*, 67:1 (Spring 1984), 91-102.

Breech's insights into the parables will guide us.[39] In the classical world there were thousands of stories with content similar to the parables of Jesus, yet Jesus' parables were unique in their plot arrangements and conclusions, says Breech. While the classical stories close with a concluding sequence of actions and events that make a moral point, Jesus' open-ended parables provide no such closure with a moral lesson.

In Jesus' parables, the immediate conflict situation is resolved, but only to open up a new unresolved situation. For instance, the good Samaritan binds up the wounds of the man beaten by robbers, deposits him with the innkeeper, and then leaves. The parable ends, and we are left not knowing the innkeeper's response. Will he nurture the beaten man until he is well? Will he evict him after the good Samaritan leaves? Will he steal his money before he evicts him? Or will the beaten man recover during the night, rob the innkeeper and flee? We find the same open-endedness in the prodigal son story. Will the prodigal son once again disappoint his father and move on to his next adventure as the picaresque rogue who never changes and who always disappoints others? Or is he a comic figure who will finally reconcile himself to his family and his world?

Although these stories are left unresolved, they do leave us with a new situation which holds new possibilities. The main characters, such as the good Samaritan and the father of the prodigal son, have freely and spontaneously acted in gracious, caring ways toward the others around them. In so doing they have created new contexts in which additional people are drawn into the sequence of events to engage in acts of loving compassion or hateful aggression. Thus new conditions are created which give birth to new possibilities for human interrelationships.

Still, the future remains uncertain and ambiguous in every instance, for we do not know how the affected characters will respond. While "angels" may emerge in the form of loving, caring responses, the way is also opened for "demons" to appear in the form of destructive actions (will the elder son embrace his prodigal brother or will he finally slay him, like Cain slew Abel?).

Breech's research into the parables convinces him that Jesus understood the dynamics of real life and created his parables to express it. Breech says, Jesus was the first narrator in the West to tell non-didactic, non-moralizing, fictional, realistic narratives," and goes on to say that if he is correct about this, "It would mean that it was Jesus who first liberated the

---

39. James Breech, *Jesus and Postmodernism* (Minneapolis: Fortress, 1989). This wonderful little book is a "must" for the thoughtful reader who is interested in the more profound meanings of the parables. Amos Wilder has this to say on the back cover of the book: "Breech's level of exploration, his *topoi*, the stakes he is playing for, the wider encounters with various authorities, with fateful agendas both moral and disciplinary—all this sets his work apart."

human imagination by communicating the truth about reality."[40]

Whether or not Jesus was the first to accomplish this, his parables do present us with life as we generally experience it, that is, life in which we can never be certain of the full consequences of our decisions and actions. Real life does not unfold along a prescribed formula; it usually fails to conform exactly to some specific plot arrangement such as comedy, tragedy, or the picaresque. In truth, most of us simply act and hope for the best, living somehow in the confidence that come what may, there is some pattern, some truth, beneath the vagaries and vicissitudes of life that correlates with our moral intuition and conforms to an ultimate system of justice and love.

Concluding Observations

On first glance, to accept Breech's view and thus affirm such an open-endedness at the core of human life may seem at odds with the gospel message. Earlier, we discussed the Christian understanding of salvation as a narrative process in which the story of Christ's life, death, and resurrection was organized around a problem and its solution that, in seeming contrast to the parables, *does* come to a moral closure. Michael Root also described for us how Christians could internalize this canonical story of Christ's mission into our personal life stories through the retelling and reliving of it. If both Breech and Root are correct, however, then we seem to be confronted with a Jesus who tells open-ended parables with an unresolved, still-unfolding plot, yet also a Jesus who himself is cast in a much larger biblical plot that is resolved in moral closure, namely, Christ's ultimate liberation of humanity from its bondage to the ambiguities and uncertainties of human sin and death.

This seeming contradiction between life stories and canonical stories may disclose the paradox at the center of the religious experience: We believe that we live open-ended lives on the one hand, while on the other hand we also believe that we live within an ultimate framework of moral closure. We move through life as if it were an avant-garde hyper-text in which we make choices leading in new directions that will open still unknown choices and directions, yet we believe the story has a final and single ending. The reflective Christian, to *be* a Christian, does seem to somehow believe there is some pattern, some truth beneath the vagaries and chances of life that correlates with our moral intuition and holds the whole human enterprise together.

We are thinking now about religious consciousness as a somewhat unique form of awareness, as a set of sensibilities that holds together different levels of consciousness in creative tension. But this is nothing new, for such a double-layered consciousness permeates the Hebrew and Christian scriptures as it does the writings of most other religions. We find this double consciousness throughout the earliest Christian literature. In fact, some of the passages expressing it are almost commonplace. In John's gospel, Christ calls

---

40. Ibid., 64.

his followers to be *in* the world but not *of* the world, for this world passes away and God's kingdom endures (Jn. 15-17). And Paul's letters constantly remind us of the double-leveled dimensions of religious experience: "Do not be conformed to this world, but be transformed by the renewal of your mind that you may prove what is the will of God" (Rm. 12:2), and "We ourselves, who have the first fruits of the Spirit groan inwardly as we wait for adoption, the redemption of our bodies" (Rm. 8:22-23., NRSV).

In this essay I have tried to show that narrative theology can help religious education bring to the surface the multilayered dimensions of religious consciousness and that it can do this through the more literary and poetic expressions of the faith that offer a kind of satisfying "soul food" that many people hunger for. By this I do not mean to suggest that other forms of teaching are not also important, such as instruction in doctrinal and theological beliefs, moral principles, and the meaning of the church and sacraments. But if the role of narrative theology in religious education is also significant, then we should develop the leadership and curriculum to provide it. More specifically, this would involve the narrative approach as a mode of teaching to bring out the internal connections between the traditional Christian message and the life stories and felt experiences of present-day teachers and students living in their community context.

Moreover, a narrative approach might provide helpful responses to some of the major problems facing religious education. Perhaps the most formidable problem is a Christian community that has lost its spiritual vitality. We have seen that a praxis understanding of education includes a social context in which the community life supports the interplay of canonical and personal life stories. But if a Christian community has lost its spiritual sense, the hard truth may sometimes be that *no* educational program can be successful. After all, tragic plots do unfold in this world. But if a vestige of spiritual awareness remains, as it almost always does, then education might begin with a congregational study of a narrative about a dying community and the impact of that death process on the community's individual members. From the Book of Genesis story of Sodom and Gomorrah to Albert Camus' novel, *The Plague*, the supply of powerful narratives is plentiful indeed.

A second problem for religious education is the apparent lack of teachers with the knowledge, talent, and interest to lead educational programs, particularly those programs that give attention to the more literary narrative approach. These teachers are presumably present in religious studies programs in colleges, universities, and seminaries, and the continuing development of such programs is a faculty responsibility. My purpose in this essay has not been to provide guidelines for the implementation of educational programs, but as I have already said, I can speak from my own experience in the local church that there *are* lay people who appreciate the role of good narratives in providing "soul food." We should seek them out and develop their teaching talents. I have found that some lay people with no formal background in literary studies have remarkable insight into literary texts once they are exposed to them. They may not have the literary training to establish themselves as leaders with technical expertise, but they have the sensibilities to join hands with others and offer guidance for a spiritual journey, for a pilgrimage.

Jack Seymour, a noted Christian educator, provides us a sensitive description of the teacher as the "guide for the journey." He says:

> The teacher functions as a guide for the learner who is on a pilgrimage toward meaning. While the teacher is clearly someone who knows something of the way, he or she travels with the learner, rather than standing ahead, beckoning, as someone who has already completed the journey; or behind pushing the learner on, as someone who does not need to go on this journey. The teacher risks participation in a mutual journey with the learner and by so doing, acts as a model. Thomas Groome suggests that the teacher be named "leading learner."[41]

Seymour's image of teacher and learner as travelers on a mutual journey suggests the narrative mode. We as travelers are the characters, and the plot unfolds as we share with one another along the pilgrimage road. Like Chaucer's pilgrims in the *Canterbury Tales*, we each have our own "story to tell." But for whatever reasons both clear and cloudy, we come together on one road for a common journey. The teachers cannot provide us with the full fruits of the destination, for that would miss the point of the pilgrimage; if the fruits of the destination were brought to us then we would not need to travel to them. Thus the plot arrangement brings us together as teachers and learner to travel the same road to a common destination. Underway, the teachers share with the learners the maps and guidebooks that relate the route to the destination. And we, learners and teachers all, remind one another where we have come from, where we are, and where we are going.

---

41. Jack L. Seymour and Donald E. Miller, *Contemporary Approaches to Christian Education* (Nashville: Abingdon, 1982), 131-132.

CHAPTER ELEVEN

Liberation Theology and Religious Education

DANIEL S. SCHIPANI

Part One

A liberative Christian education cannot be simply a tool in the hands of theology, for the latter is no longer practiced in an ivory tower divorced from the world. Theology now seeks to occupy its specific place within the global process of transformation . . . the relationship between a liberative Christian education and the theology of liberation [is dialectical in nature]. Here theology is education, and education is theological . . .

Theology draws its educative nature from this integration of faith reflection and practice. . . . It is a matter of discovering and rendering explicit, within a historical practice (however ambiguous and limited), the presence of the God of life as manifest in the struggle for justice, in order that the agent of such a practice—the people—may live this presence in a further practice. . . .

A liberative Christian education . . . must lead to an encounter with Jesus Christ in history and the liberation struggle. What Christian education is concerned with is not knowing but living, not only knowledge but action, not only interpretation but transformation. Christian education is an evangelical praxis—a process of action-reflection-action based on the liberating activity of God.[1]

INTRODUCTION

The task of relating liberation theology[2] to Christian[3] religious education is facilitated by the inherent pedagogical orientation and structure of the former.[4] Indeed, the intrinsic educational thrust and interest of liberation theology become readily apparent, among other emphases, in its focus on the normative import of the teachings of Jesus (including Jesus' way of teaching), the view of the Bible as the text of the church and God's book for the people, faith understood in terms of discipleship—i.e., committed following of Jesus Christ in light of the "curriculum" of the reign of God (e.g., the "Sermon on the Mount"), and doing theology as—essentially—an educational task for the sake of the ministry and mission of the ecclesial community in the midst of history. More fundamentally, and as highlighted in the quotation above, liberation theology draws its educative nature from the integration of faith reflection and practice.

The first part of this chapter—*Understanding Liberation Theology*—refers to several tenets, beginning with its first concern, namely, the special situation of the oppressed in God's economy. Then follow the related themes of Jesus Christ liberator and the reign of God and faithfulness reinterpreted in terms of the God's ethics and politics. Finally, there is a brief discussion of doing theology as hermeneutical and educational task in dialogue with the

---

1. Matias Preiswerk, *Educating in the Living Word: A Theoretical Framework for Christian Education*, trans. Robert R. Barr (Maryknoll, N.Y.: Orbis, 1987), 109, 112-113.

2. In this essay, "liberation theology" is used in the broad sense of a theological movement which includes a variety of types and strains. However, we will take into consideration primarily the pertinent contribution of Latin American liberation theology. There are analogous expressions of liberation theologies among African American, feminist, Hispanic, and native North Americans as well as in Asia and Africa; Latin American liberation theology has been articulated and developed more systematically than most other forms of liberation theology, and many writings of Latin American liberation theologians have been widely translated and read in the last three decades.

3. Due to personal faith commitment, academic and professional experience, and theological preference and bias, it is Christian religious education that we will be considering in this essay. Therefore, the specific context and orientation of the following discussion are primarily those of the Christian faith community; we recognize nevertheless that the concern for liberation is shared in many ways by religious educators in other faith communities as well as religious and theological traditions.

4. For a systematic and comprehensive exploration of the fruitful interplay between religious education and liberation theology—including mutual enrichment and correction—see Daniel S. Schipani, *Religious Education Encounters Liberation Theology* (Birmingham, Ala.: Religious Education Press, 1988).

Word of God. In the second part—*Liberation Theology Reshapes Religious Education*—we indicate how this theology specifically informs and orients the theory as well as the practice of the church's educational ministry.

UNDERSTANDING LIBERATION THEOLOGY

Liberation theology does not represent a school of theological theory or system as such. Instead, it constitutes a movement which integrates theology with socio-political concerns emerging from historical contexts of injustice, oppression, and massive human suffering. Liberation theology purports to be a new way of doing theology, often defined as "critical reflection on Christian praxis in the light of the Word."[5] It criticizes traditional theologies (both the "orthodox" or "conservative" as well as the "liberal" or "reformist" models)[6] and attempts to be much more than an alternative theologizing in the manner of an intellectual and academic exercise. In fact, by sponsoring active solidarity with the poor and oppressed, liberation theology advocates a *radical* model involving costly discipleship including the practical social and political implications of following and discerning the way of Jesus Christ in the real world in which we live. In other words, liberation theology is an explicitly contextual as well as committed and confessional theological task.[7]

The key interconnected features of this new paradigm (in the sense of interpretative framework and model)[8] are as follows: (1) Liberation theology focuses primarily on social contexts of human suffering as the best place—*theological locus*—and the clue to reflect on Christian faith and to test and validate its convictions, values, and actual practices. It is especially interested in that suffering which is the result of injustice, namely oppression; conse-

---

5. See Gustavo Gutiérrez, *A Theology of Liberation*, rev. ed., trans. Caridad Inda and John Eagleson (Maryknoll, N.Y.: Orbis, 1988), chap. 1.

6. For a helpful presentation and comparison of these three basic theological frameworks—orthodox, liberal, radical—see Dorothee Sölle, *Thinking About God: An Introduction to Theology*, trans. John Bowden (Philadelphia: Trinity, 1990). Within the radical paradigm, the theology of liberation redefines the task of theology itself as consisting in collaboration with God's work of liberation.

7. An insightful discussion of the contextual, confessional, and committed nature of theology is presented by Douglas John Hall, *Thinking the Faith: Christian Theology in a North American Context* (Minneapolis: Fortress, 1991), part I. Such a discussion nicely illustrates and explicates, from a North American perspective, some of the fundamental claims of liberation theology regarding contextuality and critical discernment, the necessity of compassionate involvement in our world, and the place of the theological task for the sake of the ministry of the church.

8. For a comprehensive discussion of "paradigm" in theology, see Hans Küng and David Tracy, eds., *Paradigm Change in Theology: A Symposium for the Future*, trans. Margaret Kohl (New York: Crossroad, 1989) and, especially, the essays by Küng, Matthew L. Lamb, and Leonardo Boff.

quently, commitment to and the actual quest for liberation is its central concern. (2) This theological reflection is therefore developed "from below"—from the "underside of history," i.e., the position of the oppressed, the poor, the marginated—and it is oriented toward the transformation of people as well as social structures. (3) Liberation theology operates with two fundamental assumptions, namely, that God is compassionate and liberating and the gospel news are the good news of the reign of God; and that there is an inherent human longing for freedom, justice, and peace which undergirds our vocation to struggle for humanization. (4) It emphasizes praxis—the dialectical connection of action and reflection—thus redefining faith as participation in the ethics and politics of God; and hermeneutics for transformation as an ongoing theological and educational process in dialogue with the Word of God. The significance of these key, interconnected features of liberation theology as a new theological paradigm, is presented in the following four sections.

THE OPPRESSED AND THE PEOPLE OF GOD

The Oppressed as Theological Focus

Meeting the poor and oppressed, identification with the commitment to them, is the first and indispensable movement for theological inquiry and reflection. The poor and oppressed constitute not only the necessary context and starting point, but they are also the special interlocutors of the theologians. The theological commitment presupposes the "epistemological privilege" of the oppressed. This privilege consists, first, in that their perception of the world is closer to the reality of the world than the way the rich and powerful view it (hence, the poor and oppressed can reveal more adequately what is really happening around us); second, such an advantage also connotes that they can more readily become channels of divine revelation and facilitators of transformative learnings, such as a revisioning of social reality in the direction of God's dream of freedom, peace and justice, and well-being for all (*shalom*). In fact, for liberationists, this is the key to understand Jesus' first beatitude—"blessed are you who are poor . . . ," Luke 6:20. The beatitude affirms not so much the internal spiritual disposition of the poor, but rather God's inclinations, that is to say the way in which God is predisposed on behalf of the weak, the victim, the marginal, the oppressed. In other words, this insight alludes primarily to the compassion and justice which characterizes God's reign. It follows that, as representative of Christ, the church must also affirm a *preferential option for the poor and oppressed.*

Further, theological reflection must deal responsibly with the questions raised by the oppressed peoples themselves and enter into dialogue and cooperation with them. This is the reason why, after restating the notion that every genuine theology stems from one or another concrete spirituality (that is to say, an existential encounter with God within history), liberationists can affirm that their theology "has found its cradle in the confrontation of faith with injustice perpetuated against the poor."[9] Liberation theologians understand that to assume the "place" of the oppressed is to recognize and support their interests and cause, the struggle for justice, and for new ways of realizing life in community. So this theological relocation is primarily a movement of *solidarity* which defines both praxis and reflection. In other words, the locus or context of theological inquiry and discussion correlates with involvement and participation in the actual historical settings of alienation, marginalization within which the church itself is called to adopt a new shape and orientation. In solidarity, this commitment to historical liberation praxis—i.e., salvation holistically viewed, including the socio-economic, moral, cultural, and spiritual dimensions of emancipation and enablement—constitutes the "first act" in liberationist perspective; actual theologizing in the "second act." Gustavo Gutierrez clarifies that here we are alluding to much more than methodology in a narrow sense: "When we speak of 'first act' and 'second act' . . . [we] are talking lifestyle—a way of living the faith. In the last analysis we are talking spirituality in the best and most authentic sense of the word. . . . In liberation theology, our methodology is our spirituality—a life process in the way to realization."[10]

Three implications can be drawn from the statement that the poor and oppressed constitute a special theological and religious locus, a privileged context for Christian praxis and reflection. First, the poor and oppressed constitute the place where the God of Jesus is especially present with a twofold challenge to illumination and conversion. The divine presence among the oppressed is both a prophetic (i.e., denouncing and announcing) and an apocalyptic presence which ushers in a new era. Second, "theological locus" also conveys the idea of the most appropriate and conducive situation for the religious experience of faith in Jesus Christ and the corresponding praxis of discipleship. And third, it follows that the position of the poor and oppressed is the most fitting place for reflection of discipleship. It follows that the position of the poor and oppressed is the most fitting place for reflection on Christian faith, for doing theology. Thus, for liberation theology, the optimum locus of revelation and faith is also the optimum locus of the liberating salvific praxis and theological praxis.

The Church as Base Community

In Latin America and elsewhere, the purported "new way of doing theology" on the part of liberation theologians has correlated with the proliferation of base ecclesial communities as a "new way" of being and viewing

---

9. Clodovis Boff and Leonardo Boff, *Como Hacer Teología de la Liberación* (Madrid: Ediciones Paulinas, 1986), 12.

10. Gustavo Gutiérrez, *The Power of the Poor in History*, trans. Robert R. Barr (Maryknoll, N.Y.: Orbis, 1983), 103-104.

the church.[11] The term *base* primarily refers to the poor and oppressed Christians and to those who live in solidarity with them in the contexts of worship and Bible study, mutual aid and service, and education and social action, particularly. They tend to emphasize the centrality of the gospel, a commitment in favor of the poor and oppressed, involvement in works of justice and peace as well as in education for justice and peace, and a missionary approach to ecclesiastical structures (in the sense of promoting both continuity and change in light of the current challenges and possibilities).

In the previous section there was a reference to the call the church receives to be transformed and reoriented in the face of people's suffering and God's compassion and justice. The Christian base communities represent precisely a radical reorientation of Christian practice and belief which challenges both Catholic and Protestant established churches in a number of ways: (1) These base communities are *historically* significant because they challenge the church's self-understanding, ecclesiastical institutionalism, lack of community spirit and solidarity, and centuries-old church-state alliances. (2) They are *sociologically* significant because they are a case of grassroots protest against institutional fossilization as well as a creative alternative to it. (3) Christian base communities are *ecclesiologically* significant because they confront traditional, authoritarian and pyramidal church structures. (4) They also challenge *missionary* theory and practice on the part of the Christian churches.[12]

The base communities actually display a variety of configurations, aims, and degrees of cohesion. They are composed of a number of families—usually not more than twenty—who come together on a regular basis. There is a significant degree of lay participation and direction, even in the cases in which these ecclesial groups are initiated by clergy and where priests and nuns continue to share in the leadership. The strong communitarian spirit promotes equality, mutuality, and intimacy. These are communities of religious celebration for praying, singing, reading and reflecting on the Bible, sharing meals and bread and wine—both eucharistically and informally. They foster mutual support and assistance, charitable action and service projects in a given neighborhood, as well as critical analysis of social and economic issues leading to and reflecting on diverse forms of political engagement.

In sum, grassroots Christian communities respond to a number of sociohistorical situations, including atomization, anonymity, and new forms of oppression, exploitation, and manipulation, as well as to the crises and oppor-

---

11. See Leonardo Boff, *Church: Charisma and Power: Liberation Theology and the Institutional Church*, trans. John W. Dierksmeir (New York: Crossroad, 1985), and *Ecclesiogenesis: The Base Communities Reinvent the Church*, trans. Robert R. Barr (Maryknoll, N.Y.: Orbis, 1986).

12. See Guillermo Cook, *The Expectation of the Poor: Latin American Basic Ecclesial Communities in Protestant Perspective* (Maryknoll, N.Y.: Orbis, 1985), 2-3.

tunities confronting the church.[13] As we will indicate in the second part of this chapter, whenever and wherever the church lives and ministers as an authentic base community, the church becomes a unique context for doing theology and for religious education in a liberation key.

JESUS CHRIST AND THE REIGN OF GOD

Liberation theology has recaptured the centrality of the biblical symbol of the reign (or commonwealth) of God and has suggested its fresh appropriation in the context of a keen interest in the person and ministry of Jesus according to the gospels. This theology thus underscores the political and eschatological dimensions and import of the Christian gospel in terms of a normative prophetic and utopian vision.

The focus on the reign and the justice of God carries a twofold meaning: It points to divine majesty, power, and will, and it also points to the social order and lifestyle unfolding in response to that majesty and power and in tune with the divine will for humankind and the world. Liberationists insist that not only does Jesus teach and demonstrate that the coming of God's reign creates a new and better quality of life—e.g., through healing, forgiveness and reconciliation, and empowerment to love and to create—but he also speaks of seeking (and entering) God's reign (Mt. 6:33). Thus, Jesus suggests choice, commitment, and active involvement on the part of his disciples. Further we must notice the startling contrast between Jesus' vision and teaching regarding the reign of God, and the prevailing cultural consciousness and conventional wisdom, ethics and politics. Subversively enough, Jesus criticizes traditional values, normal concerns and understanding of reality, and personal loyalties; and he announces a radically different way while inviting persons to join in his journey empowered with the new vision.[14]

The prophetic and utopian vision, so central in the ministry of Jesus, is especially affirmed in liberation christology.[15] Becoming an authentic and faithful disciple involves appropriating and proclaiming the gospel utopia, actual engagement in the praxis consistent with the politics of God, and embracing Jesus' very way of the cross and resurrection.

---

13. For compelling discussions of the pertinence of the Christian base community/liberation theology movement for North Americans, see, Richard Shaull, *Heralds of a New Reformation: The Poor of South and North America* (Maryknoll, N.Y.: Orbis, 1984) and *The Reformation and Liberation Theology—Insights for the Challenges of Today* (Louisville: WJKP, 1991); and Robert McAfee Brown, *Liberation Theology: An Introductory Guide* (Louisville: WJKP, 1993).

14. For an insightful discussion of Jesus' alternative vision in his roles as sage, revitalization movement founder, and prophet, that nicely explicates liberationists views on this matter, see Marcus J. Borg, *Jesus: A New Vision: Spirit, Culture, and the Life of Discipleship* (San Francisco: Harper & Row, 1987).

15. In the consideration of this theme we are taking into account a number of liberationist sources, especially the works of Leonardo Boff and John Sobrino.

Jesus Christ Liberator

Liberation Christology consistently presents the portrait of Jesus Christ liberator—the Jesus who challenges every social order and calls it to account before the judgment of God[16] . . . while focusing on the fundamental question, "Who is Jesus Christ for us today . . .?" The question is dealt with in the intersecting levels of description, analysis, and praxis, and from the complementary viewpoints of historicobiblical, theological, and pastoral perspectives.[17]

The christological reflection thus formulated flows naturally from the central and founding metaphor of God as liberator. That key metaphor points to the paradigmatic Exodus event and story that unites creation and redemption in the promise and hope of historical fulfillment. Given the traditional confession about Jesus of Nazareth as the Christ and the Son of God, God incarnate, and Jesus Christ as Lord, the liberation metaphor is also crucial to perceive the person and the praxis of Jesus, beginning with a candid look at the gospels in light of the present socio-historical situation. Jesus Christ effects and models liberation in his active compassion and solidarity with the poor, the oppressed, and the marginated; in his prophetic and utopian proclamation and teaching about the reign of God; in his confrontation of worldly and spiritual powers; and in his overall work for transformation and humanization in love and justice. The praxis of Jesus actually liberates, and his resurrection confirms the truth of the life of Jesus and the ultimate truth of his person.[18] The victory of the resurrection in turn sets free the power of Christian faith in the model of "Christ liberating culture" as a practical correlation between the quest for justice and the Christian praxis of solidarity with those who suffer.[19]

---

16. For a study of the images of Jesus in the history of Western culture, including a helpful presentation of Jesus as liberator, see Jaroslav Pelikan, *Jesus Through the Centuries: His Place in the History of Culture* (New Haven: Yale University Press, 1985), especially 206-219.

17. See José Míguez Bonino, "Who is Jesus Christ in America Latina?" in *Faces of Jesus: Latin American Christologies*, ed. José Míguez Bonino, trans. Robert R. Barr (Maryknoll, N.Y.: Orbis, 1984), 1-6.

18. Jon Sobrino, *Jesus in Latin America*, trans. Robert R. Barr (Maryknoll, N.Y.: Orbis, 1987), 14, 89ff.

19. This question of Christ-liberating-culture is lucidly discussed by Rebecca S. Chopp, *The Praxis of Suffering: An Interpretation of Liberation and Political Theologies* (Maryknoll, N.Y.: Orbis, 1986), chap. 7, especially 130-133. Chopp rightly observes that the model of Christ liberating culture depends on two important and specific theological arguments for liberation theologians: 1) The reason Christians relate to culture in the liberating praxis of solidarity with those who suffer is *because of God's option for the oppressed*; 2) the second argument for the Christ liberating culture model identifies *justice as a primary analogue for faith* (i.e., faith that sets free from sin and for God and world; faith working through love in bringing about human justice through structural and personal transformation).

The affirmation of Jesus Christ the liberator leads liberationists not only to denounce and negate the christologies of oppression in the actual history and experience of their people (such as those promoted by the Spanish colonizers in Latin America, beginning in 1492), but rather to suggest an alternative to the "sublime abstraction" of classic or traditional christologies.[20] Therefore, together with the critical aspect of their reflection, liberationists constructively emphasize: a) Orthopraxis as a matter of lifestyle—that is, truthful living and acting on the part of people who profess the Christian faith; the ethical and epistemological dimensions thus converge, since the only way to know Jesus is to follow after him in the real life. b) The primacy of the social and ecclesial dimensions and expression of Christian spirituality as a corrective to the individualistic and privatistic distortions of personal piety. c) A hope-filled, utopian future, ultimately as God's gift, which elicits openness to transformation.

Finally, the focus on the gospel of the reign of God—which symbolizes divine liberation and re-creating action, will, and promise, as depicted in scripture and, mainly, in light of Jesus' ministry—evokes three sets of implications,[21] as follows. (1) *Formal implications*: the centrality of the reign of God in Christian witness and theological reflection calls for affirming the normative significance of the One who reigns, and for taking history and the human community seriously; it also calls for political obedience in the manner of radical discipleship and faithful citizenship, because theology and ethics cannot be separated. (2) *Material critical implications*: God's reign presents mutually exclusive alternatives to the established order (e.g., God or wealth); the divine commonwealth is an "upside-down kingdom" that calls for personal conversion and a comprehensive restructuring of this human world (e.g., power is at the service of the common good). (3) *Material constructive implications*: the affirmation of the reign of God in deed and word invites and makes possible historical realizations of that utopia with active human involvement and participation; such a gospel offers specific criteria for discerning what is indeed consistent with the ethics and politics of God; finally, the ecclesial community is called to become a paradigm of God's reign, a sacrament of history, often as a "contrast society."

---

20. This eloquent expression comes from Jon Sobrino, *Christology at the Crossroads: A Latin American Approach*, trans. John Drury (Maryknoll, N.Y.: Orbis, 1978), xv. Sobrino's work presents two essential guidelines for a Latin American christology of liberation: 1) the centrality of the historical Jesus; 2) discipleship as the basic means for knowing Christ. These and related themes are further considered in Sobrino's *Jesus the Liberator: An Historical-Theological Reading of Jesus of Nazareth* (Maryknoll, N.Y.: Orbis, 1993).

21. For a systematic discussion of these implications, see Schipani, *Religious Education Encounters Liberation Theology*, 83-93.

FAITHFULNESS AND THE POLITICS OF GOD

Liberationists contend that *orthopraxis* rather than orthodoxy becomes the truth criterion for theology—that is, obeying the gospel rather than defining, prescribing, or even defending it. By asserting that the faithful following of Jesus is the precondition for knowing Jesus, as indicated in the previous section, they in fact restate an *epistemology of obedience*. Further, according to this view, Christian faith must be viewed as committed participation in God's liberating and recreating work for the sake of the world. Thus, in liberation theology there is a deliberate blending of a biblical understanding of knowing and faith with a notion of praxis as the dialectic of action and reflection.

A Praxis and Biblical View of Knowing

Liberation theologians have critiqued the prevailing idealist, dualist, and rationalist theological views of truth for failing to resonate with key biblical notions of knowing and faith. Their main concern in this regard is the question of the relation of truth to actual historical practice, or knowing and obedience. Thus, liberationists affirm that there is no such thing as truth outside or beyond the concrete historical situation involving human beings as agents and that, therefore, there is no meaningful knowledge except in action itself, especially in the process of transforming the world through participation in history. A major epistemological claim on their part is that a biblical view of knowing and truth must be recovered and reappropriated in theology as well as in education.

Indeed, scriptural records, especially in the prophetic writings in the Old Testament and the Johannine literature in the New Testament, point to correct or right knowing as being contingent on faithful doing. In other words, the knowledge that counts and matters—the knowledge of God—is disclosed in righteous behavior. Wrongdoing is ignorance and disbelief; further, there is no such thing as neutral knowledge (or lack of it). In this context, knowing God is not abstract theoretical knowledge but active obedience to divine will—obedience is our knowledge of God and there is not a separate noetic moment in our relationship with God.[22] Liberationists particularly highlight the prophetic identification between knowing God and practicing justice in the face of the biblical affirmation of Yahweh's own character (e.g., Je. 9:23-24). Hence, to know God is to pattern one's life after God's own way of being and acting. Authentic biblical knowledge, then, is intrinsically ethical in nature, and the juxtaposition of knowing and doing justice (e.g., Je. 22:14-16; Hos. 4:1-6; 6:6; 10:12; 12:6) is grounded in

---

22. See José Míguez Bonino, *Christians and Marxists: The Mutual Challenge to Revolution* (Grand Rapids, Mich.: Eerdmans, 1976), for a helpful discussion of liberationist epistemology.

God's nature and action in history (Hos. 14:3).

The liberationist rejection of the dominant idealistic and rationalistic theological approach includes the broader critique of European (and North American) theologies for having been, by and large, an idle, noncontextualized academic exercise.[23] Further, there is the rejection of the assumption that it is possible to acquire and develop a knowledge of truth separated from truthful action or the practice of truth, especially in the context of the ecclesial faith community (a point which includes an alternative to the traditional model of "applying" systematic theological reflection to ethical, pastoral and practical concerns). These rejections are specific expressions of the "epistemological break" consisting in the existential and historical following of Jesus Christ that yields a praxis knowing which is distinct from "natural understanding" as well as contrary to it.[24] Such a "break" also helps to redefine Christian faith itself in terms of faith-ful discipleship.

Faith Redefined: Discernment and Participation

The actual following of Jesus—discipleship—presupposes an ongoing process of discernment which is the particular quest for the will of God, not only to understand it but also to carry it out: it is a process in which God's will carried out verifies the will of God thought. Further, liberationists argue that, if being Christian means becoming children of God in the Son, then Christian discernment must have a structure analogous to the discernment of Jesus which can only be realized by faithfully following him. Jesus' own experience and praxis of discernment provides the prototype of every Christian discernment.[25]

Liberation theology presents a performative (i.e., praxis-oriented) view of faith in tune with a prophetic and utopian vision of the reign of God and the political and eschatological dimensions of the gospel. Thus it consistently proposes that the practice of justice must integrate Christian faith and love in effective responsibility for freedom at the level of society and culture. Indeed, liberation theology contends that the practice of justice defines the distinctive shape of faith in our present historical situation.

Simply stated, justice is viewed as that concrete form of love which seeks to effectively humanize, to give life in abundance to the poor and oppressed majorities of the human race; it is the form of love that is indispensable if the reign of God is to become a historical reality or if there is to be within history a reflection of the transhistorical utopian reality of

---

23. For a comparison of "European" and "Latin American" theologies as two ways of conceiving the theological task in terms of the epistemological challenges of the Enlightenment, see Jon Sobrino, *The True Church and the Poor*, trans. Matthew J. O'Connell (Maryknoll, N.Y.: Orbis, 1984), 10-38.

24. Ibid., 25.

25. Sobrino, *Jesus in Latin America*, 131. See Sobrino's discussion of the process and structure of Christian discernment in chap.5, "Following Jesus as Discernment."

that reign.[26] In short, liberationists forcefully argue that justice is a necessary and historically privileged embodiment of Christian love and the key norm and criterion for defining faithfulness.

Faith is thus a practical way of life conceived in terms of commitment, following, doing, and action, that is, discipleship oriented to the realization of God's utopia of shalom. Indeed, faith is viewed in the face of the processive nature and dynamics of the unfolding reign of God with its objective and subjective dimensions. Objectively, the faith that does justice corresponds to the mission of building God's reign which is evangelization in the fullest sense of the terms (i.e., to evangelize is to make present the Good News that is becoming a Good Reality); subjectively—in the sense of the Christian active subjects who respond to and participate in God's work—the point is that disciples are made in the very process of concrete participation in constructing that new reality. *Faith is then the present mode of participation in the ongoing creative and liberating work of God in the world*. This is the main connotation of "Christian praxis" as the object of theological reflection "in the light of the Word," which is the focus of the next section.

DOING THEOLOGY AND THE WORD OF GOD

Critical reflection and understanding for transformation constitutes another major liberation motif pointing to the question of method. The two, closely related, questions that we must consider in this regard are the liberation of theology and the liberation of the Bible.

Liberating Theology

A helpful way to overview the liberationist methodological approach consists of examining briefly the definition mentioned above—"a critical reflection on Christian praxis in the light of the Word"—while recognizing that the three dimensions included in such definition are inseparable in practice.

"A critical reflection . . ." We must reiterate that, for liberation theologians, this is not so much the beginning of the theological task as a special kind of disciplined endeavor which presupposes and necessitates a prior commitment to oppressed, suffering people and to praxis (that is, the quest for liberation and transformation). Put in simple terms, critical reflection consists of a careful analytical look at the historical situation in which Christian praxis occurs. The twofold purpose of such an observation is a) to discover and comprehend the nature and the causes of oppression; and b) to understand as fully and clearly as possible the character and dynamics of prevailing conditions (socio-economic, cultural, political structures, for instance) which generate, sustain, foster, and justify injustice and oppression. To the question of why critical reflection as a main theological task would concern itself

---

26. Sobrino, *The True Church and the Poor*, 47, 53.

and address such "temporal" matters, liberationists unanimously respond that the divine gift of salvation from sin actually consists of comprehensive, holistic liberation. Salvation is the complete and total fulfillment of humanity; conversely, injustice, poverty, and oppression are social manifestations of sin, which is the fundamental alienation from God and humanity.[27]

"... *on Christian praxis* ..." Commitment to praxis is the key because liberation theology underscores doing the truth—orthopraxis—rather than merely understanding revealed truth as the first and foremost theological task. Again, the emphasis is on orthopraxis rather than on orthodoxy. The critical reflection discussed in the previous paragraph derives from and illumines an active engagement by living out the gospel, and especially by sharing in the suffering and hope of the oppressed and the struggle for liberation and justice. Such a praxis is discerned, thoughtful action, reflectively and critically chosen, oriented and evaluated. It is a practical engagement (for instance in the planning for social change and implementation of alternative) but not as a definitive criterion of truth in itself, for praxis needs to be subject to communal assessment (and "... in the light of the Word"). The point is that liberationists see the need to encounter the reality of the present sinful situation with the explicit purpose of confronting human misery and eliminating oppression.[28]

"*in the light of the Word.*" The Word of God is the criterion liberationists bring to bear on reflection and action. That Word is first of all Jesus Christ— the Word made flesh (Jn. 1:1-14)—and it is also embodied in the church's tradition as well as in the human conscience. More specifically, the Bible witnesses to God's Word in such a way that it becomes the indispensable text for

---

27. Gustavo Gutiérrez explains that sin is at the base of all forms of alienation and, thus, it is never adequately contained in any one expression of alienation. Further, sin demands a radical global liberation (which in turn necessarily implies concrete, practical, and particular liberation). By the same token, salvation cannot be reduced or identified to any one specific instance of human transformation, fulfillment, or liberation. However, in relation to sin, salvation involves radical and practical redemptive mediations through partial fulfillment in the midst of history. The intimate connection between salvation and liberation is further illumined by Gutiérrez in his reference to the *three interconnected levels of liberation*: liberation from unjust social (political, cultural, economic, religious) structures that destroy people; liberation from the power of fate that leads to apathy or despair; and liberation from personal sin and guilt. In other words, liberation entails particular events and is intrinsic to salvation (but no single act of liberation can ever be fully identified with the depth and comprehensiveness of salvation). Consequently, liberation is viewed as inherent in the nature and purpose of history as the continual transformation of the new humanity. Liberation in concrete situations pertains to the fullness of salvation which is, ultimately, God's gift as the gift of the reign of God. In *Theology of Liberation*, 24-25, 103-104,107; see also Gutiérrez' *The Truth Shall Make You Free* (Maryknoll, N.Y.: Orbis, 1990), 121-136.

28. For a discussion of the interest in *transformation* (as opposed to mere *rationality*) on the part of liberation theologians, see Sobrino, *The True Church and the Poor*, 10-29.

the faith community, the book for the people. The scriptures play a key role in liberation theology whose main concern is, precisely, relating the gospel of the reign of God and the present historical praxis.

Liberating the Bible

The liberationist "new way of doing theology" assumes the special status of the Bible in the life and struggles of the people as well as in the theological task as such in terms of a hermeneutical process. Such a process consists of a multiway conversation involving the "pre-text" of the present historical situation, the biblical text, and the context of the faith community.[29] At the heart of the theological method, then, is hermeneutical circulation viewed and done as the interplay between the scriptures in their historical context and the interpreting community which reads the text in its own socio-historical context. The final aim of the process is not merely to better interpret the Bible but, rather, to see reality more clearly and to transform it more faithfully.

More specifically, the Bible is "liberated" by being reappropriated by the common people while the experts (teachers, scholars, and pastors) become servant-leaders and co-disciples. It is further "liberated" through communal discernment of ideological captivities which prevent us from being challenged and empowered by God's Word.[30]

Part Two

LIBERATION THEOLOGY RESHAPES RELIGIOUS EDUCATION

At the beginning of this chapter we alluded to the inherent pedagogical orientation and structure of liberation theology. From the viewpoint of religious education, we can indeed perceive a model of educational ministry which is communal in nature and shape, dialogical in spirit, prophetic and eschatological in vision, and praxis oriented and conscientizing with a dialectical-hermeneutical character.

Liberation theology can and does provide the necessary "background"

---

29. For a helpful discussion of this process in the context of grassroots ecclesial communities, see Carlos Mesters, "The Use of the Bible in Christian Communities of the Common People," in *The Challenge of Basic Christian Communities*, ed. Sergio Torres and John Eagleson, trans. John Drury (Maryknoll, N.Y.: 1981); and *Defenseless Flower* (Maryknoll, N.Y.: 1990).

30. For a provocative presentation on the Bible and ideological captivity in the context of the United States of America, see Stanley Hauerwas, *Unleashing the Scripture: Freeing the Bible from Captivity to America* (Nashville: Abingdon, 1993).

and the "clue"[31] for the educational ministry. In that capacity it can supply much of the substantive content or subject matter for the teaching-learning process and the curriculum, for instance. Thus, there is a gospel message to be rediscovered and shared; the story of the liberating and recreating work of God is to be appropriated in actual Christian praxis together with the vision of the coming reign of God. And this (substantive) content is closely linked with issues of structural content (in the sense of pedagogical strategies) as well as the contexts of education. Hence, the liberationist contribution can also play a guiding role[32] in the theological assessment of the educational ministry. Such a normative role can be seen, for example, in the theological critique of alienating doctrines regarding Christ and salvation taught, or manipulative and authoritarian instructional techniques employed; and in the theological endorsement of commitment within contexts of oppression, dialogue, critical discernment, and a transformative and hopeful orientation.

As both "background" and "clue" liberation theology reshapes our ways of viewing as well as doing Christian religious education.[33] And to a concise discussion of the theory and practice of educational ministry in a liberation key we now turn our attention.

VIEWING RELIGIOUS EDUCATION IN A LIBERATION KEY

When liberation theology is considered from the unique vantage point of the educational ministry, a number of observations can be highlighted as foundational and indispensable for refashioning that ministry. Those obser-

---

31. We are echoing Randolph Crump Miller's terms here. See his "Theology in the Background," in *Religious Education and Theology*, ed. Norma H. Thompson (Birmingham, Ala.: Religious Education Press, 1982), 17-41. Miller's position is that some kind of theology stands in the background of any religious education theory and that theology is in fact the "clue" for understanding and carrying out the religious education enterprise. The conclusion is that all religious educationists must be well aware of their own theological assumptions and foundations. See also Randolph Crump Miller, *The Theory of Christian Education Practice: How Theology Affects Christian Education* (Birmingham, Ala.: Religious Education Press, 1980), especially chaps. 3 and 9.

32. Sara Little presents five alternatives concerning the relation between theology and religious education: theology as content to be taught; theology as norm; theology as irrelevant; "doing" theology as educating; and religious education in dialogue with theology. "Theology and Religious Education," in *Foundations for Christian Education in an Era of Change*, ed. Marvin J. Taylor (Nashville: Abingdon, 1976), 30-40. It can be argued that liberation theology may relate to Christian religious education in terms of Little's categories of content, norm, theologizing, and dialogue.

33. For a Latin American presentation on Christian religious education in a liberation key, together with Preiswerk, *Educating in the Living Word,* see Enrique García Ahumada, "Qu'est-ce qu'une catéchise libératrice?," *Lumen Vitae*, 46:4, "Unir Justice et Foi" (1991), 425-436; the content of that whole volume—which includes European contributions—is pertinent for our discussion. Other European perspectives appear in Dermot A. Lane, ed. *Religious Education and the Future* (New York: Paulist, 1986).

vations include the following: a) The church—primarily as a "base community" (i.e., an efficacious sign of the presence and the reign of God in history)—is biased toward the oppressed and alienated, the stranger and marginated, and as such serves as the special *context* for religious education. b) The gospel of the reign of God establishes the *overall aim* of "discipling" (i.e., formation, transformation, and empowerment on the personal and communal levels) integral to a Christian religious education in the prophetic thrust of liberation theology; and such an overall aim points to the utopia of God's commonwealth of peace with freedom and justice (shalom). c) Faithful discipleship defines the *process and content* of praxis knowing consisting of participation in the ethics and politics of God in our world, especially for the sake of freedom, peace, and justice. d) Doing theology as educational task further illumines the process and content of the educational ministry in terms of the hermeneutical-dialectical interplay engaging the present historical situation and experience, scripture and tradition in worshipful partnership with the liberating, recreating Spirit of God. A brief discussion of such an overall revisioning of religious education in a liberation key follows.

People in Context: The Church as Base Community

This is the necessary starting point for a theory of Christian religious education inspired and oriented by liberation theology. Simply put, we must address the key and closely related, praxis questions involving *who* and *where*, such as these: who are the people that are partners to the educational process and what are their roles? Which are the places and situations most conducive to transformative learning and growth in faith? What kinds of interactions will best facilitate the learning tasks and overall experience? What features should the faith community have as a truthful context for discipling?[34] A few comments follow on how the liberationist discussion of the oppressed and the people of God begins to illumine those and related questions.

A Liberative Religious Education Calls for an Epistemological Conversion. The transformation of theological reflection postulated by liberation theology assumes the priority of an epistemological conversion. The first movement of this process consists in listening to the manifestations of the faith of the common people, especially the poor, the oppressed, and the marginated. However, the reflection stimulated by human suffering and the longing for freedom, justice, and peace is not merely an effort to explain the nature of suffering, to justify it, or to investigate its compatibility with the facts of divine revelation; it is rather an effort to confront and eliminate such suffering.

---

34. "Discipling" here stands for the multifaceted task of sponsoring human emergence according to Jesus Christ (that is, formation, transformation, and empowerment) which is the central concern of the educational ministry.

To the extent that our reality contradicts the project of the reign of God, conversion implies that even the very knowledge of that reality is to be transformed.

The integration of the expectations of compassion and obedience in solidarity corresponds to the recognition of the fundamental *authority* of the common people of God and, particularly, the oppressed. This is another way of referring to the epistemological advantage or privilege of the poor and oppressed. The common faithful people have an indirect authorship in the teaching ministry of the church to the extent that theologians and ecclesial leaders read the signs of the times adequately and become "voices of those who have no voice." Further, the oppressed people of God are, of course, also the direct authors of their own reflections, visions, and dreams, which contribute to the growth of faith and ministry of all. Thus, the importance of encountering the other oppressed is a key epistemological principle which has a theological dimension as well as a pedagogical structure and dynamic; we have here, then, a foundational principle for Christian religious education. The theological lesson is that there is divine revelation by way of encountering and commitment to the oppressed; the pedagogical lesson is that such an attentive listening and praxis (obedience) can foster transformative learning.[35]

The Church as Theological and Educational Context. The epistemological conversion that liberation theology proposes is essential for understanding the formation and transformation of the countercultural consciousness of the church as an alternative community. Further, the liberationist prophetic and utopian stance nurtures and evokes a consciousness and a perception alternative to the consciousness and perception of the dominant culture and the conventional wisdom, ethics, and politics. Theologizing and educating, so closely connected in liberation theology, thus partake of the overall discipling endeavor of formation and transformation of consciousness. The alternative or countercultural consciousness serves to critically dismantle the established, prevailing consciousness and to energize and empower the community and its people in the promise and hope for a better world toward which they move. A "better world" for the church means liberation and recreation in tune with the coming reign of God. It includes the gift and also the promise, the expectations and the demands of a new humanity according to Jesus Christ. This is why, as liberationists insist, the faith community is to attend to every aspect of human life and to seek the integration of the religious, social, political, and economic dimensions on behalf of justice and *shalom* (or fullness of life) for all people. That kind of project, needless to say,

---

35. The main themes of our brief discussion are presented by several liberationist authors, including Ignacio Ellacuría, *Conversión de la Iglesia al Reino de Dios* (Santander, Espana: Sal Terrae, 1984), Leonardo Boff, *Teología Desde el Lugar del Pobre* (Santander, Espana: Sal Terrae, 1986); Jon Sobrino, "The 'Doctrinal Authority' of the People of God in Latin America," *Concilium* (August 1985).

necessitates a common life to support such an alternative consciousness; hence, in John Westerhoff's words, the church is called to be an alternative way of seeing life (faith) and an alternative way of being (identity), especially as a community that displays a biased passion for the outsider, the stranger, and the estranged and offers people what they need, not what they "deserve."[36] And, as a unique context for Christian education which partakes of the whole nature and ministry of the church, such faith community will develop a number of features and practices especially conducive to growth in faith in light of the reign of God.[37]

The Overall Purpose: Discipling for the Reign of God

The liberationist foundations of religious education theory lead to restate its guiding principle—that is, the heart of the matter which orients the whole task of educational ministry—as well as its overall purpose, in terms of the gospel of the reign of God. The rediscovered centrality of that biblical symbol and master metaphor is thus underscored together with the gospel's witness that the reign of God is indeed the key to the content of Jesus' teaching and ministry overall.

Liberation theology emphasizes the utopian and eschatological vision of the commonwealth of God together with its interest on the historical Jesus and in the prophetic and political dimensions of the gospel in the face of today's world. That guiding principle evokes the tension between the "already" (the gifts bestowed, the dreams partially realized) and the "not yet" (the promise, the longings) of the reign of God; it also evokes alienation as well as hope in the midst of the present social structures. Further, it suggests corrective and creative alternatives to prevailing ecclesial and educational practices which foster conformity, passivity, and domestication.

Seeking and entering God's reign means, in this light, that the gift, the promise, and the demands of a new creation become the main value and focus of concern as well as the driving force in the life of the faith community and its ministry. Therefore, simply put, *the guiding principle calls for the educational task of discipling to be perceived, oriented, and evaluated in the light of the gospel of the reign of God.* And such a task, as far as the church's life and its threefold reason for being is concerned—that is, worship, community, and mission—must serve three fundamental functions: a)enabling for *worship* (lived and viewed primarily as acknowledgment and celebration of God's coming reign); b) equipping for *community* (the concrete embodiment of life as God's family and society, i.e., life as if God really reigned); c)empowering for mission (announcement and advancement of

---

36. John H. Westerhoff III, *Living the Faith Community: The Church That Makes a Difference* (Minneapolis: Winston, 1985), 83.

37. For a fuller discussion of the faith community as context for Christian religious education, see Schipani, *Religious Education Encounters Liberation Theology*, 244-250.

God's reign in presence, deeds, and words, especially in terms of freedom, peace, and justice). Simply stated, Christian religious education for the reign of God must be comprehensibly concerned with the fulfillment of the great commandment regarding love of God and neighbor.[38]

From a liberationist perspective, therefore, the historical and existential appropriation of the gospel of God's reign as overarching purpose supplies a special content to any statement of goals of Christian religious education. Such a perspective does indeed take into account not only the church's three-fold reason for being but, especially, the concrete situation of the people who participate in the educational ministry. In that light, we can suggest as summary statement that *the overall purpose is to sponsor people to appropriate the gospel of the reign of God by growing in the life of the Christian faith, and by existentially responding to the call to conversion and discipleship in the midst of the ecclesial community whose vocation is to promote faithful citizenship and social transformation for the sake of freedom, justice, and peace, make accessible knowing and loving God, and foster human emergence and wholeness.* The liberating thrust of such a comprehensive aim lies in the fact that human emergence—personal, communal, societal— is discerned and sponsored in terms of the coming reign of God.

(3) Process and Content (I): Discipling as Faith-Praxis

The liberationist contribution has much to offer also regarding the religious education questions of "how" and "what" of Christian discipling. The commitment to the ethics and politics of God in the midst of history calls for a refocusing of concerns, the development of an adequate approach, and a redefinition of Christian disciples as compassionate and responsible citizens.

Refocusing Concerns. As indicated above, one key dimension of the overall purpose of Christian religious education is promoting social transformation for the sake of freedom, justice, and peace. This specific goal of the concern with and involvement in society's political and socioeconomic realms; such a goal also calls for taking into account the systems and structures of those realms even when focusing on the special realities of persons, groups of people, or interpersonal and communal relationships. The forms and manifestations of power, the expressions of oppression and suffering as well as the quest for justice and peace, the role of ideology and interest, and the dynamics of social conflict, including political and educational strategies, must be included in a committed and contextualized religious education.

---

38. The reference to the church's threefold reason for being and the centrality of the educational ministry in the faith community stems from our recent and ongoing research on the subject. A book is being written for church leaders further spelling out the significance and implications of what we have called a congregational discipling vision and model.

Reorienting the Approach. An educational ministry in a liberation key necessitates the action-reflection-action paradigm as overarching dialectical process of learning, teaching, and transformation. More than a pedagogical strategy, this paradigm encompasses a variety of activities in tune with the very mission of the church in the world. "Believing" and "doing" must be brought together in a mutually influencing dynamic relationship. Consistent teaching principles must also be included together with the question of the place and the roles of educators as servant leaders; in other words, educators must educate for freedom, peace, and justice by educating in freedom and peace, and justly.

Christian Disciples as Responsible Citizens. Critically speaking, religious education for justice and peace amounts to confronting the dominant values and practices of contemporary American life, such as acquiescence, affluence, individualism, achievement, appearance, competition, and consumption. Indeed, the fashioning of faithful disciples involves, on the one hand, confronting domestication (i.e., strategies for mere adjustment and compliance), indifference or silence, conformity and complicity with structures of injustice and oppression. On the other hand, there is a summons for active participation in God's reign as compassionate, courageous, and caring citizens. A formidable challenge is thus presented to the church's educational ministry in terms of process and content, namely, the integration of the pedagogies of discipleship and citizenship.[39]

Process and Content (II): Doing Theology as Educational Task

The practice of liberation theology and the mode of theological reflection advocated by liberationists take on a more specific shape and significance when viewed in terms of the actual experience of the grassroot Christian communities. In fact, "critical reflection on Christian praxis in the light of the Word," becomes one special design for religious education which is strikingly analogous to the pastoral approach characterized by three movements—*seeing, judging, and acting*. In turn, the Christian education that takes place in authentic base ecclesial communities is itself the development of theology.[40]

---

39. On this topic, see John A. Coleman's excellent essay, "The Two Pedagogies: Discipleship and Citizenship," in Mary C. Boys, ed., *Education for Citizenship and Discipleship* (New York: Pilgrim Press, 1989), chap.2.

40. Reflecting on liberationist religious education in Latin America—especially the praxis of Christian base communities—Robert T. O'Gorman finds seven challenges to enrich North American Christian education: a) Both church and society are objects of transformation; b) education, as praxis, is the creation of community; c) education is central to the church; d) education is a unity of theology, organizing, research, and teaching; e) present realities, as well as those of the past tradition, are matters for teaching/learning interaction; f) religious education operates from an iconographic, or imaginal, pedagogy; g) before liberation is possible, we must discover the base on which society is formed. In

Liberationists refer to three main "mediations," in the sense of means or instruments of the theological and educational process. Briefly, those three mediations function and relate to each other in three stages as follows: (1) The socio-analytical (or historico-analytical) mediation operates in the context of the world of the oppressed; it tries to find out why the oppressed are oppressed. (2) The hermeneutical mediation operates in the sphere of God's world, metaphorically speaking, by trying to discern what God's dream and plan for the poor and oppressed is. (3) The practical mediation functions in the realm of action; it tries to discover the courses of action that need to unfold so as to overcome the situation of injustice in accordance with God's dream and plan.[41]

Content-Timing Principles. Christian religious education in a liberation key also calls for attending to the multifaceted question of "when" in light of the purpose stated above and in a comprehensive, holistic manner.[42] Thus four areas must be considered together and closely interconnected: a) The actual experience and praxis of the faith community, its past (history and tradition) and its future orientation (promise and hope, anticipation of further partnership in God's liberating and recreating work in expectation of the coming reign); and b) the "times" of the church must be discerned in relation to the situation and the flow of history in society and the world. Together with those two areas, there is c) the challenge to focus on the admittedly elusive dimension of the kairos or timing of God, in the sense of sensitivity to and readiness for the discerned divine activity in history—in both church and society as well as in the whole creation—and in tune with the eschatological view of the gospel of God's reign, as a key concern of the educational task. d) In the midst of the process, of course, there is special attention to the special agenda of human emergence both personal and communal, that is, the question of learning and growth, formation, transformation, and empowerment for faith and life.

DOING RELIGIOUS EDUCATION IN A LIBERATION KEY

In this chapter we have already established direct correlations between the key tenets of liberation theology *qua* theological reflection, as discussed in the first part, and the main features of a vision of Christian religious education in a liberation key. In this final section we will illustrate how libera-

---

"Latin American Theology and Education," *Theological Approaches to Christian Education*, ed. Jack L. Seymour and Donald E. Miller (Nashville: Abingdon, 1990), 195-215.

41. For a discussion of these questions of process and content in liberation theology, see Leonardo Boff and Clodovis Boff, *Introducing Liberation Theology* (Maryknoll, N.Y.: Orbis, 1987), chap. 3, "How Liberation Theology is Done."

42. For a fuller discussion of timing principles, see Schipani, *Religious Education Encounters Liberation Theology*, 190-194.

tion theology reshapes the actual practice of the educational ministry as further elaboration of the correlation indicated between the two disciplines and fields.

A major introductory observation is in order, in light of and in line with the "epistemological break" proposed by liberation theology, and that is the *inclusion of both action and accountability* not merely as the intended results but as integral to the educational process.[43] In other words, just as the commitment to and involvement of praxis that characterize the "practical mediation" must occur as an indispensable dimension of theological method, so must responsible action be included in the very process of transformative learning.[44] And that condition is explicitly assumed in each of the four areas briefly discussed below.

The Conscientization Model

This is a fitting starting point for us in this section, for historical reasons: Paulo Freire's work and thought provided the original and key methodological principle for liberation theology in terms of the approach and philosophy of conscientization.[45]

Originally developed by Freire and others in Brazil and Chile in the context of popular education with a Christian inspiration and base, *conscienti-*

---

43. It can be argued that one of the most crucial and lingering failures of Christian religious education in North America and elsewhere consists precisely in the lack of explicit and consistent connection and continuity between the programs and process of Christian education, such as Sunday School and CCD, and the real everyday life of Christian discipleship and citizenship of the participants.

44. On this point, from a liberationist perspective which takes seriously the "epistemological break" that moves beyond the intellectual tasks of reflection, sharing, and discussion, it must be indicated that Thomas H. Groome's "*shared praxis*" approach does not go far enough. In the conceptualization of the approach, shared *reflection* and *decision* are not necessarily accompanied and followed in the selfsame teaching/learning event and process by actual experiences of social action as something intrinsic or constitutive to the process of Christian religious education. Groome's epistemological foundations are nicely expanded and further clarified in *Sharing Faith: A Comprehensive Approach to Religious Education & Pastoral Ministry* (San Francisco: Harper & Row, 1991) in terms of "conation" as pluridimensional wisdom; however, the fifth movement of the approach is still one "that explicitly invites participants to decision about their response, individual and/or collective, as the historical *outcome* of this shared Christian praxis event." (226, emphasis added)

45. Freire's pedagogical practice together with his reflection and writing provided a timely twofold impetus in Brazil and elsewhere. The first impetus spurred on the church's involvement with the poor and oppressed. The second impetus furthered the stimulation of new insights on Christian "praxis" which became decisive in shaping the method of Latin American liberation theology. In articulating his own liberationist vision, which affirms the primacy of commitment and praxis, Freire helped to lay the foundation for the theological method adopted by liberation theologians. See Schipani, *Religious Education Encounters Liberation Theology*, chap. 1.

zation denotes an integrated process of liberative learning and teaching as well as personal and societal transformation.[46] Conscientization thus names the process of emerging critical consciousness whereby people become aware of the historical forces that shape their lives as well as their potential for freedom and creativity; the term also connotes the actual movement toward liberation and human emergence in persons, communities, and societies.

The conscientization pedagogy combines several dimensions such as: a) a collaborative and dialogical, communal context in which people can share stories and visions; b) participants engaging in critical and creative reflection beginning with problem-posing or "problematizing" their reality while; c) actively and concretely seeking better alternatives as partners in an ongoing liberation praxis. Methodologically and procedurally, the conscientization approach can take many different forms in diverse social settings while remaining as an action-reflection-action model analogous to the seeing-judging-acting process and structure. Thus, it can be seen as the inspirational centerpiece of any liberative Christian education program and pedagogy.[47] It can also be appreciated in terms of a specific pedagogy for adult religious education;[48] and as a paradigmatic expression of liberative teaching "from the heart."[49]

Contextual Dislocations as Pedagogical Strategy

Two fundamentally complementary movements must be considered in this area of concrete educational practice, which we will name "going and seeing" and "welcoming." Obviously, there is more than education (and, certainly, Christian religious education in the narrow sense of the term) involved in the situations mentioned below; but that is precisely the point of a liberation oriented vision as carried out in "doing" educational ministry in a liberation key.

Going and Seeing. One of the success stories in the area of voluntary context dislocation is that of the travel seminars model.[50] This model immerses participants in the culture of a host Third World country through visits with

---

46. See Paulo Freire, *Education for Critical Consciousness* (New York: Seabury, 1973), *Pedagogy of the Oppressed*, trans. Myra Bergman Ramos (New York: Herder, 1970), and *The Politics of Education*, trans. Donald Macedo (South Hadley, Mass.: Bergin and Garney, 1985).

47. On this topic, see Daniel S. Schipani, *Conscientization and Creativity: Paulo Freire and Christian Education* (Lanham, Md.: University Press of America, 1984).

48. See R.E.Y. Wickett, *Models of Adult Religious Education Practice* (Birmingham, Ala.: Religious Education Press, 1991), chap. 17.

49. See Mary Elizabeth Mullino Moore, *Teaching From the Heart: Theology and Educational Method* (Minneapolis: Fortress, 1991), chap. 6.

50. For a helpful presentation and discussion of this model, see Alice Frazer Evans, Robert A. Evans, & William Bean Kennedy, eds., *Pedagogies for the Non-Poor* (Maryknoll, N.Y.: Orbis, 1987), chap. 7, "Traveling for Transformation."

ordinary people as well as with key religious and political leaders who represent different approaches to a particular country's situations and problems. The design also incorporates systematic evaluative research on successive travel seminars to assess the kind and degree of impact on the participants. Participants commit themselves to covenants of preparation, living simply with their hosts, and communicating what they experience and learn when they return home. By inviting people to leave their "comfort zone" and become vulnerable in contexts of oppression and poverty, this model seeks to provide experiences which lead to significant change of views, including self-perceptions and perspectives, and of overall cultural and political appraisal and orientation.[51]

Welcoming the Stranger, the Alien, the Oppressed. A complementary movement and strategy to the one just discussed consists in the deliberate action of openly inviting and receiving people who are marginated, refugees, or otherwise victimized or oppressed, in the midst of the faith community. Two interrelated conditions, however, must be met. For one thing, such a community must move beyond the gestures of charity and assistance in attending to the physical, emotional, and spiritual needs of those persons being welcomed (although such service orientation is obviously essential too); they must confront the justice and political dimensions and issues involved, such as the questions of status of "illegal aliens," jobs and welfare system, education, health care, housing, etc. For another thing, the welcoming community will be expected to allow itself to be reshaped and even converted by the presence and participation of those "strangers"/neighbors.[52] The very life of a congregation and its practices of ministry, patterns of worship and mission may be fundamentally challenged and refashioned.

---

51. The Plowshares Institute, located in Connecticut, has made a significant contribution in terms of sponsoring seminars, workshops, and pertinent research in this area of creative dislocation for the sake of transformative and liberative learning. Another example is the Program for Conscientization for North Americans, established in Santafé de Bogotá, Colombia, and ecumenical in nature. Their month-long workshops are also designed to provide radically new experiences, alternative vantage points, and opportunities for social analysis, and for seeking ways, together with Latin American people, "to become instruments of God for justice and peace making . . . " (from the statement of objectives). The effect of analogous educational experiences made possible by the organization Witness for Peace by exposing middle-class North Americans to the realities of the Central American situation, including the impact of United States policies of domination and war, is also well documented. Interestingly enough, the content of the resulting conscientization process in all these cases often includes not only new insights, attitudes, and choices regarding other people's oppression and its causes, but new realization on one's own alienation and oppression.

52. Such a reshaping and conversion are actually documented, for example, in the case of many faith communities in Canada and the United States which welcomed significant numbers of people coming to North America as refugees from Asia and Latin America particularly.

In other words, the friendly space of Christian hospitality may thus become a privileged context for transformation, both within the contours of the caring faith community as well as in the public arena with a pertinent witness to the commonwealth of freedom, justice, and peace, and well-being for all.[53]

There are also a number of pedagogical strategies and methods which combine or alternate the "going" and the "welcoming" dimensions of context dislocations. One of these consists in deliberate and focused encounters between middle- and low-income groups. Those encounters require careful preparation to facilitate a situation of trust and respect. Further, the encounters are structured in ways that include sharing and hearing stories, actual entering into the reality of poor and oppressed people (e.g., by visiting homes, moving to a certain neighborhood) and sharing activities and experiences such as meals, fellowship, worship, entertaining, and others, and working on a common project. Process and evaluation of the encounters, and further commitment to peace and justice, are also essential.[54]

Education for Peace and Justice

Seen and carried out in a liberation key, Christian religious education points to peace and justice not only as a major, indispensable goal but also as a matter of substantive content and teaching-learning process as well. Indeed, the whole of the church curriculum will thus be fashioned and will unfold in light of faith as participation in God's reign.[55] More specifically, most of doing liberation-oriented Christian education consists of the opportune and pertinent practices and tasks of the "curriculum of service" (*diakonia*), including, in Maria Harris' terms, such forms as social care, social ritual, social empowerment, and social legislation.[56] Further, a number of specific approaches and methodologies have been recently developed for the sake of discipling for justice and peace.[57] Two illustrations follow,

---

53. See Nelle G. Slater, ed. *Tension Between Citizenship and Discipleship: A Case Study* (New York: Pilgrim Press, 1989) for the study and multilayered analysis of "The Church of the Covenant" and its experience of becoming a sanctuary church. The theme of the relationship and tension between the church's mission and its educational ministry, as well as the educational dimensions and significance of a number of settings and process in the ecclesial ecology, are nicely illuminated in this book.

54. On this subject of encounters between groups, see Gerald W. Schlabach, *And Who is My Neighbor?—Poverty, Privilege, and the Gospel of Christ* (Scottdale, Pa.: Herald, 1990), 197-206.

55. For a discussion of justice and peace as constitutive in religious education, see Groome, *Sharing Faith*, 397-406.

56. Maria Harris, *Fashion Me a People: Curriculum in the Church* (Louisville: WJKP, 1989), chap. 8.

57. One of the best examples of creative appropriation and development of approaches and methodologies in education for peace and justice in a North American context, is the book by Schlabach, *And Who is My Neighbor?*

The **"Spirals of Praxis**." This model combines pastoral and educational ministry and has been explicitly connected with the Latin American liberationist contributions of Paulo Freire and the pastoral theologians engaged in biblical hermeneutics.[58] Four interconnected movements are identified in terms of mediations of experience, simply stated as follows: 1) insertion, that is the actual, live commitment and engagement within contexts of injustice and oppression; 2) social analysis, consisting in placing that experience of engagement into a wider framework of understanding; 3) theological reflection, by focusing on the questions of significance and implications regarding faith and praxis; and 4) pastoral planning oriented toward long-term change. We call this a "spiral" of praxis—that is, the action-reflection dialectic—because the process keeps breaking new ground in the manner of an ongoing seeing-judging-acting dynamic.[59]

Awareness, Concern, and Action. This approach, designed especially for education for peace and justice, explicitly assumes that lifestyle, methodology and content cannot be separated.[60] Its overall goal is expressed in a way that reveals the methodological components—awareness-concern-action. a) Awareness (cognitive goals) includes the dimensions of self (people's giftedness, self-worth, etc.), peace and justice issues, manipulation and propaganda, sources of injustice, church teaching, and how change take place. b) Concern (affective goals) includes nurturing a sense and disposition of solidarity that effectively embraces awareness and action. As a form of education of the heart, several dimensions of an ongoing conversion process are included, such as experiencing a spiritual vocation, being "touched" by the victims of injustice as well as the advocates for justice, and being supported by a caring, discipling faith community. c) Action (behavioral goals) refers to actions of direct service— "works of mercy"—as well as social and structural change—"works of justice;" also, actions focusing on both the local and the global dimensions of the same issue (e.g., issues of violence and conflict resolution). The design also indicates specific guidelines to carry out, to facilitate and to evaluate the actual process of faith education for peace and justice.

---

58. The clearest version of this model is articulated by Joe Holland and Peter Henriot as the "pastoral circle," in *Social Analysis-Linking Faith and Justice* (Maryknoll, N.Y.: Orbis, 1983), chap. 1. In our brief discussion in this section, we utilize their conceptualization.

59. The Lumko Institute of South Africa designed an adaptation of this model which, interestingly enough, was then reappropriated by the United Church of Christ-Board of World Ministries, and disseminated with the publication by Robin Petersen and Lou Ann Parsons, "See-Judge-Act: Pastoral Planning for a Prophetic Church," (1991).

60. See James McGinnis, "Toward Compassionate and Courageous Action: A Methodology for Educating for Peace and Justice" (St. Louis: Institute for Peace and Justice, 1987). We will summarize the main section of this booklet.

Liberating Bible Study

A final point on doing religious education in a liberation key concerns the twofold affirmation that the Bible is the book for the people of God to be read in context and that the hermeneutical circulation process is pivotal in both education and theology. Therefore, two brief and interconnected considerations are now in order regarding location and process for liberating Bible study.[61]

Location: Unexpected News. One of the specific emphases coming from Latin American grassroots ecclesial communities is that the Bible can function primarily as a mirror in which the faithful will see their own reality reflected and also expect to learn about themselves in the process. However, there is the requirement of a prayerful approach and spirit coupled with profound humility, in the framework of a worshipful hermeneutic community, committed to the ethics and politics of God, as already indicated. The claim is, then, that in such a context it will be possible, by the Spirit's grace, to begin to see and hear God's Word afresh, with new eyes and ears. A deliberate and disciplined change of vantage point and perspective can take place (for instance by explicitly seeking to be informed and challenged by Third World Christians or oppressed groups at home) which is potentially transformative, especially in terms of an action-reflection circulation process engaging the scriptures.[62]

In Dialogue with the Word: A Multiway Conversation. Together with the specific guidelines mentioned above, we must briefly consider the grassroots hermeneutics of the Bible circles in Latin America[63] as suggesting further principles for liberation discipling . In short, such hermeneutics consist of a community of people who, while reading the Bible, inject concrete reality and their own existential situation into the process. The three main dimensions of that liberationist scripture study are, then: the Bible itself, the Christian faith community, and the reality of the surrounding world. A multiway conversation thus becomes possible in which each of the three dimensions or factors—the text, the "pre-test" of the real life situation, and the context of the ecclesial community—is deemed indispensable for authentically hearing and responding to God's Word today. Furthermore, it does not matter whether the group starts with the reality of the "pre-text," with the

---

61. For these and related topics, see Norman K. Gottwald and Richard Horsley, eds., *The Bible and Liberation: Political and Social Hermeneutics*, rev. ed. (Maryknoll, N.Y.: Orbis, 1991).

62. An example of and resource for liberating Bible study explicitly involving alternative locations and perspectives, is Robert McAfee Brown, *Unexpected News: Reading the Bible With Third World Eyes* (Philadelphia: Westminster, 1984). And for a helpful discussion of "liberating exegesis" as foundational for Christian religious education, see *Liberating Exegesis: The Challenge of Liberation Theology to Biblical Studies* (Louisville: WJKP, 1989).

63. The main source here is Mesters, "The Use of the Bible," and *Defenseless Flower*.

Bible, or with the church community they represent. What is crucial in biblical interpretation as liberative educational process is to include all three dimensions while the participants are assisted (and mutually help one another) to make their own discoveries and to integrate their learnings. In this light, the reading and interpretation of scripture makes no real progress, and even becomes distorted, whenever one of those factors is missing. The dynamic interplay and integration of Bible, real-life situation, and ecclesial community facilitates a process of transformative learning which always includes the praxis component as ongoing dialogue with the creative and liberating Word of God.

CONCLUSION

Our discussion throughout this chapter suggests that liberation theology can provide an essential background and frame of reference for viewing as well as doing Christian religious education. We do not assume, however, that liberation theology by itself can serve as the sufficient theological foundation of both theory and practice.[64] Nevertheless, we do claim that this theological movement provides a necessary and, indeed, indispensable contribution for the educational ministry of the church in North America and elsewhere in a rapidly changing world.[65] The challenge for the Christian community to embrace a consistent commitment to holistic liberation—that is, freedom with justice and peace—and social and personal transformation, certainly points in that direction as we approach the third millennium.

---

64. The richness demonstrated by the plurality of theological views and approaches, and the potential complementarity among them—including mutual correction and enhancement—is, of course, nicely illustrated in this book. We would argue that further research and dialogue focused on such potential complementarity, is still a challenge before us.

65. Two general considerations are pertinent here. For one thing, on the global scene, the so-called "new world order" does not appear to foster real justice, humanization, and well-being but rather to exacerbate conditions of poverty and oppression; thus, diverse forms of liberation theology will keep being necessary in the face of massive human suffering. For another thing, and more specifically in the North American context, we witness a paradigm shift in historical consciousness toward , among other things, a post-Christian, relatively un-churched, and post-Constantinian (i.e., where the state no longer supports Christian faith and the church) culture; it is our claim that, in the midst of this historical situation, the church must reclaim its identity and place as a faithful, prophetic minority for the sake of God's ethics and politics in the manner advocated by liberation theology.

CHAPTER TWELVE

Black Theology and Religious Education

GRANT S. SHOCKLEY

INTRODUCTION

The objectives of this chapter on black theology and religious education are two: (1) to explore the background and current situation in black theology and (2) to discuss the impact and implications of black theology for the theory and practice of religious education primarily in black churches. The background and content section will discuss: the origins of black theology; reactions to black theology; definition and sources of black theology; black theologies and theologians; and an assessment of black theology. The impact and implication section will discuss: A new black church paradigm; challenge and assumptions; the search for models toward a new paradigm and an ethnocultural black church education-for-liberation paradigm.

Part One

ORIGINS OF BLACK THEOLOGY

Black theology has been aptly referred to as the most fruitful and exciting theological development in North America. It had its inception with the publication of the Black Power Statement by the National Committee of Negro Churchmen in 1966. This statement had come as the result of a decision of a group of black clergy to endorse the then-emerging Black Power movement. The argument of the statement was a deep concern that the "important human realities" in the controversy about black power not be ignored because of . . . militant rhetoric and strident language. "The fundamental distortion facing us on the controversy of black power," they said, "is rooted in a gross imbalance of power and conscience between Negro and White Americans."[1] Further, these clergy made it clear that they would no longer abide by the assumption

> that white people are justified in getting what they want through the use of power, but that Negro Americans must, either by nature or by circumstances, make their appeal only through conscience. As a result . . . the power of white men is corrupted because it meets little resistance. . . . The conscience of black men is corrupted because, having no power to implement the demands of conscience, the concern for justice is transmuted into a distorted form of love, which in the absence of justice, becomes chaotic self-surrender. Powerlessness creates a race of beggars. We are faced now with a situation where conscience-less power meets powerless conscience, threatening the very foundations of our nation.[2]

Much of the tumult surrounding black theology centered around this early association with Black Power and the continued insistence "that black people must have the capacity to participate with power, i.e., organized political and economic strength to really influence people with whom . . . [they] . . . interact."

A second major goal of the black theology movement was the eradication of racism in the general society as well as in white church structures. Defined by the Uppsala Assembly of the World Council of Churches in 1968 as "ethnocentric pride" . . . with the "thrust to discriminate against and exclude,"[3] this social cancer has wrought havoc with the lives and hopes of the rejected and powerless for centuries.

Under the guise of "Manifest Destiny" it has condoned and allowed white settlers in America to confiscate from the Indians most of the land which now comprises the United States.[4] Racism contributed to the corruption of the social, economic, and political structure of the nation (North and South) through the system of chattel slave labor, "the vilest that ever saw the sun."[5]

---

1. "Black Power: Statement by National Committee of Negro Churchmen," *New York Times,* 31 July 1966, E5.

2. Ibid.

3. "The Uppsala 68 Report," World Council of Churches, Geneva, Switzerland, 1968, 241.

4. Dee Brown, *Bury My Heart at Wounded Knee* (New York: Holt, Rinehart and Winston, 1971), chap. 1-2.

5. *The Works of John Wesley,* vol. 13 (Grand Rapids, Mich.: Zondervan, n.d.), 153.

Spanish American lands were taken in illegal wars of "territorial expansion," and Asian Americans, whose poorly paid labor developed much of the west and its farmlands, were "rewarded" with racist-inspired exclusion acts and relocation (detention camps) center.[6]

The classic and most dramatic example of racism in America was its black population who, since the early seventeenth century, had endured in both the churches and the general society every conceivable form of abuse. They were considered only three-fifths human in the Constitution of "the most enlightened democracy on earth." In 1854 the Supreme Court maintained that black people "had no rights that whites were bound to respect." In 1896 the Supreme Court legalized the segregation of its "free" citizens on the basis of skin color. The United Nations was not three years old (1947) when it received from the black constituency of the United States, a charter member, a document entitled "A Statement on the Denial of Human Rights to Minorities in the Case of Citizens of Negro Descent in the United States of America and an Appeal for Redress." It was 1954 before the Supreme Court recognized that the 1896 decision was a travesty upon justice and that separate in an open society is by definition "unequal." In 1964 and 1965 Congress legislated its first comprehensive civil rights bills in a century, including the right of franchise for millions of disfranchised black people in the South.

The years 1964-66 were years of disenchantment. The Civil Rights movement crested with Martin Luther King's eloquent "I Have a Dream" address (Washington, D.C., 1963). In 1964-65 deep frustration developed as unenforceable laws were substituted for justice and tokenism in employment for comprehensive fair-employment practices.

Succinctly, by the late 1960s, the extremity of most black patience, with gradualism, legalism, tinkering reform, and conciliation was reached. Then it came—the black revolution for power—Black Power! This movement galvanized the white (and some sectors of the black) community. It was a totally new, "audacious" way for black people to act. It meant a new assessment of power—not only to achieve equality of opportunity but to achieve equality of advantage and results. With this new concept of power other insights were born. Black power came to signify a new understanding of one's blackness, worth, dignity, and heritage. It meant affirmation rather than negation, activity rather than passivity, self-pride instead of self-hate. In this new light, black survival meant black control. Educational, economic, social, political, and religious institutions must become imbued with black self-determination.

------

6. Milton L. Barron, ed., *Minorities in a Changing World* (New York: Knopf, 1967), chaps. 3,4; George E. Simpson and J. Milton Yinger, *Racial and Cultural Minorities* (New York: Harper and Bros., 1953), chaps. 11-15; Philip Hayasaka, "The Asian Experience in White America," *Journal of Intergroup Relations* 2 (Spring 1973), 67-73.

REACTIONS TO BLACK THEOLOGY

Generally, what had been the witness of the churches in the long struggle for black civil rights and liberation from white racism? At best it had been paternalistic. But in terms of the mandate of the gospel it had been (and still is) reluctant. It had acquiesced in segregation, failed to identify, define, or articulate critically or challenge effectively a single aspect of the problem of racism faced by almost 15 percent of its national population, 80 percent of whom were fellow Christians.

While the churches did produce, periodically, sincere dissenting voices who exerted a positive though not a crucial influence, it is only honest to say that this was the limit of their participation. Further, as the black revolution escalated in the direction of challenging the root systems of power that enabled racism and called to accountability the centers of power that supported it, most, though not all, of the white "liberal" voices receded into the background. At this point, two things became clear. The black struggle for justice and liberation must become independent. There could be no sure reliance on white "reformers." The struggle would have to seek a base of support within the black community and most likely in the black churches. Second, the black churches themselves would have to be committed to the black masses and their liberation. A new generation of black youth began to question the credentials of an institution that could not or would not act courageously on issues it claimed were aborting its mission, violating its fellowship, and mocking its witness. It was this situation in the general society and in the church which gave birth to a liberation movement of its own, one that would combine the yet remaining faith of black people in the black church and their new determination to obtain corrective justice.

DEFINITION AND SOURCES OF BLACK THEOLOGY

Black theology became the name of the movement that "religiocified" Black Power. It was a unique and indigenous development on the American theological scene. More than a "blackenized" version of Euro-American theology, it was a new way of "doing" theology. Its mission was to raise new questions, develop novel concepts, and pattern new motifs about the basic nature of the Christian faith in relation to the black experience, forcing a reconsideration "if not a redefinition of every major theological category." James Cone states the matter very clearly in an early definition:

What is Black Theology? Black Theology is that theology which arises out of the need to articulate the significance of Black presence in a hostile white world. It is Black people reflecting religiously on the Black experience, attempting to redefine the relevance of the Christian Gospel for their lives.[7]

Originating in the midst of the black struggle for liberation, black theology, not only developed a unique objective and definition but a novel set of sources as well. These are identifiable as the following: (1) the Civil Rights movement; (2) Joseph Washington's *Black Religion* (1964); (3) the Black Revolution (1966) and (4) the dialogue among theologians outside the United States.

The Civil Rights struggle for equality was a primary source for developing a black theology. Its data began with fierce resistance to enslavement, slave rebellions, Underground Railroad escapes, and Civil War participation. In this century every known form of protest including litigation at every judicial level was explored. Since 1950 there have been additional strategic expressions in the liberation struggle. The first of these was the Freedom Movement (1955-1965). This brought the politicization of the black masses and the rise of a strong black leadership class personified in the brilliant leadership of Martin Luther King Jr. (1929-1968).

The publication of *Black Religion*[8] by Joseph Washington (1964) ushered in another critical period in the black struggle for liberation. Often referred to as "one of the most important works in the history of black theology" it was a pivotal source for later black religion and theology protest writers such as Vincent Harding, Charles Long, and especially James Cone. A brief summary of the contents of Washington's *Black Religion* illustrates its importance as a point of departure for Cone, Long, and others. Washington makes several assertions: (1) Black people are not a part of the "mainstream" Christian tradition in theology; (2) nor do they have "authentic" roots in the historical Christian tradition; (3) they seem to lack an ecumenical vision; and (4) for all practical purposes they do not exclude non-blacks but neither do they seem to intentionally include them. Agreement or disagreement with Washington's allegations aside, his work made a necessary critique of the nascent black theology movement. It did this by raising fundamental questions about the nature, purpose, and forms of black religion. These questions initiated a dialogue which preoccupied black theology for at least two decades.

Not long after Washington's *Black Religion* created its sensational stir, the Black Revolution enveloped the black community. Much of the 1966-1976 decade witnessed the escalation of essentially nonviolent but confrontational strategies in the achievement of black liberation goals. A new and fiercely independent black leadership cadre spoke of "black identity," "black self-deter-

---

7. James H. Cone, "Black Consciousness and the Black Church: A Historical-Theological Interpretation," *Annals of the American Academy of Political and Social Science* 387 (January 1970), 33.

8. Joseph R. Washington, *Black Religion* (Boston: Beacon Press, 1964).

mination," and "black power." Interracial dialogues were often replaced by painful periods of "strategic disengagement" with whites. Black church "caucuses" were initiated. Black heritage reclamation and black cultural indigenization became normative. Politicization had become radicalization. Needless to say this traumatic period provided the definitive input for the then emerging black theology paradigm.[9]

A fourth source that influenced the development of black theology was the many dialogues with theologians outside the United States. Teaching exchanges, conferences, and publications between African European, Asian, Latin American, and North American theologians and black theologians (since about 1976) served to broaden and deepen the study of black theology.[10]

The fifth and most recent source of influence in the development of black theology has been the growing conversation with black women. The recent publication of Jacqueline Grant's influential essay, "White Woman's Christ and Black Woman's Jesus: Feminine Christology and Womanist Response," has done much to visiblize and critique black male predominance in the theological arena. More than that, however, it has called into question several assumptions about women in liberation theology and especially black theology.

BLACK THEOLOGIES AND THEOLOGIANS

The Civil Rights Movement, anti-civil rights intransigence, sexism, and white church reluctance to move beyond rhetoric and the safe confines of pious liberal pronouncements to basic reform, forced black people to reconsider, redefine, and reconstruct their worldview and religious faith. The result of this new mood in the secular sphere was the cry for Black Power. In the religious domain it was black theology.

James Cone, in his pivotal volume *Black Theology and Black Power*, outlined the direction of this new departure in American theological thought, the first ever to challenge its dominance from a social perspective. He made several definitive assertions: (1) theology can be done independently of any previous paradigm, and it can be done from a black perspective; (2) black theology is and ought to be a theology of and for the oppressed; (3) black theology originated in the struggle of the black church on behalf of the black masses; (4) black theology is a valid explication of the role that God has always played in the history of his people.

Cone's "theology of black power" for black liberation became the major

---

9. See *Black Theology: A Critical Assessment*, comp. James H. Evans Jr. (New York: Greenwood Press, 1987) for an excellent coverage of the literature of black theology.

10. See James H. Cone and Gayraud S. Wilmore, eds, *Black Theology: A Documentary History, 1966-1979*, vol. 1 (Maryknoll, N.Y.: Orbis, 1993), especially Part VI, 349-454.

voice in the black theology movement. There were and are other positions, however. Albert Cleage in his *Black Messiah* (1968) provided a thoroughly black nationalist interpretation of both black religion and the black church. J. Deotis Roberts in his *Liberation and Reconciliation: A Black Theology* (1971), while not denying the importance of liberation, insists that it must be preceded by reconciliation. Major Jones, theologizing from a "theology of hope" position in his *Black Awareness: A Theology of Hope* (1971), believed that black theology is valid as it moves the black church toward the new community beyond racism of any kind. Charles Long in key articles (1971 and 1975) questions the very legitimacy of black theology if based on Western rather than African theological thought. Gayraud Wilmore, basically agreeing with Long but still adhering to James Cone's black theology tradition, contends in his *Black Religion and Black Radicalism* (1972) that black radicalism can best be validated in a black theology based on black religion rather than on a "black version of white theology based on Black Power." Cecil Cone, the brother of James Cone, adds a significant statement to the black theology discussion with his position that black theology grows out of African Christian, black religious and black church roots.[13] Yet another voice is heard on the black theology issue. William Jones in *Is God a White Racist?* (1973) introduces the problem of suffering into the black theology discussion. He holds the position, from a black humanistic perspective, that black theology is an anomaly since it cannot be empirically demonstrated that God either exists or has ever really delivered black people from oppression.

AN ASSESSMENT OF BLACK THEOLOGY

The prior brief look at the background, growth, and development of black theology leads naturally to an assessment of its value, worth, and relevance to the black church and to religious education. It has done several things. *First*, it has challenged the black church to engage itself effectively in the liberation of oppressed black people. This challenge has historic significance. It marks for the first time in the history of church life in America that a radical minority group or movement has aggressively challenged the theological assumptions of the Christian faith on the basis of its own ethic of inclusiveness and justice. Also it is the first time that a color-minority has articulated such a protest in the form of a radically alternative system and church style, i.e., black theology and a public program of social liberation.

11. See Ibid., Part V, 279-348. For the best available coverage of black theology and women's issues.

12. James H. Cone, *Black Theology and Black Power* (New York: Seabury, 1969). Also see Cone's *A Black Theology of Liberation* (Philadelphia: Westminster, 1970).

13. See Cecil W. Cone, *Identity Crisis in Black Theology* (Nashville: African Methodist Espiscopal Church, 1975).

Second, black theology has caused the black church to see religious education from a entirely new perspective. Black theology suggests that there is now "a felt need to reconstruct a worldview as it concerns an entire people."[14] That worldview illuminates a new future that black people can have. It is a future in which they believe and know that they can be free if they want that freedom enough to suffer, sacrifice, and perhaps even die for it.

Third, black theology teaches black people that they must develop and initiate a black agenda. Liberation begins with "me" and with "us." It is not something that can be done for us. In solidarity with others in similar situations of oppression—women, Asians, Latinos, Native Americans—"consciousness" must be raised, identity must be self-affirmed and liberation—our liberation—must be claimed.

Fourth, black theology has confronted black people with the realization that religious education in our context must include transformation as well as information. Religious education fulfills a highly normative function when it seeks to guide the teaching learning process to the end that justice and a new humanity may emerge.

Finally, black theology has been instructive at the point of letting us know that any religious education program that might be constructed must grow out of and center around the experiences, relationships, and situational dilemmas that black people face in their day-to-day struggle to survive, develop, and progress in an often hostile, uncaring, majority-dominated society. A corollary to this is a continuous and faithful search for practices, methods, and techniques that embody, complement, and reinforce this principle.

Part Two

NEW BLACK CHURCH PARADIGM

The black church that emerged from the black revolution of the late 1960s was a surprisingly timely response to the pre-black revolution traditional black church. It was not only a response to the triumphant cry for identity, equality, and self-determination, it was a viable alternative to white Christianity and white American theology constructs which historically had held that black religion, generally, was "defective." Additionally, it was a response to either the unwillingness or the inability of white North American

---

14. Leon E. Wright, "Black Theology or Black Experience?" *Journal of Religious Thought* (Summer 1969), 46.

Christianity to offer more than rhetoric to the challenge of inclusiveness, white ethnocentrism, and racism.

What was the outline of the new Black Church Paradigm claiming a holistic approach to a ministry with the oppressed? Gayraud Wilmore identified four axioms of an autonomous, free-standing system. He emphasized:

1. The renewal and enhancement of the black church in terms of its liturgical life, its theological interpretation [and], its understanding of its mission. . . .
2. The development of the black church, not only as a religious fellowship, but as a community organization . . . which uses its resources . . . the black community.
3. The projection of a new quality of church life which would equip and strengthen the church as custodian and interpreter of that cultural heritage which is rooted and in the peculiar experience of black people . . . and the faith that has sustained them.
4. The contribution of the black church, out of its experience of suffering and the yearning for freedom, of that quality of faith, hope, and love which can activate, empower, renew, and unite the whole church of Christ.[15]

This "paradigm shift, embodying a new set of conceptual, methodological, and theoretical assumptions,"[16] significantly reoriented the black church and gave it a widely acclaimed self-authenticating mandate to "do" ministry contextually, i.e., in distinctive and unique ways. This "praxis" move by an appreciable number of black churches was not precipitous. It was made with the full realization that it would alienate many nonradicalized black clergy and lay persons as well as many so-called liberal whites in biracial denominations. It was made because a majority of forward-thinking black church leaders knew, in Gayraud Wilmore's words, that "it may be the last opportunity for the church to break out of its symbolic commitment to the illusionary goal of one-way integration and permeate the black community with a positive concept of power and sense of transcendent vocation that will serve the purposes of justice and freedom."[17]

---

15. Gayraud S. Wilmore, "The Case for a New Black Church Style," in *The Black Experience and Religion*, ed. C. Eric Lincoln (Garden City, N.Y.: Doubleday, 1974), 33-44.

16. Ian G. Barbour, *Myths, Models and Paradigms: A Study in Science and Religion* (New York: Harper & Row, 1974), 8.

17. K.B. Cully and F. Niles Harper, *Will the Church Lose the City?* (New York: World, 1969).

Part Two

A BLACK CHURCH EDUCATION LIBERATION DESIGN

Against the background presented in the paragraphs above we are now ready to discuss some necessary components of a religious education design that would implement a black liberation theology. Additionally we will share a search for models amidst several theorists working in the field of social justice concerns. But first the challenge and assumptions.

CHALLENGE AND ASSUMPTIONS

The overall challenge of the New Black Church to religious education is to assist it in reconstructing its entire church-community ministry and relationship to reflect the reuniting of the "spiritual-evangelical" and the "social-liberation" intent of the gospel. Several assumptions undergirding this overall task should be highlighted.

Assumption I: Education for change: The New Black Church challenges religious education to teach its members to live and minister as Christians in and through a church that is open to changing demands, sensitive to emerging issues, and resilient to shock and reversals. It must be proactive in relation to change, shaping it for responsible engagement with "open" and "possible" futures.

Assumption II: Prophetic education: The New Black Church challenges religious education to be prophetic, to continually be aware of the responsibility of the black church to resist being used to exploit or to be merely conservators of the "status quo." The black church is always obligated to challenge "faddish" values and "conventional" wisdom and in the spirit of Jürgen Moltmann, to confront the present as one who shall bring to pass what God has promised in the future.

Assumption III: Education for liberation: Following the thought of Paulo Freire, it is being assumed that neutrality in education is a fiction. All education ultimately is for either domination or liberation, it cannot be for both. The challenge of the New Black Church to religious education at this point is unmistakably clear. Spirituality and personal salvation not withstanding, a major and controlling responsibility of the black church has been, is, and will continue to be the humanization of the dehumanized and the liberation of the oppressed.

Assumption IV: Education for mission: C.D. Coleman states the "mission assumption" for black theology's challenge to religious education. The New Black Church should be mission-oriented rather than "institution" oriented. Further, he admonishes the black church to "cease being pre-occupied with its institutional status and image and seize the opportunity to formulate an agenda which will bring the black community to its divine destiny of redeeming and remaking a spiritually denuded society."[18]

Assumption V: The genius of the black church is its historic and current capacity for relevance and resiliency. Whatever the need and/or circumstance of the black community might be—survival, protest, consciousness-raising, reform, or revolution—the black church and its resources has been (and will be) an ever-present foundation.

THE SEARCH FOR MODELS

The search for models that embody the radical visioning, commitment, awareness, reflection, and intentionality that are necessary for the development of a black theology-inspired educational approach was difficult. The result is a composite of concepts, constructs, experimental programs, and theories which have addressed education for liberation in culturally diverse communities by black and white educationists and religious educators.

It is now our task to interrelate these various fragments into an ethnocultural black church education-for-liberation-paradigm for predominantly, but not exclusively, black congregations.

UNDERLYING ASSUMPTION

Undergirding the design that is being presented is the assumption that a crucial and definitive aspect of the nature and purpose of the church is to be revolutionizing as well as a reconciling presence in the personal, social, and world-life of the church. The new situation in the church and in society requires a critical theological and educational analysis such as black theology has suggested. Again, congregations must be radicalized over the issues of racism and national, economic, and social development. Robert McAfee Brown suggests that "we are called upon to develop a theology of the world, more than theology of the church; or if it is to be a theology for the church, it must be a theology for the church-that-exists-not-for-itself-but-for-the-sake-of-the-world."[19]

---

18. Ceasar D. Coleman, "Agenda for the Black Church," *Religious Education* 64 (November-December 1969), 441-446.

19. Robert McAfee Brown, "Doing Theology Today: Some Footnotes on Theological Method," *Action-Reaction* (Summer 1969), 3; ibid., p. 4.

TRANSFORMATIVE EDUCATION

A complementary educational philosophy for black theology could well be Paulo Freire's "transformational learning." Resting firmly on a humanist belief that education should be an instrument of liberation for the oppressed and the oppressor, Freire insists that both the oppressed and the oppressor "name" their world. This is basic for authentic humanity. With this new power to name their world they may also discern previously unrealized options and voluntarily pursue courses of action to obtain and maintain their freedom. The method by which this can be accomplished involves four steps: (1) an acute sense of awareness of one's oppression and oppressors; (2) a realistic analysis of the extent and impact of the "limit situations" imposed and the "limit acts" required for liberation; (3) an articulation of the critical action or praxis that must follow analysis if education is to be more than intellectual emptiness; (4) verification or ascertaining that the "new" person born in this process is "no longer oppressor or oppressed, but . . . in the process of achieving freedom."[20]

HOLISTIC CHURCH EDUCATION

Black church education for liberation suggests the need for a holistic approach, i.e., an approach concerned with the entire system in question. Dieter Hessel's holistic or integrated model for implementing the liberation education program is well-suited to do this. Applied to black churches interested in a liberation model of education it would have several implications.

First, it would be in basic agreement with Susan Thistlethwaite that justice (in this case liberation) must become an identity for the churches desiring such a ministry and not just a panel of issues.[21] Second, as Hessel suggests, each ministry of the church, e.g., preaching, teaching, worship, etc., should have some "liberation education" character. Third, in implementing Hessel's approach the lectionary for the Christian year would be used (see Hessel's *Social Themes of the Church Year*). This ecumenical commentary on the lectionary of the Christian year explores potential uses and meanings for teaching about social justice issues on an annual basis.

There are five foundations for Hessel's holistic approach: (1) critical reflection on ministry including linkage "between worship, teaching, and public engagement"; (2) scriptural grounding "in the biblical story of the social God" who "creates us with promise, commissions us by grace, and sends us into mission"; (3) an insistence that no distinction be made between

---

20. Paulo Freire, *Pedagogy of the Oppressed* (New York: Herder and Herder, 1970), 33-34.

21. Susan Thistlewaite, "Peace and Justice, Not Issues but Identities for the Church," *Engage/Social Action* (January 1987), 33.

the personal and social aspects for the Christian faith; (4) faithfulness to the gospel involving "public engagement simultaneously with personal integration"; (5) participation in the life of the "church redemptive" as the singular authentic center of "God's transforming activity."[22]

TEACHING AND LEARNING FOR DISCIPLESHIP

Sara Little's "discipleship" model offers interesting insights for black liberation theology and the teaching-learning process. It does so, however, by raising a difficult question. She asks, "How does one include actual acts of effecting social justice as teaching." She goes on to question whether just "doing" is "doing the truth" to use a phrase of Thomas Groome. Little believes that "simulating," "planning," and "contriving" experiences is not too meaningful. She is convinced that it is important to work with persons and situations "to help . . . [them] relate the gospel to their situation, learning with them and working to move toward 'responsible freedom.'" Her process for achieving this is a four-phase one: Awareness; Analysis; Action; Reflection:

Awareness: A learning process phase designed to increase levels of awareness and understanding in reference to "God's intention and purpose for human life" and "the Christian's responsibility to be involved. . . ."

Analysis: A learning process phase in which information and facts are gathered, explored, and perceived in relation to goals, resources, alternatives, urgency, and the integrity of the gospel.

Action: A learning process phase in which participative individual personal and/or corporate action "consistent with the Christian ethic" and directed toward the establishment of social justice (liberation) is enacted.

Reflection: A learning process phase in which planned-for theological reflection on the praxis experience is held "to test the ethical assumption of our perception of God's will on which the action was based."[23]

RELATIONAL TEACHING FOR PEACE AND JUSTICE

Working from within a somewhat different educational construct, James McGinnis projects a "relational" model, i.e., one that "moves from awareness to concern to action" in a program "to educate for peace and justice." Premised on the belief that peace (and other social justice concerns) is not simply a con-

---

22. Dieter T. Hessel, *Social Ministry* (Philadelphia: Westminster, 1982), 198.
23. Sara Little, *To Set One's Heart: Belief and Teaching in the Church* (Atlanta: John Knox Press, 1983), 76-79.

cept to be taught, but a reality to be lived, awareness, concern, and action are deployed as the basis for conscientious decision making in the following ways:

> *Awareness* of social justice issues and the disposition to work for change would be encouraged by "promoting a sense of self-esteem" and a feeling that our "gifts" should be shared with others for the good of all.

> *Concern* about social issues is to be nurtured into a sense of solidarity with the victims of injustices. Such link is crucial for action.

> *Action* itself should eventuate from concern. It may take the form of direct service, acting on local issues and/or action within one's "Zones of freedom."[24]

TEACHING FOR SYSTEMIC CHANGE

A final allied approach to liberation education with black theology as a base could be Suzanne Toton's Systemic Change Model.[25]

In a courageous attempt to confront and answer the question, "What would it mean to respond seriously to the turmoil and suffering of our world," Suzanne Toton is convinced that religious education must go beyond the domestic issues of church education and even beyond "consciousness raising" and "value change" learning. Her insightful thesis is "that if justice is to be central to religious education, it must play a role in effecting structural and systemic change." More explicitly, educational efforts to change individual attitudes and value systems must be realistically viewed in relation to "the nature of social structures and the web of structural relationships that make up the social order." In her food crisis research, for an example, she found that national policy and legislation on this issue "is structured primarily to meet the economic interests of our country and only secondarily to meet the needs of hungry people." Implicit in this critique is a basic issue for religious education in reference to social justice. Can structures and systems be placed beyond criticism and succumbed to as a patriotic duty? Further, can Christians do this?

Toton offers several suggestions toward engaging the problem of the systemic nature of injustice. Commencing with a distinction between religious and general or public education she asserts that the peculiar task of religious education regarding injustice is to stand with them "to create a world of jus-

---

24. James B. McGinnis, "Educating for Peace and Justice," *Religious Education* (Summer 1986), 446-465.

25. See Suzanne Toton, "Structural Change: The Next Step in Justice Education," *Religious Education* (Summer 1985).

tice, peace, and love (and) to remove whatever breeds oppression, be it personal, structural, or systemic."

TOWARD A NEW PARADIGM

This closing section of the chapter dealing with black theology and religious education will cite four black church liberation education models sympathetic to if not oriented in black theology assumptions. At the conclusion of these model-presentations a black church education-for liberation paradigm will be suggested. Including segments and insights from non-black as well as black religious educators, it will reflect an ethnocultural approach to the theory and practice of religious education in black churches. But first a critique of the models just discussed.

CRITIQUE OF WHITE CHURCHES

In black perspective, the models for social justice ministries previously discussed the need to be critiqued. Essentially, while helpful, suggestive, and even provocative, they yield less than adequate solutions to the problems faced by black churches committed to black theology: Several things may account for this:

First, social justice and especially black liberation ministries are rarely, if ever, central in mission, ministry, or program in non-black churches. This being the case they are routinely marginalized and low-prioritized. Peter Berger is perhaps correct when in referring to white Christianity he says, religion is "functional" rather than "dysfunctional" in reference to the status quo. It tends to provide the "integrating" symbols rather than the "symbols of revolution."[26]

Second, there is little hard evidence to believe that racial majority churches are ready, willing, or able to go beyond their customary "ministries of intervention" and seriously challenge the violent and persistent structures and systems that are the root causes of injustice, oppression, and racism and that causes the underclasses to suffer.

Third, the churches of the oppressors do not deal on a face-to-face or day-to-day basis with the oppressed. Their contact is impersonal and buffered. Further, their institutions, especially their churches, are usually safely distanced from the consequences of their behavior or policies.

For these and similar reasons black theology has found it almost universally necessary to create and develop support systems and strategies for liberation ministries outside of white colleague-churches.

---

26. Peter Berger, *The Precarious Vision* (New York: Doubleday, 1961), 111.

BLACK CHURCH LIBERATION EDUCATION MODELS

Since the black revolution of the late 1960s several black religious educators have advanced church/congregational models for church education. One of the earliest of these models had been projected by Yvonne Delk (United Church of Christ) in the late 1960s. The rationale for coming forth with this model was Delk's sense of the need to confront the lack of identity, self-worth and self-esteem in black children, youth, and adults. From her point of view a four-point program of religious education was needed to correct these omissions: (1) the rehearsal of the story of "who we are" through study-reflection-action modules based on African and African-American history and religious faith; (2) a recovery of the positive values of learning reflected in the African oral tradition; (3) the reexploration of the values in intergenerational learning and teaching in black churches, and (4) serious, personalized, and relevant Bible study as a grounding for religious education. Strategic themes for this biblical curriculum are: "hearing the word; "interpreting the word," "living the word" and "acting the word."[27]

SATURDAY ETHNIC SCHOOL MODEL

Concurrently with the work of Yvonne Delk was the contribution of Olivia Stokes, the first black person to be appointed to the professional staff of the National Council of Church's Division of Christian Education. Through the "Black Christian Education Project" Stokes assisted in setting the direction of religious education for a decade with the following definition of the task of religious education in the black church. Consonant with the substance of the black theology statements of the time she said in essence that the task was to join theological reflection with those processes which expose the structures which enslave, to develop techniques for freedom, and give structure to those values of the black experience for building community for God's people.[28]

Stokes was also largely responsible for initiating and implementing the Saturday Ethnic School model. The following are its objectives:

To develop a curriculum emphasizing black church history, black history, and contemporary issues.

---

27. The pioneering work of Yvonne Delk is related by Delores H. Carpenter in an article, "Interpreting the History of Religious Education in the Twentieth Century," *Religious Education* 88:4 (Fall 1993), 622-623.

28. For additional information see Olivia P. Stokes, "Black Theology: A Challenge to Religious Education," in *Religious Education and Theology*, ed. Norma H. Thompson (Birmingham, Ala.: Religious Education Press, 1982).

To develop creativity within its members enabling them to express their religious feelings through drama, music, painting, poetry, and creative writing.

To provide a forum for youth and adult expression of the need for community development, social and political solidarity, and other liberation issues.

To provide a Black Resource Center for the black community. In such a center African and African American culture and heritage would be studied and taught, greatly enhancing the self-esteem and self-development of African American students and others.

ORAL TRADITION MODEL

Based on several years of study, teaching, research, and travel in Africa, especially West Africa, Ella Mitchell[29] developed a contextual education model for religious education in the black church. For Mitchell "contextual" means the structuring, guidance, and interpretation of what goes on in the home, community, and society as a matter of course. In her words, "Both words and living examples are effective, whether formally or informally given, because they occur in the midst of a related experience." Several insights came out of Mitchell's work both here in the United States and in Africa:

1. The basic pattern of oral communication and learning are rooted in African rather than African American culture.
2. Many "so-called" illiterate cultures communicate their religious beliefs more effectively than some "so-called" literate one.
3. The oral process of learning is a legitimate system of teaching and retention. Its methodology should and could be extrapolated into African American educational experience.
4. Early African and early African American teaching and learning was "contextual," i.e., carried on in relation to ongoing life experiences.
5. Contextual/oral tradition learning data and methods included: slave cabin life; slave field conversation; mealtime table talk; the secret "church" meeting; plantation churches; storytelling, music, dancing, proverbial sayings, etc.

---

29. Ella P. Mitchell discusses her contextual mode in some detail in her article: "Oral Tradition: Legacy of Faith for the Black Church," *Religious Education* 81:1 (Winter 1986), 93-112.

AFRICAN AMERICAN MODEL

Joseph Crockett, Director of United Methodist Racial and Ethnic congregations before assuming a teaching position at Colgate/Rochester Divinity School, raised a number of questions about teaching/learning scripture among African Americans. What influences their learning? How is scripture taught? What is the role and function of cultural heritage in church education?

These questions and further issues of content and interpretation lie behind his development of an African American teaching-learning model.

Three general principles govern this effort toward multicultural curriculum design:

The inseparability but distinguishability between African American sources of religious experience.

The necessity of approaching the interpretation task with openness rather than preconcluded views.

The "weighing of scripture in relation to African Americans' personal and communal feelings, thoughts, and life tasks."

In concluding this African American approach, four functional strategies are suggested:

The *story* strategy integrating identity and vocation issues through storytelling.

The *exile* strategy focusing on heritage, tradition, and God's loving care and call to Christian community.

The *Exodus* strategy emphasizing the unique missional, justice, and social engagement responsibility of the African American Church.

The *sanctuary* strategy acknowledging the central place of the church community in African American life, especially in its worship aspect.[30]

AN ETHNOCULTURAL BLACK CHURCH
EDUCATION-FOR-LIBERATION PARADIGM

The resultant composite ethnocultural black church education-for-liberation model will be discussed under several headings: challenge; mission,

---

30. In his *Teaching Scripture from an African-American Perspective* (Nashville: Discipleship Resources, 1990). Joseph V. Crockett gives careful attention to use of the Bible in the black educational experience.

guidelines; church involvement; teaching; learning; curriculum contraction; leadership development.

Challenge: The black church must set itself to deal with several major issues in this closing decade of the century. Otherwise it may not continue to command the respect and credibility of many of its followers:

> It must respond more unequivocally to the continuing and desperate demands of the vast numbers of what William Julius Wilson calls "the truly disadvantaged," i.e., the growing underclass, the homeless, the many new types of families, victims of AIDS, the black poor and others crying for assistance.[31]

> Second, it must renew the waning enthusiasm for black pride, self-esteem, cultural integrity, and indigeneity. This must be done while not failing to pursue what Walter Brueggemann has so aptly called the "central vision of world history in the Bible, namely, that . . . of every creature in community with every other living in harmony and security toward the joy and well-being of every other creature."[32]

> Third, it must position itself to offer to black and other Christians alike a new understanding of black theology which Rosemary Ruether has called "a possible form of theology as a whole."

> Fourth, the churches and their people must disengage themselves from parochialism and racism and intentionally engage in the personal and social transforming ministries of the gospel that alone can reconcile all persons in Christ.

Mission: The black church cannot assume universally that its members understand, accept, and proactively pursue a central tenet of the church universal to be a revolutionary force not only in personal lives but society as well. Many black members as well as white may not realize with Paul Lehman that the "Christian should have known about revolution all along . . . and only the non-Christian . . . (be) surprised at revolution."[33]

Guidelines: Several guidelines are being suggested for black churches and other churches wishing to align black theology and religious education in the local church:

---

31. See William Julius Wilson, *The Truly Disadvantaged* (Chicago: University of Chicago Press, 1987).

32. See Walter Brueggemann, *Living Toward a Vision* (New York: United Church Press, 1982), 15.

33. Paul L. Lehmann, "The Shape of Theology for a World in Revolution," *Motive* (April 1965), 9.

"Black theology and religious education can find a common base in their common task, i.e., to respond to the call to social engagement by God who is fully social and radically present in the world."[34] Such a response "frontlines" social and political involvement and gives the church an "identity" as an advocate of liberation.

Church Involvement: If, as black theology cogently states, God acts in history to redeem the oppressed and that he has acted decisively in the Incarnation to demonstrate this, churches must be involved in the black struggle for liberation. As the continuing presence of Christ on earth, their ministries represent Christ and what they do represents him as well. It is reasonable, then, to expect the church through its educational program to strive to accomplish what Christ would accomplish, especially among the oppressed. This holistic ministry by the whole congregation to the whole person in his/her whole context, then, calls the church to be the "people of God."[35] Randolph Crump Miller interprets this to mean that "one finds . . . vocation at the centers of power, that the ministry of the laity is crucial in terms of the religious issues in political action, economic decisions, and social concerns."[36]

Teaching-Learning: The educational foundation for a black liberation-oriented religious education is praxis-learning, i.e., interactive reflection toward the actual transformation of an actual situation. Unless this crucial motif is in the design of the black church's ministry and intentionally pursued, the heart of Christian teaching is being denied. Paulo Freire speaks to this: "Within the word we find two dimensions, reflection and action in such radical interaction that if one is sacrificed . . . the other immediately suffers. There is no true word that is not at the same time a praxis."[37]

Curriculum Construction: There are three major objectives in constructing a curriculum and developing curriculum resources for an ethno-cultural black church education-for-liberation educational experience:

Biblical/Theological/Historical Integrity: The black religious experience is replete with Old and New Testament references and images of God's concern for justice, righteousness, and freedom. In the life and teachings of Jesus, examples of Jesus' concern for persons and human need abound, for example, his solidarity with the poor, his association with the outcast, and his identification with the "marginal" people of his

---

34. Dieter T. Hessel, *Social Ministry* (Philadelphia: Westminster, 1982), 18.

35. George E. Koehler, "Some Methodist Hopes for a New Educational Ministry," *Religious Education* (May-June 1966).

36. Randolph C. Miller, "From Where I Sit: Some Issues in Christian Education," *Religious Education* (March-April 1965), 101.

37. Freire, *Pedagogy of the Oppressed*, 75.

day. These modules are basic for curriculum construction for all ages and groups in the black church liberation thrust. Essential themes to be emphasized are: God is the Lord of history; God is concerned about and involved in history; God is the God of the oppressed; and God came to liberate all oppressed and oppressors in the historical person of Jesus Christ.

Contextual Reality: Curriculum construction must take the context (setting) of black religious experience seriously. It should teach believing that the activity of God primarily occurs in the midst of the trials and tribulations of the oppressed of every kind. James Cone explains this when he defines black theology as "that theology which arises out of the need to articulate the significance of black presence in a hostile white world." William Jones makes the same point when saying, "each Black Theology presents itself, implicitly or explicitly as a specific strategy for black liberation."[38]

Systemic Engagement: Biblical integrity and contextual reality lead to a third crucial foundation of the curriculum—systemic engagement. Essentially this means that students should learn to identify, analyze, correct, or eliminate restraining or destructive structures and/or systems that support and sustain oppression, racism, or sexism. This was Martin Luther King's concern. "King's perception of the human problem . . . led him to emphasize . . . that his struggle was directed against the forces, or structure of evil itself rather than against the person or group . . . doing the evil."[39]

Leadership Development: Discovering, enlisting, training, and supporting teachers and leaders for an ethnocultural black church education-for-liberation program presents a unique challenge. In addition to the standard qualifications expected from those who will direct an/or lead groups, e.g., visioning group goals, sensing skill limits and potential, image and self-esteem building, initiative, group participation skills, etc., liberation oriented leaders-educators will possibly need still other abilities.

Liberation-oriented education in the local congregation will require a unique enabling style of leadership, committed to the concept of the black

---

38. William R. Jones, "Toward An Interim Assessment of Black Theology," *Christian Century* 89, 3 May 1972, 513-517.

39. Herbert Richardson as quoted in *Roots of Resistance: The Non-Violent Ethic of Martin Luther King, Jr.*, by William D. Wately (Valley Forge, Pa.: Judson Press, 1985), 15.

church as a potential agency for basic social change and to the belief that persons must and can come to a realization of the need for change. Black parents, teachers, group leaders, officials, and clergy in black churches will need immersion in and exposure to a variety of learning theories and leadership styles from which to glean and construct a personally meaningful style of leadership and learning method.

CHAPTER THIRTEEN

Ecological Theology and Religious Education

RANDOLPH CRUMP MILLER

Part One

Our goal in this chapter is to derive a theological position on the basis of our experience of the ecology of the world. It starts with an examination of the evidence available from experts in ecology and relates this evidence to various theological positions, from which we can derive educational theory and practice.

Theology has a problem with nature and the environment. In earlier times, nature was included in God's activities, as the stories in Genesis indicate. Lynn White about fifty years ago exposed the long-standing indifference of theologians to ecology. Nature was considered something to be used for the convenience of human beings, not only plants and animals but the earth itself. It was thought that nature was able to withstand any abuse and that human beings, as the top of the ladder, could do anything they wanted, for the creation story said that human beings had dominance over all created beings and inanimate matter.

The model of God according to this kind of thinking is of an absolute sovereign, separated from the world and its inhabitants, but benevolent in relation to the world, especially human beings. God controls everything, either through intervention or predestination. God is in heaven and all is right—in heaven. This position enforces a dualism between God and the world, male and female, human and nonhuman, organic and inorganic, and ultimately between one race and another, between you and me.[1]

This monarchical model arose early in the Christian tradition. Instead of building a model of God in terms of the teachings in the gospels, it rejected the model of persuasive love in favor of those of a pharaoh, emperor, king, and even a dictator (Barth called God "der Führer"). This view has dominated theology throughout the past centuries. It failed to provide ways of facing the problem of evil, the powers of nature, concern for the environment, and human freedom.

Ecology has emerged only in recent years as a challenge to traditional theology. The problem facing theologians in this period of history is to develop a theology which takes into account the possibility of the destruction of nature as we know it and even of turning the earth into a lifeless planet. Human beings have the capability of doing this, and unless there is a change in theology and the development of a new ethics that deals with the cosmic environment, this destruction may occur.

ECOLOGY

Ernst Haeckel (1870) first used the word ecology to

mean the body of knowledge concerning the economy of nature—the investigation of the total relations of the animal both to its inorganic and to its organic environment; including above all, its friendly and inimical relations with those animals and plants with which it comes directly or indirectly into contact.[2]

Birch and Cobb add that "it is a study not only of what keeps species extant but what makes them extinct."[3]

As nature has been investigated and interpreted, Charles Darwin's insights have been assimilated by the present culture. In the struggle for existence, taught Darwin, there are chance variations. The natural selection of these variations made evolution and ultimately freedom possible. Also, the interrelatedness and interdependence of all organic processes help to sustain life. The richness of nature has led to enormous waste through the millions of years, with new life and new species filling the gaps.

Human societies are also helped by chance events and are wasteful. Nature's waste is recyclable, but human waste has been sheer waste and led to nonrecyclable garbage. "What was a self-sustaining system has been con-

---

1. See Sallie McFague, "Imaging a Theology of Nature," in *Liberating Life*, ed. Charles Birch, William Eakin, and Jay B. McDaniel (Maryknoll, N.Y.: Orbis, 1990), 209-210.

2. Charles Birch and John B. Cobb Jr., *The Liberation of Life* (Cambridge: Cambridge University Press, 1981), 29, quoting Haeckel.

3. Ibid.

verted into an unsustainable one.''[4] Thus we find that we are short of nonre-
newable resources, such as fossil fuels. We let pollution increase without
limit and use renewable materials so rapidly that nature cannot renew or
sustain them.

This is nothing new. As far back as the Hebrew prophets, Isaiah saw the
problem and the dangers:

> The earth lies polluted
> under its inhabitants;
> for they have transgressed laws,
> violated the statutes,
> broken the everlasting covenant.
> Therefore a curse devours the earth,
> and its inhabitants suffer for their guilt.
> Therefore the inhabitants of the earth dwindled,
> and a few people are left.
> The wine dries up,
> the vine languishes
> all the merry-hearted sigh.
> The mirth of the cymbals is stilled,
> the noise of the jubilant has ceased,
> Desolation is left in the city,
> the gates are battered into ruins,
> For thus it shall be on the earth
> and among the nations.
> (Is. 24:5-8; 12-13a, NRSV).

The earliest human beings were hunters and gatherers. Following this
came the development of small settlements and local agriculture, leading
to the cutting of nearby forests. Already sheep had been domesticated by
about 9000 BC. By 7000 BC Jericho was a flourishing town. Soon came
the domestication of pigs and cattle, the creation of pottery, and by 5000
BC the first use of irrigation in Khuziztan. Diets improved as millet, rice, pep-
pers, tomatoes, squash, gourds, and maize were grown.[5]

As deforestation continued, Plato in his *Critias* wrote:

What now remains compared with what then existed is like the skeleton of
a sick man, all the fat and soft earth having wasted away, and only the
bare framework of the land being left. There are some mountains which
have nothing but food for bees, but they had trees not very long ago. . . .

---

4. Ibid., 36.
5. See Clive Ponting, *A Green History of the World* (New York: St. Martin's Press,
1991), 53.

Moreover, it was enriched by yearly rains from Zeus, which were not lost to it, as now, by flowing from the bare land into the sea.[6]

Birch and Cobb described the sustainability of nature by looking at the cell, the organism, and the population. Relationships are essential to our understanding of these events. There are relationships between molecules in the cell. Organisms have ecological relations with the environment, other organisms, and elements which lead to increase in the population. Ecology is a means by which we understand these relationships. This process results in decreasing entropy and increasing order.[7]

Order emerges, maintains itself, and finally disappears. All life is a constant process of emerging and perishing. Among living organisms life is much less fixed than in simpler orders for

> the key idea here is the "struggle for existence" which includes among its strategies individual adaptation and spreading of risks. From these dynamic processes emerges the principle of independence of living organisms and their environment.[8]

This relation is under attack from human beings and only they can restore it.

Human beings are part of nature and the ecosystem. They have penetrated all parts of the eco-system, even the seas, and have used technology to alter the system. Most obviously, the population explosion of humanity exacerbates all the other threats and contributes to the lack of sustainability. Even without other environmental dangers, the resources of the planet may not be able to sustain the increasing millions of the the human species. Pressures are leading to shortage of food, degradation of soil, overfishing in the seas, and pollution of water, air, and forests.

Technology has brought many benefits, especially to the First World, but environmental costs have been obscured and ignored. The industrial revolution, on which our current culture is based, has threatened us with global warming, ozone depletion, deforestation, and soil erosion, leading to dangers to the health of plants and animals, including the permanent loss of many species.

The increase in human power, especially through modern science and technology, has led to widespread toxic waste, including nuclear waste, the devastation of indigenous people and their cultures, often with the help of Christian missionaries, as well as the suffering and poverty of those in inner-city ghettos. When added to this the often corrupt and totalitarian nature of government, the increase in human suffering as well as damage to the environment are colossal. But this same increase in human power and knowledge

---

6. Quoted by Ponting, ibid., 76.
7. See Birch and Cobb, *Liberation of Life*, 42.
8. Ibid., 43.

has led to the amenities of modern life, especially for the favored few, the improvement in intercultural and international relations, and the overcoming of many diseases among animals, plants, and human beings.

Economics has developed as an independent discipline. In the United States, emphasis is on the gross national product, a way of establishing human welfare in monetary terms. It is restricted to the way goods are exchanged, profit and loss, and capital costs and depletion. It ignores whatever is beyond this central focus, so that environmental costs are disregarded (except when clean-up is mandated). The depletion of reserves, such as oil, coal, and water, is omitted from the GNP. There is here the fallacy of misplaced concreteness (to use Whitehead's phrase).

Herman Daly, quoting Sismondi (1827), writes that "humanity should be on guard against all generalization of ideas that cause us to lose sight of the facts, and above all the error of identifying the public good with wealth, abstracted from the suffering of human beings who create it."[9] Thus, economics, by ignoring the ecological and cultural costs of production, fails to establish standards for the increasing welfare of the earth. The closing down of basic life systems is an economic as well as an ecological deficit and disaster.

In much current thinking, in spite of the findings of biology and other sciences, humanity is often divorced from the rest of nature. A dualism has infected our perspective, and instead of seeing humanity as part of the animal kingdom, it has been given dominance over nature. Albert Gore sees this clearly:

Whatever verses are selected in an effort to lend precision to the Judeo-Christian definition of life's purpose, that purpose is clearly inconsistent with the reckless destruction of that which belongs to God and which has been seen as "good." How can one glorify the Creator while heaping contempt on the creation? How can one walk humbly with nature's God while wreaking havoc on nature?[10]

Humanity is an evolving creature, the product of chance mutations that led to new forms of life. Chance and necessity together provide the basic principles of evolution. Beyond this is the intelligence and purpose of animals that aid in the struggle for existence. Thus human beings are continuous with the rest of nature.[11] There was a slow evolution of the human brain, and human beings evolved as a group rather than through one individual. This development can only be understood in terms of purposive behavior. Evolution

---

9. Herman E. Daly and John B. Cobb Jr., *For the Common Good* (Boston: Beacon Press, 1988), 36; see pp. 62-63.

10. Albert Gore, *Earth in the Balance* (New York: Houghton, Mifflin, 1992), 244. See "Earth in the Balance," *Christian Century*, 8 April 1992, 368-374.

11. See Birch and Cobb, *Liberation of Life*, 44-45.

continues, and ecology and evolution belong together. The development of human culture, with the freedom and purpose that humanity provides, introduces new elements into the web of life.[12]

Birch and Cobb suggest that an ecological model needs to be a major element in thinking about reality. The mechanical model has its usefulness in dealing with aspects of the nonliving world, but even a stone in its environment and the effect of its environment demands use of an ecological model. For practical purposes the mechanical model works in a limited manner. The ecological model sees events as primary "and substantial objects are to be viewed as enduring patterns among changing events."[13]

The human reaction, at first, to both the environmental crisis and a change in religious outlook is denial. We are addicted, in the Western world, to a lifestyle that ignores any threat to its continuance. Although our way of life is not sustainable in the long run and future generations will suffer if no changes are made (and ultimately may perish), we deny this evidence. We use any claims we can find or manufacture to support our present rate of consumption. We reassert our claimed dominion over nature and rely on our technologies to maintain that dominance, but this claim needs clarifying. As Daly and Cobb state, "Any improvement of the relations between human and other species will come about by better ways of exercising dominion, not by renouncing it."[14]

Most people take little notice of what is happening to the environment. They may be aware of aspects of deterioration, as when there is a threat of a nearby nuclear waste disposal, or when some catastrophe such as Love Canal occurs, or the ozone hole over Australia, but they are so conditioned by confidence in technology or the demands for economic well-being (their own) that they ignore other signs of trouble. The findings of ecologists and environmentalists are of events too far away to be a major concern.

THEOLOGY

Current theology, on the whole, has not been ready for this challenge, Thomas Berry has suggested that Christianity has emphasized redemption, which is an anthropocentric concept, at the cost of ignoring creation as the center. "The natural world is the largest sacred community to which we belong."[15]

Larry Rasmussen writes that almost all previous theology and current theology has centered on the *imago dei* of human beings, thus placing human

---

12. See ibid., 64-65. See Philip Hefner, *The Human Factor* (Minneapolis: Fortress, 1993), 28-31.

13. Birch and Cobb, *Liberation of Life*, 95.

14. Daly and Cobb, *For the Common Good*, 387.

15. Thomas Berry, *The Dream of Earth* (San Francisco: Sierra Club Books, 1989), 79.

beings somewhere between nature and God, rather than within the natural order. For Rudolf Bultmann and Søren Kierkegaard, nature and human freedom were on different planes, history was separated from nature, and the emphasis was on human redemption. Neighbor love "never includes five to ten million other species of God's fecund imagination. . . . Luminaries of no less magnitude than Karl Barth and Rienhold Niebuhr joined Bultmann in drawing the line at the same place. This may explain why so few systematic theologians are interested in the ecocrisis or know what to do with it theologically."[16] So Rasmussen turns to process theology. He writes, "Process theology has vaulted from the minor leagues to the majors, largely because nature abhors a theological vacuum too."[17]

Chief Seattle's pleading to white culture said:

This we know. The earth does not belong to man: man belongs to the earth. This we know. All things are connected like the blood which unites one family. All things are connected. Whatever befalls the earth befalls the sons of earth. Man did not weave the web of life, he is merely a strand in it. Whatever he does to the web he does to himself.[18]

Empirical theology provides one starting point. F.S.C. Northrop speaks of an "undifferentiated aesthetic continuum" with the emphasis on "undifferentiated,"[19] by which he means a genuine human experience which cannot be broken down into any parts but of which one is aware either consciously or unconsciously. It may or may not be termed mystical. H.D. Lewis points to "the peculiar undiversified awareness of there being some 'beyond' in which such limitations (hidden and invisible) are superseded."[20] There is, says William James, "a mystical germ. It is a very common germ. It creates the rank and file of believers." By religious experience, James meant "any moment of life that brings the reality of spiritual things 'home' to one."[21]

This may be a beginning for understanding how God works among persons, but it does not necessarily lead to an understanding of the cosmos or ecology. It depends on how theology emerges from such a starting point.

Henry Nelson Weiman was an empiricist and a naturalistic theist. In his ear-

---

16. Larry Rasmussen, "Ecocrisis and Theology's Quest," *Christianity and Crisis*, 16 March 1992, 85.

17. Ibid.

18. Quoted by Albert Gore, in "Earth in Balance," 259.

19. F. S. C. Northrop, *Man, Nature, and God* (New York: Pocket Books, 1962), 242.

20. Hywel D. Lewis, "God and Mystery," in *Prospect for Metaphysics*, ed. Ian T. Ramsey (London: Allen and Unwin, 1961), 231.

21. *The Letters of William James*, ed. Henry James, vol. II (Boston: Atlantic Monthly Press, 1920), 211, 215. See William James, *Pragmatism* (New York: Longmans, Green, 1907), 154-155.

lier writings he was sympathetic to Whitehead's metaphysics, which does provide a basis for understanding the world in which we live. Later, Wieman specifically rejected this approach and restricted his empirical evidence to "creative interchange" as experienced by human beings. The "creative event" was more than humanity, but Wieman was not interested in the God of animals, plants, or nature as a whole. God is the source of good for *human* beings.

However, Wieman was aware of the possibility of ecological disaster. He knew how destructive human beings can be. This destructiveness has been built up, he wrote, by a failure of commitment to creative interchange. When the commitment is "to some created system, intellectual, political, economic, or the system of [one's] own ego," a person or group "is doomed." Human power is misused and many evils result. "Only when creative interchange is made dominant over all else can we be secure."[22] It is an illusion that anyone can find support outside "the potentiality of human existence. This excludes the subhuman cosmos except as it supports human existence; and the same applies to the ground of all being."[23]

Sallie McFague has developed a theology for an ecological, nuclear age that deals directly with the problem as we have described it. She reminds us that models and metaphors are never to be taken literally, but that they suggest the reality that cannot be described in prosaic and literal language. Further, no one model can carry the weight of the meaning of God. Her approach at this point reminds one of Horace Bushnell's insistence that many images be used and that all of them have a portion of truth. He warned his colleagues of the danger of becoming one-word theologians and preachers.[24]

All theological terms are based on primary models and in essence are metaphysical. McFague has centered on the world as God's body. She reminds us how frequently Christian tradition has used body language: resurrection of the body, body and blood in Holy Communion, the church as the body of Christ: metaphors all. But the model of the world as God's body is beyond Christian imagery and can be used by religious people throughout the world.

This imagery overcomes the dualism of body and spirit, of mind and matter, and provides an organic view of God's relation to the world. The world becomes "a sacrament of the invisible God." Such a deity is vulnerable and at risk, for it may be abused, neglected, or destroyed by just one creature:

22. Henry Nelson Wieman, *Religious Inquiry* (Boston: Beacon Press, 1969), 211.

23. Henry Nelson Wieman, *Seeking a Faith for a New Age*, ed. Cedric Hepler (Metuchen, N.J.: Scarecrow Press, 1975), 266; see Frederick Ferré, "The Integrity of Creation," in *Empirical Theology: A Handbook*, ed. Randolph C. Miller (Birmingham, Ala.: Religious Education Press, 1992), 230-232.

24. Horace Bushnell, *God in Christ* (New York: Scribner's, 1876), 48-50; H. Shelton Smith, ed., *Horace Bushnell* (New York: Oxford University Press, 1965), 92-93.

human beings. Yet God is willing to suffer in the body of the world and to take the risk that God's body will be cared for. "What the experiment regarding the world as God's body comes to, finally, is an awareness, both chilling and breathtaking, that we, as worldly, bodily beings, are in God's presence."[25] This is a nonheirarchical image that leads to human responsibility for the cosmos. We become sensitive to the loss of one individual or of one species.

McFague is always creative and persuasive in her theology, and the model of the world as God's body awakens us to the failure of the mechanical model. Ian Barbour, however, claims that it is "no more compatible with human freedom and responsibility than the monarchical model."[26] Furthermore, it does not allow for any reality beyond God's body, thus suggesting a closed, monistic universe. It is a form of panentheism approaching pantheism, which she clearly rejects.

Other models suggested by McFague provide for human freedom, but they do not face the issue of ecology. Rather, they provide helpful and creative ways of thinking about God as one whom we address, but these models only clarify the relations between God and human beings. Perhaps McFague has provided for a combination of models that will provide another step in the relation of God to the environment. Is there a sense that God is other than the world and that human beings can act freely on and within God's body?

Ian Barbour considers McFague's model of God's body and moves to a broader process view, which is more social and pluralistic. He suggests that "we can think of God as *the leader of a cosmic community*."[27] By using interpersonal models in a pluralistic world, which include freedom and intention, God is seen to be deeply involved in the total cosmos as its leader. The

---

25. Sallie McFague, "The World as God's Body," *Christian Century*, July 20-27, 1988, 672. *Models of God* (Philadelphia: Fortress, 1987), 181: She suggests several models: "When we address God as mother, father, lover, friend, or as judge, healer, liberator, companion, or yet again as sun, moon, fortress, shield, or even as creator, redeemer, and sustainer, we know that these are not descriptions of God. When we speak to God, we are most conscious of how inadequate our language is for God, something we most easliy forget when we speak about God—that is, when we are doing theology." See *National Catholic Reporter*, 25 March 1994, 20-24 for an interpretation of McFague's eco-theology.

26. Ian Barbour, *Religion in an Age of Science* (San Francisco: Harper & Row, 1990), 50-51. But McFague does mention freedom: "Self-consciousness is the basis of free will, imagination, choice, or whatever one calls that dimension of human beings that makes us capable of changing ourselves and our world" (*The Body of God* [Minneapolis: Fortress, 1993], 123). "Life, diversity, complexity, novelty—and even our free will—all rest on the randomness of natural selection as well as the diminishment, waste, and death of its processes. And yet, while accepting the inevitability of this pattern, we grieve for and suffer with—as God does also in the cosmic Christ—those who are diminished and wasted" (Ibid, 176).

27. Barbour, *Religion in an Age of Science*, 260.

cosmos is still incomplete and coming into being, and the outcome is unpredictable and open. Human nature is part of this natural community.

> All creatures are intrinsically valuable because each is a center of experience, though there are enormous gradations in the complexity and intensity of experience. In addition, by balancing immanence and transcendence, process thought encourages respect for nature.[28]

This allows for the combination of law and chance as a basis for facing an open future.

Bernard Loomer has stirred theological thinking with his claim that ambiguity is the empirical answer to the world situation. The measure for God is "size," which means the capacity to include both good and evil and to keep one's integrity. He interprets this evidence within a pantheistic worldview, with both God and the world as ambiguous. If empiricism means to account for all that is experienced, it must lead to ambiguity as the key. To reduce God to mere goodness is a false abstraction from the concrete experience of the whole.

Loomer writes that tragedy

> is not overcome. It is not overcomable, any more than ambiguity is overcomable in the divine life. . . . It is my contention that, for the most part, process thinkers, who pride themselves on overcoming the basic dichotomies of modern theology, still remain guilty of committing the greatest dichotomy, namely the dichotomy between God and evil. So in this sense, you don't associate God simply and clearly on the side of good. And the evil is something outside. You have to affirm both. And if you have to exorcise evil, you end up cutting the guts out of goodness.[29]

Loomer's suggestions are persuasive and realistic, but many questions remain unanswered. Is an ambiguous deity valid only in a pantheistic world? Is a concrete deity an empirical concept or a false abstraction? Is Loomer's view necessary in a pluralistic, process view?

Bernard Meland called himself an empirical realist. Meland used the term "dissonance" in contrast with "coherence" in picturing the world. This is Meland's equivalent to Loomer's ambiguity. Meland is aware of tragedy

---

28. Ibid., 262.

29. Bernard Loomer, in *American Journal of Theology and Philosophy* (May-September, 1984), 141-142. See William Dean, "Empiricism and God," in *Empirical Theology: A Handbook*, 126. See Tyron Inbody, 26-27; Marjorie Hewitt Suchocki, 100-104; Dean, 125-127, in ibid. See Bernard Loomer, *The Size of God*, ed. William Dean and Larry Axel (Macon, Ga.: Mercer University Press, 1987), esp. 20-51; Douglas A. Fox, "Bernard Loomer's Concept of Interconnectedness," in *God, Values, and Empiricism*, ed. Creighton Peden and Larry Axel (Macon, Ga.: Mercer University Press, 1989), 53-63.

and despair. He starts by taking human kinship with the earth seriously. His theology starts with

> a creaturely awareness of a Sensitivity within Nature, burdened with much the same anguish that attends those who attend these lived experiences, yet, impelled with growth and renewal through the efficacy of its own indominable intent and redemptive lure, imparts a persistent intent and lure to our own sense of creaturehood.

Being aware of tragedy and despair "need not preclude a creaturely sense of trust, realistically embraced."[30]

There is a mystical naturalism at the base of Meland's theology. It is an awareness by the appreciative consciousness of the mystery of God. For Meland, the word "God" is a "collective term" and refers to the plurality of functions to which we relate. God is worshiped as one and is served through the wealth of reality expressed in a plurality of activities. Meland differed from other empirical and process theologians at this point. He proceeded as time went on to stress the victory of tenderness over force, on sensitivity at the heart of nature conceived as an organism, and persuasion as God's primary way of influencing both nature and humanity. Meland wrote that his mood "has altered from a cosmic to a cultural orientation" as he became more concerned with the "troubling and haunting realities of these lived experiences." His development of the image of the "Creative Passage" "implies a reorientation of the remote cosmic mystery as a depth of Ultimacy within the immediacies of experience."[31]

Meland's final position provides a theology for an ecological age. God is at work pluralistically in a pluralistic universe in which human beings have responsibility for the health of the universe as well as for each other. His position avoids the weakness of a philosophy of organicism in which, as Frederick Ferré writes, evolutionary naturalism depends on a ruthless elimination of those less equipped to survive. Survival of the species at the expense of individuals is the norm. This can lead to a demonic totalitarianism at the human level.[32]

A limited deity in a pluralistic world is evident in Meland's position. It also emerges in the work of Birch and Cobb, but not so obviously. It is clearly the position of William James, who wrote that the only way to deal with the

---

30. Bernard Meland, *American Journal of Theology and Philosophy* (May-September 1984), 77.

31. Ibid., 98-99. See Bernard Meland, *Modern Man's Worship* (New York: Harper & Bros., 1934), 171-181; *The Reawakening of Christian Faith* (New York: Macmillan, 1949), 95-100; *The Secularization of Modern Culture* (New York: Oxford, 1966), 121; *Fallible Forms and Symbols* (Philadelphia: Fortress, 1976), 168.

32. Bernard Meland, *American Journal of Theology and Philosophy* (May-September 1984), 113.

problems of monism "is to be frankly pluralistic and assume that the super-human consciousness, however vast it may be, has itself an external environment, and consequently is finite."[33]

For James, God is conceived as working within an environment, within nature, within the strictures of time and history, and thus free from any time-less, abstract absolute. Because of his radical empiricism which includes experience of both inner and external relations, this leads to an organismic view of reality. We live in a "multiverse" rather than a universe, but "it is nei-ther a universe pure and simple nor a multiverse pure and simple."[34] It is a mul-tiverse that hangs together in what can be called "the strung-along type, the type of continuity, contiguity, or concatenation." "This fact of next to next in concrete experience" makes empiricism radical, recognizing the experience of relations as basic.[35]

> I am willing that there should be real losses and real losers, and no total preservation of all that is. When the cup is poured off, the dregs are left behind forever, but the possibility of what is poured off is sweet enough to accept.[36]

This is also true of God, who "having an environment, being in time, and working in history just like ourselves . . . escapes from the foreignness of all that is human, of the static timeless perfect absolute,"[37] and from the ambi-guity of an enclosed world.

In the best interpretation of James that I know of, Nancy Frankenberry writes,

> By counting conjunctive, no less than disjunctive, relations as *given* in experience, and felt *as* given, James corrected classical empiricism's dis-jointed world and at the same time obviated the need for rationalism's pos-tulation of a transcendental agent of unification. He thereby affected a stunning shift of emphasis with respect to the locus of religious attention and interest: away from absolutes and toward relativities: away from the focus on sense experience and toward the background of fringe experiences. Not another world, but a *wider* world is the focus of religious interest.[38]

---

33. William James, *A Pluralistic Universe* (New York: Longmans, Green, 1909), 310-311; see Randolph C. Miller, *The American Spirit in Theology* (Philadelphia: Pilgrim Press, 1974), 29-44, 231-232.

34. James, *Pragmatism*, 148. See my chapter on "Empirical Theology and Religious Education," above, chap. VI.

35. James, *A Pluralistic Universe*, 325.

36. James, *Pragmatism*, 295.

37. James, *A Pluralistic Universe*, 318.

38. Nancy Frankenberry, *Religion and Radical Pluralism* (Albany, N.Y.: SUNY, 1987), 103-104; See Nancy Frankenberry, "Consequences of William James's Pragmatism to Religion," in *God, Values, and Empiricism*, 64-72.

"God is in the world, or nowhere," said Whitehead, "creating in us and around us."[39] The Episcopal *Book of Common Prayer* includes a prayer that relates to ecology. It is addressed to God.

> At your command all things came to be: the vast expanse of interstellar space, galaxies, suns, the planets in their courses, and this fragile earth, our island home. . . . From the primal elements you brought forth the human race, and blessed us with memory, reason, and skill. You made us the rulers of creation. But we turned against you, and betrayed your trust; and we turned against one another. . . . Again and again, you called us to return. Through prophets and sages you revealed your righteous law. And in the fullness of time you sent your only Son, born of a woman, to fulfill your law, to open for us the way of freedom and peace.[40]

Here in a few words is a central element of Christianity and its relation to ecology. It is best understood in the theologies we have listed. As we listen to Sallie McFague, Ian Barbour, Bernard Loomer, Bernard Meland, and especially William James, we will have a theological background for interpreting religious education in relation to ecological issues.

Part Two

THEORIES OF RELIGIOUS EDUCATION

We turn now to the relation of an ecological theology to religious education theory. If ecology is the center of interest in the development of a theory of religious education, we can start with some objectives arising from the concern for ecology. The Parliament of the World's Religions stressed many things to be done, including striving for a more just social order. Chiefly, they wrote that

> earth cannot be changed for the better unless the consciousness of individuals is changed first. . . . We commit our selves to this global ethic, to understand one another, and to socially beneficial, peace-fostering and nature-friendly ways of life. We invite all people, religious or not, to do the same.[41]

---

39. *Dialogues of Alfred North Whitehead*, as recorded by Lucian Price (Boston: Little, Brown, 1954), 370.

40. *Book of Common Prayer* (New York: Church Pension Fund, 1976), 370.

41. *USA Weekend*, 17-19 December 1993, 11.

We can adapt some of Thomas Berry's suggestions to develop some objectives. We can educate people to achieve:

1. An understanding of human and earth technologies.
2. A transformation of thinking about the relation of human behavior to the needs and health of the planet.
3. A sense of the entire earth community and the basis for its sustainability.
4. A new approach to the handling of waste products, including nuclear waste, to protect both land and sea from undue pollution.
5. An interpretation of reverence for the earth to "consider that the universe, the earth, the sequence of living forms, and the human mode of consciousness have from the beginning had a psycho-spiritual as well as a physical-material aspect."
6. A recognition that nature is both benign and violent. We need to find protection against the assaults of nature, disease, earthquakes, hurricanes, and other disasters.
7. We need new and healing technologies that operate within a bioregional context, taking into consideration the location, climates, sources, animals, plants, and general needs of a region.
8. We need to change the direction of our technologies, for we know "that our sciences and technologies are needed more than ever; we can do nothing adequate toward human survival or toward the healing of the planet without our technologies. Extensive scientific research is needed if we are to appreciate the integral functioning of the basic life systems of the planet and enter into a mutually enhancing relationship."[42]
9. We need a theology that builds from these issues and provides an interpretation of God and nature that encompasses the insights of other theological systems.
10. Finally, we need an educational theory that sees such a theology as background, and works in practice to guide the learner to ecological responsibility.

Frederick Ferré suggests that "any lasting solutions will need to deal with illiteracy, in particular the education of women and men in the importance of methods of reforestation, in family planning and birth control, and the use of appropriate technology in the family setting."[43]

---

42. Berry, *Dream of Earth*, 65-69.
43. Ferré, "Integrity of Creation," 243; Brian Swimme writes, "No tribal myth, no matter how wild, ever imagined a more profound relationship connecting all things in an internal way right from the beginning of time. All thinking must begin with this cosmic genetic relatedness." (Brian Swimme, "Science: A Partner in Creating the Vision," in *Thomas Berry and the New Cosmology*, ed. Anne Lonergan and Caroline Richards [Mystic, Conn.: Twenty-Third Publications, 1987], 87). Quoted by McFague, *The Body of God*; 106.

There is no common human outlook on either the environmental or ethical side. There is still a split between human nature and nature; between human beings and other animals; between human needs and the needs of the environment. The dangers warned against by ecologists still exist in most parts of the world. What is needed is acceptance of an ecological model which places a demand on educational theory and practice. But to achieve this goal, a more profound understanding of the genetic and cultural evolution of human beings is necessary.

Birch and Cobb write that

> the full grasp of what is involved in the (ecological) model is possible only when human beings take themselves in the concreteness of immediate experience as illustrating and illuminating the model. The argument is not that understanding the nonhuman world provides the categories by which human experience can be understood. But rather the nonhuman world can only be adequately understood in terms of what human beings know directly and immediately—human experience.[44]

What, then, are the issues to be faced in an ecological model for theology? With a theological background such as we have suggested, we can move to ethical questions as an approach to education. Birch and Cobb write that the focus must be on rights and duties. If animals are considered true subjects, this will expand our concepts of rights and duties to include a sense of the interconnectness of all. Human beings act out of inclination more than the sense of moral responsibility. This complicates matters, but it fails to deal with the reality of moral freedom. "We want to change to more appropriate ways of acting, but we do not know what they are. What we lack is not the inclination but the guidance."[45] Bernard Meland and other empiricists have suggested that human evolution is a movement toward greater "richness of experience," which is a vague term for the enhancement of life. What can we do to make the enhancement of life available to other animals?

The Mosaic decalogue is an early example of relationships between individual persons whose values as ends are recognized. But there is no such interpretation placed on land, except as something purely economic. Persons, animals, and things have value to God.

---

44. Birch and Cobb, *Liberation of Life*, 139.
45. Ibid., 145. Related Bible passages for study: Gen 1:1-2:4; 2:4-24; 3:1-4:25; Ex. 33:20-33 (see McFague, *The Body of God*, 131-136); Is. 25:5-19, 19-20; Mt. 13:18-51; Acts 17:22-34; Rom. 1:18-25; Rom. 8:18-28; Eph. 4:11-14; Psalms 8, 9, 24, 39, 103, 139:1-17, 150. For the Exile, see Donald B. Rogers, *Religious Education* (Summer 1990), 412-423. Topics for further study: ozone depletion, acid rain, air pollution, justice and the food supply, farms and care of the soil, irrigation and water shortages, sustainability of the earth, population control, birth control, abortion, technology, income distribution, ecology and reform of style of living, ecology model for the earth ecology and our understanding of God. (See McFague, *The Body of God*, 202-205).

Jesus expressed the divine concern for the sparrow and even the grasses in the field. If a [person] is worth many sparrows then a sparrow's worth is not zero. But the Christian tradition did not live up to the conviction of its founder.[46]

With the failure to see the evolutionary relationships between human beings and animals, people have advocated kindness and compassion for animals and societies have arisen to protect them, but people have evaluated animals only in terms of their value to human beings. What is needed is to see animals as both means and ends, which changes the traditional viewpoint. There are, however, scales of values and levels of richness of experience. Thus, porpoises would outrank sharks.

Human beings, like other animals, are also both means and ends. The difference is due to the greater cultural evolution and therefore greater richness of experience. Most animals seeks to satisfy the body, but human beings are conscious of themselves and seek richness of experience, including mental experience, so that they are ends, and when used should retain their sense of intrinsic worth. There are differences among human beings, but the difference is in instrumental value, and the claim is for equality of intrinsic worth. In daily life this seems to be impossible, for there are genetic differences, cultural opportunities and deprivations, and accidents or such incidents as drug addicted parents giving birth to drug addicted babies.

Educationally, this is a call for justice, which means that we share each other's fate. There are inequalities of opportunity among peasants, slaves (still), women, ethnic minorities, and those suffering from ethnic cleansing. This unbalance provides a challenge to right the wrongs of society. This includes facing the problems of abortion and the right to die, both of which are high on the agendas in some countries.[47]

When we turn to the biosphere, we face a different category of problems. Individuals can do much less, and group action is desirable and necessary. The humane treatment of animals, for example, means not changing them genetically to take away their opportunity to live in conditions more or less natural. When we radically alter their habitats, they can quickly become extinct. In most instances, the individual animal counts for little, and the emphasis should be on species rights. A specific case is the chimpanzee, who can be used to develop and test a new vaccine. Since only about 50,000 chimpanzees are still in the wild and are an endangered species, it is, then, our responsibility to protect their environments and to limit our medical testing, even though the vaccine has great value for human well-being.[48]

Birch and Cobb write,

---

46. See Birch and Cobb, *Liberation of Life*, 147.
47. Ibid., 162-168.
48. Ibid., 170.

At this point, a sense of the web of life, the value of diversity, and the way people are constituted by internal relations to others, will guide the imagination. In addition it is necessary to take into account the relation of intrinsic and instrumental value.[49]

This promises new ways of enhancing life for all. There are ways to do this, but most of us in the Western world are attempting to maximize the richness of our experience. The first requirement would be for the fortunate few to live more frugally, thus making possible greater richness of experience for others throughout the earth. Changes in farming practices would free up land for other uses, including more space for wildlife. Tropical rainforests could be restored by intelligent planting and planning. A reversal in the human birth rate would come from better economic conditions and education. Birth control has worked only in highly educated countries, and greater cooperation between church and state is essential for more widespread education and use.

Kenneth Peter suggests two approaches to education for ecology, for there are two types of domination.[50] The first he describes as vainglory which centers on the human need for power. Individuals express this in many ways, both good and bad. It is a passionate drive that can be controlled, and moral education can be effective. There is evidence of the partial success of this approach. However, when anthropocentrism controls human activities, the relations between human beings and other people as well as with nature can be destructive competition.

The other approach is more impersonal, and refers to belief in progress, advances in technology, and to the development of rational-legal institutions such as various bureaucracies. Power operates through human organizations in order to dominate others. Bureaucracy becomes a legalistic machine of rule and laws. Human behavior is rationalized without being rational. Peter quotes Max Weber:

When asceticism was carried out of monastic cells into everyday life, and began to dominate worldly morality, it did its part in building the tremendous cosmos of the modern economic order. This order is not bound to the technical and economic conditions of machine production which today determine the lives of all the individuals who are born into this mechanism . . . with irresistible force.[51]

Peter brings alive both of these approaches. Teddy Roosevelt was called the first conservationist president, and he earned this title through the devel-

---

49. Ibid.

50. Kenneth Peter, "Domination of Nature: Hobbesian Vainglory and Military Herrschaft," *Journal of Political and Military Sociology* 21 (Winter) 1993, 181-195.

51. Ibid., 187; Max Weber, *The Protestant Ethic and the Spirit of Capitalism*, trans. Talcott Parsons (New York: Scribner's, 1958), 181.

opment of expanded national parks, the nationalized national forests, and his support of Gifford Pinchot. But this was based on stewardship for human good and not for the sake of the environment. He was willing to sell public lands to raise money to build irrigation dams and even had one built in his honor. He was also a hunter, who rejoiced in killing animals and gathering trophies of his kills. As Peter writes:

> While Roosevelt's *vainglory* could preserve parks for human enjoyment, it also produced a century of economically questionable and ecologically disastrous reclamation, of nationally organized tree-farming, and public policies promoting the extermination of "dangerous or noxious animals, like the bear, cougar, and wolf."[52]

It is this contradiction that needs to be faced as an educational goal. Attitudes can be changed by effective moral education, which churches are admirably equipped to do, and more can be achieved along these lines.

The other kind of situation, which is impersonal and bureaucratic, cannot be approached through education, for we face impersonal corporations, governmental policies, and the alienation of people from facing such obstacles. It is similar to Eisenhower's military-industrial complex. The clearest example is the military.

It is obvious that war damages the environment, but we ignore the damage by the military during peace time. It holds large areas for training purposes, and the environment suffers. It consumes many natural resources and deposits huge amounts of nuclear and other waste. This is not due to any antisocial or anti-environmental attitudes by the military or industrial forces, but the results are endemic to the system.

Education of individuals is not going to touch this portion of the environmental problem. Education at this point must concentrate on the need for social and political change. Machines cannot be educated, but their use can be redirected. A radical restructuring of society will ultimately be necessary to change the ecology of today's culture. Thus, education must seek ways to bring political pressure on the organizations, both governmental and industrial, to make the changes necessary to safeguard the environment. This is no easy task, and the churches, certainly, are not up to the challenge today. The unanswered question remains: How can concerned people find ways to organize to seek cooperation with or bring pressure on those impersonal complexes that can change in such a way that the environment will be protected from deterioration?[53]

A curriculum drawn from such suggestions would need the backing of a theology oriented to ecology, such as we have suggested.

---

52. Peter, "Domination of Nature," 190.
53. See ibid., 193.

FAITH IN LIFE

The word "Life" for Birch and Cobb is another way of speaking of God, but it avoids the missapprehensions of a traditional doctrine of God. Life is life-giving, persuasive, and loving, but it is not all-powerful. It takes account of evil and suffering, and yet it is creative and makes possible both value and freedom. It brings order out of chaos. This creativity is at the center of all that human beings can become.[54]

Henry Nelson Wieman makes a distinction between creative good and the created good. If one gives loyalty to the created good, this is a stopping place that leads no further. It is a kind of idolatry. This blocks the working of the creative good. "Creative good is identified with Life. It is Life that is to be trusted and served."[55]

Education helps us bring to the present our feelings and purposes from the past and use them as background for new stimuli, thus blending past and present in compatible elements. We may screen out anything that is new, or we may move to new personal goals. This is a novel and unforeseeable possibility which is the working of Life. The emerging novelty which is the gift of Life is more than simple change, for it offers new possibilities for enriching experience.[56]

This emphasis on creative novelty does not counteract the need to develop habits. As Williams James taught us, habits are central to good education, for they free us to develop new habits and to attend to the novel elements in life. "Learning, therefore, is a twofold process: We learn to make the processes of deliberate thought 'instinctive' and automatic, and we learn to make automatic and instinctive processes the subject of discriminating thought. It is in this latter process that Life is most fully present."[57]

This approach affects our attitude toward our bodies. Life is present in our cells. We are not a dualism of mind and body, but a society of living cells affected by tenseness, anxiety, and control. When we gladly serve the body, the whole community of cells is freed to operate to our health and benefit.

To trust Life, or God as defined, is to be open-ended about our future and the future of society and nature. There is a "not yet" in every hope for the future. The world we hope to build is also open-ended, or its static nature would kill hope. Life does not force us to follow the right path, and we can choose a rigid, static world which will die or a world in which there is a permanent becoming and perishing.[58]

---

54. Birch and Cobb, *Liberation of Life*, 192.
55. Ibid., 180.
56. Ibid., 183-185.
57. Ibid., 186.
58. Ibid., 186-187.

Life, or God, as Birch and Cobb see it, is interpreted in terms of Whitehead's process philosophy, which is a theological position that fits well with our understanding of ecology. The theological positions of McFague, Loomer, Meland, and James, described in the first section of this chapter are consistent with the insights of process theology, and our educational theory for ecology can be backed by this movement in theology.

PRACTICE

At an early age, I learned a poem by Tennyson that has influenced my theology and my approach to ecology:

> Flower in the crannied wall,
> I pluck you out of the crannies;
> Hold you here, root and all, in my hand.
> Little flower—but if I could understand
> What you are, root and all, and all in all,
> I should know what God and man is.[59]

It could be the starting point for the study of ecology and theology for the very young. As children have the opportunity to pluck some flowers and examine the roots and the soil, and then are helped to look back at the water, the rain, the sky, the sun, and the moon, it may dawn on them that all things are interconnected. This order in nature is aesthetic, and "the aesthetic order is derived from the immanence of God," according to Whitehead.[60] Older students could benefit from a similar approach.

Often worship is considered a key experience in religious education. It may occur at any point in the educational process, and most naturally prior to classes on a Sunday morning. Some parishes have developed a tradition of families worship together in a brief service (30-35 minutes) geared primarily to the children. Suitable traditional hymns reflecting ecological issues are hard to find.

Jeffery Rowthorn has written a hymn that reflects a process view and an ecological outlook:

> Creating God, your fingers trace
> the bold designs of farthest space;

---

59. Randolph C. Miller, *The Language Gap and God* (Philadelphia: Pilgrim Press, 1970), 149-150, from *The Poetical Works of Alfred Tennyson* (Boston: Osgood, 1875), 416. Children especially need exposure to what they can touch and see: field trips to gardens, petting zoos, wild animal zoos in natural settings, plus exposure to other cultures. This is especially true for inner-city children.

60. Alfred North Whitehead, *Religion in the Making* (New York: Macmillan, 1926), 105.

let sun and moon and stars and light
and what lies hidden praise your might.

Sustaining God, your hands uphold
earth's mysteries known or yet untold;
let water's fragile blend with air,
enabling life, proclaim your care.

Redeeming God, your arms embrace
all now despised for creed or race;
let peace, descending like a dove,
make known on earth your healing love.

Indwelling God, your gospel claims
one family with a billion names;
let every life be touched by grace
until we praise you face to face.[61]

William De Witt Hyde wrote a hymn about creation:

Creation's Lord, we give thee thanks
That this thy world is incomplete;
That battle calls our marshalled ranks;
That work awaits our hands and feet.
That thou hast not yet finished man;
That we are in the making still.
As friends who share the Maker's plan,
As sons who know the Father's will. [62]

Here are two more or less traditional prayers that deal with nature:

We give you thanks, most gracious God, for the beauty of the earth and sky and sea; for the richness of mountains, plain, and rivers; for the songs of birds and the loveliness of flowers. We praise you for these good gifts, and pray that we may safeguard them for posterity. Grant that we may continue to grow in our grateful enjoyment of your abundant creation, to the honor and glory of your Name, now and forever.[63]

God, in giving us dominion over things of earth, you made us fellow work-

---

61. From *The Hymnal 1992*, #394. By Jeffery Rowthorn, copyright © 1979 by the Hymn Society. Used by permission. Other suitable hymns are "Fairest Lord Jesus," "All things bright and beautiful," "This is my Father's world," and "O beautiful for spacious skies."

62. From *The Hymnal 1940*, copyright Church Pension Fund. By William DeWitt Hyde, 1943, #548. Used by permission.

63. *Book of Common Prayer*, 1986, 840.

ers in your creation: Give us wisdom and reverence so to use the resources of nature, that no one may suffer from our abuse of them, and that generations yet to come may continue to praise you for your bounty; through Jesus Christ our Lord.[64]

A stranger wandered into the Episcopal Cathedral of St. John in New York City on St. Francis Day. The service was a celebration of creation. The celebration focused on the *Missa Gaia* (Earth Mass); it was created by Paul Winters, artist-in-residence. It included the sounds of the endangered wolf and whale, along with St. Francis' "Canticle of the Sun" and prayers for peace. Winter's soprano saxophone, pounding tribal rhythms and dancers performing around the altar, and a solemn procession were part of the service. The sermon called for the care for all creatures. Many people had brought pets to be blessed. Then the great bronze doors were opened for the entrance of an elephant, a camel, and a llama, a person with a flask of algae, and another with a banana topped by a flower. James Parks Morton, the Dean, says that "religion binds the whole cosmos starting from above; ecology binds the whole cosmos starting from below."

Much else related to ecology goes on at the cathedral. Every Sunday there are prayers for endangered species. Environmental activities are encouraged. An ecological think tank tries to connect intellectual and spiritual decision about ecology. There is a large recycling center on the grounds. There are services incorporating Native American concerns. A blue crab lives in the cathedral, and it dances with fingerling, striped bass, mussels and other creatures of the Hudson River. As Dean Morton says, "Every created thing is joined into the whole through the compassion of God, just as every sinuous joint of the rose window is interconnected through the Christ at its center."[65]

The average congregation lacks the resources to imitate many of the practices in the cathedral, but some of the ideas can be adapted to the average congregation. A little imagination and a knowledge of ecology can stimulate the worshipers to think and feel ecologically, especially if the theology is ecologically responsible, as it is at the cathedral.

Anne Rowthorn has proposed ten commandments for ecological responsibility. Keeping those commandments depends on one's view of nature and of God's relation to the cosmos. Unless God is working to create and sustain the world, there is little to challenge our despair. But if God is the divine MORE, at work as the Creative Passage in all of nature, at work in a pluralistic multiverse that is still a universe, there is a basis for both hope and human responsibility. A Christian education for ecology can draw on these insights for guidance.

---

64. *Book of Common Prayer*, 1986, 827.
65. See the report in *National Catholic Reporter*, 25 March 1964, 19.

Rowthorn suggests that we start (1) with repenting for ignoring the needs of creation. This can lead to a change of attitude and action away from those that endanger the environment, especially the danger of devastation (even from the peaceful use of nuclear power and its waste products). (2) Listening to talk, hearing of the dangers of certain kinds of industrial work, injustice within the workplace, oppression, unemployment, and harassment, with special attention to conditions in Third World countries. (3) Praying for and trying to love our enemies, which are often industrial giants on which we depend for our economic well-being, but which oppose the economic costs of sustaining the environment. (4) Participating in the rituals which sharpen our wits and establish unity among those who participate. These include fiestas, country fairs, liturgies both secular and religious, which alert us to the positive and negative aspects of our ecological adventures. (5) Learning from others, especially those who have served in the Peace Corps, student exchanges, or volunteers for church ministry at home and abroad. Cross-cultural learning is essential to an environmental ethics. (6) Acting when the opportunity arises and seeking such opportunities. The church at this point is not an escape hatch for those who may hear and clearly do not respond. As we recognize the seduction of these people by the anti-environmentalists, we need to participate in politics and community action. (7) Uniting our personal morality with the search for the common good. As an example, the search for moral standards for sexuality has bedeviled the church in recent years. Liberation theology has dealt with the misery of the oppressed, not only the homeless and the starving, not only in South and Latin America and North Africa, but even in wealthy countries. (8) Willingness to sacrifice in order to heal what has already been done to the integrity of creation. Our decisions from now on will have to deal with the costs in suffering, degradation, and unnecessary deaths. We can help avoid such results with right decisions, especially by making economic and political decisions at the cost of a lower standard of living for the favored few. (9) Seeing the service to a just and sustainable world as a religious act. A faith in God who is at work in the natural world as well as in history and interpersonal relations would lead to a new type of lay or ordained ministry that lets creativity lead to continuous richness of experience for both human beings and the other animal species. (10) Finally, watching as creation is healed, giving thanks to God and to those who have worked in many ways to eliminate our nuclear waste and stopped many ways of polluting the earth and the cosmos in which we and God are active agents. There are signs of renewal and reform that may let the earth heal itself.[66]

A Christian education geared to such a theology as we have described, with the resulting educational theory and practice, may arm us to defend the integrity of creation.

---

66. Anne Rowthorn, *Caring for Creation* (Wilton, Conn.: Morehouse, 1989), 111-143.

Contributors

MARY C. BOYS, S.N.J.M., author of *Biblical Interpretation in Religious Education and Educating in Faith: Maps and Visions*, has moved from Boston College to Union Theological Seminary, New York City, to become Skinner and McAlpin Professor of Practical Theology. Among other professional memberships, she belongs to the Christian Scholars Group on Judaism and the Jewish People.

KENNETH O. GANGEL serves as Vice President for Academic Affairs, Academic Dean, and Senior Professor of Christian Education at Dallas Theological Seminary. He has authored multiple books and articles in the field of Christian Education, including *Building Leaders for Church Education* and *Christian Education: Its History and Philosophy* (co-authored with Warren Benson). He is also co-editing *The Christian Educator's Hand-book* series.

HELEN GOGGIN is Professor of Christian Education at Knox College, The Toronto School of Theology, at the University of Toronto in Canada. She is an ordained minister in the Presbyterian Church in Canada and served as the Minister of Education in a congregation for nineteen years prior to going to Ewart College, in Toronto, to teach Christian Education. In 1990 the College was amalgamated with Knox College. Helen continues to be involved in lay education at the congregational and conference levels and is always happy to find someone who wants to talk about process theology or postmodernism.

ELIZABETH DODSON GRAY is a feminist theologian. She is a graduate of Yale Divinity School (B. Div. 1954) and has taught at MIT's Sloan School of Management, Williams College, Boston College, and Antioch New England Graduate School. Since 1978 she has been Coordinator of the Theological Opportunities Program at Harvard Divinity School. She is the author of *Green Paradise Lost* (1979), *Patriarchy as a Conceptual Trap* (1982), and editor of *Sacred Dimensions of Women's Experience*. She also wrote with her husband *Children of Joy: Raising Your Own Home-Grown Christians* (1976). In 1989 the National Film Board of Canada released a twenty-minute film, "Adam's World," about her work.

MARK HEATH O.P. is presently instructor in theology in the Archdiocese of Washington Permanent Deacon Formation Program and also Director of Development of the Dominican House of Studies in Washington. In the past he has served as director of the graduate studies programs in religious education at La Salle University and Providence College and Professor of Religious Education and President at the Dominican House of Studies in Washington. He has also been a member and board member of the Religious Education Association (REA) and the Association of Professors and Researchers in Religious Education (APRRE). He served also as pastor of St. Louis Bertrand Parish in Louisville, Kentucky.

SARA LITTLE is Professor of Christian Education, Emerita, at Union Theological Seminary in Virginia. Since retirement in 1989, she has taught at Columbia Seminary in Decatur, Georgia, and has served as interim Dean and Vice-President of Academic Affairs at Pacific School of Religion in Berkeley, California. She is now Distinguished Visiting Professor of Christian Education at Presbyterian School of Christian Education. Her Ph. D. is from Yale University, where she worked with Randolph C. Miller. Her most recent book is *To Set One's Heart: Belief and Teaching in the Church.*

RANDOLPH CRUMP MILLER is Horace Bushnell Professor of Christian Nurture, Emeritus, at Yale University Divinity School, and Editor Emeritus of *Religious Education*. From 1936 to 1952, he taught at the Church Divinity School of the Pacific in Berkeley, California and at Yale until he retired in 1981. His most recent book was editor, *Empirical Theology: A Handbook.* He and his wife, Elizabeth, reside in New Haven, Connecticut.

FRANK ROGERS JR. is Assistant Professor at the School of Theology at Claremont. He has taught at Seattle University and Princeton Theological Seminary. He has led parish programs and done pulpit supply work and youth ministry in several parishes. His most recent article appeared in *Religious Education.*

DANIEL S. SCHIPANI is a native of Argentina. He is Professor of Christian Education and Personality at the Associated Mennonite Biblical Seminary. He also serves as Affiliate Professor of Christian Education and Pastoral Care at Northern Baptist Theological Seminary and as visiting professor at several institutions in Latin America and the Caribbean. He is a graduate of the University of Buenos Aires (Lic. Psy.), Catholic University of Argentina (Dr. Psy.), Goshen Biblical Seminary (M.A. Peace Studies), and Princeton Theological Seminary (Ph. D.). He is the author of several books in Spanish and in English, including *Conscientization and Creativity, Religious Education Encounters Liber-ation Theology,* and *Freedom and Discipleship.*

GRANT S. SHOCKLEY is Professor Emeritus of Christian Education, the Divinity School, Duke University, and visiting professor, religion and philosophy, Clark Atlanta University. He has served as professor of religious education at Gammon Theological Seminary, at Garrett Theological Seminary, at Candler School of Theology, and at Duke. He was president of The Interdenominational Center, Atlanta, 1975-1979, and of Philander Smith College, Little Rock, 1979-1983. He and his wife reside in Atlanta.

JERRY H. STONE is Adjunct Professor of Religion Emeritus at Illinois Wesleyan University. In addition to teaching courses in the religion department, he participated for many years in designing, staffing, and teaching in interdisciplinary team-taught humanities courses including art, history, literature, and religion, hence his interest in narrative theology and the broader aesthetic dimensions of theology and religious education. He has published in *Soundings: An Interdisciplinary Journal, Christian Century*, an essay in an edited book of essays entitled *Legal Hermeneutics: History, Theory, and Practice*, several entries in *Harper's Encyclopedia of Religious Education*, and book reviews in the area of art and religion.

CHRISTY SULLIVAN serves as Director of External Studies and as Adjunct Teacher in Christian Education at Dallas Theological Seminary. Her work includes oversight of the distant education programs.

CONSTANCE J. TARASAR is Associate for Faith and Order of the National Council of Churches and holds membership on the Faith and Order Plenary Commission of the World Council of Churches. She serves as Unit Coordinator of the Orthodox Church in America's Unit on Education and Community Life Ministries and is lecturer in religious education at St. Vladimir's Orthodox Seminary, Crestwood, N.Y. An author of numerous articles, educational publications, and religious education materials for children and adults, she now serves as a consultant for Orthodox Churches in Eastern Europe.

DAVID F. WHITE is a candidate for the Ph. D. at the School of Theology in Claremont. In the past he has written curriculum for the United Methodist Church, served as a missionary in Alaska, and is currently developing youth ministry models. He is working with Mary Elizabeth Moore in co-editing a book about six ethnic youth groups.

Index of Names
(The important references are in boldface.)

Index of Subjects
(The important references are in boldface.)

371